THE ROBERT FROST READER

THE
Robert Frost READER

Poetry and Prose

Edited by Edward Connery Lathem
and Lawrance Thompson

An Owl Book
Henry Holt and Company   New York

Henry Holt and Company, LLC
Publishers since 1866
115 West 18th Street
New York, New York 10011

Henry Holt® is a registered trademark of
Henry Holt and Company, LLC.

Library of Congress Cataloging-in-Publication Data
Frost, Robert, 1874–1963.
    [Selections. 2002]
    The Robert Frost reader : poetry and prose /
    edited by Edward Connery Lathem and Lawrance Thompson.
        p.   cm.
    "An Owl book."
    ISBN 0-8050-7021-4 (pbk.)
     I. Lathem, Edward Connery.   II. Thompson, Lawrance.
    III. Title.

    PS3511.R94 A6   2002
    811'.52—dc21   2001044578

First published in hardcover in 1973
as *Robert Frost: Poetry and Prose*
by Holt, Rinehart and Winston
First Owl Books Edition 1984

Reissued 2002

Designed by Paula Russell Szafranski

Printed in the United States of America

10   9   8   7   6   5

THE AMHERST STUDENT
for the letter which appeared in the March 25, 1935, issue.

THE CHRISTIAN SCIENCE MONITOR
for "Education by Presence" (originally "Robert Frost Interprets His Teaching Method"), an interview by Janet Mabie, issue of December 24, 1925.

DARTMOUTH ALUMNI MAGAZINE
for "Don't Get Converted. Stay," an address delivered at the Dartmouth commencement of June 1955, and published in the issue of July 1955; "On Extravagance," a talk delivered at Dartmouth on November 27, 1962, and published in the issue of March 1963.

THE MACMILLAN COMPANY
for Robert Frost's introduction to *King Jasper*. Reprinted with permission of The Macmillan Company from *King Jasper* by Edwin Arlington Robinson. Copyright 1935 by Edwin Arlington Robinson, renewed 1963 by The Macmillan Company.

MASSACHUSETTS LIBRARY ASSOCIATION
for Robert Frost's list of "Ten Favorite Books" in *Books We Like* (1936).

MIDDLEBURY COLLEGE
for "The Doctrine of Excursions," a Preface by Robert Frost to the *Bread Loaf Anthology* published in 1939.

THE NEW YORK TIMES
for "We Seem to Lack the Courage to Be Ourselves" (originally "Robert Frost Relieves His Mind"), an interview by Rose C. Feld, issue of October 21, 1923. © 1923 by The New York Times Company. Reprinted by permission.

NEW YORK UNIVERSITY PRESS
for Robert Frost's Introduction to *A Swinger of Birches* by Sidney Cox. © 1957 by New York University Press, Inc. Reprinted by permission of the Press.

OBERLIN ALUMNI MAGAZINE
for "What Became of New England?"—an address delivered at the Oberlin commencement of June 1937; published in the issue of May 1938.

THE TEXAS QUARTERLY
for a letter from Robert Frost to Wilbert Snow, dated January 2, 1938, quoted by Snow in his article "The Robert Frost I Knew" in *The Texas Quarterly*, Vol. XI, No. 3 (Autumn 1968).

Contents

Introduction

Robert Frost continues to be recognized and cherished as America's favorite poet. Few readers are familiar, however, with the diversity of his literary achievement, and it is the purpose of this volume to reveal something of that many-sidedness by presenting selections from his remarkable prose as well as from his highly regarded poetry.

Frost liked to declare that one reads poem A the better to read poem B, one reads poem B the better to read C, C the better to read D, and D the better to return and get something more from A. This circular representation of an exploratory action was Frost's way of emphasizing that the comprehension and aesthetic pleasure derived from any text is increased by—is even substantially dependent upon—a knowledge of pertinent contexts.

For those who wish to extend their understanding and enjoyment of Robert Frost's poetry this book provides an opportunity to consider some of his best and best-known poems against a background of his other writings, many of them little known and some, indeed, heretofore unpublished. Part I includes selections from Frost's individual books of new verse, *A Boy's Will* (1913) through *In the Clearing* (1962). Part II includes—arranged successively in a roughly chronological order—examples of his earliest known writings in poetry and in prose, narratives he wrote for his children, stories he published in poultry magazines while he himself was a farm-poultryman, a one-act play, extracts from his correspondence, formal essays, public talks, conversations with interviewers, excerpts from his notebooks, and certain pieces of his uncollected verse. Never before have so many different sides of the poet-as-literary-artist been made available.

These texts and contexts are allowed to speak for themselves. The editors have deliberately avoided making interpretations, and have given in their notes only basic information for the identification of the materials presented. They have provided, for the user's convenience of reference, a brief chronology, as well as a selected bibliography and a comprehensive index.

Edward Connery Lathem
Lawrance Thompson

A Brief Chronology

1874   Robert Lee Frost is born at San Francisco, California, on the twenty-sixth of March.

1885   RF's mother, Isabelle Moodie Frost, upon the death of her husband, William Prescott Frost, Jr., travels with her son and daughter (Jeanie Florence Frost, born 1876) to Lawrence, Massachusetts, her husband's boyhood home; after a brief interval in Lawrence she moves with her two children to Salem, New Hampshire, to begin teaching in the town schools there.

1888   RF begins his high school course at Lawrence, commuting from Salem.

1890   RF's first poem, "La Noche Triste," is published in the Lawrence *High School Bulletin*.

1892   RF is graduated from Lawrence High School, sharing valedictory honors with Elinor Miriam White; is chosen Class Poet; enters Dartmouth College, remaining there less than a semester.

1893   Begins period devoted to teaching, mill work, newspaper reporting, and odd jobs.

1894 "My Butterfly," RF's first poem in a publication of national circulation, appears in *The Independent* (New York), November 8.

1895 Marries Elinor Miriam White in Lawrence, December 19.

1897 Enters Harvard College as a special student, formally withdrawing in March 1899.

1900 Moves with his family to Derry, New Hampshire, to engage in chicken farming.

1906 Begins teaching at Pinkerton Academy in Derry.

1911 Resigns from Pinkerton Academy staff and then moves to Plymouth, New Hampshire, to join the faculty of the New Hampshire State Normal School there.

1912 Goes with his family to live in England.

1913 *A Boy's Will* is published in London by David Nutt and Company.

1914 *North of Boston* is published by Nutt.

1915 Returns to America; both *North of Boston* and *A Boy's Will* are published in New York by Henry Holt and Company, RF's principal publisher henceforth; purchases farm at Franconia, New Hampshire.

1916 *Mountain Interval* is published by Holt.

1917 Begins teaching at Amherst College.

1920 Resigns from Amherst College faculty; returns to Franconia, New Hampshire; then moves to South Shaftsbury, Vermont.

1921 Accepts appointment as Poet in Residence at University of Michigan.

1922 Is reappointed for a second year on University of Michigan staff, as Fellow in Creative Arts.

1923 The first of RF's several editions of *Selected Poems* is published; *New Hampshire* is published (Pulitzer Prize 1924); returns to a professorship at Amherst College.

1925 Leaves Amherst College to return to University of Michigan as Fellow in Letters.

1926 Resigns from University of Michigan and returns again to an Amherst College professorship.

1928 Goes abroad, visiting France, England, and Ireland; *West-Running Brook* is published.

1930 RF's first *Collected Poems* is published (Pulitzer Prize 1931).

1931 Receives Russell Loines Poetry Prize from National Institute of Arts and Letters.

1936 Serves as Charles Eliot Norton Professor of Poetry at Harvard University (while still on Amherst College faculty), delivering lecture series there; *A Further Range* is published (Pulitzer Prize 1937).

1938 Mrs. Frost dies in Gainesville, Florida, March 21; RF resigns professorship at Amherst College; sells home in Amherst, Massachusetts, and returns to South Shaftsbury, Vermont; subsequently rents apartment in Boston.

1939 Is appointed Ralph Waldo Emerson Fellow in Poetry at Harvard University; purchases Homer Noble Farm in Ripton, Vermont.

1940 Purchases property in South Miami, Florida.

1941 Is awarded Gold Medal by Poetry Society of America; purchases home in Cambridge, Massachusetts.

1942 *A Witness Tree* is published (Pulitzer Prize 1943).

1943 Terminates his Harvard University assignment; becomes George Ticknor Fellow in the Humanities at Dartmouth College.

1945 *A Masque of Reason* is published.

1947 *Steeple Bush* and *A Masque of Mercy* are published.

1949 *Complete Poems* (1949) is published; accepts life appointment as Simpson Lecturer in Literature at Amherst College.

1953 Receives award from American Academy of Poets.

1954 *Aforesaid,* a limited edition of selected poetry, is published on RF's eightieth birthday; he is sent by U.S. Department of State as a delegate to the World Congress of Writers at São Paulo, Brazil.

1957 Goes to Britain and Ireland on "good will mission" for U.S. Department of State.

1958 Is named to term as Consultant in Poetry at the Library of Congress; receives awards from several sources, including Poetry Society of America, American Academy of Arts and Sciences, and Huntington Hartford Foundation.

1961 Participates in President John F. Kennedy's Inauguration; goes to Israel and Greece; designated Poet Laureate of Vermont by legislative act.

1962 Marks eighty-eighth birthday by receiving gold medal bestowed by U.S. Congress and by celebrating publication of *In the Clearing;* goes to Russia on "good will mission" for U.S. Department of State; receives Edward MacDowell Medal.

1963 Dies at Boston, Massachusetts, January 29.

I
POETRY

SELECTIONS FROM ELEVEN BOOKS

In 1912, shortly after his arrival in England from America,
Robert Frost gathered together a group of his lyrics—poems
written, chiefly, while he was living on his farm at Derry, New
Hampshire. He submitted the resulting manuscript to a
London publisher, David Nutt and Company, and soon
learned that it had been accepted by the firm. *A Boy's Will,*
Frost's first regularly published volume, appeared during the
spring of 1913.

On the pages that follow, within this opening section, a
representative selection is provided of poems drawn from *A
Boy's Will* and from the contents of all ten of Frost's
subsequent individual books of new verse, *North of Boston*
(1914) through *In the Clearing* (1962).

INTO MY OWN

One of my wishes is that those dark trees,
So old and firm they scarcely show the breeze,
Were not, as 'twere, the merest mask of gloom,
But stretched away unto the edge of doom.

I should not be withheld but that some day   5
Into their vastness I should steal away,
Fearless of ever finding open land,
Or highway where the slow wheel pours the sand.

I do not see why I should e'er turn back,
Or those should not set forth upon my track   10
To overtake me, who should miss me here
And long to know if still I held them dear.

They would not find me changed from him they knew—
Only more sure of all I thought was true.

GHOST HOUSE

I dwell in a lonely house I know
That vanished many a summer ago,
      And left no trace but the cellar walls,
      And a cellar in which the daylight falls
And the purple-stemmed wild raspberries grow.   5

O'er ruined fences the grapevines shield
The woods come back to the mowing field;
      The orchard tree has grown one copse

Of new wood and old where the woodpecker chops;
The footpath down to the well is healed.   10

I dwell with a strangely aching heart
In that vanished abode there far apart
   On that disused and forgotten road
   That has no dust-bath now for the toad.
Night comes; the black bats tumble and dart;   15

The whippoorwill is coming to shout
And hush and cluck and flutter about:
   I hear him begin far enough away
   Full many a time to say his say
Before he arrives to say it out.   20

It is under the small, dim, summer star.
I know not who these mute folk are
   Who share the unlit place with me—
   Those stones out under the low-limbed tree
Doubtless bear names that the mosses mar.   25

They are tireless folk, but slow and sad—
Though two, close-keeping, are lass and lad—
   With none among them that ever sings,
   And yet, in view of how many things,
As sweet companions as might be had.   30

MY NOVEMBER GUEST

My Sorrow, when she's here with me,
   Thinks these dark days of autumn rain
Are beautiful as days can be;
She loves the bare, the withered tree;
   She walks the sodden pasture lane.   5

Her pleasure will not let me stay.
　　She talks and I am fain to list:
She's glad the birds are gone away,
She's glad her simple worsted gray
　　Is silver now with clinging mist.　　　　10

The desolate, deserted trees,
　　The faded earth, the heavy sky,
The beauties she so truly sees,
She thinks I have no eye for these,
　　And vexes me for reason why.　　　　15

Not yesterday I learned to know
　　The love of bare November days
Before the coming of the snow,
But it were vain to tell her so,
　　And they are better for her praise.　　　　20

LOVE AND A QUESTION

A Stranger came to the door at eve,
　　And he spoke the bridegroom fair.
He bore a green-white stick in his hand,
　　And, for all burden, care.
He asked with the eyes more than the lips　　　　5
　　For a shelter for the night,
And he turned and looked at the road afar
　　Without a window light.

The bridegroom came forth into the porch
　　With, "Let us look at the sky,　　　　10
And question what of the night to be,
　　Stranger, you and I."
The woodbine leaves littered the yard,

(5)

The woodbine berries were blue,
Autumn, yes, winter was in the wind;   15
   "Stranger, I wish I knew."

Within, the bride in the dusk alone
   Bent over the open fire,
Her face rose-red with the glowing coal
   And the thought of the heart's desire.   20
The bridegroom looked at the weary road,
   Yet saw but her within,
And wished her heart in a case of gold
   And pinned with a silver pin.

The bridegroom thought it little to give   25
   A dole of bread, a purse,
A heartfelt prayer for the poor of God,
   Or for the rich a curse;
But whether or not a man was asked
   To mar the love of two   30
By harboring woe in the bridal house,
   The bridegroom wished he knew.

STORM FEAR

When the wind works against us in the dark,
And pelts with snow
The lower-chamber window on the east,
And whispers with a sort of stifled bark,
The beast,   5
"Come out! Come out!"—
It costs no inward struggle not to go,
Ah, no!
I count our strength,

Two and a child,   10
Those of us not asleep subdued to mark
How the cold creeps as the fire dies at length—
How drifts are piled,
Dooryard and road ungraded,
Till even the comforting barn grows far away,   15
And my heart owns a doubt
Whether 'tis in us to arise with day
And save ourselves unaided.

TO THE THAWING WIND

Come with rain, O loud Southwester!
Bring the singer, bring the nester;
Give the buried flower a dream;
Make the settled snowbank steam;
Find the brown beneath the white;   5
But whate'er you do tonight,
Bathe my window, make it flow,
Melt it as the ice will go;
Melt the glass and leave the sticks
Like a hermit's crucifix;   10
Burst into my narrow stall;
Swing the picture on the wall;
Run the rattling pages o'er;
Scatter poems on the floor;
Turn the poet out of door.   15

A PRAYER IN SPRING

Oh, give us pleasure in the flowers today;
And give us not to think so far away

As the uncertain harvest; keep us here
All simply in the springing of the year.

Oh, give us pleasure in the orchard white, 5
Like nothing else by day, like ghosts by night;
And make us happy in the happy bees,
The swarm dilating round the perfect trees.

And make us happy in the darting bird
That suddenly above the bees is heard, 10
The meteor that thrusts in with needle bill,
And off a blossom in mid-air stands still.

For this is love and nothing else is love,
The which it is reserved for God above
To sanctify to what far ends He will, 15
But which it only needs that we fulfill.

FLOWER-GATHERING

I left you in the morning,
And in the morning glow
You walked a way beside me
To make me sad to go.
Do you know me in the gloaming, 5
Gaunt and dusty gray with roaming?
Are you dumb because you know me not,
Or dumb because you know?

All for me? And not a question
For the faded flowers gay 10
That could take me from beside you
For the ages of a day?
They are yours, and be the measure

Of their worth for you to treasure,
The measure of the little while 15
That I've been long away.

A DREAM PANG

I had withdrawn in forest, and my song
Was swallowed up in leaves that blew alway;
And to the forest edge you came one day
(This was my dream) and looked and pondered long,
But did not enter, though the wish was strong: 5
You shook your pensive head as who should say,
"I dare not—too far in his footsteps stray—
He must seek me would he undo the wrong."

Not far, but near, I stood and saw it all,
Behind low boughs the trees let down outside; 10
And the sweet pang it cost me not to call
And tell you that I saw does still abide.
But 'tis not true that thus I dwelt aloof,
For the wood wakes, and you are here for proof.

IN NEGLECT

They leave us so to the way we took,
  As two in whom they were proved mistaken,
That we sit sometimes in the wayside nook,
With mischievous, vagrant, seraphic look,
  And *try* if we cannot feel forsaken. 5

MOWING

There was never a sound beside the wood but one,
And that was my long scythe whispering to the ground.

What was it it whispered? I knew not well myself;
Perhaps it was something about the heat of the sun,
Something, perhaps, about the lack of sound—   5
And that was why it whispered and did not speak.
It was no dream of the gift of idle hours,
Or easy gold at the hand of fay or elf:
Anything more than the truth would have seemed too weak
To the earnest love that laid the swale in rows,   10
Not without feeble-pointed spikes of flowers
(Pale orchises), and scared a bright green snake.
The fact is the sweetest dream that labor knows.
My long scythe whispered and left the hay to make.

REVELATION

We make ourselves a place apart
    Behind light words that tease and flout,
But oh, the agitated heart
    Till someone really find us out.

'Tis pity if the case require   5
    (Or so we say) that in the end
We speak the literal to inspire
    The understanding of a friend.

But so with all, from babes that play
    At hide-and-seek to God afar,   10
So all who hide too well away
    Must speak and tell us where they are.

THE TRIAL BY EXISTENCE

Even the bravest that are slain
    Shall not dissemble their surprise

On waking to find valor reign,
 Even as on earth, in paradise;
And where they sought without the sword   5
 Wide fields of asphodel fore'er,
To find that the utmost reward
 Of daring should be still to dare.

The light of heaven falls whole and white
 And is not shattered into dyes,   10
The light forever is morning light;
 The hills are verdured pasturewise;
The angel hosts with freshness go,
 And seek with laughter what to brave—
And binding all is the hushed snow   15
 Of the far-distant breaking wave.

And from a cliff top is proclaimed
 The gathering of the souls for birth,
The trial by existence named,
 The obscuration upon earth.   20
And the slant spirits trooping by
 In streams and cross- and counter-streams
Can but give ear to that sweet cry
 For its suggestion of what dreams!

And the more loitering are turned   25
 To view once more the sacrifice
Of those who for some good discerned
 Will gladly give up paradise.
And a white shimmering concourse rolls
 Toward the throne to witness there   30
The speeding of devoted souls
 Which God makes His especial care.

And none are taken but who will,
  Having first heard the life read out
That opens earthward, good and ill,   35
  Beyond the shadow of a doubt;
And very beautifully God limns,
  And tenderly, life's little dream,
But naught extenuates or dims,
  Setting the thing that is supreme.   40

Nor is there wanting in the press
  Some spirit to stand simply forth,
Heroic in its nakedness,
  Against the uttermost of earth.
The tale of earth's unhonored things   45
  Sounds nobler there than 'neath the sun;
And the mind whirls and the heart sings,
  And a shout greets the daring one.

But always God speaks at the end:
  "One thought in agony of strife   50
The bravest would have by for friend,
  The memory that he chose the life;
But the pure fate to which you go
  Admits no memory of choice,
Or the woe were not earthly woe   55
  To which you give the assenting voice."

And so the choice must be again,
  But the last choice is still the same;
And the awe passes wonder then,
  And a hush falls for all acclaim.   60
And God has taken a flower of gold
  And broken it, and used therefrom

The mystic link to bind and hold
　　Spirit to matter till death come.

'Tis of the essence of life here,   65
　　Though we choose greatly, still to lack
The lasting memory at all clear,
　　That life has for us on the wrack
Nothing but what we somehow chose;
　　Thus are we wholly stripped of pride   70
In the pain that has but one close,
　　Bearing it crushed and mystified.

THE TUFT OF FLOWERS

I went to turn the grass once after one
Who mowed it in the dew before the sun.

The dew was gone that made his blade so keen
Before I came to view the leveled scene.

I looked for him behind an isle of trees;   5
I listened for his whetstone on the breeze.

But he had gone his way, the grass all mown,
And I must be, as he had been—alone,

"As all must be," I said within my heart,
"Whether they work together or apart."   10

But as I said it, swift there passed me by
On noiseless wing a bewildered butterfly,

Seeking with memories grown dim o'er night
Some resting flower of yesterday's delight.

(13)

And once I marked his flight go round and round,   15
As where some flower lay withering on the ground.

And then he flew as far as eye could see,
And then on tremulous wing came back to me.

I thought of questions that have no reply,
And would have turned to toss the grass to dry;   20

But he turned first, and led my eye to look
At a tall tuft of flowers beside a brook,

A leaping tongue of bloom the scythe had spared
Beside a reedy brook the scythe had bared.

The mower in the dew had loved them thus,   25
By leaving them to flourish, not for us,

Nor yet to draw one thought of ours to him,
But from sheer morning gladness at the brim.

The butterfly and I had lit upon,
Nevertheless, a message from the dawn,   30

That made me hear the wakening birds around,
And hear his long scythe whispering to the ground,

And feel a spirit kindred to my own;
So that henceforth I worked no more alone;

But glad with him, I worked as with his aid,   35
And weary, sought at noon with him the shade;

And dreaming, as it were, held brotherly speech
With one whose thought I had not hoped to reach.

"Men work together," I told him from the heart,
"Whether they work together or apart."   40

THE DEMIURGE'S LAUGH

It was far in the sameness of the wood;
   I was running with joy on the Demon's trail,
Though I knew what I hunted was no true god.
   It was just as the light was beginning to fail
That I suddenly heard—all I needed to hear: 5
It has lasted me many and many a year.

The sound was behind me instead of before,
   A sleepy sound, but mocking half,
As of one who utterly couldn't care.
   The Demon arose from his wallow to laugh,   10
Brushing the dirt from his eye as he went;
And well I knew what the Demon meant.

I shall not forget how his laugh rang out.
   I felt as a fool to have been so caught,
And checked my steps to make pretense   15
   It was something among the leaves I sought
(Though doubtful whether he stayed to see).
Thereafter I sat me against a tree.

OCTOBER

O hushed October morning mild,
Thy leaves have ripened to the fall;
Tomorrow's wind, if it be wild,
Should waste them all.
The crows above the forest call;   5
Tomorrow they may form and go.
O hushed October morning mild,
Begin the hours of this day slow.
Make the day seem to us less brief.

Hearts not averse to being beguiled,   10
Beguile us in the way you know.
Release one leaf at break of day;
At noon release another leaf;
One from our trees, one far away.
Retard the sun with gentle mist;   15
Enchant the land with amethyst.
Slow, slow!
For the grapes' sake, if they were all,
Whose leaves already are burnt with frost,
Whose clustered fruit must else be lost—   20
For the grapes' sake along the wall.

RELUCTANCE

Out through the fields and the woods
    And over the walls I have wended;
I have climbed the hills of view
    And looked at the world, and descended;
I have come by the highway home,   5
    And lo, it is ended.

The leaves are all dead on the ground,
    Save those that the oak is keeping
To ravel them one by one
    And let them go scraping and creeping   10
Out over the crusted snow,
    When others are sleeping.

And the dead leaves lie huddled and still,
    No longer blown hither and thither;
The last lone aster is gone;   15
    The flowers of the witch hazel wither;

The heart is still aching to seek,
    But the feet question "Whither?"

Ah, when to the heart of man
    Was it ever less than a treason   20
To go with the drift of things,
    To yield with a grace to reason,
And bow and accept the end
    Of a love or a season?

THE PASTURE

I'm going out to clean the pasture spring;
I'll only stop to rake the leaves away
(And wait to watch the water clear, I may):
I shan't be gone long.—You come too.

I'm going out to fetch the little calf   5
That's standing by the mother. It's so young
It totters when she licks it with her tongue.
I shan't be gone long.—You come too.

MENDING WALL

Something there is that doesn't love a wall,
That sends the frozen-ground-swell under it
And spills the upper boulders in the sun,
And makes gaps even two can pass abreast.
The work of hunters is another thing: 5
I have come after them and made repair
Where they have left not one stone on a stone,
But they would have the rabbit out of hiding,
To please the yelping dogs. The gaps I mean,
No one has seen them made or heard them made,   10
But at spring mending-time we find them there.
I let my neighbor know beyond the hill;
And on a day we meet to walk the line
And set the wall between us once again.
We keep the wall between us as we go.   15

To each the boulders that have fallen to each.
And some are loaves and some so nearly balls
We have to use a spell to make them balance:
"Stay where you are until our backs are turned!"
We wear our fingers rough with handling them. 20
Oh, just another kind of outdoor game,
One on a side. It comes to little more:
There where it is we do not need the wall:
He is all pine and I am apple orchard.
My apple trees will never get across 25
And eat the cones under his pines, I tell him.
He only says, "Good fences make good neighbors."
Spring is the mischief in me, and I wonder
If I could put a notion in his head:
"*Why* do they make good neighbors? Isn't it 30
Where there are cows? But here there are no cows.
Before I built a wall I'd ask to know
What I was walling in or walling out,
And to whom I was like to give offense.
Something there is that doesn't love a wall, 35
That wants it down." I could say "Elves" to him,
But it's not elves exactly, and I'd rather
He said it for himself. I see him there,
Bringing a stone grasped firmly by the top
In each hand, like an old-stone savage armed. 40
He moves in darkness as it seems to me,
Not of woods only and the shade of trees.
He will not go behind his father's saying,
And he likes having thought of it so well
He says again, "Good fences make good neighbors." 45

THE DEATH OF THE HIRED MAN

Mary sat musing on the lamp-flame at the table,
Waiting for Warren. When she heard his step,
She ran on tiptoe down the darkened passage
To meet him in the doorway with the news
And put him on his guard. "Silas is back."   5
She pushed him outward with her through the door
And shut it after her. "Be kind," she said,
She took the market things from Warren's arms
And set them on the porch, then drew him down
To sit beside her on the wooden steps.   10

"When was I ever anything but kind to him?
But I'll not have the fellow back," he said.
"I told him so last haying, didn't I?
If he left then, I said, that ended it.
What good is he? Who else will harbor him   15
At his age for the little he can do?
What help he is there's no depending on.
Off he goes always when I need him most.
He thinks he ought to earn a little pay,
Enough at least to buy tobacco with,   20
So he won't have to beg and be beholden.
'All right,' I say, 'I can't afford to pay
Any fixed wages, though I wish I could.'
'Someone else can.' 'Then someone else will have to.'
I shouldn't mind his bettering himself   25
If that was what it was. You can be certain,
When he begins like that, there's someone at him
Trying to coax him off with pocket money—
In haying time, when any help is scarce.
In winter he comes back to us. I'm done."   30

"Sh! not so loud: he'll hear you," Mary said.

"I want him to: he'll have to soon or late."

"He's worn out. He's asleep beside the stove.
When I came up from Rowe's I found him here,
Huddled against the barn door fast asleep,   35
A miserable sight, and frightening, too—
You needn't smile—I didn't recognize him—
I wasn't looking for him—and he's changed.
Wait till you see."

                "Where did you say he'd been?"

"He didn't say, I dragged him to the house,   40
And gave him tea and tried to make him smoke.
I tried to make him talk about his travels.
Nothing would do: he just kept nodding off."

"What did he say? Did he say anything?"

"But little."

           "Anything? Mary, confess   45
He said he'd come to ditch the meadow for me."

"Warren!"

           "But did he? I just want to know."

"Of course he did. What would you have him say?
Surely you wouldn't grudge the poor old man
Some humble way to save his self-respect.   50
He added, if you really care to know,
He meant to clear the upper pasture, too.
That sounds like something you have heard before?
Warren, I wish you could have heard the way

He jumbled everything. I stopped to look   55
Two or three times—he made me feel so queer—
To see if he was talking in his sleep.
He ran on Harold Wilson—you remember—
The boy you had in haying four years since.
He's finished school, and teaching in his college.   60
Silas declares you'll have to get him back.
He says they two will make a team for work:
Between them they will lay this farm as smooth!
The way he mixed that in with other things.
He thinks young Wilson a likely lad, though daft   65
On education—you know how they fought
All through July under the blazing sun,
Silas up on the cart to build the load,
Harold along beside to pitch it on."

"Yes, I took care to keep well out of earshot."   70

"Well, those days trouble Silas like a dream.
You wouldn't think they would. How some things linger!
Harold's young college-boy's assurance piqued him.
After so many years he still keeps finding
Good arguments he sees he might have used.   75
I sympathize. I know just how it feels
To think of the right thing to say too late.
Harold's associated in his mind with Latin.
He asked me what I thought of Harold's saying
He studied Latin, like the violin,   80
Because he liked it—that an argument!
He said he couldn't make the boy believe
He could find water with a hazel prong—
Which showed how much good school had ever done him.
He wanted to go over that. But most of all   85

He thinks if he could have another chance
To teach him how to build a load of hay——"

"I know, that's Silas' one accomplishment.
He bundles every forkful in its place,
And tags and numbers it for future reference,   90
So he can find and easily dislodge it
In the unloading. Silas does that well.
He takes it out in bunches like big birds' nests.
You never see him standing on the hay
He's trying to lift, straining to lift himself."   95

"He thinks if he could teach him that, he'd be
Some good perhaps to someone in the world.
He hates to see a boy the fool of books.
Poor Silas, so concerned for other folk,
And nothing to look backward to with pride,   100
And nothing to look forward to with hope,
So now and never any different."

Part of a moon was falling down the west,
Dragging the whole sky with it to the hills.
Its light poured softly in her lap. She saw it   105
And spread her apron to it. She put out her hand
Among the harplike morning-glory strings,
Taut with the dew from garden bed to eaves,
As if she played unheard some tenderness
That wrought on him beside her in the night.   110
"Warren," she said, "he has come home to die:
You needn't be afraid he'll leave you this time."

"Home," he mocked gently.

                          "Yes, what else but home?

It all depends on what you mean by home.
Of course he's nothing to us, any more   115
Than was the hound that came a stranger to us
Out of the woods, worn out upon the trail."

"Home is the place where, when you have to go there,
They have to take you in."

                              "I should have called it
Something you somehow haven't to deserve."   120

Warren leaned out and took a step or two,
Picked up a little stick, and brought it back
And broke it in his hand and tossed it by.
"Silas has better claim on us you think
Than on his brother? Thirteen little miles   125
As the road winds would bring him to his door.
Silas has walked that far no doubt today.
Why doesn't he go there? His brother's rich,
A somebody—director in the bank."

"He never told us that."

                              "We know it, though."   130

"I think his brother ought to help, of course.
I'll see to that if there is need. He ought of right
To take him in, and might be willing to—
He may be better than appearances.
But have some pity on Silas. Do you think   135
If he had any pride in claiming kin
Or anything he looked for from his brother,
He'd keep so still about him all this time?"

"I wonder what's between them."

                        "I can tell you.

Silas is what he is—we wouldn't mind him—   140
But just the kind that kinsfolk can't abide.
He never did a thing so very bad.
He don't know why he isn't quite as good
As anybody. Worthless though he is,
He won't be made ashamed to please his brother."   145

"*I* can't think Si ever hurt anyone."

"No, but he hurt my heart the way he lay
And rolled his old head on that sharp-edged chair-back.
He wouldn't let me put him on the lounge.
You must go in and see what you can do.   150
I made the bed up for him there tonight.
You'll be surprised at him—how much he's broken.
His working days are done; I'm sure of it."

"I'd not be in a hurry to say that."

"I haven't been. Go, look, see for yourself.   155
But, Warren, please remember how it is:
He's come to help you ditch the meadow.
He has a plan. You mustn't laugh at him.
He may not speak of it, and then he may.
I'll sit and see if that small sailing cloud   160
Will hit or miss the moon."

                   It hit the moon.
Then there were three there, making a dim row,
The moon, the little silver cloud, and she.

Warren returned—too soon, it seemed to her—
Slipped to her side, caught up her hand and waited.   165

"Warren?" she questioned.

"Dead," was all he answered.

THE MOUNTAIN

The mountain held the town as in a shadow.
I saw so much before I slept there once:
I noticed that I missed stars in the west,
Where its black body cut into the sky.
Near me it seemed: I felt it like a wall   5
Behind which I was sheltered from a wind.
And yet between the town and it I found,
When I walked forth at dawn to see new things,
Were fields, a river, and beyond, more fields.
The river at the time was fallen away,   10
And made a widespread brawl on cobblestones;
But the signs showed what it had done in spring:
Good grassland gullied out, and in the grass
Ridges of sand, and driftwood stripped of bark.
I crossed the river and swung round the mountain.   15
And there I met a man who moved so slow
With white-faced oxen, in a heavy cart,
It seemed no harm to stop him altogether.

"What town is this?" I asked.

"This? Lunenburg."

Then I was wrong: the town of my sojourn,   20
Beyond the bridge, was not that of the mountain,
But only felt at night its shadowy presence.
"Where is your village? Very far from here?"

(26)

"There is no village—only scattered farms.
We were but sixty voters last election.   25
We can't in nature grow to many more:
That thing takes all the room!" He moved his goad.
The mountain stood there to be pointed at.
Pasture ran up the side a little way,
And then there was a wall of trees with trunks;   30
After that only tops of trees, and cliffs
Imperfectly concealed among the leaves.
A dry ravine emerged from under boughs
Into the pasture.

                    "That looks like a path.
Is that the way to reach the top from here?—   35
Not for this morning, but some other time:
I must be getting back to breakfast now."

"I don't advise your trying from this side.
There is no proper path, but those that *have*
Been up, I understand, have climbed from Ladd's.   40
That's five miles back. You can't mistake the place:
They logged it there last winter some way up.
I'd take you, but I'm bound the other way."

"You've never climbed it?"

                          "I've been on the sides,
Deer-hunting and trout-fishing. There's a brook   45
That starts up on it somewhere—I've heard say
Right on the top, tip-top—a curious thing.
But what would interest you about the brook,
It's always cold in summer, warm in winter.
One of the great sights going is to see   50

It steam in winter like an ox's breath,
Until the bushes all along its banks
Are inch-deep with the frosty spines and bristles—
You know the kind. Then let the sun shine on it!"

"There ought to be a view around the world   55
From such a mountain—if it isn't wooded
Clear to the top." I saw through leafy screens
Great granite terraces in sun and shadow,
Shelves one could rest a knee on getting up—
With depths behind him sheer a hundred feet—   60
Or turn and sit on and look out and down,
With little ferns in crevices at his elbow.

"As to that I can't say. But there's the spring,
Right on the summit, almost like a fountain.
That ought to be worth seeing."

                              "If it's there.   65
You never saw it?"

                    "I guess there's no doubt
About its being there. I never saw it.
It may not be right on the very top:
It wouldn't have to be a long way down
To have some head of water from above,   70
And a *good distance* down might not be noticed
By anyone who'd come a long way up.
One time I asked a fellow climbing it
To look and tell me later how it was."

"What did he say?"

                    "He said there was a lake   75
Somewhere in Ireland on a mountain top."

(28)

"But a lake's different. What about the spring?"

"He never got up high enough to see.
That's why I don't advise your trying this side.
He tried this side. I've always meant to go   80
And look myself, but you know how it is:
It doesn't seem so much to climb a mountain
You've worked around the foot of all your life.
What would I do? Go in my overalls,
With a big stick, the same as when the cows   85
Haven't come down to the bars at milking time?
Or with a shotgun for a stray black bear?
'Twouldn't seem real to climb for climbing it."

"I shouldn't climb it if I didn't want to—
Not for the sake of climbing. What's its name?"   90

"We call it Hor: I don't know if that's right."

"Can one walk around it? Would it be too far?"

"You can drive round and keep in Lunenburg,
But it's as much as ever you can do,
The boundary lines keep in so close to it.   95
Hor is the township, and the township's Hor—
And a few houses sprinkled round the foot,
Like boulders broken off the upper cliff,
Rolled out a little farther than the rest."

"Warm in December, cold in June, you say?"   100

"I don't suppose the water's changed at all.
You and I know enough to know it's warm
Compared with cold, and cold compared with warm.
But all the fun's in how you say a thing."

"You've lived here all your life?"

"Ever since Hor
Was no bigger than a——" What, I did not hear.
He drew the oxen toward him with light touches
Of his slim goad on nose and offside flank,
Gave them their marching orders and was moving.

HOME BURIAL

He saw her from the bottom of the stairs
Before she saw him. She was starting down,
Looking back over her shoulder at some fear.
She took a doubtful step and then undid it
To raise herself and look again. He spoke   5
Advancing toward her: "What is it you see
From up there always?—for I want to know."
She turned and sank upon her skirts at that,
And her face changed from terrified to dull.
He said to gain time: "What is it you see?"   10
Mounting until she cowered under him.
"I will find out now—you must tell me, dear."
She, in her place, refused him any help,
With the least stiffening of her neck and silence.
She let him look, sure that he wouldn't see,   15
Blind creature; and awhile he didn't see.
But at last he murmured, "Oh," and again, "Oh."

"What is it—what?" she said.

"Just that I see."

"You don't," she challenged. "Tell me what it is."

(3 0)

"The wonder is I didn't see at once.   20
I never noticed it from here before.
I must be wonted to it—that's the reason.
The little graveyard where my people are!
So small the window frames the whole of it.
Not so much larger than a bedroom, is it?   25
There are three stones of slate and one of marble,
Broad-shouldered little slabs there in the sunlight
On the sidehill. We haven't to mind *those*.
But I understand: it is not the stones,
But the child's mound——"
                                      "Don't, don't, don't,
                                            don't," she cried.   30

She withdrew, shrinking from beneath his arm
That rested on the banister, and slid downstairs;
And turned on him with such a daunting look,
He said twice over before he knew himself:
"Can't a man speak of his own child he's lost?"   35

"Not you!—Oh, where's my hat? Oh, I don't need it!
I must get out of here. I must get air.—
I don't know rightly whether any man can."

"Amy! Don't go to someone else this time.
Listen to me. I won't come down the stairs."   40
He sat and fixed his chin between his fists.
"There's something I should like to ask you, dear."

"You don't know how to ask it."

                                      "Help me, then."

Her fingers moved the latch for all reply.

(3 1)

"My words are nearly always an offense.   45
I don't know how to speak of anything
So as to please you. But I might be taught,
I should suppose. I can't say I see how.
A man must partly give up being a man
With womenfolk. We could have some arrangement   50
By which I'd bind myself to keep hands off
Anything special you're a-mind to name.
Though I don't like such things 'twixt those that love.
Two that don't love can't live together without them.
But two that do can't live together with them."   55
She moved the latch a little. "Don't—don't go.
Don't carry it to someone else this time.
Tell me about it if it's something human.
Let me into your grief. I'm not so much
Unlike other folks as your standing there   60
Apart would make me out. Give me my chance.
I do think, though, you overdo it a little.
What was it brought you up to think it the thing
To take your mother-loss of a first child
So inconsolably—in the face of love.   65
You'd think his memory might be satisfied——"

"There you go sneering now!"

                              "I'm not, I'm not!
You make me angry. I'll come down to you.
God, what a woman! And it's come to this,
A man can't speak of his own child that's dead."   70

"You can't because you don't know how to speak.
If you had any feelings, you that dug
With your own hand—how could you?—his little grave;

(32)

I saw you from that very window there,
Making the gravel leap and leap in air,   75
Leap up, like that, like that, and land so lightly
And roll back down the mound beside the hole.
I thought, Who is that man? I didn't know you.
And I crept down the stairs and up the stairs
To look again, and still your spade kept lifting.   80
Then you came in. I heard your rumbling voice
Out in the kitchen, and I don't know why,
But I went near to see with my own eyes.
You could sit there with the stains on your shoes
Of the fresh earth from your own baby's grave   85
And talk about your everyday concerns.
You had stood the spade up against the wall
Outside there in the entry, for I saw it."

"I shall laugh the worst laugh I ever laughed.
I'm cursed, God, if I don't believe I'm cursed."   90

"I can repeat the very words you were saying:
'Three foggy mornings and one rainy day
Will rot the best birch fence a man can build.'
Think of it, talk like that at such a time!
What had how long it takes a birch to rot   95
To do with what was in the darkened parlor?
You *couldn't* care! The nearest friends can go
With anyone to death, comes so far short
They might as well not try to go at all.
No, from the time when one is sick to death,   100
One is alone, and he dies more alone.
Friends make pretense of following to the grave,
But before one is in it, their minds are turned
And making the best of their way back to life

(33)

And living people, and things they understand.   105
But the world's evil. I won't have grief so
If I can change it. Oh, I won't, I won't!"

"There, you have said it all and you feel better.
You won't go now. You're crying. Close the door.
The heart's gone out of it: why keep it up?   110
Amy! There's someone coming down the road!"

"*You*—oh, you think the talk is all. I must go—
Somewhere out of this house. How can I make you——"

"If—you—do!" She was opening the door wider.
"Where do you mean to go? First tell me that.   115
I'll follow and bring you back by force. I *will!*—"

A SERVANT TO SERVANTS

I didn't make you know how glad I was
To have you come and camp here on our land.
I promised myself to get down some day
And see the way you lived, but I don't know!
With a houseful of hungry men to feed   5
I guess you'd find. . . . It seems to me
I can't express my feelings, any more
Than I can raise my voice or want to lift
My hand (oh, I can lift it when I have to).
Did ever you feel so? I hope you never.   10
It's got so I don't even know for sure
Whether I *am* glad, sorry, or anything.
There's nothing but a voice-like left inside
That seems to tell me how I ought to feel,
And would feel if I wasn't all gone wrong.   15
You take the lake. I look and look at it.

I see it's a fair, pretty sheet of water.
I stand and make myself repeat out loud
The advantages it has, so long and narrow,
Like a deep piece of some old running river   20
Cut short off at both ends. It lies five miles
Straightaway through the mountain notch
From the sink window where I wash the plates,
And all our storms come up toward the house,
Drawing the slow waves whiter and whiter and whiter.   25
It took my mind off doughnuts and soda biscuit
To step outdoors and take the water dazzle
A sunny morning, or take the rising wind
About my face and body and through my wrapper,
When a storm threatened from the Dragon's Den,   30
And a cold chill shivered across the lake.
I see it's a fair, pretty sheet of water,
Our Willoughby! How did you hear of it?
I expect, though, everyone's heard of it.
In a book about ferns? Listen to that!   35
You let things more like feathers regulate
Your going and coming. And you like it here?
I can see how you might. But I don't know!
It would be different if more people came,
For then there would be business. As it is,   40
The cottages Len built, sometimes we rent them,
Sometimes we don't. We've a good piece of shore
That ought to be worth something, and may yet.
But I don't count on it as much as Len.
He looks on the bright side of everything,   45
Including me. He thinks I'll be all right
With doctoring. But it's not medicine—
Lowe is the only doctor's dared to say so—

It's rest I want—there, I have said it out—
From cooking meals for hungry hired men   50
And washing dishes after them—from doing
Things over and over that just won't stay done.
By good rights I ought not to have so much
Put on me, but there seems no other way.
Len says one steady pull more ought to do it.   55
He says the best way out is always through.
And I agree to that, or in so far
As that I can see no way out but through—
Leastways for me—and then they'll be convinced.
It's not that Len don't want the best for me.   60
It was his plan our moving over in
Beside the lake from where that day I showed you
We used to live—ten miles from anywhere.
We didn't change without some sacrifice,
But Len went at it to make up the loss.   65
His work's a man's, of course, from sun to sun,
But he works when he works as hard as I do—
Though there's small profit in comparisons.
(Women and men will make them all the same.)
But work ain't all. Len undertakes too much.   70
He's into everything in town. This year
It's highways, and he's got too many men
Around him to look after that make waste.
They take advantage of him shamefully,
And proud, too, of themselves for doing so.   75
We have four here to board, great good-for-nothings,
Sprawling about the kitchen with their talk
While I fry their bacon. Much they care!
No more put out in what they do or say
Than if I wasn't in the room at all.   80

Coming and going all the time, they are:
I don't learn what their names are, let alone
Their characters, or whether they are safe
To have inside the house with doors unlocked.
I'm not afraid of them, though, if they're not   85
Afraid of me. There's two can play at that.
I have my fancies: it runs in the family.
My father's brother wasn't right. They kept him
Locked up for years back there at the old farm.
I've been away once—yes, I've been away.   90
The State Asylum. I was prejudiced;
I wouldn't have sent anyone of mine there;
You know the old idea—the only asylum
Was the poorhouse, and those who could afford,
Rather than send their folks to such a place,   95
Kept them at home; and it does seem more human.
But it's not so: the place is the asylum.
There they have every means proper to do with,
And you aren't darkening other people's lives—
Worse than no good to them, and they no good   100
To you in your condition; you can't know
Affection or the want of it in that state.
I've heard too much of the old-fashioned way.
My father's brother, he went mad quite young.
Some thought he had been bitten by a dog,   105
Because his violence took on the form
Of carrying his pillow in his teeth;
But it's more likely he was crossed in love,
Or so the story goes. It was some girl.
Anyway all he talked about was love.   110
They soon saw he would do someone a mischief
If he wa'n't kept strict watch of, and it ended

In father's building him a sort of cage,
Or room within a room, of hickory poles,
Like stanchions in the barn, from floor to ceiling— 115
A narrow passage all the way around.
Anything they put in for furniture
He'd tear to pieces, even a bed to lie on.
So they made the place comfortable with straw,
Like a beast's stall, to ease their consciences. 120
Of course they had to feed him without dishes.
They tried to keep him clothed, but he paraded
With his clothes on his arm—all of his clothes.
Cruel—it sounds. I s'pose they did the best
They knew. And just when he was at the height, 125
Father and mother married, and mother came,
A bride, to help take care of such a creature,
And accommodate her young life to his.
That was what marrying father meant to her.
She had to lie and hear love things made dreadful 130
By his shouts in the night. He'd shout and shout
Until the strength was shouted out of him,
And his voice died down slowly from exhaustion.
He'd pull his bars apart like bow and bowstring,
And let them go and make them twang, until 135
His hands had worn them smooth as any oxbow.
And then he'd crow as if he thought that child's play—
The only fun he had. I've heard them say, though,
They found a way to put a stop to it.
He was before my time—I never saw him; 140
But the pen stayed exactly as it was,
There in the upper chamber in the ell,
A sort of catchall full of attic clutter.

I often think of the smooth hickory bars.
It got so I would say—you know, half fooling—   145
"It's time I took my turn upstairs in jail"—
Just as you will till it becomes a habit.
No wonder I was glad to get away.
Mind you, I waited till Len said the word.
I didn't want the blame if things went wrong.   150
I was glad though, no end, when we moved out,
And I looked to be happy, and I was,
As I said, for a while—but I don't know!
Somehow the change wore out like a prescription.
And there's more to it than just window views   155
And living by a lake. I'm past such help—
Unless Len took the notion, which he won't,
And I won't ask him—it's not sure enough.
I s'pose I've got to go the road I'm going:
Other folks have to, and why shouldn't I?   160
I almost think if I could do like you,
Drop everything and live out on the ground—
But it might be, come night, I shouldn't like it,
Or a long rain. I should soon get enough,
And be glad of a good roof overhead.   165
I've lain awake thinking of you, I'll warrant,
More than you have yourself, some of these nights.
The wonder was the tents weren't snatched away
From over you as you lay in your beds.
I haven't courage for a risk like that.   170
Bless you, of course you're keeping me from work,
But the thing of it is, I need to *be* kept.
There's work enough to do—there's always that;
But behind's behind. The worst that you can do

Is set me back a little more behind.   175
I shan't catch up in this world, anyway.
I'd *rather* you'd not go unless you must.

AFTER APPLE-PICKING

My long two-pointed ladder's sticking through a tree
Toward heaven still,
And there's a barrel that I didn't fill
Beside it, and there may be two or three
Apples I didn't pick upon some bough.   5
But I am done with apple-picking now.
Essence of winter sleep is on the night,
The scent of apples: I am drowsing off.
I cannot rub the strangeness from my sight
I got from looking through a pane of glass   10
I skimmed this morning from the drinking trough
And held against the world of hoary grass.
It melted, and I let it fall and break.
But I was well
Upon my way to sleep before it fell,   15
And I could tell
What form my dreaming was about to take.
Magnified apples appear and disappear,
Stem end and blossom end,
And every fleck of russet showing clear.   20
My instep arch not only keeps the ache,
It keeps the pressure of a ladder-round.
I feel the ladder sway as the boughs bend.
And I keep hearing from the cellar bin
The rumbling sound   25
Of load on load of apples coming in.

For I have had too much
Of apple-picking: I am overtired
Of the great harvest I myself desired.
There were ten thousand thousand fruit to touch, 30
Cherish in hand, lift down, and not let fall.
For all
That struck the earth,
No matter if not bruised or spiked with stubble,
Went surely to the cider-apple heap 35
As of no worth.
One can see what will trouble
This sleep of mine, whatever sleep it is.
Were he not gone,
The woodchuck could say whether it's like his 40
Long sleep, as I describe its coming on,
Or just some human sleep.

THE CODE

There were three in the meadow by the brook
Gathering up windrows, piling cocks of hay,
With an eye always lifted toward the west
Where an irregular sun-bordered cloud
Darkly advanced with a perpetual dagger 5
Flickering across its bosom. Suddenly
One helper, thrusting pitchfork in the ground,
Marched himself off the field and home. One stayed.
The town-bred farmer failed to understand.

"What is there wrong?"

                  "Something you just now said." 10

"What did I say?"

"About our taking pains."

"To cock the hay?—because it's going to shower?
I said that more than half an hour ago.
I said it to myself as much as you."

"You didn't know. But James is one big fool.   15
He thought you meant to find fault with his work.
That's what the average farmer would have meant.
James would take time, of course, to chew it over
Before he acted: he's just got round to act."

"He *is* a fool if that's the way he takes me."   20

"Don't let it bother you. You've found out something.
The hand that knows his business won't be told
To do work better or faster—those two things.
I'm as particular as anyone:
Most likely I'd have served you just the same.   25
But I know you don't understand our ways.
You were just talking what was in your mind,
What was in all our minds, and you weren't hinting.
Tell you a story of what happened once:
I was up here in Salem, at a man's   30
Named Sanders, with a gang of four or five
Doing the haying. No one liked the boss.
He was one of the kind sports call a spider,
All wiry arms and legs that spread out wavy
From a humped body nigh as big's a biscuit.   35
But work! that man could work, especially
If by so doing he could get more work
Out of his hired help. I'm not denying

(42)

He was hard on himself. I couldn't find
That he kept any hours—not for himself. 40
Daylight and lantern-light were one to him:
I've heard him pounding in the barn all night.
But what he liked was someone to encourage.
Them that he couldn't lead he'd get behind
And drive, the way you can, you know, in mowing— 45
Keep at their heels and threaten to mow their legs off.
I'd seen about enough of his bulling tricks
(We call that bulling). I'd been watching him.
So when he paired off with me in the hayfield
To load the load, thinks I, Look out for trouble. 50
I built the load and topped it off; old Sanders
Combed it down with a rake and says, 'O.K.'
Everything went well till we reached the barn
With a big jag to empty in a bay.
You understand that meant the easy job 55
For the man up on top, of throwing *down*
The hay and rolling it off wholesale,
Where on a mow it would have been slow lifting.
You wouldn't think a fellow'd need much urging
Under those circumstances, would you now? 60
But the old fool seizes his fork in both hands,
And looking up bewhiskered out of the pit,
Shouts like an army captain, 'Let her come!'
Thinks I, D'ye mean it? 'What was that you said?'
I asked out loud, so's there'd be no mistake, 65
'Did you say, "Let her come"?' 'Yes, let her come.'
He said it over, but he said it softer.
Never you say a thing like that to a man,
Not if he values what he is. God, I'd as soon
Murdered him as left out his middle name. 70

I'd built the load and knew right where to find it.
Two or three forkfuls I picked lightly round for
Like meditating, and then I just dug in
And dumped the rackful on him in ten lots.
I looked over the side once in the dust 75
And caught sight of him treading-water-like,
Keeping his head above. 'Damn ye,' I says,
'That gets ye!' He squeaked like a squeezed rat.
That was the last I saw or heard of him.
I cleaned the rack and drove out to cool off. 80
As I sat mopping hayseed from my neck,
And sort of waiting to be asked about it,
One of the boys sings out, 'Where's the old man?'
'I left him in the barn under the hay.
If ye want him, ye can go and dig him out.' 85
They realized from the way I swabbed my neck
More than was needed, something must be up.
They headed for the barn; I stayed where I was.
They told me afterward. First they forked hay,
A lot of it, out into the barn floor. 90
Nothing! They listened for him. Not a rustle.
I guess they thought I'd spiked him in the temple
Before I buried him, or I couldn't have managed.
They excavated more. 'Go keep his wife
Out of the barn.' Someone looked in a window, 95
And curse me if he wasn't in the kitchen
Slumped way down in a chair, with both his feet
Against the stove, the hottest day that summer.
He looked so clean disgusted from behind
There was no one that dared to stir him up, 100
Or let him know that he was being looked at.
Apparently I hadn't buried him

(I may have knocked him down); but my just trying
To bury him had hurt his dignity.
He had gone to the house so's not to meet me. 105
He kept away from us all afternoon.
We tended to his hay. We saw him out
After a while picking peas in his garden:
He couldn't keep away from doing something."

"Weren't you relieved to find he wasn't dead?" 110

"No! and yet I don't know—it's hard to say.
I went about to kill him fair enough."

"You took an awkward way. Did he discharge you?"

"Discharge me? No! He knew I did just right."

THE HOUSEKEEPER

I let myself in at the kitchen door.

"It's you," she said. "I can't get up. Forgive me
Not answering your knock. I can no more
Let people in than I can keep them out.
I'm getting too old for my size, I tell them. 5
My fingers are about all I've the use of
So's to take any comfort. I can sew:
I help out with this beadwork what I can."

"That's a smart pair of pumps you're beading there.
Who are they for?"

           "You mean?—oh, for some miss. 10
I can't keep track of other people's daughters.
Lord, if I were to dream of everyone

Whose shoes I primped to dance in!"

"And where's John?"

"Haven't you seen him? Strange what set you off
To come to his house when he's gone to yours.   15
You can't have passed each other. I know what:
He must have changed his mind and gone to Garland's.
He won't be long in that case. You can wait.
Though what good you can be, or anyone—
It's gone so far. You've heard? Estelle's run off."   20

"Yes, what's it all about? When did she go?"

"Two weeks since."

"She's in earnest, it appears."

"I'm sure she won't come back. She's hiding somewhere.
I don't know where myself. John thinks I do.
He thinks I only have to say the word,   25
And she'll come back. But, bless you, I'm her mother—
I can't talk to her, and, Lord, if I could!"

"It will go hard with John. What will he do?
He can't find anyone to take her place."

"Oh, if you ask me that, what *will* he do?   30
He gets some sort of bakeshop meals together,
With me to sit and tell him everything,
What's wanted and how much and where it is.
But when I'm gone—of course I can't stay here:
Estelle's to take me when she's settled down.   35
He and I only hinder one another.
I tell them they can't get me through the door, though:

(46)

I've been built in here like a big church organ.
We've been here fifteen years."

                              "That's a long time
To live together and then pull apart.   40
How do you see him living when you're gone?
Two of you out will leave an empty house."

"I don't just see him living many years,
Left here with nothing but the furniture.
I hate to think of the old place when we're gone,   45
With the brook going by below the yard,
And no one here but hens blowing about.
If he could sell the place, but then, he can't:
No one will ever live on it again.
It's too run down. This is the last of it.   50
What I think he will do, is let things smash.
He'll sort of swear the time away. He's awful!
I never saw a man let family troubles
Make so much difference in his man's affairs.
He's just dropped everything. He's like a child.   55
I blame his being brought up by his mother.
He's got hay down that's been rained on three times.
He hoed a little yesterday for me:
I thought the growing things would do him good.
Something went wrong. I saw him throw the hoe   60
Sky-high with both hands. I can see it now—
Come here—I'll show you—in that apple tree.
That's no way for a man to do at his age:
He's fifty-five, you know, if he's a day."

"Aren't you afraid of him? What's that gun for?"   65

"Oh, that's been there for hawks since chicken-time.
John Hall touch me! Not if he knows his friends.
I'll say that for him, John's no threatener
Like some menfolk. No one's afraid of him;
All is, he's made up his mind not to stand   70
What he has got to stand."

                    "Where is Estelle?
Couldn't one talk to her? What does she say?
You say you don't know where she is."

                            "Nor want to!
She thinks if it was bad to live with him,
It must be right to leave him."

                    "Which is wrong!"   75

"Yes, but he should have married her."

                            "I know."

"The strain's been too much for her all these years:
I can't explain it any other way.
It's different with a man, at least with John:
He knows he's kinder than the run of men.   80
Better than married ought to be as good
As married—that's what he has always said.
I know the way he's felt—but all the same!"

"I wonder why he doesn't marry her
And end it."

                    "Too late now: she wouldn't have him.   85
He's given her time to think of something else.
That's his mistake. The dear knows my interest
Has been to keep the thing from breaking up.

(48)

This is a good home: I don't ask for better.
But when I've said, Why shouldn't they be married?   90
He'd say, Why should they?—no more words than that."

"And after all why should they? John's been fair
I take it. What was his was always hers.
There was no quarrel about property."

"Reason enough, there was no property.   95
A friend or two as good as own the farm,
Such as it is. It isn't worth the mortgage."

"I mean Estelle has always held the purse."

"The rights of that are harder to get at.
I guess Estelle and I have filled the purse.   100
'Twas we let him have money, not he us.
John's a bad farmer. I'm not blaming him.
Take it year in, year out, he doesn't make much.
We came here for a home for me, you know,
Estelle to do the housework for the board   105
Of both of us. But look how it turns out:
She seems to have the housework, and besides,
Half of the outdoor work, though as for that,
He'd say she does it more because she likes it.
You see our pretty things are all outdoors.   110
Our hens and cows and pigs are always better
Than folks like us have any business with.
Farmers around twice as well off as we
Haven't as good. They don't go with the farm.
One thing you can't help liking about John,   115
He's fond of nice things—too fond, some would say.
But Estelle don't complain: she's like him there.
She wants our hens to be the best there are.

You never saw this room before a show,
Full of lank, shivery, half-drowned birds   120
In separate coops, having their plumage done.
The smell of the wet feathers in the heat!
You spoke of John's not being safe to stay with.
You don't know what a gentle lot we are:
We wouldn't hurt a hen! You ought to see us   125
Moving a flock of hens from place to place.
We're not allowed to take them upside down,
All we can hold together by the legs.
Two at a time's the rule, one on each arm,
No matter how far and how many times   130
We have to go."

     "You mean that's John's idea."

"And we live up to it; or I don't know
What childishness he wouldn't give way to.
He manages to keep the upper hand
On his own farm. He's boss. But as to hens: 135
We fence our flowers in and the hens range.
Nothing's too good for them. We say it pays.
John likes to tell the offers he has had,
Twenty for this cock, twenty-five for that.
He never takes the money. If they're worth   140
That much to sell, they're worth as much to keep.
Bless you, it's all expense, though. Reach me down
The little tin box on the cupboard shelf—
The upper shelf, the tin box. That's the one.
I'll show you. Here you are."

     "What's this?"

       "A bill—   145

(50)

For fifty dollars for one Langshang cock—
Receipted. And the cock is in the yard."

"Not in a glass case, then?"

                    "He'd need a tall one:
He can eat off a barrel from the ground.
He's been in a glass case, as you may say,   150
The Crystal Palace, London. He's imported.
John bought him, and we paid the bill with beads—
Wampum, I call it. Mind, we don't complain.
But you see, don't you, we take care of him."

"And like it, too. It makes it all the worse."   155

"It seems as if. And that's not all: he's helpless
In ways that I can hardly tell you of.
Sometimes he gets possessed to keep accounts
To see where all the money goes so fast.
You know how men will be ridiculous.   160
But it's just fun the way he gets bedeviled—
If he's untidy now, what will he be——?"

"It makes it all the worse. You must be blind."

"Estelle's the one. You needn't talk to me."

"Can't you and I get to the root of it?   165
What's the real trouble? What will satisfy her?"

"It's as I say: she's turned from him, that's all."

"But why, when she's well off? Is it the neighbors,
Being cut off from friends?"

"We have our friends.
That isn't it. Folks aren't afraid of us."   170

"She's let it worry her. You stood the strain,
And you're her mother."

                    "But I didn't always.
I didn't relish it along at first.
But I got wonted to it. And besides—
John said I was too old to have grandchildren.   175
But what's the use of talking when it's done?
She won't come back—it's worse than that—she can't."

"Why do you speak like that? What do you know?
What do you mean?—she's done harm to herself?"

"I mean she's married—married someone else."   180

"Oho, oho!"

                    "You don't believe me."

                              "Yes, I do,
Only too well. I knew there must be something!
So that was what was back. She's bad, that's all!"

"Bad to get married when she had the chance?"

"Nonsense! See what she's done! But who, but who——?"   185

"Who'd marry her straight out of such a mess?
Say it right out—no matter for her mother.
The man was found. I'd better name no names.
John himself won't imagine who he is."

"Then it's all up. I think I'll get away.   190
You'll be expecting John. I pity Estelle;

I suppose she deserves some pity, too.
You ought to have the kitchen to yourself
To break it to him. You may have the job."

"You needn't think you're going to get away. 195
John's almost here. I've had my eye on someone
Coming down Ryan's Hill. I thought 'twas him.
Here he is now. This box! Put it away.
And this bill."

      "What's the hurry? He'll unhitch."

"No, he won't, either. He'll just drop the reins 200
And turn Doll out to pasture, rig and all.
She won't get far before the wheels hang up
On something—there's no harm. See, there he is!
My, but he looks as if he must have heard!"

John threw the door wide but he didn't enter. 205
"How are you, neighbor? Just the man I'm after.
Isn't it Hell?" he said. "I want to know.
Come out here if you want to hear me talk.—
I'll talk to you, old woman, afterward.—
I've got some news that maybe isn't news. 210
What are they trying to do to me, these two?"

"Do go along with him and stop his shouting."
She raised her voice against the closing door:
"Who wants to hear your news, you—dreadful fool?"

THE FEAR

A lantern-light from deeper in the barn
Shone on a man and woman in the door
And threw their lurching shadows on a house

Nearby, all dark in every glossy window.
A horse's hoof pawed once the hollow floor,   5
And the back of the gig they stood beside
Moved in a little. The man grasped a wheel.
The woman spoke out sharply, "Whoa, stand still!—
I saw it just as plain as a white plate,"
She said, "as the light on the dashboard ran   10
Along the bushes at the roadside—a man's face.
You *must* have seen it too."

              "I didn't see it.

Are you sure——"

         "Yes, I'm sure!"

             "—it was a face?"

"Joel, I'll have to look. I can't go in,
I can't, and leave a thing like that unsettled.   15
Doors locked and curtains drawn will make no difference.
I always have felt strange when we came home
To the dark house after so long an absence,
And the key rattled loudly into place
Seemed to warn someone to be getting out   20
At one door as we entered at another.
What if I'm right, and someone all the time—
Don't hold my arm!"

        "I say it's someone passing."

"You speak as if this were a traveled road.
You forget where we are. What is beyond   25
That he'd be going to or coming from

At such an hour of night, and on foot too?
What was he standing still for in the bushes?"

"It's not so very late—it's only dark.
There's more in it than you're inclined to say.
Did he look like——?"   30

                    "He looked like anyone.
I'll never rest tonight unless I know.
Give me the lantern."

                    "You don't want the lantern."

She pushed past him and got it for herself.

"You're not to come," she said. "This is my business.   35
If the time's come to face it, I'm the one
To put it the right way. He'd never dare—
Listen! He kicked a stone. Hear that, hear that!
He's coming towards us. Joel, *go* in—please.
Hark!—I don't hear him now. But please go in."   40

"In the first place you can't make me believe it's——"

"It is—or someone else he's sent to watch.
And now's the time to have it out with him
While we know definitely where he is.
Let him get off and he'll be everywhere   45
Around us, looking out of trees and bushes
Till I shan't dare to set a foot outdoors.
And I can't stand it. Joel, let me go!"

"But it's nonsense to think he'd care enough."

"You mean you couldn't understand his caring.   50
Oh, but you see he hadn't had enough—

Joel, I won't—I won't—I promise you.
We mustn't say hard things. You mustn't either."

"I'll be the one, if anybody goes!
But you give him the advantage with this light.　　　55
What couldn't he do to us standing here!
And if to see was what he wanted, why,
He has seen all there was to see and gone."

He appeared to forget to keep his hold,
But advanced with her as she crossed the grass.　　　60

"What do you want?" she cried to all the dark.
She stretched up tall to overlook the light
That hung in both hands, hot against her skirt.

"There's no one; so you're wrong," he said.

　　　　　　　　　　　　　"There is.—
What do you want?" she cried, and then herself　　　65
Was startled when an answer really came.

"Nothing." It came from well along the road.

She reached a hand to Joel for support:
The smell of scorching woolen made her faint.
"What are you doing round this house at night?"　　　70

"Nothing." A pause: there seemed no more to say.

And then the voice again: "You seem afraid.
I saw by the way you whipped up the horse.
I'll just come forward in the lantern-light
And let you see."

　　　　　　　　　"Yes, do.—Joel, go back!"　　　75

She stood her ground against the noisy steps
That came on, but her body rocked a little.

"You see," the voice said.

           "Oh." She looked and looked.

"You don't see—I've a child here by the hand.
A robber wouldn't have his family with him."   80

"What's a child doing at this time of night——?"

"Out walking. Every child should have the memory
Of at least one long-after-bedtime walk.
What, son?"

       "Then I should think you'd try to find
Somewhere to walk——"

              "The highway, as it happens— 85
We're stopping for the fortnight down at Dean's."

"But if that's all—Joel—you realize—
You won't think anything. You understand?
You understand that we have to be careful.
This is a very, very lonely place.—   90
Joel!" She spoke as if she couldn't turn.
The swinging lantern lengthened to the ground,
It touched, it struck, it clattered and went out.

THE WOOD-PILE

Out walking in the frozen swamp one gray day,
I paused and said, "I will turn back from here.
No, I will go on farther—and we shall see."

The hard snow held me, save where now and then
One foot went through. The view was all in lines 5
Straight up and down of tall slim trees
Too much alike to mark or name a place by
So as to say for certain I was here
Or somewhere else: I was just far from home.
A small bird flew before me. He was careful 10
To put a tree between us when he lighted,
And say no word to tell me who he was
Who was so foolish as to think what *he* thought.
He thought that I was after him for a feather—
The white one in his tail; like one who takes 15
Everything said as personal to himself.
One flight out sideways would have undeceived him.
And then there was a pile of wood for which
I forgot him and let his little fear
Carry him off the way I might have gone, 20
Without so much as wishing him good-night.
He went behind it to make his last stand.
It was a cord of maple, cut and split
And piled—and measured, four by four by eight.
And not another like it could I see. 25
No runner tracks in this year's snow looped near it.
And it was older sure than this year's cutting,
Or even last year's or the year's before.
The wood was gray and the bark warping off it
And the pile somewhat sunken. Clematis 30
Had wound strings round and round it like a bundle.
What held it, though, on one side was a tree
Still growing, and on one a stake and prop,
These latter about to fall. I thought that only
Someone who lived in turning to fresh tasks 35

Could so forget his handiwork on which
He spent himself, the labor of his ax,
And leave it there far from a useful fireplace
To warm the frozen swamp as best it could
With the slow smokeless burning of decay.   40

THE ROAD NOT TAKEN

Two roads diverged in a yellow wood,
And sorry I could not travel both
And be one traveler, long I stood
And looked down one as far as I could
To where it bent in the undergrowth;   5

Then took the other, as just as fair,
And having perhaps the better claim,
Because it was grassy and wanted wear;
Though as for that, the passing there
Had worn them really about the same,   10

And both that morning equally lay
In leaves no step had trodden black.
Oh, I kept the first for another day!
Yet knowing how way leads on to way,
I doubted if I should ever come back.   15

I shall be telling this with a sigh
Somewhere ages and ages hence:
Two roads diverged in a wood, and I—
I took the one less traveled by,
And that has made all the difference.   20

AN OLD MAN'S WINTER NIGHT

All out-of-doors looked darkly in at him
Through the thin frost, almost in separate stars,
That gathers on the pane in empty rooms.

What kept his eyes from giving back the gaze
Was the lamp tilted near them in his hand. 5
What kept him from remembering what it was
That brought him to the creaking room was age.
He stood with barrels round him—at a loss.
And having scared the cellar under him
In clomping here, he scared it once again 10
In clomping off—and scared the outer night,
Which has its sounds, familiar, like the roar
Of trees and crack of branches, common things,
But nothing so like beating on a box.
A light he was to no one but himself 15
Where now he sat, concerned with he knew what,
A quiet light, and then not even that.
He consigned to the moon—such as she was,
So late-arising—to the broken moon,
As better than the sun in any case 20
For such a charge, his snow upon the roof,
His icicles along the wall to keep;
And slept. The log that shifted with a jolt
Once in the stove, disturbed him and he shifted,
And eased his heavy breathing, but still slept. 25
One aged man—one man—can't keep a house,
A farm, a countryside, or if he can,
It's thus he does it of a winter night.

THE TELEPHONE

"When I was just as far as I could walk
From here today,
There was an hour
All still

(61)

When leaning with my head against a flower   5
I heard you talk.
Don't say I didn't, for I heard you say—
You spoke from that flower on the windowsill—
Do you remember what it was you said?"

"First tell me what it was you thought you heard."   10

"Having found the flower and driven a bee away,
I leaned my head,
And holding by the stalk,
I listened and I thought I caught the word—
What was it? Did you call me by my name?   15
Or did you say—
Someone said 'Come'—I heard it as I bowed."

"I may have thought as much, but not aloud."

"Well, so I came."

HYLA BROOK

By June our brook's run out of song and speed.
Sought for much after that, it will be found
Either to have gone groping underground
(And taken with it all the Hyla breed
That shouted in the mist a month ago,   5
Like ghost of sleigh bells in a ghost of snow)—
Or flourished and come up in jewelweed,
Weak foliage that is blown upon and bent,
Even against the way its waters went.
Its bed is left a faded paper sheet   10
Of dead leaves stuck together by the heat—
A brook to none but who remember long.

This as it will be seen is other far
Than with brooks taken otherwhere in song.
We love the things we love for what they are.   15

THE OVEN BIRD

There is a singer everyone has heard,
Loud, a mid-summer and a mid-wood bird,
Who makes the solid tree trunks sound again.
He says that leaves are old and that for flowers
Mid-summer is to spring as one to ten.   5
He says the early petal-fall is past,
When pear and cherry bloom went down in showers
On sunny days a moment overcast;
And comes that other fall we name the fall.
He says the highway dust is over all.   10
The bird would cease and be as other birds
But that he knows in singing not to sing.
The question that he frames in all but words
Is what to make of a diminished thing.

BIRCHES

When I see birches bend to left and right
Across the lines of straighter darker trees,
I like to think some boy's been swinging them.
But swinging doesn't bend them down to stay
As ice storms do. Often you must have seen them   5
Loaded with ice a sunny winter morning
After a rain. They click upon themselves
As the breeze rises, and turn many-colored
As the stir cracks and crazes their enamel
Soon the sun's warmth makes them shed crystal shells   10

(6 3)

Shattering and avalanching on the snow crust—
Such heaps of broken glass to sweep away
You'd think the inner dome of heaven had fallen.
They are dragged to the withered bracken by the load,
And they seem not to break; though once they are bowed   15
So low for long, they never right themselves:
You may see their trunks arching in the woods
Years afterwards, trailing their leaves on the ground
Like girls on hands and knees that throw their hair
Before them over their heads to dry in the sun.   20
But I was going to say when Truth broke in
With all her matter of fact about the ice storm,
I should prefer to have some boy bend them
As he went out and in to fetch the cows—
Some boy too far from town to learn baseball,   25
Whose only play was what he found himself,
Summer or winter, and could play alone.
One by one he subdued his father's trees
By riding them down over and over again
Until he took the stiffness out of them,   30
And not one but hung limp, not one was left
For him to conquer. He learned all there was
To learn about not launching out too soon
And so not carrying the tree away
Clear to the ground. He always kept his poise   35
To the top branches, climbing carefully
With the same pains you use to fill a cup
Up to the brim, and even above the brim.
Then he flung outward, feet first, with a swish,
Kicking his way down through the air to the ground.   40
So was I once myself a swinger of birches.
And so I dream of going back to be.

It's when I'm weary of considerations,
And life is too much like a pathless wood
Where your face burns and tickles with the cobwebs   45
Broken across it, and one eye is weeping
From a twig's having lashed across it open.
I'd like to get away from earth awhile
And then come back to it and begin over.
May no fate willfully misunderstand me   50
And half grant what I wish and snatch me away
Not to return. Earth's the right place for love:
I don't know where it's likely to go better.
I'd like to go by climbing a birch tree,
And climb black branches up a snow-white trunk   55
Toward heaven, till the tree could bear no more,
But dipped its top and set me down again.
That would be good both going and coming back.
One could do worse than be a swinger of birches.

THE COW IN APPLE TIME

Something inspires the only cow of late
To make no more of a wall than an open gate,
And think no more of wall-builders than fools.
Her face is flecked with pomace and she drools
A cider syrup. Having tasted fruit,   5
She scorns a pasture withering to the root.
She runs from tree to tree where lie and sweeten
The windfalls spiked with stubble and worm-eaten.
She leaves them bitten when she has to fly.
She bellows on a knoll against the sky.   10
Her udder shrivels and the milk goes dry.

The Hill Wife

I. LONELINESS

Her Word

One ought not to have to care
    So much as you and I
Care when the birds come round the house
    To seem to say good-by;

Or care so much when they come back   5
    With whatever it is they sing;
The truth being we are as much
    Too glad for the one thing

As we are too sad for the other here—
    With birds that fill their breasts   10
But with each other and themselves
    And their built or driven nests.

II. HOUSE FEAR

Always—I tell you this they learned—
Always at night when they returned
To the lonely house from far away,
To lamps unlighted and fire gone gray,
They learned to rattle the lock and key   5
To give whatever might chance to be,
Warning and time to be off in flight:
And preferring the out- to the indoor night,
They learned to leave the house door wide
Until they had lit the lamp inside.   10

III. THE SMILE

Her Word

I didn't like the way he went away.
That smile! It never came of being gay.
Still he smiled—did you see him?—I was sure!
Perhaps because we gave him only bread
And the wretch knew from that that we were poor.   5
Perhaps because he let us give instead
Of seizing from us as he might have seized.
Perhaps he mocked at us for being wed,
Or being very young (and he was pleased
To have a vision of us old and dead).   10
I wonder how far down the road he's got.
He's watching from the woods as like as not.

IV. THE OFT-REPEATED DREAM

She had no saying dark enough
    For the dark pine that kept
Forever trying the window latch
    Of the room where they slept.

The tireless but ineffectual hands   5
    That with every futile pass
Made the great tree seem as a little bird
    Before the mystery of glass!

It never had been inside the room,
    And only one of the two   10
Was afraid in an oft-repeated dream
    Of what the tree might do.

V. THE IMPULSE

It was too lonely for her there,
   And too wild,
And since there were but two of them,
   And no child,

And work was little in the house,   5
   She was free,
And followed where he furrowed field,
   Or felled tree.

She rested on a log and tossed
   The fresh chips,   10
With a song only to herself
   On her lips.

And once she went to break a bough
   Of black alder.
She strayed so far she scarcely heard   15
   When he called her—

And didn't answer—didn't speak—
   Or return.
She stood, and then she ran and hid
   In the fern.   20

He never found her, though he looked
   Everywhere,
And he asked at her mother's house
   Was she there.

Sudden and swift and light as that   25
   The ties gave,
And he learned of finalities
   Besides the grave.

"OUT, OUT—"

The buzz saw snarled and rattled in the yard
And made dust and dropped stove-length sticks of wood,
Sweet-scented stuff when the breeze drew across it.
And from there those that lifted eyes could count
Five mountain ranges one behind the other   5
Under the sunset far into Vermont.
And the saw snarled and rattled, snarled and rattled,
As it ran light, or had to bear a load.
And nothing happened: day was all but done.
Call it a day, I wish they might have said   10
To please the boy by giving him the half hour
That a boy counts so much when saved from work.
His sister stood beside them in her apron
To tell them "Supper." At the word, the saw,
As if to prove saws knew what supper meant,   15
Leaped out at the boy's hand, or seemed to leap—
He must have given the hand. However it was,
Neither refused the meeting. But the hand!
The boy's first outcry was a rueful laugh,
As he swung toward them holding up the hand,   20
Half in appeal, but half as if to keep
The life from spilling. Then the boy saw all—
Since he was old enough to know, big boy
Doing a man's work, though a child at heart—
He saw all spoiled. "Don't let him cut my hand off—   25
The doctor, when he comes. Don't let him, sister!"
So. But the hand was gone already.
The doctor put him in the dark of ether.
He lay and puffed his lips out with his breath.
And then—the watcher at his pulse took fright.   30

No one believed. They listened at his heart.
Little—less—nothing!—and that ended it.
No more to build on there. And they, since they
Were not the one dead, turned to their affairs.

THE SOUND OF TREES

I wonder about the trees.
Why do we wish to bear
Forever the noise of these
More than another noise
So close to our dwelling place?   5
We suffer them by the day
Till we lose all measure of pace,
And fixity in our joys,
And acquire a listening air.
They are that that talks of going   10
But never gets away;
And that talks no less for knowing,
As it grows wiser and older,
That now it means to stay.
My feet tug at the floor   15
And my head sways to my shoulder
Sometimes when I watch trees sway,
From the window or the door.
I shall set forth for somewhere,
I shall make the reckless choice   20
Some day when they are in voice
And tossing so as to scare
The white clouds over them on.
I shall have less to say,
But I shall be gone.   25

NEW HAMPSHIRE

I met a lady from the South who said
(You won't believe she said it, but she said it):
"None of my family ever worked, or had
A thing to sell." I don't suppose the work
Much matters. You may work for all of me.   5
I've seen the time I've had to work myself.
The having anything to sell is what
Is the disgrace in man or state or nation.

I met a traveler from Arkansas
Who boasted of his state as beautiful   10
For diamonds and apples. "Diamonds
And apples in commercial quantities?"
I asked him, on my guard. "Oh, yes," he answered,
Off his. The time was evening in the Pullman.
"I see the porter's made your bed," I told him.   15

I met a Californian who would
Talk California—a state so blessed,
He said, in climate, none had ever died there
A natural death, and Vigilance Committees
Had had to organize to stock the graveyards   20
And vindicate the state's humanity.
"Just the way Stefansson runs on," I murmured,
"About the British Arctic. That's what comes
Of being in the market with a climate."

I met a poet from another state,   25
A zealot full of fluid inspiration,

Who in the name of fluid inspiration,
But in the best style of bad salesmanship,
Angrily tried to make me write a protest
(In verse I think) against the Volstead Act. 30
He didn't even offer me a drink
Until I asked for one to steady *him*.
This is called having an idea to sell.

It never could have happened in New Hampshire.

The only person really soiled with trade 35
I ever stumbled on in old New Hampshire
Was someone who had just come back ashamed
From selling things in California.
He'd built a noble mansard roof with balls
On turrets, like Constantinople, deep 40
In woods some ten miles from a railroad station,
As if to put forever out of mind
The hope of being, as we say, received.
I found him standing at the close of day
Inside the threshold of his open barn, 45
Like a lone actor on a gloomy stage—
And recognized him, through the iron gray
In which his face was muffled to the eyes,
As an old boyhood friend, and once indeed
A drover with me on the road to Brighton. 50
His farm was "grounds," and not a farm at all;
His house among the local sheds and shanties
Rose like a factor's at a trading station.
And he was rich, and I was still a rascal.
I couldn't keep from asking impolitely 55
Where had he been and what had he been doing?
How did he get so? (Rich was understood.)

In dealing in "old rags" in San Francisco.
Oh, it was terrible as well could be.
We both of us turned over in our graves.   60

Just specimens is all New Hampshire has,
One each of everything as in a showcase,
Which naturally she doesn't care to sell.

She had one President. (Pronounce him Purse,
And make the most of it for better or worse.   65
He's your one chance to score against the state.)
She had one Daniel Webster. He was all
The Daniel Webster ever was or shall be,
She had the Dartmouth needed to produce him.

I call her old. She has one family   70
Whose claim is good to being settled here
Before the era of colonization,
And before that of exploration even.
John Smith remarked them as he coasted by,
Dangling their legs and fishing off a wharf   75
At the Isles of Shoals, and satisfied himself
They weren't Red Indians but veritable
Pre-primitives of the white race, dawn people,
Like those who furnished Adam's sons with wives;
However uninnocent they may have been   80
In being there so early in our history.
They'd been there then a hundred years or more.
Pity he didn't ask what they were up to
At that date with a wharf already built,
And take their name. They've since told me their name—   85
Today an honored one in Nottingham.
As for what they were up to more than fishing—

(73)

Suppose they weren't behaving Puritanly,
The hour had not yet struck for being good,
Mankind had not yet gone on the Sabbatical. 90
It became an explorer of the deep
Not to explore too deep in others' business.

Did you but know of him, New Hampshire has
One real reformer who would change the world
So it would be accepted by two classes, 95
Artists the minute they set up as artists,
Before, that is, they are themselves accepted,
And boys the minute they get out of college.
I can't help thinking those are tests to go by.

And she has one I don't know what to call him, 100
Who comes from Philadelphia every year
With a great flock of chickens of rare breeds
He wants to give the educational
Advantages of growing almost wild
Under the watchful eye of hawk and eagle— 105
Dorkings because they're spoken of by Chaucer,
Sussex because they're spoken of by Herrick.

She has a touch of gold. New Hampshire gold—
You may have heard of it. I had a farm
Offered me not long since up Berlin way 110
With a mine on it that was worked for gold;
But not gold in commercial quantities,
Just enough gold to make the engagement rings
And marriage rings of those who owned the farm.
What gold more innocent could one have asked for? 115
One of my children ranging after rocks
Lately brought home from Andover or Canaan

A specimen of beryl with a trace
Of radium. I know with radium
The trace would have to be the merest trace   120
To be below the threshold of commercial;
But trust New Hampshire not to have enough
Of radium or anything to sell.

A specimen of everything, I said.
She has one witch—old style. She lives in Colebrook.   125
(The only other witch I ever met
Was lately at a cut-glass dinner in Boston.
There were four candles and four people present.
The witch was young, and beautiful (new style),
And open-minded. She was free to question   130
Her gift for reading letters locked in boxes.
Why was it so much greater when the boxes
Were metal than it was when they were wooden?
It made the world seem so mysterious.
The S'ciety for Psychical Research   135
Was cognizant. Her husband was worth millions.
I think he owned some shares in Harvard College.)

New Hampshire *used* to have at Salem
A company we called the White Corpuscles,
Whose duty was at any hour of night   140
To rush in sheets and fool's caps where they smelled
A thing the least bit doubtfully perscented
And give someone the Skipper Ireson's Ride.

One each of everything as in a showcase.

More than enough land for a specimen   145
You'll say she has, but there there enters in
Something else to protect her from herself.

There quality makes up for quantity.
Not even New Hampshire farms are much for sale.
The farm I made my home on in the mountains   150
I had to take by force rather than buy.
I caught the owner outdoors by himself
Raking up after winter, and I said,
"I'm going to put you off this farm: I want it."
"Where are you going to put me? In the road?"   155
"I'm going to put you on the farm next to it."
"Why won't the farm next to it do for you?"
"I like this better." It was really better.

Apples? New Hampshire has them, but unsprayed,
With no suspicion in stem end or blossom end   160
Of vitriol or arsenate of lead,
And so not good for anything but cider.
Her unpruned grapes are flung like lariats
Far up the birches out of reach of man.

A state producing precious metals, stones,   165
And—writing; none of these except perhaps
The precious literature in quantity
Or quality to worry the producer
About disposing of it. Do you know,
Considering the market, there are more   170
Poems produced than any other thing?
No wonder poets sometimes have to *seem*
So much more businesslike than businessmen.
Their wares are so much harder to get rid of.

She's one of the two best states in the Union.   175
Vermont's the other. And the two have been
Yokefellows in the sap yoke from of old

In many Marches. And they lie like wedges,
Thick end to thin end and thin end to thick end,
And are a figure of the way the strong   180
Of mind and strong of arm should fit together,
One thick where one is thin and vice versa.
New Hampshire raises the Connecticut
In a trout hatchery near Canada,
But soon divides the river with Vermont.   185
Both are delightful states for their absurdly
Small towns—Lost Nation, Bungey, Muddy Boo,
Poplin, Still Corners (so called not because
The place is silent all day long, nor yet
Because it boasts a whisky still—because   190
It set out once to be a city and still
Is only corners, crossroads in a wood).
And I remember one whose name appeared
Between the pictures on a movie screen
Election night once in Franconia,   195
When everything had gone Republican
And Democrats were sore in need of comfort:
Easton goes Democratic, Wilson 4
Hughes 2. And everybody to the saddest
Laughed the loud laugh the big laugh at the little.   200
New York (five million) laughs at Manchester,
Manchester (sixty or seventy thousand) laughs
At Littleton (four thousand), Littleton
Laughs at Franconia (seven hundred), and
Franconia laughs, I fear—did laugh that night—   205
At Easton. What has Easton left to laugh at,
And like the actress exclaim "Oh, my God" at?
There's Bungey; and for Bungey there are towns,
Whole townships named but without population.

Anything I can say about New Hampshire   210
Will serve almost as well about Vermont,
Excepting that they differ in their mountains.
The Vermont mountains stretch extended straight;
New Hampshire mountains curl up in a coil.

I had been coming to New Hampshire mountains.   215
And here I am and what am I to say?
Here first my theme becomes embarrassing.
Emerson said, "The God who made New Hampshire
Taunted the lofty land with little men."
Another Massachusetts poet said,   220
"I go no more to summer in New Hampshire.
I've given up my summer place in Dublin."
But when I asked to know what ailed New Hampshire,
She said she couldn't stand the people in it,
The little men (it's Massachusetts speaking).   225
And when I asked to know what ailed the people,
She said, "Go read your own books and find out."
I may as well confess myself the author
Of several books against the world in general.
To take them as against a special state   230
Or even nation's to restrict my meaning.
I'm what is called a sensibilitist,
Or otherwise an environmentalist.
I refuse to adapt myself a mite
To any change from hot to cold, from wet   235
To dry, from poor to rich, or back again.
I make a virtue of my suffering
From nearly everything that goes on round me.
In other words, I know wherever I am,

Being the creature of literature I am,   240
I shall not lack for pain to keep me awake.
Kit Marlowe taught me how to say my prayers:
"Why, this is Hell, nor am I out of it."
Samoa, Russia, Ireland I complain of,
No less than England, France, and Italy.   245
Because I wrote my novels in New Hampshire
Is no proof that I aimed them at New Hampshire.

When I left Massachusetts years ago
Between two days, the reason why I sought
New Hampshire, not Connecticut,   250
Rhode Island, New York, or Vermont was this:
Where I was living then, New Hampshire offered
The nearest boundary to escape across.
I hadn't an illusion in my handbag
About the people being better there   255
Than those I left behind. I thought they weren't.
I thought they couldn't be. And yet they were.
I'd sure had no such friends in Massachusetts
As Hall of Windham, Gay of Atkinson,
Bartlett of Raymond (now of Colorado),   260
Harris of Derry, and Lynch of Bethlehem.

The glorious bards of Massachusetts seem
To want to make New Hampshire people over.
They taunt the lofty land with little men.
I don't know what to say about the people.   265
For art's sake one could almost wish them worse
Rather than better. How are we to write
The Russian novel in America
As long as life goes so unterribly?

There is the pinch from which our only outcry 270
In literature to date is heard to come.
We get what little misery we can
Out of not having cause for misery.
It makes the guild of novel writers sick
To be expected to be Dostoievskis 275
On nothing worse than too much luck and comfort.
This is not sorrow, though; it's just the vapors,
And recognized as such in Russia itself
Under the new regime, and so forbidden.
If well it is with Russia, then feel free 280
To say so or be stood against the wall
And shot. It's Pollyanna now or death.
This, then, is the new freedom we hear tell of;
And very sensible. No state can build
A literature that shall at once be sound 285
And sad on a foundation of well-being.

To show the level of intelligence
Among us: it was just a Warren farmer
Whose horse had pulled him short up in the road
By me, a stranger. This is what he said, 290
From nothing but embarrassment and want
Of anything more sociable to say:
"You hear those hound dogs sing on Moosilauke?
Well, they remind me of the hue and cry
We've heard against the Mid-Victorians 295
And never rightly understood till Bryan
Retired from politics and joined the chorus.
The matter with the Mid-Victorians
Seems to have been a man named John L. Darwin."
"Go 'long," I said to him, he to his horse. 300

I knew a man who failing as a farmer
Burned down his farmhouse for the fire insurance,
And spent the proceeds on a telescope
To satisfy a lifelong curiosity
About our place among the infinities.
And how was that for otherworldliness?   305

If I must choose which I would elevate—
The people or the already lofty mountains,
I'd elevate the already lofty mountains.
The only fault I find with old New Hampshire   310
Is that her mountains aren't quite high enough.
I was not always so; I've come to be so.
How, to my sorrow, how have I attained
A height from which to look down critical
On mountains? What has given me assurance   315
To say what height becomes New Hampshire mountains,
Or any mountains? Can it be some strength
I feel, as of an earthquake in my back,
To heave them higher to the morning star?
Can it be foreign travel in the Alps?   320
Or having seen and credited a moment
The solid molding of vast peaks of cloud
Behind the pitiful reality
Of Lincoln, Lafayette, and Liberty?
Or some such sense as says how high shall jet   325
The fountain in proportion to the basin?
No, none of these has raised me to my throne
Of intellectual dissatisfaction,
But the sad accident of having seen
Our actual mountains given in a map   330
Of early times as twice the height they are—

(81)

Ten thousand feet instead of only five—
Which shows how sad an accident may be.
Five thousand is no longer high enough.
Whereas I never had a good idea   335
About improving people in the world,
Here I am overfertile in suggestion,
And cannot rest from planning day or night
How high I'd thrust the peaks in summer snow
To tap the upper sky and draw a flow   340
Of frosty night air on the vale below
Down from the stars to freeze the dew as starry.

The more the sensibilitist I am
The more I seem to want my mountains wild;
The way the wiry gang-boss liked the log jam.   345
After he'd picked the lock and got it started,
He dodged a log that lifted like an arm
Against the sky to break his back for him,
Then came in dancing, skipping with his life
Across the roar and chaos, and the words   350
We saw him say along the zigzag journey
Were doubtless as the words we heard him say
On coming nearer: "Wasn't she an *i*-deal
Son-of-a-bitch? You bet she was an *i*-deal."

For all her mountains fall a little short,   355
Her people not quite short enough for Art,
She's still New Hampshire, a most restful state.

Lately in converse with a New York alec
About the new school of the pseudo-phallic,
I found myself in a close corner where   360
I had to make an almost funny choice.

"Choose you which you will be—a prude, or puke,
Mewling and puking in the public arms."
"Me for the hills where I don't have to choose."
"But if you had to choose, which would you be?"   365
I wouldn't be a prude afraid of nature.
I know a man who took a double ax
And went alone against a grove of trees;
But his heart failing him, he dropped the ax
And ran for shelter quoting Matthew Arnold: 370
"'Nature is cruel, man is sick of blood';
There's been enough shed without shedding mine.
Remember Birnam Wood! The wood's in flux!"
He had a special terror of the flux
That showed itself in dendrophobia.   375
The only decent tree had been to mill
And educated into boards, he said.
He knew too well for any earthly use
The line where man leaves off and nature starts,
And never overstepped it save in dreams.   380
He stood on the safe side of the line talking—
Which is sheer Matthew Arnoldism,
The cult of one who owned himself "a foiled
Circuitous wanderer," and "took dejectedly
His seat upon the intellectual throne"—   385
Agreed in frowning on these improvised
Altars the woods are full of nowadays,
Again as in the days when Ahaz sinned
By worship under green trees in the open.
Scarcely a mile but that I come on one,   390
A black-cheeked stone and stick of rain-washed charcoal.
Even to say the groves were God's first temples
Comes too near to Ahaz' sin for safety.

Nothing not built with hands of course is sacred.
But here is not a question of what's sacred;   395
Rather of what to face or run away from.
I'd hate to be a runaway from nature.
And neither would I choose to be a puke
Who cares not what he does in company,
And when he can't do anything, falls back   400
On words, and tries his worst to make words speak
Louder than actions, and sometimes achieves it.
It seems a narrow choice the age insists on.
How about being a good Greek, for instance?
That course, they tell me, isn't offered this year.   405
"Come, but this isn't choosing—puke or prude?"
Well, if I have to choose one or the other,
I choose to be a plain New Hampshire farmer
With an income in cash of, say, a thousand
(From, say, a publisher in New York City).   410
It's restful to arrive at a decision,
And restful just to think about New Hampshire.
At present I am living in Vermont.

A STAR IN A STONEBOAT

For Lincoln MacVeagh

Never tell me that not one star of all
That slip from heaven at night and softly fall
Has been picked up with stones to build a wall.

Some laborer found one faded and stone-cold,
And saving that its weight suggested gold   5
And tugged it from his first too certain hold,

He noticed nothing in it to remark.
He was not used to handling stars thrown dark
And lifeless from an interrupted arc.

He did not recognize in that smooth coal   10
The one thing palpable besides the soul
To penetrate the air in which we roll.

He did not see how like a flying thing
It brooded ant eggs, and had one large wing,
One not so large for flying in a ring,   15

And a long Bird of Paradise's tail
(Though these when not in use to fly and trail
It drew back in its body like a snail);

Nor know that he might move it from the spot—
The harm was done: from having been star-shot   20
The very nature of the soil was hot

And burning to yield flowers instead of grain,
Flowers fanned and not put out by all the rain
Poured on them by his prayers prayed in vain.

He moved it roughly with an iron bar,   25
He loaded an old stoneboat with the star
And not, as you might think, a flying car,

Such as even poets would admit perforce
More practical than Pegasus the horse
If it could put a star back in its course.   30

He dragged it through the plowed ground at a pace
But faintly reminiscent of the race
Of jostling rock in interstellar space.

It went for building stone, and I, as though
Commanded in a dream, forever go   35
To right the wrong that this should have been so.

Yet ask where else it could have gone as well,
I do not know—I cannot stop to tell:
He might have left it lying where it fell.

From following walls I never lift my eye,   40
Except at night to places in the sky
Where showers of charted meteors let fly.

Some may know what they seek in school and church,
And why they seek it there; for what I search
I must go measuring stone walls, perch on perch;   45

Sure that though not a star of death and birth,
So not to be compared, perhaps, in worth
To such resorts of life as Mars and Earth—

Though not, I say, a star of death and sin,
It yet has poles, and only needs a spin   50
To show its worldly nature and begin

To chafe and shuffle in my calloused palm
And run off in strange tangents with my arm,
As fish do with the line in first alarm.

Such as it is, it promises the prize   55
Of the one world complete in any size
That I am like to compass, fool or wise.

THE STAR-SPLITTER

"You know Orion always comes up sideways.
Throwing a leg up over our fence of mountains,

And rising on his hands, he looks in on me
Busy outdoors by lantern-light with something
I should have done by daylight, and indeed,   5
After the ground is frozen, I should have done
Before it froze, and a gust flings a handful
Of waste leaves at my smoky lantern chimney
To make fun of my way of doing things,
Or else fun of Orion's having caught me.   10
Has a man, I should like to ask, no rights
These forces are obliged to pay respect to?"
So Brad McLaughlin mingled reckless talk
Of heavenly stars with hugger-mugger farming,
Till having failed at hugger-mugger farming   15
He burned his house down for the fire insurance
And spent the proceeds on a telescope
To satisfy a lifelong curiosity
About our place among the infinities.

"What do you want with one of those blame things?"   20
I asked him well beforehand. "Don't you get one!"

"Don't call it blamed; there isn't anything
More blameless in the sense of being less
A weapon in our human fight," he said.
"I'll have one if I sell my farm to buy it."   25
There where he moved the rocks to plow the ground
And plowed between the rocks he couldn't move,
Few farms changed hands; so rather than spend years
Trying to sell his farm and then not selling,
He burned his house down for the fire insurance   30
And bought the telescope with what it came to.
He had been heard to say by several:
"The best thing that we're put here for's to see;

The strongest thing that's given us to see with's
A telescope. Someone in every town   35
Seems to me owes it to the town to keep one.
In Littleton it may as well be me."
After such loose talk it was no surprise
When he did what he did and burned his house down.

Mean laughter went about the town that day   40
To let him know we weren't the least imposed on,
And he could wait—we'd see to him tomorrow.
But the first thing next morning we reflected
If one by one we counted people out
For the least sin, it wouldn't take us long   45
To get so we had no one left to live with.
For to be social is to be forgiving.
Our thief, the one who does our stealing from us,
We don't cut off from coming to church suppers,
But what we miss we go to him and ask for.   50
He promptly gives it back, that is if still
Uneaten, unworn out, or undisposed of.
It wouldn't do to be too hard on Brad
About his telescope. Beyond the age
Of being given one for Christmas gift,   55
He had to take the best way he knew how
To find himself in one. Well, all we said was
He took a strange thing to be roguish over.
Some sympathy was wasted on the house,
A good old-timer dating back along;   60
But a house isn't sentient; the house
Didn't feel anything. And if it did,
Why not regard it as a sacrifice,

And an old-fashioned sacrifice by fire,
Instead of a new-fashioned one at auction? 65

Out of a house and so out of a farm
At one stroke (of a match), Brad had to turn
To earn a living on the Concord railroad,
As under-ticket-agent at a station
Where his job, when he wasn't selling tickets, 70
Was setting out, up track and down, not plants
As on a farm, but planets, evening stars
That varied in their hue from red to green.

He got a good glass for six hundred dollars.
His new job gave him leisure for stargazing. 75
Often he bid me come and have a look
Up the brass barrel, velvet black inside,
At a star quaking in the other end.
I recollect a night of broken clouds
And underfoot snow melted down to ice, 80
And melting further in the wind to mud.
Bradford and I had out the telescope.
We spread our two legs as we spread its three,
Pointed our thoughts the way we pointed it,
And standing at our leisure till the day broke, 85
Said some of the best things we ever said.
That telescope was christened the Star-Splitter,
Because it didn't do a thing but split
A star in two or three, the way you split
A globule of quicksilver in your hand 90
With one stroke of your finger in the middle.
It's a star-splitter if there ever was one,

And ought to do some good if splitting stars
'Sa thing to be compared with splitting wood.

We've looked and looked, but after all where are we? 95
Do we know any better where we are,
And how it stands between the night tonight
And a man with a smoky lantern chimney?
How different from the way it ever stood?

WILD GRAPES

What tree may not the fig be gathered from?
The grape may not be gathered from the birch?
It's all you know the grape, or know the birch.
As a girl gathered from the birch myself
Equally with my weight in grapes, one autumn, 5
I ought to know what tree the grape is fruit of.
I was born, I suppose, like anyone,
And grew to be a little boyish girl
My brother could not always leave at home.
But that beginning was wiped out in fear 10
The day I swung suspended with the grapes,
And was come after like Eurydice
And brought down safely from the upper regions;
And the life I live now's an extra life
I can waste as I please on whom I please. 15
So if you see me celebrate two birthdays,
And give myself out as two different ages,
One of them five years younger than I look—

One day my brother led me to a glade
Where a white birch he knew of stood alone, 20
Wearing a thin headdress of pointed leaves,

And heavy on her heavy hair behind,
Against her neck, an ornament of grapes.
Grapes, I knew grapes from having seen them last year.
One bunch of them, and there began to be   25
Bunches all round me growing in white birches,
The way they grew round Leif the Lucky's German;
Mostly as much beyond my lifted hands, though,
As the moon used to seem when I was younger,
And only freely to be had for climbing.   30
My brother did the climbing; and at first
Threw me down grapes to miss and scatter
And have to hunt for in sweet fern and hardhack;
Which gave him some time to himself to eat,
But not so much, perhaps, as a boy needed.   35
So then, to make me wholly self-supporting,
He climbed still higher and bent the tree to earth
And put it in my hands to pick my own grapes.
"Here, take a treetop, I'll get down another.
Hold on with all your might when I let go."   40
I said I had the tree. It wasn't true.
The opposite was true. The tree had me.
The minute it was left with me alone,
It caught me up as if I were the fish
And it the fishpole. So I was translated,   45
To loud cries from my brother of "Let go!
Don't you know anything, you girl? Let go!"
But I, with something of the baby grip
Acquired ancestrally in just such trees
When wilder mothers than our wildest now   50
Hung babies out on branches by the hands
To dry or wash or tan, I don't know which
(You'll have to ask an evolutionist)—

I held on uncomplainingly for life.
My brother tried to make me laugh to help me.   55
"What are you doing up there in those grapes?
Don't be afraid. A few of them won't hurt you.
I mean, they won't pick you if you don't them."
Much danger of my picking anything!
By that time I was pretty well reduced   60
To a philosophy of hang-and-let-hang.
"Now you know how it feels," my brother said,
"To be a bunch of fox grapes, as they call them,
That when it thinks it has escaped the fox
By growing where it shouldn't—on a birch,   65
Where a fox wouldn't think to look for it—
And if he looked and found it, couldn't reach it—
Just then come you and I to gather it.
Only you have the advantage of the grapes
In one way: you have one more stem to cling by,   70
And promise more resistance to the picker."

One by one I lost off my hat and shoes,
And still I clung. I let my head fall back,
And shut my eyes against the sun, my ears
Against my brother's nonsense. "Drop," he said,   75
I'll catch you in my arms. It isn't far."
(Stated in lengths of him it might not be.)
"Drop or I'll shake the tree and shake you down."
Grim silence on my part as I sank lower,
My small wrists stretching till they showed the banjo strings.   80
"Why, if she isn't serious about it!
Hold tight awhile till I think what to do.
I'll bend the tree down and let you down by it."
I don't know much about the letting down;

But once I felt ground with my stocking feet   85
And the world came revolving back to me,
I know I looked long at my curled-up fingers,
Before I straightened them and brushed the bark off.
My brother said: "Don't you weigh anything?
Try to weigh something next time, so you won't   90
Be run off with by birch trees into space."

It wasn't my not weighing anything
So much as my not knowing anything—
My brother had been nearer right before.
I had not taken the first step in knowledge;   95
I had not learned to let go with the hands,
As still I have not learned to with the heart,
And have no wish to with the heart—nor need,
That I can see. The mind—is not the heart.
I may yet live, as I know others live,   100
To wish in vain to let go with the mind—
Of cares, at night, to sleep; but nothing tells me
That I need learn to let go with the heart.

THE WITCH OF COÖS

I stayed the night for shelter at a farm
Behind the mountain, with a mother and son,
Two old-believers. They did all the talking.

MOTHER.   Folks think a witch who has familiar spirits
She could call up to pass a winter evening,   5
But won't, should be burned at the stake or something.
Summoning spirits isn't "Button, button,
Who's got the button," I would have them know.

SON.   Mother can make a common table rear
And kick with two legs like an army mule.   10

MOTHER.   And when I've done it, what good have I done?
Rather than tip a table for you, let me
Tell you what Ralle the Sioux Control once told me.
He said the dead had souls, but when I asked him
How could that be—I thought the dead were souls—   15
He broke my trance. Don't that make you suspicious
That there's something the dead are keeping back?
Yes, there's something the dead are keeping back.

SON.   You wouldn't want to tell him what we have
Up attic, mother?

MOTHER.   Bones—a skeleton.   20

SON.   But the headboard of mother's bed is pushed
Against the attic door: the door is nailed.
It's harmless. Mother hears it in the night,
Halting perplexed behind the barrier
Of door and headboard. Where it wants to get   25
Is back into the cellar where it came from.

MOTHER.   We'll never let them, will we, son? We'll never!

SON.   It left the cellar forty years ago
And carried itself like a pile of dishes
Up one flight from the cellar to the kitchen,   30
Another from the kitchen to the bedroom,
Another from the bedroom to the attic,
Right past both father and mother, and neither stopped it.
Father had gone upstairs; mother was downstairs.
I was a baby: I don't know where I was.   35

MOTHER. The only fault my husband found with me—
I went to sleep before I went to bed,
Especially in winter when the bed
Might just as well be ice and the clothes snow.
The night the bones came up the cellar stairs   40
Toffile had gone to bed alone and left me,
But left an open door to cool the room off
So as to sort of turn me out of it.
I was just coming to myself enough
To wonder where the cold was coming from,   45
When I heard Toffile upstairs in the bedroom
And thought I heard him downstairs in the cellar.
The board we had laid down to walk dry-shod on
When there was water in the cellar in spring
Struck the hard cellar bottom. And then someone   50
Began the stairs, two footsteps for each step,
The way a man with one leg and a crutch,
Or a little child, comes up. It wasn't Toffile:
It wasn't anyone who could be there.
The bulkhead double doors were double-locked   55
And swollen tight and buried under snow.
The cellar windows were banked up with sawdust
And swollen tight and buried under snow.
It was the bones. I knew them—and good reason.
My first impulse was to get to the knob   60
And hold the door. But the bones didn't try
The door; they halted helpless on the landing,
Waiting for things to happen in their favor.
The faintest restless rustling ran all through them.
I never could have done the thing I did   65
If the wish hadn't been too strong in me

To see how they were mounted for this walk.
I had a vision of them put together
Not like a man, but like a chandelier.
So suddenly I flung the door wide on him.   70
A moment he stood balancing with emotion,
And all but lost himself. (A tongue of fire
Flashed out and licked along his upper teeth.
Smoke rolled inside the sockets of his eyes.)
Then he came at me with one hand outstretched,   75
The way he did in life once; but this time
I struck the hand off brittle on the floor,
And fell back from him on the floor myself.
The finger-pieces slid in all directions.
(Where did I see one of those pieces lately?   80
Hand me my button box—it must be there.)
I sat up on the floor and shouted, "Toffile,
It's coming up to you." It had its choice
Of the door to the cellar or the hall.
It took the hall door for the novelty,   85
And set off briskly for so slow a thing,
Still going every which way in the joints, though,
So that it looked like lightning or a scribble,
From the slap I had just now given its hand.
I listened till it almost climbed the stairs   90
From the hall to the only finished bedroom,
Before I got up to do anything;
Then ran and shouted, "Shut the bedroom door,
Toffile, for my sake!" "Company?" he said,
"Don't make me get up; I'm too warm in bed."   95
So lying forward weakly on the handrail
I pushed myself upstairs, and in the light
(The kitchen had been dark) I had to own

I could see nothing. "Toffile, I don't see it.
It's with us in the room, though. It's the bones." 100
"What bones?" "The cellar bones—out of the grave."
That made him throw his bare legs out of bed
And sit up by me and take hold of me.
I wanted to put out the light and see
If I could see it, or else mow the room, 105
With our arms at the level of our knees,
And bring the chalk-pile down. "I'll tell you what—
It's looking for another door to try.
The uncommonly deep snow has made him think
Of his old song, 'The Wild Colonial Boy,' 110
He always used to sing along the tote road.
He's after an open door to get outdoors.
Let's trap him with an open door up attic."
Toffile agreed to that, and sure enough,
Almost the moment he was given an opening, 115
The steps began to climb the attic stairs.
I heard them. Toffile didn't seem to hear them.
"Quick!" I slammed to the door and held the knob.
"Toffile, get nails." I made him nail the door shut
And push the headboard of the bed against it. 120
Then we asked was there anything
Up attic that we'd ever want again.
The attic was less to us than the cellar.
If the bones liked the attic, let them have it.
Let them stay in the attic. When they sometimes 125
Come down the stairs at night and stand perplexed
Behind the door and headboard of the bed,
Brushing their chalky skull with chalky fingers,
With sounds like the dry rattling of a shutter,
That's what I sit up in the dark to say— 130

To no one anymore since Toffile died.
Let them stay in the attic since they went there.
I promised Toffile to be cruel to them
For helping them be cruel once to him.

SON.   We think they had a grave down in the cellar.   135

MOTHER.   We know they had a grave down in the cellar.

SON.   We never could find out whose bones they were.

MOTHER.   Yes, we could too, son. Tell the truth for once.
They were a man's his father killed for me.
I mean a man he killed instead of me.   140
The least I could do was help dig their grave.
We were about it one night in the cellar.
Son knows the story: but 'twas not for him
To tell the truth, suppose the time had come.
Son looks surprised to see me end a lie   145
We'd kept up all these years between ourselves
So as to have it ready for outsiders.
But tonight I don't care enough to lie—
I don't remember why I ever cared.
Toffile, if he were here, I don't believe   150
Could tell you why he ever cared himself. . . .

She hadn't found the finger-bone she wanted
Among the buttons poured out in her lap.
I verified the name next morning: Toffile.
The rural letter box said Toffile Lajway.   155

AN EMPTY THREAT

I stay;
But it isn't as if

(98)

There wasn't always Hudson's Bay
And the fur trade,
A small skiff   5
And a paddle blade.

I can just see my tent pegged,
And me on the floor,
Cross-legged,
And a trapper looking in at the door   10
With furs to sell.

His name's Joe,
Alias John,
And between what he doesn't know
And won't tell   15
About where Henry Hudson's gone,
I can't say he's much help;
But we get on.

The seal yelp
On an ice cake.   20
It's not men by some mistake?

No,
There's not a soul
For a windbreak
Between me and the North Pole—   25

Except always John-Joe,
My French Indian Esquimaux,
And he's off setting traps—
In one himself perhaps.

Give a headshake   30
Over so much bay

Thrown away
In snow and mist
That doesn't exist,
I was going to say,   35
For God, man, or beast's sake,
Yet does perhaps for all three.

Don't ask Joe
What it is to him.
It's sometimes dim   40
What it is to me,
Unless it be
It's the old captain's dark fate
Who failed to find or force a strait
In its two-thousand-mile coast;   45
And his crew left him where he failed,
And nothing came of all he sailed.

It's to say, "You and I—"
To such a ghost—
"You and I   50
Off here
With the dead race of the Great Auk!"
And, "Better defeat almost,
If seen clear,
Than life's victories of doubt   55
That need endless talk-talk
To make them out."

I WILL SING YOU ONE-O

It was long I lay
Awake that night

Wishing the tower
Would name the hour
And tell me whether   5
To call it day
(Though not yet light)
And give up sleep.
The snow fell deep
With the hiss of spray;   10
Two winds would meet,
One down one street,
One down another,
And fight in a smother
Of dust and feather.   15
I could not say,
But feared the cold
Had checked the pace
Of the tower clock
By tying together
Its hands of gold   20
Before its face.

Then came one knock!
A note unruffled
Of earthly weather,   25
Though strange and muffled.
The tower said, "One!"
And then a steeple.
They spoke to themselves
And such few people   30
As winds might rouse
From sleeping warm
(But not unhouse).

They left the storm
That struck en masse   35
My window glass
Like a beaded fur.
In that grave One
They spoke of the sun
And moon and stars,   40
Saturn and Mars
And Jupiter.
Still more unfettered,
They left the named
And spoke of the lettered,   45
The sigmas and taus
Of constellations.
They filled their throats
With the furthest bodies
To which man sends his   50
Speculation,
Beyond which God is;
The cosmic motes
Of yawning lenses.
Their solemn peals   55
Were not their own:
They spoke for the clock
With whose vast wheels
Theirs interlock.
In that grave word   60
Uttered alone
The utmost star
Trembled and stirred,
Though set so far
Its whirling frenzies   65

Appear like standing
In one self station.
It has not ranged,
And save for the wonder
Of once expanding   70
To be a nova,
It has not changed
To the eye of man
On planets over,
Around, and under   75
It in creation
Since man began
To drag down man
And nation nation.

FIRE AND ICE

Some say the world will end in fire,
Some say in ice.
From what I've tasted of desire
I hold with those who favor fire.
But if it had to perish twice,   5
I think I know enough of hate
To say that for destruction ice
Is also great
And would suffice.

DUST OF SNOW

The way a crow
Shook down on me
The dust of snow
From a hemlock tree

Has given my heart   5
A change of mood
And saved some part
Of a day I had rued.

NOTHING GOLD CAN STAY

Nature's first green is gold,
Her hardest hue to hold.
Her early leaf's a flower;
But only so an hour.
Then leaf subsides to leaf.   5
So Eden sank to grief,
So dawn goes down to day.
Nothing gold can stay.

THE RUNAWAY

Once when the snow of the year was beginning to fall,
We stopped by a mountain pasture to say, "Whose colt?"
A little Morgan had one forefoot on the wall,
The other curled at his breast. He dipped his head
And snorted at us. And then he had to bolt.   5
We heard the miniature thunder where he fled,
And we saw him, or thought we saw him, dim and gray,
Like a shadow against the curtain of falling flakes.
"I think the little fellow's afraid of the snow.
He isn't winter-broken. It isn't play   10
With the little fellow at all. He's running away.
I doubt if even his mother could tell him, 'Sakes,
It's only weather.' He'd think she didn't know!
Where is his mother? He can't be out alone."

And now he comes again with clatter of stone,   15
And mounts the wall again with whited eyes
And all his tail that isn't hair up straight.
He shudders his coat as if to throw off flies.
"Whoever it is that leaves him out so late,
When other creatures have gone to stall and bin,   20
Ought to be told to come and take him in."

THE AIM WAS SONG

Before man came to blow it right
    The wind once blew itself untaught,
And did its loudest day and night
    In any rough place where it caught.

Man came to tell it what was wrong: 5
    It hadn't found the place to blow;
It blew too hard—the aim was song.
    And listen—how it ought to go!

He took a little in his mouth,
    And held it long enough for north   10
To be converted into south,
    And then by measure blew it forth.

By measure. It was word and note,
    The wind the wind had meant to be—
A little through the lips and throat.   15
    The aim was song—the wind could see.

STOPPING BY WOODS
ON A SNOWY EVENING

Whose woods these are I think I know.
His house is in the village, though;
He will not see me stopping here
To watch his woods fill up with snow.

My little horse must think it queer   5
To stop without a farmhouse near
Between the woods and frozen lake
The darkest evening of the year.

He gives his harness bells a shake
To ask if there is some mistake.   10
The only other sound's the sweep
Of easy wind and downy flake.

The woods are lovely, dark, and deep,
But I have promises to keep,
And miles to go before I sleep,   15
And miles to go before I sleep.

FOR ONCE, THEN, SOMETHING

Others taunt me with having knelt at well-curbs
Always wrong to the light, so never seeing
Deeper down in the well than where the water
Gives me back in a shining surface picture
Me myself in the summer heaven, godlike,   5
Looking out of a wreath of fern and cloud puffs.
Once, when trying with chin against a well-curb,
I discerned, as I thought, beyond the picture,
Through the picture, a something white, uncertain,

Something more of the depths—and then I lost it.   10
Water came to rebuke the too clear water.
One drop fell from a fern, and lo, a ripple
Shook whatever it was lay there at bottom,
Blurred it, blotted it out. What was that whiteness?
Truth? A pebble of quartz? For once, then, something.   15

THE ONSET

Always the same, when on a fated night
At last the gathered snow lets down as white
As may be in dark woods, and with a song
It shall not make again all winter long
Of hissing on the yet uncovered ground,   5
I almost stumble looking up and round,
As one who overtaken by the end
Gives up his errand, and lets death descend
Upon him where he is, with nothing done
To evil, no important triumph won,   10
More than if life had never been begun.

Yet all the precedent is on my side:
I know that winter death has never tried
The earth but it has failed: the snow may heap
In long storms an undrifted four feet deep   15
As measured against maple, birch, and oak,
It cannot check the peeper's silver croak;
And I shall see the snow all go downhill
In water of a slender April rill
That flashes tail through last year's withered brake   20
And dead weeds, like a disappearing snake.
Nothing will be left white but here a birch,
And there a clump of houses with a church.

TO EARTHWARD

Love at the lips was touch
As sweet as I could bear;
And once that seemed too much;
I lived on air

That crossed me from sweet things,   5
The flow of—was it musk
From hidden grapevine springs
Downhill at dusk?

I had the swirl and ache
From sprays of honeysuckle   10
That when they're gathered shake
Dew on the knuckle.

I craved strong sweets, but those
Seemed strong when I was young;
The petal of the rose   15
It was that stung.

Now no joy but lacks salt,
That is not dashed with pain
And weariness and fault;
I crave the stain   20

Of tears, the aftermark
Of almost too much love,
The sweet of bitter bark
And burning clove.

When stiff and sore and scarred   25
I take away my hand
From leaning on it hard
In grass and sand,

The hurt is not enough:
I long for weight and strength   30
To feel the earth as rough
To all my length.

NOT TO KEEP

They sent him back to her. The letter came
Saying. . . . And she could have him. And before
She could be sure there was no hidden ill
Under the formal writing, he was there,
Living. They gave him back to her alive—   5
How else? They are not known to send the dead.—
And not disfigured visibly. His face?
His hands? She had to look, to look and ask,
"What is it, dear?" And she had given all
And still she had all—*they* had—they the lucky!   10
Wasn't she glad now? Everything seemed won,
And all the rest for them permissible ease.
She had to ask, "What was it, dear?"

                                        "Enough,
Yet not enough. A bullet through and through,
High in the breast. Nothing but what good care   15
And medicine and rest, and you a week,
Can cure me of to go again." The same
Grim giving to do over for them both.
She dared no more than ask him with her eyes
How was it with him for a second trial.   20
And with his eyes he asked her not to ask.
They had given him back to her, but not to keep.

(109)

THE LOCKLESS DOOR

It went many years,
But at last came a knock,
And I thought of the door
With no lock to lock.

I blew out the light,
I tiptoed the floor,   5
And raised both hands
In prayer to the door.

But the knock came again.
My window was wide;   10
I climbed on the sill
And descended outside.

Back over the sill
I bade a "Come in"
To whatever the knock   15
At the door may have been.

So at a knock
I emptied my cage
To hide in the world
And alter with age.   20

THE NEED OF BEING VERSED
IN COUNTRY THINGS

The house had gone to bring again
To the midnight sky a sunset glow.
Now the chimney was all of the house that stood,
Like a pistil after the petals go.

The barn opposed across the way,   5
That would have joined the house in flame
Had it been the will of the wind, was left
To bear forsaken the place's name.

No more it opened with all one end
For teams that came by the stony road   10
To drum on the floor with scurrying hoofs
And brush the mow with the summer load.

The birds that came to it through the air
At broken windows flew out and in,
Their murmur more like the sigh we sigh   15
From too much dwelling on what has been.

Yet for them the lilac renewed its leaf,
And the aged elm, though touched with fire;
And the dry pump flung up an awkward arm;
And the fence post carried a strand of wire.   20

For them there was really nothing sad.
But though they rejoiced in the nest they kept,
One had to be versed in country things
Not to believe the phoebes wept.

SPRING POOLS

These pools that, though in forests, still reflect
The total sky almost without defect,
And like the flowers beside them, chill and shiver,
Will like the flowers beside them soon be gone,
And yet not out by any brook or river,   5
But up by roots to bring dark foliage on.

The trees that have it in their pent-up buds
To darken nature and be summer woods—
Let them think twice before they use their powers
To blot out and drink up and sweep away   10
These flowery waters and these watery flowers
From snow that melted only yesterday.

DEVOTION

The heart can think of no devotion
Greater than being shore to the ocean—
Holding the curve of one position,
Counting an endless repetition.

ON GOING UNNOTICED

As vain to raise a voice as a sigh
In the tumult of free leaves on high.
What are you, in the shadow of trees
Engaged up there with the light and breeze?

Less than the coralroot, you know,   5
That is content with the daylight low,

And has no leaves at all of its own;
Whose spotted flowers hang meanly down.

You grasp the bark by a rugged pleat,
And look up small from the forest's feet.   10
The only leaf it drops goes wide,
Your name not written on either side.

You linger your little hour and are gone,
And still the woods sweep leafily on,
Not even missing the coralroot flower   15
You took as a trophy of the hour.

A PASSING GLIMPSE

*To Ridgely Torrence
on last looking into his "'Hesperides"*

I often see flowers from a passing car
That are gone before I can tell what they are.

I want to get out of the train and go back
To see what they were beside the track.

I name all the flowers I am sure they weren't: 5
Not fireweed loving where woods have burnt—

Not bluebells gracing a tunnel mouth—
Not lupine living on sand and drouth.

Was something brushed across my mind
That no one on earth will ever find?   10

Heaven gives its glimpses only to those
Not in position to look too close.

ONCE BY THE PACIFIC

The shattered water made a misty din.
Great waves looked over others coming in,
And thought of doing something to the shore
That water never did to land before.
The clouds were low and hairy in the skies,   5
Like locks blown forward in the gleam of eyes.
You could not tell, and yet it looked as if
The shore was lucky in being backed by cliff,
The cliff in being backed by continent;
It looked as if a night of dark intent   10
Was coming, and not only a night, an age.
Someone had better be prepared for rage.
There would be more than ocean-water broken
Before God's last *Put out the Light* was spoken.

LODGED

The rain to the wind said,
"You push and I'll pelt."
They so smote the garden bed
That the flowers actually knelt,
And lay lodged—though not dead.   5
I know how the flowers felt.

A MINOR BIRD

I have wished a bird would fly away,
And not sing by my house all day;

Have clapped my hands at him from the door
When it seemed as if I could bear no more.

(114)

The fault must partly have been in me.   5
The bird was not to blame for his key.

And of course there must be something wrong
In wanting to silence any song.

BEREFT

Where had I heard this wind before
Change like this to a deeper roar?
What would it take my standing there for,
Holding open a restive door,
Looking downhill to a frothy shore?   5
Summer was past and day was past.
Somber clouds in the west were massed.
Out in the porch's sagging floor
Leaves got up in a coil and hissed,
Blindly struck at my knee and missed.   10
Something sinister in the tone
Told me my secret must be known:
Word I was in the house alone
Somehow must have gotten abroad,
Word I was in my life alone,   15
Word I had no one left but God.

TREE AT MY WINDOW

Tree at my window, window tree,
My sash is lowered when night comes on;
But let there never be curtain drawn
Between you and me.

Vague dream-head lifted out of the ground,   5
And thing next most diffuse to cloud,

Not all your light tongues talking aloud
Could be profound.

But, tree, I have seen you taken and tossed,
And if you have seen me when I slept,　　　　　　10
You have seen me when I was taken and swept
And all but lost.

That day she put our heads together,
Fate had her imagination about her,
Your head so much concerned with outer,　　　　15
Mine with inner, weather.

THE PEACEFUL SHEPHERD

If heaven were to do again,
And on the pasture bars
I leaned to line the figures in
Between the dotted stars,

I should be tempted to forget,　　　　　　　　5
I fear, the Crown of Rule,
The Scales of Trade, the Cross of Faith,
As hardly worth renewal.

For these have governed in our lives,
And see how men have warred.　　　　　　　　10
The Cross, the Crown, the Scales may all
As well have been the Sword.

THE THATCH

Out alone in the winter rain,
Intent on giving and taking pain.
But never was I far out of sight

Of a certain upper-window light.
The light was what it was all about: 5
I would not go in till the light went out;
It would not go out till I came in.
Well, we should see which one would win,
We should see which one would be first to yield.
The world was a black invisible field.   10
The rain by rights was snow for cold.
The wind was another layer of mold.
But the strangest thing: in the thick old thatch,
Where summer birds had been given hatch,
Had fed in chorus, and lived to fledge,   15
Some still were living in hermitage.
And as I passed along the eaves
So low I brushed the straw with my sleeves,
I flushed birds out of hole after hole,
Into the darkness. It grieved my soul,   20
It started a grief within a grief,
To think their case was beyond relief—
They could not go flying about in search
Of their nest again, nor find a perch.
They must brood where they fell in mulch and mire,   25
Trusting feathers and inward fire
Till daylight made it safe for a flyer.
My greater grief was by so much reduced
As I thought of them without nest or roost.
That was how that grief started to melt.   30
They tell me the cottage where we dwelt,
Its wind-torn thatch goes now unmended;
Its life of hundreds of years has ended
By letting the rain I knew outdoors
In onto the upper chamber floors.   35

(117)

A WINTER EDEN

A winter garden in an alder swamp,
Where conies now come out to sun and romp,
As near a paradise as it can be
And not melt snow or start a dormant tree.

It lifts existence on a plane of snow 5
One level higher than the earth below,
One level nearer heaven overhead,
And last year's berries shining scarlet red.

It lifts a gaunt luxuriating beast
Where he can stretch and hold his highest feast 10
On some wild apple-tree's young tender bark,
What well may prove the year's high girdle mark.

So near to paradise all pairing ends:
Here loveless birds now flock as winter friends,
Content with bud-inspecting. They presume 15
To say which buds are leaf and which are bloom.

A feather-hammer gives a double knock.
This Eden day is done at two o'clock.
An hour of winter day might seem too short
To make it worth life's while to wake and sport. 20

ACQUAINTED WITH THE NIGHT

I have been one acquainted with the night.
I have walked out in rain—and back in rain.
I have outwalked the furthest city light.

I have looked down the saddest city lane.
I have passed by the watchman on his beat 5
And dropped my eyes, unwilling to explain.

I have stood still and stopped the sound of feet
When far away an interrupted cry
Came over houses from another street,

But not to call me back or say good-by;   10
And further still at an unearthly height
One luminary clock against the sky

Proclaimed the time was neither wrong nor right.
I have been one acquainted with the night.

THE LOVELY SHALL BE CHOOSERS

The Voice said, "Hurl her down!"

The Voices, "How far down?"

"Seven levels of the world."

"How much time have we?"

"Take twenty years.   5
She *would* refuse love safe with wealth and honor!
The lovely shall be choosers, shall they?
Then let them choose!"

"Then we shall let her choose?"

"Yes, let her choose.
Take up the task beyond her choosing."   10

Invisible hands crowded on her shoulder
In readiness to weigh upon her.
But she stood straight still,
In broad round earrings, gold and jet with pearls,   15

(119)

And broad round suchlike brooch,
Her cheeks high-colored,
Proud and the pride of friends.

The Voice asked, "You can let her choose?"

"Yes, we can let her and still triumph." 20

"Do it by joys, and leave her always blameless.
Be her first joy her wedding,
That though a wedding,
Is yet—well, something they know, he and she.
And after that her next joy 25
That though she grieves, her grief is secret:
Those friends know nothing of her grief to make it shameful.
Her third joy that though now they cannot help but know,
They move in pleasure too far off
To think much or much care. 30
Give her a child at either knee for fourth joy
To tell once and once only, for them never to forget,
How once she walked in brightness,
And make them see it in the winter firelight.
But give her friends, for then she dare not tell 35
For their foregone incredulousness.
And be her next joy this:
Her never having deigned to tell them.
Make her among the humblest even
Seem to them less than they are. 40
Hopeless of being known for what she has been,
Failing of being loved for what she is,
Give her the comfort for her sixth of knowing
She fails from strangeness to a way of life
She came to from too high too late to learn. 45

Then send some *one* with eyes to see
And wonder at her where she is,
And words to wonder in her hearing how she came there,
But without time to linger for her story.
Be her last joy her heart's going out to this one   50
So that she almost speaks.
You know them—seven in all."

"Trust us," the Voices said.

WEST-RUNNING BROOK

"Fred, where is north?"

                    "North? North is there, my love.
The brook runs west."

                    "West-Running Brook then call it."
(West-Running Brook men call it to this day.)
"What does it think it's doing running west
When all the other country brooks flow east   5
To reach the ocean? It must be the brook
Can trust itself to go by contraries
The way I can with you—and you with me—
Because we're—we're—I don't know what we are.
What are we?"

            "Young or new?"

                    "We must be something.   10
We've said we two. Let's change that to we three.
As you and I are married to each other,
We'll both be married to the brook. We'll build
Our bridge across it, and the bridge shall be

(1 2 1)

Our arm thrown over it asleep beside it.   15
Look, look, it's waving to us with a wave
To let us know it hears me."

                              "Why, my dear,
That wave's been standing off this jut of shore—"
(The black stream, catching on a sunken rock,
Flung backward on itself in one white wave,   20
And the white water rode the black forever,
Not gaining but not losing, like a bird
White feathers from the struggle of whose breast
Flecked the dark stream and flecked the darker pool
Below the point, and were at last driven wrinkled   25
In a white scarf against the far-shore alders.)
"That wave's been standing off this jut of shore
Ever since rivers, I was going to say,
Were made in heaven. It wasn't waved to us."

"It wasn't, yet it was. If not to you,   30
It was to me—in an annunciation."

"Oh, if you take it off to lady-land,
As't were the country of the Amazons
We men must see you to the confines of
And leave you there, ourselves forbid to enter—   35
It is your brook! I have no more to say."

"Yes, you have, too. Go on. You thought of something."

"Speaking of contraries, see how the brook
In that white wave runs counter to itself.
It is from that in water we were from   40
Long, long before we were from any creature.

Here we, in our impatience of the steps,
Get back to the beginning of beginnings,
The stream of everything that runs away.
Some say existence like a Pirouot 45
And Pirouette, forever in one place,
Stands still and dances, but it runs away;
It seriously, sadly, runs away
To fill the abyss's void with emptiness.
It flows beside us in this water brook, 50
But it flows over us. It flows between us
To separate us for a panic moment.
It flows between us, over us, and *with* us.
And it is time, strength, tone, light, life, and love—
And even substance lapsing unsubstantial; 55
The universal cataract of death
That spends to nothingness—and unresisted,
Save by some strange resistance in itself,
Not just a swerving, but a throwing back,
As if regret were in it and were sacred. 60
It has this throwing backward on itself
So that the fall of most of it is always
Raising a little, sending up a little.
Our life runs down in sending up the clock.
The brook runs down in sending up our life. 65
The sun runs down in sending up the brook.
And there is something sending up the sun.
It is this backward motion toward the source,
Against the stream, that most we see ourselves in,
The tribute of the current to the source. 70
It is from this in nature we are from.
It is most us."

"Today will be the day
You said so."

"No, today will be the day
You said the brook was called West-Running Brook."

"Today will be the day of what we both said."   75

SAND DUNES

Sea waves are green and wet,
But up from where they die
Rise others vaster yet,
And those are brown and dry.

They are the sea made land   5
To come at the fisher town
And bury in solid sand
The men she could not drown.

She may know cove and cape,
But she does not know mankind   10
If by any change of shape
She hopes to cut off mind.

Men left her a ship to sink:
They can leave her a hut as well;
And be but more free to think   15
For the one more cast-off shell.

A SOLDIER

He is that fallen lance that lies as hurled,
That lies unlifted now, come dew, come rust,
But still lies pointed as it plowed the dust.

If we who sight along it round the world,
See nothing worthy to have been its mark,   5
It is because like men we look too near,
Forgetting that as fitted to the sphere,
Our missiles always make too short an arc.
They fall, they rip the grass, they intersect
The curve of earth, and striking, break their own;   10
They make us cringe for metal-point on stone.
But this we know, the obstacle that checked
And tripped the body, shot the spirit on
Further than target ever showed or shone.

THE DOOR IN THE DARK

In going from room to room in the dark
I reached out blindly to save my face,
But neglected, however lightly, to lace
My fingers and close my arms in an arc.
A slim door got in past my guard,   5
And hit me a blow in the head so hard
I had my native simile jarred.
So people and things don't pair anymore
With what they used to pair with before.

SITTING BY A BUSH
IN BROAD SUNLIGHT

When I spread out my hand here today,
I catch no more than a ray
To feel of between thumb and fingers;
No lasting effect of it lingers.

There was one time and only the one   5
When dust really took in the sun;

(125)

And from that one intake of fire
All creatures still warmly suspire.

And if men have watched a long time
And never seen sun-smitten slime   10
Again come to life and crawl off,
We must not be too ready to scoff.

God once declared He was true
And then took the veil and withdrew,
And remember how final a hush   15
Then descended of old on the bush.

God once spoke to people by name.
The sun once imparted its flame.
One impulse persists as our breath;
The other persists as our faith.   20

RIDERS

The surest thing there is is we are riders,
And though none too successful at it, guiders,
Through everything presented, land and tide
And now the very air, of what we ride.

What is this talked-of mystery of birth   5
But being mounted bareback on the earth?
We can just see the infant up astride,
His small fist buried in the bushy hide.

There is our wildest mount—a headless horse.
But though it runs unbridled off its course,   10
And all our blandishments would seem defied,
We have ideas yet that we haven't tried.

(126)

ON LOOKING UP BY CHANCE
AT THE CONSTELLATIONS

You'll wait a long, long time for anything much
To happen in heaven beyond the floats of cloud
And the Northern Lights that run like tingling nerves.
The sun and moon get crossed, but they never touch,
Nor strike out fire from each other, nor crash out loud.   5
The planets seem to interfere in their curves,
But nothing ever happens, no harm is done.
We may as well go patiently on with our life,
And look elsewhere than to stars and moon and sun
For the shocks and changes we need to keep us sane.   10
It is true the longest drouth will end in rain,
The longest peace in China will end in strife.
Still it wouldn't reward the watcher to stay awake
In hopes of seeing the calm of heaven break
On his particular time and personal sight.   15
That calm seems certainly safe to last tonight.

THE BEAR

The bear puts both arms around the tree above her
And draws it down as if it were a lover
And its chokecherries lips to kiss good-by,
Then lets it snap back upright in the sky.
Her next step rocks a boulder on the wall   5
(She's making her cross-country in the fall).
Her great weight creaks the barbed wire in its staples
As she flings over and off down through the maples,
Leaving on one wire tooth a lock of hair.
Such is the uncaged progress of the bear.   10

(127)

The world has room to make a bear feel free;
The universe seems cramped to you and me.
Man acts more like the poor bear in a cage,
That all day fights a nervous inward rage,
His mood rejecting all his mind suggests.   15
He paces back and forth and never rests
The toenail click and shuffle of his feet,
The telescope at one end of his beat,
And at the other end the microscope,
Two instruments of nearly equal hope,   20
And in conjunction giving quite a spread.
Or if he rests from scientific tread,
'Tis only to sit back and sway his head
Through ninety-odd degrees of arc, it seems,
Between two metaphysical extremes.   25
He sits back on his fundamental butt
With lifted snout and eyes (if any) shut
(He almost looks religious but he's not),
And back and forth he sways from cheek to cheek,
At one extreme agreeing with one Greek,   30
At the other agreeing with another Greek,
Which may be thought, but only so to speak.
A baggy figure, equally pathetic
When sedentary and when peripatetic.

A Further Range   1936

TWO TRAMPS IN MUD TIME

Out of the mud two strangers came
And caught me splitting wood in the yard.
And one of them put me off my aim
By hailing cheerily "Hit them hard!"
I knew pretty well why he dropped behind   5
And let the other go on a way.
I knew pretty well what he had in mind:
He wanted to take my job for pay.

Good blocks of oak it was I split,
As large around as the chopping block;   10
And every piece I squarely hit
Fell splinterless as a cloven rock.
The blows that a life of self-control
Spares to strike for the common good,
That day, giving a loose to my soul,   15
I spent on the unimportant wood.

The sun was warm but the wind was chill.
You know how it is with an April day
When the sun is out and the wind is still,
You're one month on in the middle of May.   20
But if you so much as dare to speak,
A cloud comes over the sunlit arch,
A wind comes off a frozen peak,
And you're two months back in the middle of March.

A bluebird comes tenderly up to alight   25
And turns to the wind to unruffle a plume,

His song so pitched as not to excite
A single flower as yet to bloom.
It is snowing a flake: and he half knew
Winter was only playing possum.   30
Except in color he isn't blue,
But he wouldn't advise a thing to blossom.

The water for which we may have to look
In summertime with a witching wand,
In every wheelrut's now a brook,   35
In every print of a hoof a pond.
Be glad of water, but don't forget
The lurking frost in the earth beneath
That will steal forth after the sun is set
And show on the water its crystal teeth.   40

The time when most I loved my task
These two must make me love it more
By coming with what they came to ask.
You'd think I never had felt before
The weight of an ax-head poised aloft,   45
The grip on earth of outspread feet,
The life of muscles rocking soft
And smooth and moist in vernal heat.

Out of the woods two hulking tramps
(From sleeping God knows where last night,   50
But not long since in the lumber camps).
They thought all chopping was theirs of right.
Men of the woods and lumberjacks,
They judged me by their appropriate tool.
Except as a fellow handled an ax   55
They had no way of knowing a fool.

Nothing on either side was said.
They knew they had but to stay their stay
And all their logic would fill my head:
As that I had no right to play   60
With what was another man's work for gain.
My right might be love but theirs was need.
And where the two exist in twain
Theirs was the better right—agreed.

But yield who will to their separation,   65
My object in living is to unite
My avocation and my vocation
As my two eyes make one in sight.
Only where love and need are one,
And the work is play for mortal stakes,   70
Is the deed ever really done
For Heaven and the future's sakes.

THE WHITE-TAILED HORNET

The white-tailed hornet lives in a balloon
That floats against the ceiling of the woodshed.
The exit he comes out at like a bullet
Is like the pupil of a pointed gun.
And having power to change his aim in flight,   5
He comes out more unerring than a bullet.
Verse could be written on the certainty
With which he penetrates my best defense
Of whirling hands and arms about the head
To stab me in the sneeze-nerve of a nostril.   10
Such is the instinct of it I allow.
Yet how about the insect certainty
That in the neighborhood of home and children

Is such an execrable judge of motives
As not to recognize in me the exception   15
I like to think I am in everything—
One who would never hang above a bookcase
His Japanese crepe-paper globe for trophy?
He stung me first and stung me afterward.
He rolled me off the field head over heels   20
And would not listen to my explanations.

That's when I went as visitor to his house.
As visitor at my house he is better.
Hawking for flies about the kitchen door,
In at one door perhaps and out another,   25
Trust him then not to put you in the wrong.
He won't misunderstand your freest movements.
Let him light on your skin unless you mind
So many prickly grappling feet at once.
He's after the domesticated fly   30
To feed his thumping grubs as big as he is.
Here he is at his best, but even here—
I watched him where he swooped, he pounced, he struck;
But what he found he had was just a nailhead.
He struck a second time. Another nailhead.   35
"Those are just nailheads. Those are fastened down."
Then disconcerted and not unannoyed,
He stooped and struck a little huckleberry
The way a player curls around a football.
"Wrong shape, wrong color, and wrong scent," I said.   40
The huckleberry rolled him on his head.
At last it was a fly. He shot and missed;
And the fly circled round him in derision.
But for the fly he might have made me think

He had been at his poetry, comparing   45
Nailhead with fly and fly with huckleberry:
How like a fly, how very like a fly.
But the real fly he missed would never do;
The missed fly made me dangerously skeptic.

Won't this whole instinct matter bear revision?   50
Won't almost any theory bear revision?
To err is human, not to, animal.
Or so we pay the compliment to instinct,
Only too liberal of our compliment
That really takes away instead of gives.   55
Our worship, humor, conscientiousness
Went long since to the dogs under the table.
And served us right for having instituted
Downward comparisons. As long on earth
As our comparisons were stoutly upward   60
With gods and angels, we were men at least,
But little lower than the gods and angels.
But once comparisons were yielded downward,
Once we began to see our images
Reflected in the mud and even dust,   65
'Twas disillusion upon disillusion.
We were lost piecemeal to the animals,
Like people thrown out to delay the wolves.
Nothing but fallibility was left us,
And this day's work made even that seem doubtful.   70

A BLUE RIBBON AT AMESBURY

Such a fine pullet ought to go
All coiffured to a winter show,

And be exhibited, and win.
The answer is this one has been—

And come with all her honors home.   5
Her golden leg, her coral comb,
Her fluff of plumage, white as chalk,
Her style, were all the fancy's talk.

It seems as if you must have heard.
She scored an almost perfect bird.   10
In her we make ourselves acquainted
With one a Sewell might have painted.

Here common with the flock again,
At home in her abiding pen,
She lingers feeding at the trough,   15
The last to let night drive her off.

The one who gave her ankle-band,
Her keeper, empty pail in hand,
He lingers too, averse to slight
His chores for all the wintry night.   20

He leans against the dusty wall,
Immured almost beyond recall,
A depth past many swinging doors
And many litter-muffled floors.

He meditates the breeder's art.   25
He has a half a mind to start,
With her for Mother Eve, a race
That shall all living things displace.

'Tis ritual with her to lay
The full six days, then rest a day;   30

At which rate barring broodiness
She well may score an egg-success.

The gatherer can always tell
Her well-turned egg's brown sturdy shell,
As safe a vehicle of seed   35
As is vouchsafed to feathered breed.

No human specter at the feast
Can scant or hurry her the least.
She takes her time to take her fill.
She whets a sleepy sated bill.   40

She gropes across the pen alone
To peck herself a precious stone.
She waters at the patent fount.
And so to roost, the last to mount.

The roost is her extent of flight.   45
Yet once she rises to the height,
She shoulders with a wing so strong
She makes the whole flock move along.

The night is setting in to blow.
It scours the windowpane with snow,   50
But barely gets from them or her
For comment a complacent chirr.

The lowly pen is yet a hold
Against the dark and wind and cold
To give a prospect to a plan   55
And warrant prudence in a man.

A DRUMLIN WOODCHUCK

One thing has a shelving bank,
Another a rotting plank,
To give it cozier skies
And make up for its lack of size.

My own strategic retreat   5
Is where two rocks almost meet,
And still more secure and snug,
A two-door burrow I dug.

With those in mind at my back
I can sit forth exposed to attack,   10
As one who shrewdly pretends
That he and the world are friends.

All we who prefer to live
Have a little whistle we give,
And flash, at the least alarm   15
We dive down under the farm.

We allow some time for guile
And don't come out for a while,
Either to eat or drink.
We take occasion to think.   20

And if after the hunt goes past
And the double-barreled blast
(Like war and pestilence
And the loss of common sense),

If I can with confidence say   25
That still for another day,

Or even another year,
I will be there for you, my dear,

It will be because, though small
As measured against the All,   30
I have been so instinctively thorough
About my crevice and burrow.

IN TIME OF CLOUDBURST

Let the downpour roil and toil!
The worst it can do to me
Is carry some garden soil
A little nearer the sea.

'Tis the world-old way of the rain   5
When it comes to a mountain farm
To exact for a present gain
A little of future harm.

And the harm is none too sure,
For when all that was rotted rich   10
Shall be in the end scoured poor,
When my garden has gone down ditch,

Some force has but to apply,
And summits shall be immersed,
The bottom of seas raised dry—   15
The slope of the earth reversed.

Then all I need do is run
To the other end of the slope,
And on tracts laid new to the sun,
Begin all over to hope.   20

Some worn old tool of my own
Will be turned up by the plow,
The wood of it changed to stone,
But as ready to wield as now.

May my application so close   25
To so endless a repetition
Not make me tired and morose
And resentful of man's condition.

DEPARTMENTAL

An ant on the tablecloth
Ran into a dormant moth
Of many times his size.
He showed not the least surprise.
His business wasn't with such.   5
He gave it scarcely a touch,
And was off on his duty run.
Yet if he encountered one
Of the hive's enquiry squad
Whose work is to find out God   10
And the nature of time and space,
He would put him onto the case.
Ants are a curious race;
One crossing with hurried tread
The body of one of their dead   15
Isn't given a moment's arrest—
Seems not even impressed.
But he no doubt reports to any
With whom he crosses antennae,
And they no doubt report   20
To the higher-up at court.

(138)

Then word goes forth in Formic:
"Death's come to Jerry McCormic,
Our selfless forager Jerry.
Will the special Janizary   25
Whose office it is to bury
The dead of the commissary
Go bring him home to his people.
Lay him in state on a sepal.
Wrap him for shroud in a petal.   30
Embalm him with ichor of nettle.
This is the word of your Queen."
And presently on the scene
Appears a solemn mortician;
And taking formal position,   35
With feelers calmly atwiddle,
Seizes the dead by the middle,
And heaving him high in air,
Carries him out of there.
No one stands round to stare.   40
It is nobody else's affair.

It couldn't be called ungentle.
But how thoroughly departmental.

DESERT PLACES

Snow falling and night falling fast, oh, fast
In a field I looked into going past,
And the ground almost covered smooth in snow,
But a few weeds and stubble showing last.

The woods around it have it—it is theirs.   5
All animals are smothered in their lairs.

I am too absent-spirited to count;
The loneliness includes me unawares.

And lonely as it is, that loneliness
Will be more lonely ere it will be less—   10
A blanket whiteness of benighted snow
With no expression, nothing to express.

They cannot scare me with their empty spaces
Between stars—on stars where no human race is.
I have it in me so much nearer home   15
To scare myself with my own desert places.

THEY WERE WELCOME TO THEIR BELIEF

Grief may have thought it was grief.
Care may have thought it was care.
They were welcome to their belief,
The overimportant pair.

No, it took all the snows that clung   5
To the low roof over his bed,
Beginning when he was young,
To induce the one snow on his head.

But whenever the roof came white
The head in the dark below   10
Was a shade less the color of night,
A shade more the color of snow.

Grief may have thought it was grief.
Care may have thought it was care.
But neither one was the thief   15
Of his raven color of hair.

(140)

NEITHER OUT FAR NOR IN DEEP

The people along the sand
All turn and look one way.
They turn their back on the land.
They look at the sea all day.

As long as it takes to pass   5
A ship keeps raising its hull;
The wetter ground like glass
Reflects a standing gull.

The land may vary more;
But wherever the truth may be—   10
The water comes ashore,
And the people look at the sea.

They cannot look out far.
They cannot look in deep.
But when was that ever a bar   15
To any watch they keep?

DESIGN

I found a dimpled spider, fat and white,
On a white heal-all, holding up a moth
Like a white piece of rigid satin cloth—
Assorted characters of death and blight
Mixed ready to begin the morning right,   5
Like the ingredients of a witches' broth—
A snow-drop spider, a flower like a froth,
And dead wings carried like a paper kite.

What had that flower to do with being white,
The wayside blue and innocent heal-all?   10

What brought the kindred spider to that height,
Then steered the white moth thither in the night?
What but design of darkness to appall?—
If design govern in a thing so small.

ON A BIRD SINGING IN ITS SLEEP

A bird half wakened in the lunar noon
Sang halfway through its little inborn tune.
Partly because it sang but once all night
And that from no especial bush's height,
Partly because it sang ventriloquist   5
And had the inspiration to desist
Almost before the prick of hostile ears,
It ventured less in peril than appears.
It could not have come down to us so far,
Through the interstices of things ajar   10
On the long bead chain of repeated birth,
To be a bird while we are men on earth,
If singing out of sleep and dream that way
Had made it much more easily a prey.

AFTERFLAKES

In the thick of a teeming snowfall
I saw my shadow on snow.
I turned and looked back up at the sky,
Where we still look to ask the why
Of everything below.   5

If I shed such a darkness,
If the reason was in me,
That shadow of mine should show in form

(142)

Against the shapeless shadow of storm,
How swarthy I must be.   10

I turned and looked back upward.
The whole sky was blue;
And the thick flakes floating at a pause
Were but frost knots on an airy gauze,
With the sun shining through.   15

NOT QUITE SOCIAL

Some of you will be glad I did what I did,
And the rest won't want to punish me too severely
For finding a thing to do that though not forbid
Yet wasn't enjoined and wasn't expected, clearly.

To punish me overcruelly wouldn't be right   5
For merely giving you once more gentle proof
That the city's hold on a man is no more tight
Than when its walls rose higher than any roof.

You may taunt me with not being able to flee the earth.
You have me there, but loosely, as I would be held.   10
The way of understanding is partly mirth.
I would not be taken as ever having rebelled.

And anyone is free to condemn me to death—
If he leaves it to nature to carry out the sentence.
I shall will to the common stock of air my breath   15
And pay a death tax of fairly polite repentance.

PROVIDE, PROVIDE

The witch that came (the withered hag)
To wash the steps with pail and rag
Was once the beauty Abishag,

The picture pride of Hollywood.
Too many fall from great and good   5
For you to doubt the likelihood.

Die early and avoid the fate.
Or if predestined to die late,
Make up your mind to die in state.

Make the whole stock exchange your own!   10
If need be occupy a throne,
Where nobody can call *you* crone.

Some have relied on what they knew,
Others on being simply true.
What worked for them might work for you.   15

No memory of having starred
Atones for later disregard
Or keeps the end from being hard.

Better to go down dignified
With boughten friendship at your side   20
Than none at all. Provide, provide!

PRECAUTION

I never dared be radical when young
For fear it would make me conservative when old.

THE SPAN OF LIFE

The old dog barks backward without getting up.
I can remember when he was a pup.

THE HARDSHIP OF ACCOUNTING

Never ask of money spent
Where the spender thinks it went.
Nobody was ever meant
To remember or invent
What he did with every cent.   5

NOT ALL THERE

I turned to speak to God
About the world's despair;
But to make bad matters worse
I found God wasn't there.

God turned to speak to me   5
(Don't anybody laugh);
God found I wasn't there—
At least not over half.

BUILD SOIL

A political pastoral

Why, Tityrus! But you've forgotten me.
I'm Meliboeus the potato man,
The one you had the talk with, you remember,
Here on this very campus years ago.
Hard times have struck me and I'm on the move.   5
I've had to give my interval farm up
For interest, and I've bought a mountain farm
For nothing down, all-out-doors of a place,
All woods and pasture only fit for sheep.
But sheep is what I'm going into next.   10

(145)

I'm done forever with potato crops
At thirty cents a bushel. Give me sheep.
I know wool's down to seven cents a pound.
But I don't calculate to sell my wool.
I didn't my potatoes. I consumed them.   15
I'll dress up in sheep's clothing and eat sheep.
The Muse takes care of you. You live by writing
Your poems on a farm and call that farming.
Oh, I don't blame you. I say take life easy.
I should myself, only I don't know how.   20
But have some pity on us who have to work.
Why don't you use your talents as a writer
To advertise our farms to city buyers,
Or else write something to improve food prices.
Get in a poem toward the next election.   25

Oh, Meliboeus, I have half a mind
To take a writing hand in politics.
Before now poetry has taken notice
Of wars, and what are wars but politics
Transformed from chronic to acute and bloody?   30

I may be wrong, but, Tityrus, to me
The times seem revolutionary bad.

The question is whether they've reached a depth
Of desperation that would warrant poetry's
Leaving love's alternations, joy and grief,   35
The weather's alternations, summer and winter,
Our age-long theme, for the uncertainty
Of judging who is a contemporary liar—
Who in particular, when all alike
Get called as much in clashes of ambition.   40

Life may be tragically bad, and I
Make bold to sing it so, but do I dare
Name names and tell you who by name is wicked?
Whittier's luck with Skipper Ireson awes me—
Many men's luck with Greatest Washington   45
(Who sat for Stuart's portrait, but who sat
Equally for the nation's Constitution).
I prefer to sing safely in the realm
Of types, composite and imagined people:
To affirm there is such a thing as evil   50
Personified, but ask to be excused
From saying on a jury "Here's the guilty."

I doubt if you're convinced the times are bad.

I keep my eye on Congress, Meliboeus.
They're in the best position of us all   55
To know if anything is very wrong.
I mean they could be trusted to give the alarm
If earth were thought about to change its axis,
Or a star coming to dilate the sun.
As long as lightly all their livelong sessions,   60
Like a yardful of schoolboys out at recess
Before their plays and games were organized,
They yelling mix tag, hide-and-seek, hopscotch,
And leapfrog in each other's way—all's well.
Let newspapers profess to fear the worst!   65
Nothing's portentous, I am reassured.

Is socialism needed, do you think?

We have it now. For socialism is
An element in any government.
There's no such thing as socialism pure—   70

Except as an abstraction of the mind.
There's only democratic socialism,
Monarchic socialism, oligarchic—
The last being what they seem to have in Russia.
You often get it most in monarchy,   75
Least in democracy. In practice, pure,
I don't know what it would be. No one knows.
I have no doubt like all the loves when
Philosophized together into one—
One sickness of the body and the soul.   80
Thank God our practice holds the loves apart,
Beyond embarrassing self-consciousness
Where natural friends are met, where dogs are kept,
Where women pray with priests. There is no love.
There's only love of men and women, love   85
Of children, love of friends, of men, of God:
Divine love, human love, parental love,
Roughly discriminated for the rough.

Poetry, itself once more, is back in love.

Pardon the analogy, my Meliboeus,   90
For sweeping me away. Let's see, where was I?

But don't you think more should be socialized
Than is?

            What should you mean by socialized?

Made good for everyone—things like inventions—
Made so we all should get the good of them—   95
All, not just great exploiting businesses.

We sometimes only get the bad of them.
In your sense of the word ambition has

Been socialized—the first propensity
To be attempted. Greed may well come next.   100
But the worst one of all to leave uncurbed,
Unsocialized, is ingenuity;
Which for no sordid self-aggrandizement,
For nothing but its own blind satisfaction
(In this it is as much like hate as love),   105
Works in the dark as much against as for us.
Even while we talk some chemist at Columbia
Is stealthily contriving wool from jute
That when let loose upon the grazing world
Will put ten thousand farmers out of sheep.   110
Everyone asks for freedom for himself,
The man free love, the businessman free trade,
The writer and talker free speech and free press.
Political ambition has been taught,
By being punished back, it is not free: 115
It must at some point gracefully refrain.
Greed has been taught a little abnegation
And shall be more before we're done with it.
It is just fool enough to think itself
Self-taught. But our brute snarling and lashing taught it.   120
None shall be as ambitious as he can.
None should be as ingenious as he could,
Not if I had my say. Bounds should be set
To ingenuity for being so cruel
In bringing change unheralded on the unready.   125

I elect you to put the curb on it.

Were I dictator, I'll tell you what I'd do.

What should you do?

I'd let things take their course
And then I'd claim the credit for the outcome.

You'd make a sort of safety-first dictator. 130

Don't let the things I say against myself
Betray you into taking sides against me,
Or it might get you into trouble with me.
I'm not afraid to prophesy the future,
And be judged by the outcome, Meliboeus. 135
Listen and I will take my dearest risk.
We're always too much out or too much in.
At present from a cosmical dilation
We're so much out that the odds are against
Our ever getting inside in again. 140
But inside in is where we've got to get.
My friends all know I'm interpersonal.
But long before I'm interpersonal,
Away 'way down inside I'm personal.
Just so before we're international, 145
We're national and act as nationals.
The colors are kept unmixed on the palette,
Or better on dish plates all around the room,
So the effect when they are mixed on canvas
May seem almost exclusively designed. 150
Some minds are so confounded intermental
They remind me of pictures on a palette:
"Look at what happened. Surely some god *pinxit*.
Come look at my significant mud pie."
It's hard to tell which is the worse abhorrence, 155
Whether it's persons pied or nations pied.
Don't let me seem to say the exchange, the encounter,
May not be the important thing at last.

It well may be. We meet—I don't say when—
But must bring to the meeting the maturest,   160
The longest-saved-up, raciest, localest
We have strength of reserve in us to bring.

Tityrus, sometimes I'm perplexed myself
To find the good of commerce. Why should I
Have to sell you my apples and buy yours?   165
It can't be just to give the robber a chance
To catch them and take toll of them in transit.
Too mean a thought to get much comfort out of.
I figure that like any bandying
Of words or toys, it ministers to health.   170
It very likely quickens and refines us.

To market 'tis our destiny to go.
But much as in the end we bring for sale there,
There is still more we never bring or should bring;
More that should be kept back—the soil for instance,   175
In my opinion—though we both know poets
Who fall all over each other to bring soil
And even subsoil and hardpan to market.
To sell the hay off, let alone the soil,
Is an unpardonable sin in farming.   180
The moral is, make a late start to market.
Let me preach to you, will you, Meliboeus?

Preach on. I thought you were already preaching.
But preach and see if I can tell the difference.

Needless to say to you, my argument   185
Is not to lure the city to the country.
Let those possess the land, and only those,
Who love it with a love so strong and stupid

(151)

That they may be abused and taken advantage of
And made fun of by business, law, and art;   190
They still hang on. That so much of earth's
Unoccupied need not make us uneasy.
We don't pretend to complete occupancy.
The world's one globe, human society
Another softer globe that slightly flattened   195
Rests on the world, and clinging slowly rolls.
We have our own round shape to keep unbroken.
The world's size has no more to do with us
Than has the universe's. We are balls,
We are round from the same source of roundness.   200
We are both round because the mind is round,
Because all reasoning is in a circle.
At least that's why the universe is round.

If what you're preaching is a line of conduct,
Just what am I supposed to do about it?   205
Reason in circles?

                              No, refuse to be
Seduced back to the land by any claim
The land may seem to have on man to use it.
Let none assume to till the land but farmers.
I only speak to you as one of them.   210
You shall go to your run-out mountain farm,
Poor castaway of commerce, and so live
That none shall ever see you come to market—
Not for a long, long time. Plant, breed, produce,
But what you raise or grow, why, feed it out,   215
Eat it or plow it under where it stands,
To build the soil. For what is more accursed
Than an impoverished soil, pale and metallic?

What cries more to our kind for sympathy?
I'll make a compact with you, Meliboeus,   220
To match you deed for deed and plan for plan.
Friends crowd around me with their five-year plans
That Soviet Russia has made fashionable.
You come to me and I'll unfold to you
A five-year plan I call so not because   225
It takes ten years or so to carry out,
Rather because it took five years at least
To think it out. Come close, let us conspire—
In self-restraint, if in restraint of trade.
You will go to your run-out mountain farm   230
And do what I command you. I take care
To command only what you meant to do
Anyway. That is my style of dictator.
Build soil. Turn the farm in upon itself
Until it can contain itself no more,   235
But sweating-full, drips wine and oil a little.
I will go to my run-out social mind
And be as unsocial with it as I can.
The thought I have, and my first impulse is
To take to market—I will turn it under.   240
The thought from that thought—I will turn it under.
And so on to the limit of my nature.
We are too much out, and if we won't draw in
We shall be driven in. I was brought up
A state-rights free-trade Democrat. What's that?   245
An inconsistency. The state shall be
Laws to itself, it seems, and yet have no
Control of what it sells or what it buys.
Suppose someone comes near me who in rate
Of speech and thinking is so much my better   250

I am imposed on, silenced and discouraged.
Do I submit to being supplied by him
As the more economical producer,
More wonderful, more beautiful producer?
No. I unostentatiously move off   255
Far enough for my thought-flow to resume.
Thought product and food product are to me
Nothing compared to the producing of them.
I sent you once a song with the refrain:

    Let me be the one   260
    To do what is done—

My share at least, lest I be empty-idle.
Keep off each other and keep each other off.
You see the beauty of my proposal is
It needn't wait on general revolution.   265
I bid you to a one-man revolution—
The only revolution that is coming.
We're too unseparate out among each other—
With goods to sell and notions to impart.
A youngster comes to me with half a quatrain   270
To ask me if I think it worth the pains
Of working out the rest, the other half.
I am brought guaranteed young prattle poems
Made publicly in school, above suspicion
Of plagiarism and help of cheating parents.   275
We congregate embracing from distrust
As much as love, and too close in to strike
And be so very striking. Steal away,
The song says. Steal away and stay away.
Don't join too many gangs. Join few if any.   280
Join the United States and join the family—

But not much in between unless a college.
Is it a bargain, Shepherd Meliboeus?

Probably, but you're far too fast and strong
For my mind to keep working in your presence. 285
I can tell better after I get home,
Better a month from now when cutting posts
Or mending fence it all comes back to me
What I was thinking when you interrupted
My life-train logic. I agree with you 290
We're too unseparate. And going home
From company means coming to our senses.

A Witness Tree   1942

BEECH

Where my imaginary line
Bends square in woods, an iron spine
And pile of real rocks have been founded.
And off this corner in the wild,
Where these are driven in and piled,   5
One tree, by being deeply wounded,
Has been impressed as Witness Tree
And made commit to memory
My proof of being not unbounded.
Thus truth's established and borne out,   10
Though circumstanced with dark and doubt—
Though by a world of doubt surrounded.

—The Moodie Forester

THE SILKEN TENT

She is as in a field a silken tent
At midday when a sunny summer breeze
Has dried the dew and all its ropes relent,
So that in guys it gently sways at ease,
And its supporting central cedar pole,   5
That is its pinnacle to heavenward
And signifies the sureness of the soul,
Seems to owe naught to any single cord,
But strictly held by none, is loosely bound
By countless silken ties of love and thought   10
To everything on earth the compass round,
And only by one's going slightly taut

In the capriciousness of summer air
Is of the slightest bondage made aware.

ALL REVELATION

A head thrusts in as for the view,
But where it is it thrusts in from
Or what it is it thrusts into
By that Cyb'laean avenue,
And what can of its coming come,   5

And whither it will be withdrawn,
And what take hence or leave behind,
These things the mind has pondered on
A moment and still asking gone.
Strange apparition of the mind!   10

But the impervious geode
Was entered, and its inner crust
Of crystals with a ray cathode
At every point and facet glowed
In answer to the mental thrust.   15

Eyes seeking the response of eyes
Bring out the stars, bring out the flowers,
Thus concentrating earth and skies
So none need be afraid of size.
All revelation has been ours.   20

HAPPINESS MAKES UP IN HEIGHT
FOR WHAT IT LACKS IN LENGTH

O stormy, stormy world,
The days you were not swirled

Around with mist and cloud,
Or wrapped as in a shroud,
And the sun's brilliant ball   5
Was not in part or all
Obscured from mortal view—
Were days so very few
I can but wonder whence
I get the lasting sense   10
Of so much warmth and light.
If my mistrust is right
It may be altogether
From one day's perfect weather,
When starting clear at dawn   15
The day swept clearly on
To finish clear at eve.
I verily believe
My fair impression may
Be all from that one day   20
No shadow crossed but ours
As through its blazing flowers
We went from house to wood
For change of solitude.

COME IN

As I came to the edge of the woods,
Thrush music—hark!
Now if it was dusk outside,
Inside it was dark.

Too dark in the woods for a bird   5
By sleight of wing

To better its perch for the night,
Though it still could sing.

The last of the light of the sun
That had died in the west   10
Still lived for one song more
In a thrush's breast.

Far in the pillared dark
Thrush music went—
Almost like a call to come in   15
To the dark and lament.

But no, I was out for stars;
I would not come in.
I meant not even if asked,
And I hadn't been.   20

CARPE DIEM

Age saw two quiet children
Go loving by at twilight,
He knew not whether homeward,
Or outward from the village,
Or (chimes were ringing) churchward.   5
He waited (they were strangers)
Till they were out of hearing
To bid them both be happy.
"Be happy, happy, happy,
And seize the day of pleasure."   10
The age-long theme is Age's.
'Twas Age imposed on poems
Their gather-roses burden

To warn against the danger
That overtaken lovers   15
From being overflooded
With happiness should have it
And yet not know they have it.
But bid life seize the present?
It lives less in the present   20
Than in the future always,
And less in both together
Than in the past. The present
Is too much for the senses,
Too crowding, too confusing—   25
Too present to imagine.

THE MOST OF IT

He thought he kept the universe alone;
For all the voice in answer he could wake
Was but the mocking echo of his own
From some tree-hidden cliff across the lake.
Some morning from the boulder-broken beach   5
He would cry out on life, that what it wants
Is not its own love back in copy speech,
But counter-love, original response.
And nothing ever came of what he cried
Unless it was the embodiment that crashed   10
In the cliff's talus on the other side,
And then in the far-distant water splashed,
But after a time allowed for it to swim,
Instead of proving human when it neared
And someone else additional to him,   15
As a great buck it powerfully appeared,

Pushing the crumpled water up ahead,
And landed pouring like a waterfall,
And stumbled through the rocks with horny tread,
And forced the underbrush—and that was all.   20

THE SUBVERTED FLOWER

She drew back; he was calm:
"It is this that had the power."
And he lashed his open palm
With the tender-headed flower.
He smiled for her to smile,   5
But she was either blind
Or willfully unkind.
He eyed her for a while
For a woman and a puzzle.
He flicked and flung the flower,   10
And another sort of smile
Caught up like fingertips
The corners of his lips
And cracked his ragged muzzle.
She was standing to the waist   15
In goldenrod and brake,
Her shining hair displaced.
He stretched her either arm
As if she made it ache
To clasp her—not to harm;   20
As if he could not spare
To touch her neck and hair.
"If this has come to us
And not to me alone——"
So she thought she heard him say;   25

Though with every word he spoke
His lips were sucked and blown
And the effort made him choke
Like a tiger at a bone.
She had to lean away.   30
She dared not stir a foot,
Lest movement should provoke
The demon of pursuit
That slumbers in a brute,
It was then her mother's call   35
From inside the garden wall
Made her steal a look of fear
To see if he could hear
And would pounce to end it all
Before her mother came.   40
She looked and saw the shame:
A hand hung like a paw,
An arm worked like a saw
As if to be persuasive,
An ingratiating laugh   45
That cut the snout in half,
An eye become evasive.
A girl could only see
That a flower had marred a man,
But what she could not see   50
Was that the flower might be
Other than base and fetid:
That the flower had done but part,
And what the flower began
Her own too meager heart   55
Had terribly completed.
She looked and saw the worst.

And the dog or what it was,
Obeying bestial laws,
A coward save at night,   60
Turned from the place and ran.
She heard him stumble first
And use his hands in flight.
She heard him bark outright.
And oh, for one so young   65
The bitter words she spit
Like some tenacious bit
That will not leave the tongue.
She plucked her lips for it,
And still the horror clung.   70
Her mother wiped the foam
From her chin, picked up her comb,
And drew her backward home.

WILLFUL HOMING

It is getting dark and time he drew to a house,
But the blizzard blinds him to any house ahead.
The storm gets down his neck in an icy souse
That sucks his breath like a wicked cat in bed.

The snow blows on him and off him, exerting force   5
Downward to make him sit astride a drift,
Imprint a saddle, and calmly consider a course.
He peers out shrewdly into the thick and swift.

Since he means to come to a door he will come to a door,
Although so compromised of aim and rate   10
He may fumble wide of the knob a yard or more,
And to those concerned he may seem a little late.

THE DISCOVERY OF THE MADEIRAS

A rhyme of Hakluyt

A stolen lady was coming on board,
But whether stolen from her wedded lord
Or from her own self against her will
Was not set forth in the lading bill.
A stolen lady was all it said.   5
She came down weakly and blindly led
To the darkening, windy village slip.
She would not look at the fateful ship.
Her lover to make the ordeal swift
Had to give her the final lift   10
And force her farewell step off shore.
The way she clung to him the more
Seemed to argue perhaps she went
Not entirely without consent.
But with no companion of womankind   15
To leave the English law behind
And sail for some vague Paphian bourn
Began already to seem forlorn.

It did more distance up and down,
Their little stormy ship, than on.   20
Now it took a fitful run;
Now standing cracked its sail and spun;
Now stood upon its bulging prow
Till the pirate sailors made a vow
Of where they would go on pilgrimage   25
If God would spare them to die of age.
When the clap of two converging waves
Failed to crush their barrel staves

Or the wind to snap their walking stick,
They laughed as if they had turned a trick.   30

This was no lady's time of year.
For long the lady would disappear,
And might be rolling dead below
For all the crew were let to know.
But when the ocean's worst had passed   35
She was carried out beside the mast,
Where all day long she lay and dozed.
Or she and her lover would sit opposed
And darkly drink each other's eyes
With faint headshakings, no more wise.   40
The most he asked her eyes to grant
Was that in what she does not want
A woman wants to be overruled.
Or was the instinct in him fooled?
He knew not, neither of them knew.   45
They could only say like any two,
"You tell me and I'll tell you."

Sometimes, with her permissive smile,
He left her to her thoughts awhile
And went to lean against the rail,   50
And let the captain tell him a tale.
(He had to keep the captain's favor.)
The ship it seemed had been a slaver.
And once they had shipped a captive pair
Whose love was such they didn't care   55
Who took in them onlooker's share.
Well, when at length the fever struck
That spoils the nigger-trader's luck
The man was among the first it took.

"Throw him over alive," they said,   60
"Before the thing has time to spread.
You've got to keep the quarters clean."
But the girl fought them and made a scene.
She was a savage jungle cat
It was easy to be angry at;   65
Which put the thought into someone's head
Of the ocean bed for a marriage bed.
Some Tom said to Dick or Harry:
"Apparently these two ought to marry.
We get plenty funerals at sea.   70
How for a change would a wedding be?—
Or a combination of the two,
How would a funeral-wedding do?
It's gone so far she's probably caught
Whatever it is the nigger's got."   75
They bound them naked so they faced
With a length of cordage about the waist.
Many lovers have been divorced
By having what is free enforced.
But presence of love these had in death   80
To kiss and drink each other's breath
Before they were hurled from the slaver's deck.
They added clasps about the neck
And went embraced to the cold and dark
To be their own marriage feast for the shark.   85

When after talk with other men
A man comes back to a woman again
He tells her as much of blood and dirt
As he thinks will do her not too much hurt.

"What was the pirate captain's chaff?   90
He laughed but he did not make you laugh.
The jest seemed his and the plaudits his,
I heard him shout 'What a thing it is!'
Some standing jest between you men?
Don't tell me if you don't want to, then."   95
Whereat in a moment of cross unruth
He thought, All right, if you want the truth!

"I don't believe it! It isn't true!
It never happened! Did it, you?"
Seeing no help in wings or feet   100
She withdrew back in self-retreat
Till her heart almost ceased to beat.
Her spirit faded as far away
As the living ever go yet stay,
And her thought was she had had her pay.   105

He said to the captain, "Give command,
And bring us to the nearest land;
And let us try an untossed place
And see if it will help her case."
They brought her to a nameless isle.   110
And the ship lay in the bay for a while
Waiting to see if she would mend;
But sailed and left them in the end.
Her lover saw them sail away,
But dared not tell her all one day.   115
For slowly even her sense of him
And love itself were growing dim.
He no more drew the smile he sought.
The story is she died of thought.

(167)

And when her lover was left alone   120
He stayed long enough to carve on stone
The name of the lady with his own
To be her only marriage lines.
And carved them round with a scroll of vines.
Then he gouged a clumsy sailing trough   125
From a fallen tree and pushing off
Safely made the African shore;
Where he fell a prisoner to the Moor.
But the Moor strangely enough believed
The tale of the voyage he had achieved,   130
And sent him to the King to admire.
He came at last to his native shire.
The island he found was verified.
And the bay where his stolen lady died
Was named for him instead of her.   135
But so is history like to err.
And soon it is neither here nor there
Whether time's rewards are fair or unfair.

THE GIFT OUTRIGHT

The land was ours before we were the land's.
She was our land more than a hundred years
Before we were her people. She was ours
In Massachusetts, in Virginia,
But we were England's, still colonials,   5
Possessing what we still were unpossessed by,
Possessed by what we now no more possessed.
Something we were withholding made us weak
Until we found out that it was ourselves
We were withholding from our land of living,   10

And forthwith found salvation in surrender.
Such as we were we gave ourselves outright
(The deed of gift was many deeds of war)
To the land vaguely realizing westward,
But still unstoried, artless, unenhanced,   15
Such as she was, such as she would become.

OUR HOLD ON THE PLANET

We asked for rain. It didn't flash and roar.
It didn't lose its temper at our demand
And blow a gale. It didn't misunderstand
And give us more than our spokesman bargained for;
And just because we owned to a wish for rain,   5
Send us a flood and bid us be damned and drown.
It gently threw us a glittering shower down.
And when we had taken that into the roots of grain,
It threw us another and then another still,
Till the spongy soil again was natal wet.   10
We may doubt the just proportion of good to ill.
There is much in nature against us. But we forget:
Take nature altogether since time began,
Including human nature, in peace and war,
And it must be a little more in favor of man,   15
Say a fraction of one percent at the very least,
Or our number living wouldn't be steadily more,
Our hold on the planet wouldn't have so increased.

THE LESSON FOR TODAY

If this uncertain age in which we dwell
Were really as dark as I hear sages tell,
And I convinced that they were really sages,

I should not curse myself with it to hell,
But leaving not the chair I long have sat in   5
I should betake me back ten thousand pages
To the world's undebatably dark ages,
And getting up my medieval Latin,
Seek converse common cause and brotherhood
(By all that's liberal—I should, I should)   10
With poets who could calmly take the fate
Of being born at once too early and late,
And for these reasons kept from being great.
Yet singing but Dione in the wood
And *ver aspergit terram floribus*   15
They slowly led old Latin verse to rhyme
And to forget the ancient lengths of time,
And so began the modern world for us.

    I'd say, O Master of the Palace School,
You were not Charles' nor anybody's fool: 20
Tell me as pedagogue to pedagogue,
You did not know that since King Charles did rule
You had no chance but to be minor, did you?
Your light was spent perhaps as in a fog
That at once kept you burning low and hid you.   25
The age may very well have been to blame
For your not having won to Virgil's fame.
But no one ever heard you make the claim.
You would not think you knew enough to judge
The age when full upon you. That's my point.   30
We have today and I could call their name
Who know exactly what is out of joint
To make their verse and their excuses lame.
They've tried to grasp with too much social fact

Too large a situation. You and I   35
Would be afraid if we should comprehend
And get outside of too much bad statistics,
Our muscles never could again contract:
We never could recover human shape,
But must live lives out mentally agape   40
Or die of philosophical distention.
That's how we feel—and we're no special mystics.

    We can't appraise the time in which we act.
But for the folly of it, let's pretend
We know enough to know it for adverse.   45
One more millennium's about to end.
Let's celebrate the event, my distant friend,
In publicly disputing which is worse,
The present age or your age. You and I
As schoolmen of repute should qualify   50
To wage a fine scholastical contention
As to whose age deserves the lower mark,
Or should I say the higher one, for dark.
I can just hear the way you make it go:
There's always something to be sorry for,   55
A sordid peace or an outrageous war.
Yes, yes, of course. We have the same convention.
The groundwork of all faith is human woe.
It was well worth preliminary mention.
There's nothing but injustice to be had,   60
No choice is left a poet, you might add,
But how to take the curse, tragic or comic.
It was well worth preliminary mention.
But let's go on to where our cases part,
If part they do. Let me propose a start.   65

(171)

(We're rivals in the badness of our case,
Remember, and must keep a solemn face.)
Space ails us moderns: we are sick with space.
Its contemplation makes us out as small
As a brief epidemic of microbes   70
That in a good glass may be seen to crawl
The patina of this the least of globes.
But have we there the advantage after all?
You were belittled into vilest worms
God hardly tolerated with his feet;   75
Which comes to the same thing in different terms.
We both are the belittled human race,
One as compared with God and one with space.
I had thought ours the more profound disgrace;
But doubtless this was only my conceit.   80
The cloister and the observatory saint
Take comfort in about the same complaint.
So science and religion really meet.

    I can just hear you call your Palace class:
Come learn the Latin *eheu* for alas.   85
You may not want to use it and you may.
O paladins, the lesson for today
Is how to be unhappy yet polite.
And at the summons Roland, Olivier,
And every sheepish paladin and peer,   90
Being already more than proved in fight,
Sits down in school to try if he can write
Like Horace in the true Horatian vein,
Yet like a Christian disciplined to bend
His mind to thinking always of the end.   95
Memento mori and obey the Lord.

Art and religion love the somber chord.
Earth's a hard place in which to save the soul,
And could it be brought under state control,
So automatically we all were saved,   100
Its separateness from Heaven could be waived;
It might as well at once be kingdom-come.
(Perhaps it will be next millennium.)

But these are universals, not confined
To any one time, place, or human kind.   105
We're either nothing or a God's regret.
As ever when philosophers are met,
No matter where they stoutly mean to get,
Nor what particulars they reason from,
They are philosophers, and from old habit   110
They end up in the universal Whole
As unoriginal as any rabbit.

One age is like another for the soul.
I'm telling you. You haven't said a thing,
Unless I put it in your mouth to say.   115
I'm having the whole argument my way—
But in your favor—please to tell your King—
In having granted you all ages shine
With equal darkness, yours as dark as mine.
I'm liberal. You, you aristocrat,   120
Won't know exactly what I mean by that.
I mean so altruistically moral
I never take my own side in a quarrel.
I'd lay my hand on his hand on his staff,
Lean back and have my confidential laugh,   125
And tell him I had read his Epitaph.

(173)

It sent me to the graves the other day.
The only other there was far away
Across the landscape with a watering pot
At his devotions in a special plot. 130
And he was there resuscitating flowers
(Make no mistake about its being bones);
But I was only there to read the stones
To see what on the whole they had to say
About how long a man may think to live, 135
Which is becoming my concern of late.
And very wide the choice they seemed to give;
The ages ranging all the way from hours
To months and years and many, many years.
One man had lived one hundred years and eight. 140
But though we all may be inclined to wait
And follow some development of state,
Or see what comes of science and invention,
There is a limit to our time extension.
We all are doomed to broken-off careers, 145
And so's the nation, so's the total race.
The earth itself is liable to the fate
Of meaninglessly being broken off.
(And hence so many literary tears
At which my inclination is to scoff.) 150
I may have wept that any should have died
Or missed their chance, or not have been their best,
Or been their riches, fame, or love denied;
On me as much as any is the jest.
I take my incompleteness with the rest. 155
God bless himself can no one else be blessed.

I hold your doctrine of *Memento Mori*.
And were an epitaph to be my story
I'd have a short one ready for my own.
I would have written of me on my stone: 160
I had a lover's quarrel with the world.

A CONSIDERABLE SPECK

(Microscopic)

A speck that would have been beneath my sight
On any but a paper sheet so white
Set off across what I had written there.
And I had idly poised my pen in air
To stop it with a period of ink,   5
When something strange about it made me think.
This was no dust speck by my breathing blown,
But unmistakably a living mite
With inclinations it could call its own.
It paused as with suspicion of my pen,   10
And then came racing wildly on again
To where my manuscript was not yet dry;
Then paused again and either drank or smelt—
With loathing, for again it turned to fly.
Plainly with an intelligence I dealt.   15
It seemed too tiny to have room for feet,
Yet must have had a set of them complete
To express how much it didn't want to die.
It ran with terror and with cunning crept.
It faltered: I could see it hesitate;   20
Then in the middle of the open sheet
Cower down in desperation to accept

Whatever I accorded it of fate.
I have none of the tenderer-than-thou
Collectivistic regimenting love 25
With which the modern world is being swept.
But this poor microscopic item now!
Since it was nothing I knew evil of
I let it lie there till I hope it slept.

I have a mind myself and recognize 30
Mind when I meet with it in any guise.
No one can know how glad I am to find
On any sheet the least display of mind.

NOVEMBER

We saw leaves go to glory,
Then almost migratory
Go part way down the lane,
And then to end the story
Get beaten down and pasted 5
In one wild day of rain.
We heard " 'Tis over" roaring.
A year of leaves was wasted.
Oh, we make a boast of storing,
Of saving and of keeping, 10
But only by ignoring
The waste of moments sleeping,
The waste of pleasure weeping,
By denying and ignoring
The waste of nations warring. 15

THE RABBIT-HUNTER

Careless and still
The hunter lurks
With gun depressed,
Facing alone
The alder swamps   5
Ghastly snow-white.
And his hound works
In the offing there
Like one possessed,
And yelps delight   10
And sings and romps,
Bringing him on
The shadowy hare
For him to rend
And deal a death   15
That he nor it
(Nor I) have wit
To comprehend.

IT IS ALMOST THE YEAR TWO THOUSAND

To start the world of old
We had one age of gold
Not labored out of mines,
And some say there are signs
The second such has come,   5
The true Millennium,
The final golden glow
To end it. And if so
(And science ought to know)

We well may raise our heads 10
From weeding garden beds
And annotating books
To watch this end deluxe.

IN A POEM

The sentencing goes blithely on its way
And takes the playfully objected rhyme
As surely as it keeps the stroke and time
In having its undeviable say.

A QUESTION

A voice said, Look me in the stars
And tell me truly, men of earth,
If all the soul-and-body scars
Were not too much to pay for birth.

BOEOTIAN

I love to toy with the Platonic notion
That wisdom need not be of Athens Attic,
But well may be Laconic, even Boeotian.
At least I will not have it systematic.

THE SECRET SITS

We dance round in a ring and suppose,
But the Secret sits in the middle and knows.

AN ANSWER

But Islands of the Blessèd, bless you, son,
I never came upon a blessèd one.

A SERIOUS STEP LIGHTLY TAKEN

Between two burrs on the map
Was a hollow-headed snake.
The burrs were hills, the snake was a stream,
And the hollow head was a lake.

And the dot in *front* of a name   5
Was what should be a town.
And there might be a house we could buy
For only a dollar down.

With two wheels low in the ditch
We left our boiling car   10
And knocked at the door of a house we found,
And there today we are.

It is turning three hundred years
On our cisatlantic shore
For family after family name.   15
We'll make it three hundred more

For our name farming here,
Aloof yet not aloof,
Enriching soil and increasing stock,
Repairing fence and roof;   20

A hundred thousand days
Of front-page paper events,
A half a dozen major wars,
And forty-five presidents.

A YOUNG BIRCH

The birch begins to crack its outer sheath
Of baby green and show the white beneath,
As whosoever likes the young and slight
May well have noticed. Soon entirely white
To double day and cut in half the dark   5
It will stand forth, entirely white in bark,
And nothing but the top a leafy green—
The only native tree that dares to lean,
Relying on its beauty, to the air.
(Less brave perhaps than trusting are the fair.)   10
And someone reminiscent will recall
How once in cutting brush along the wall
He spared it from the number of the slain,
At first to be no bigger than a cane,
And then no bigger than a fishing pole,   15
But now at last so obvious a bole
The most efficient help you ever hired
Would know that it was there to be admired,
And zeal would not be thanked that cut it down
When you were reading books or out of town.   20
It was a thing of beauty and was sent
To live its life out as an ornament.

DIRECTIVE

Back out of all this now too much for us,
Back in a time made simple by the loss
Of detail, burned, dissolved, and broken off
Like graveyard marble sculpture in the weather,

There is a house that is no more a house   5
Upon a farm that is no more a farm
And in a town that is no more a town.
The road there, if you'll let a guide direct you
Who only has at heart your getting lost,
May seem as if it should have been a quarry—   10
Great monolithic knees the former town
Long since gave up pretense of keeping covered.
And there's a story in a book about it:
Besides the wear of iron wagon wheels
The ledges show lines ruled southeast-northwest,   15
The chisel work of an enormous Glacier
That braced his feet against the Arctic Pole.
You must not mind a certain coolness from him
Still said to haunt this side of Panther Mountain.
Nor need you mind the serial ordeal   20
Of being watched from forty cellar holes
As if by eye pairs out of forty firkins.
As for the woods' excitement over you
That sends light rustle rushes to their leaves,
Charge that to upstart inexperience.   25
Where were they all not twenty years ago?
They think too much of having shaded out
A few old pecker-fretted apple trees.
Make yourself up a cheering song of how
Someone's road home from work this once was,   30
Who may be just ahead of you on foot
Or creaking with a buggy load of grain.
The height of the adventure is the height
Of country where two village cultures faded
Into each other. Both of them are lost.   35
And if you're lost enough to find yourself

(181)

By now, pull in your ladder road behind you
And put a sign up CLOSED to all but me.
Then make yourself at home. The only field
Now left's no bigger than a harness gall.   40
First there's the children's house of make-believe,
Some shattered dishes underneath a pine,
The playthings in the playhouse of the children.
Weep for what little things could make them glad.
Then for the house that is no more a house,   45
But only a belilaced cellar hole,
Now slowly closing like a dent in dough.
This was no playhouse but a house in earnest.
Your destination and your destiny's
A brook that was the water of the house,   50
Cold as a spring as yet so near its source,
Too lofty and original to rage.
(We know the valley streams that when aroused
Will leave their tatters hung on barb and thorn.)
I have kept hidden in the instep arch   55
Of an old cedar at the waterside
A broken drinking goblet like the Grail
Under a spell so the wrong ones can't find it,
So can't get saved, as Saint Mark says they mustn't.
(I stole the goblet from the children's playhouse.)   60
Here are your waters and your watering place.
Drink and be whole again beyond confusion.

THE NIGHT LIGHT

She always had to burn a light
Beside her attic bed at night.
It gave bad dreams and broken sleep,

But helped the Lord her soul to keep.
Good gloom on her was thrown away.   5
It is on me by night or day,
Who have, as I suppose, ahead
The darkest of it still to dread.

BRAVADO

Have I not walked without an upward look
Of caution under stars that very well
Might not have missed me when they shot and fell?
It was a risk I had to take—and took.

A MOOD APART

Once down on my knees to growing plants
I prodded the earth with a lazy tool
In time with a medley of sotto chants;
But becoming aware of some boys from school
Who had stopped outside the fence to spy,   5
I stopped my song and almost heart,
For any eye is an evil eye
That looks in onto a mood apart.

THE FEAR OF GOD

If you should rise from Nowhere up to Somewhere,
From being No one up to being Someone,
Be sure to keep repeating to yourself
You owe it to an arbitrary god
Whose mercy to you rather than to others   5
Won't bear too critical examination.
Stay unassuming. If for lack of license

To wear the uniform of who you are,
You should be tempted to make up for it
In a subordinating look or tone, 10
Beware of coming too much to the surface
And using for apparel what was meant
To be the curtain of the inmost soul.

IOTA SUBSCRIPT

Seek not in me the big I capital,
Nor yet the little dotted in me seek.
If I have in me any I at all,
'Tis the iota subscript of the Greek.

So small am I as an attention beggar. 5
The letter you will find me subscript to
Is neither alpha, eta, nor omega,
But upsilon which is the Greek for you.

IT BIDS PRETTY FAIR

The play seems out for an almost infinite run.
Don't mind a little thing like the actors fighting.
The only thing I worry about is the sun.
We'll be all right if nothing goes wrong with the lighting.

A CASE FOR JEFFERSON

Harrison loves my country too,
But wants it all made over new.
He's Freudian Viennese by night,
By day he's Marxian Muscovite.
It isn't because he's Russian Jew. 5

(184)

He's Puritan Yankee through and through.
He dotes on Saturday pork and beans.
But his mind is hardly out of his teens:
With him the love of country means
Blowing it all to smithereens 10
And having it all made over new.

WHY WAIT FOR SCIENCE

Sarcastic Science, she would like to know,
In her complacent ministry of fear,
How we propose to get away from here
When she has made things so we have to go
Or be wiped out. Will she be asked to show 5
Us how by rocket we may hope to steer
To some star off there, say, a half light-year
Through temperature of absolute zeró?
Why wait for Science to supply the how
When any amateur can tell it now? 10
The way to go away should be the same
As fifty million years ago we came—
If anyone remembers how that was.
I have a theory, but it hardly does.

AN IMPORTER

Mrs. Someone's been to Asia.
What she brought back would amaze ye.
Bamboos, ivories, jades, and lacquers,
Devil-scaring firecrackers,
Recipes for tea with butter, 5
Sacred rigmaroles to mutter,

Subterfuge for saving faces,
A developed taste in vases,
Arguments too stale to mention
'Gainst American invention— 10
Most of all the mass production
Destined to prove our destruction.
What are telephones, skyscrapers,
Safety razors, Sunday papers
But the silliest evasion 15
Of the truths we owe an Asian?
But the best of her exhibit
Was a prayer machine from Tibet
That by brook power in the garden
Kept repeating Pardon, pardon; 20
And as picturesque machinery
Beat a sundial in the scenery—
The most primitive of engines
Mass-producing with a vengeance.
Teach those Asians mass production? 25
Teach your grandmother egg suction.

NO HOLY WARS FOR THEM

States strong enough to do good are but few.
Their number would seem limited to three.
Good is a thing that they, the great, can do,
But puny little states can only be.
And being good for these means standing by 5
To watch a war in nominal alliance,
And when it's over watch the world's supply
Get parceled out among the winning giants.

God, have You taken cognizance of this?
And what on this is Your divine position? 10
That nations like the Cuban and the Swiss
Can never hope to wage a Global Mission.
No Holy Wars for them. The most the small
Can ever give us is a nuisance brawl.

TAKE SOMETHING LIKE A STAR

O Star (the fairest one in sight),
We grant your loftiness the right
To some obscurity of cloud—
It will not do to say of night,
Since dark is what brings out your light. 5
Some mystery becomes the proud.
But to be wholly taciturn
In your reserve is not allowed.
Say something to us we can learn
By heart and when alone repeat. 10
Say something! And it says, "I burn."
But say with what degree of heat.
Talk Fahrenheit, talk Centigrade.
Use language we can comprehend.
Tell us what elements you blend. 15
It gives us strangely little aid,
But does tell something in the end.
And steadfast as Keats' Eremite,
Not even stooping from its sphere,
It asks a little of us here. 20
It asks of us a certain height,
So when at times the mob is swayed

To carry praise or blame too far,

We may take something like a star

To stay our minds on and be staid. 25

[Not initially included among the poems published in *Steeple Bush* (1947), "Take Something Like a Star" did appear in *Complete Poems of Robert Frost* (1949) within a section entitled "An Afterword," immediately following the *Steeple Bush* poems. It was continued in that position in subsequent editions of Frost's selected and collected verse.]

In the Clearing 1962

But God's own descent
Into flesh was meant
As a demonstration
That the supreme merit
Lay in risking spirit
In substantiation.
Spirit enters flesh
And for all it's worth
Charges into earth
In birth after birth
Ever fresh and fresh.
We may take the view
That its derring-do
Thought of in the large
Is one mighty charge
On our human part
Of the soul's ethereal
Into the material.

—FRONTISPIECE

AWAY!

Now I out walking
The world desert,
And my shoe and my stocking
Do me no hurt.

I leave behind   5
Good friends in town.
Let them get well-wined
And go lie down.

(189)

Don't think I leave
For the outer dark   10
Like Adam and Eve
Put out of the Park.

Forget the myth.
There is no one I
Am put out with   15
Or put out by.

Unless I'm wrong
I but obey
The urge of a song:
"I'm—bound—away!"   20

And I may return
If dissatisfied
With what I learn
From having died.

A CABIN IN THE CLEARING

For Alfred Edwards

MIST.   I don't believe the sleepers in this house
Know where they are.

SMOKE.   They've been here long enough
To push the woods back from around the house
And part them in the middle with a path.

MIST.   And still I doubt if they know where they are.   5
And I begin to fear they never will.
All they maintain the path for is the comfort

Of visiting with the equally bewildered.
Nearer in plight their neighbors are than distance.

SMOKE.   I am the guardian wraith of starlit smoke   10
That leans out this and that way from their chimney.
I will not have their happiness despaired of.

MIST.   No one—not I—would give them up for lost
Simply because they don't know where they are.
I am the damper counterpart of smoke,   15
That gives off from a garden ground at night
But lifts no higher than a garden grows.
I cotton to their landscape. That's who I am.
I am no further from their fate than you are.

SMOKE.   They must by now have learned the native tongue.   20
Why don't they ask the Red Man where they are?

MIST.   They often do, and none the wiser for it.
So do they also ask philosophers
Who come to look in on them from the pulpit.
They will ask anyone there is to ask—   25
In the fond faith accumulated fact
Will of itself take fire and light the world up.
Learning has been a part of their religion.

SMOKE.   If the day ever comes when they know who
They are, they may know better where they are.   30
But who they are is too much to believe—
Either for them or the onlooking world.
They are too sudden to be credible.

MIST.   Listen, they murmur talking in the dark
On what should be their daylong theme continued.   35
Putting the lamp out has not put their thought out.
Let us pretend the dewdrops from the eaves
Are you and I eavesdropping on their unrest—
A mist and smoke eavesdropping on a haze—
And see if we can tell the bass from the soprano.   40

Than smoke and mist who better could appraise
The kindred spirit of an inner haze?

CLOSED FOR GOOD

Much as I own I owe
The passers of the past
Because their to and fro
Has cut this road to last,
I owe them more today   5
Because they've gone away

And come not back with steed
And chariot to chide
My slowness with their speed
And scare me to one side.   10
They have found other scenes
For haste and other means.

They leave the road to me
To walk in saying naught
Perhaps but to a tree   15
Inaudibly in thought,

"From you the road receives
A priming coat of leaves.

"And soon for lack of sun,
The prospects are in white   20
It will be further done,
But with a coat so light
The shape of leaves will show
Beneath the brush of snow."

And so on into winter   25
Till even I have ceased
To come as a foot printer,
And only some slight beast
So mousy or so foxy
Shall print there as my proxy.   30

ONE MORE BREVITY

I opened the door so my last look
Should be taken outside a house and book.
Before I gave up seeing and slept
I said I would see how Sirius kept
His watchdog eye on what remained   5
To be gone into if not explained.
But scarcely was my door ajar,
When past the leg I thrust for bar
Slipped in to be my problem guest,
Not a heavenly dog made manifest,   10
But an earthly dog of the carriage breed;
Who, having failed of the modern speed,
Now asked asylum—and I was stirred
To be the one so dog-preferred.

He dumped himself like a bag of bones, 15
He sighed himself a couple of groans,
And head to tail then firmly curled
Like swearing off on the traffic world.
I set him water, I set him food.
He rolled an eye with gratitude 20
(Or merely manners it may have been),
But never so much as lifted chin.
His hard tail loudly smacked the floor
As if beseeching me, "Please, no more;
I can't explain—tonight at least." 25
His brow was perceptibly trouble-creased.
So I spoke in terms of adoption thus:
"Gustie, old boy, Dalmatian Gus,
You're right, there's nothing to discuss.
Don't try to tell me what's on your mind, 30
The sorrow of having been left behind,
Or the sorrow of having run away.
All that can wait for the light of day.
Meanwhile feel obligation-free.
Nobody has to confide in me." 35
'Twas too one-sided a dialogue,
And I wasn't sure I was talking dog.
I broke off baffled. But all the same,
In fancy I ratified his name,
Gustie—Dalmatian Gus, that is— 40
And started shaping my life to his,
Finding him in his right supplies
And sharing his miles of exercise.

Next morning the minute I was about
He was at the door to be let out 45

With an air that said, "I have paid my call.
You mustn't feel hurt if now I'm all
For getting back somewhere or further on."
I opened the door and he was gone.
I was to taste in little the grief   50
That comes of dogs' lives being so brief,
Only a fraction of ours at most.
He might have been the dream of a ghost
In spite of the way his tail had smacked
My floor so hard and matter-of-fact.   55
And things have been going so strangely since,
I wouldn't be too hard to convince,
I might even claim, he was Sirius
(Think of presuming to call him Gus),
The star itself—Heaven's greatest star,   60
Not a meteorite, but an avatar—
Who had made an overnight descent
To show by deeds he didn't resent
My having depended on him so long,
And yet done nothing about it in song.   65
A symbol was all he could hope to convey,
An intimation, a shot of ray,
A meaning I was supposed to seek,
And finding, wasn't disposed to speak.

ESCAPIST—NEVER

He is no fugitive —escaped, escaping.
No one has seen him stumble looking back.
His fear is not behind him but beside him
On either hand to make his course perhaps
A crooked straightness yet no less a straightness.   5

(195)

He runs face forward. He is a pursuer.
He seeks a seeker who in his turn seeks
Another still, lost far into the distance.
Any who seek him seek in him the seeker.
His life is a pursuit of a pursuit forever.   10
It is the future that creates his present.
All is an interminable chain of longing.

ACCIDENTALLY ON PURPOSE

The Universe is but the Thing of things,
The things but balls all going round in rings.
Some of them mighty huge, some mighty tiny,
All of them radiant and mighty shiny.

They mean to tell us all was rolling blind   5
Till accidentally it hit on mind
In an albino monkey in a jungle,
And even then it had to grope and bungle,

Till Darwin came to earth upon a year
To show the evolution how to steer.   10
They mean to tell us, though, the Omnibus
Had no real purpose till it got to us.

Never believe it. At the very worst
It must have had the purpose from the first
To produce purpose as the fitter bred: 15
We were just purpose coming to a head.

Whose purpose was it? His or Hers or Its?
Let's leave that to the scientific wits.
Grant me intention, purpose, and design—
That's near enough for me to the Divine.   20

And yet for all this help of head and brain
How happily instinctive we remain,
Our best guide upward further to the light,
Passionate preference such as love at sight.

A NEVER NAUGHT SONG

There was never naught,
There was always thought.
But when noticed first
It was fairly burst
Into having weight.   5
It was in a state
Of atomic One.
Matter was begun—
And in fact complete,
One and yet discrete   10
To conflict and pair.
Everything was there,
Every single thing
Waiting was to bring,
Clear from hydrogen   15
All the way to men.
It is all the tree
It will ever be,
Bole and branch and root
Cunningly minute.   20
And this gist of all
Is so infra-small
As to blind our eyes
To its every guise
And so render nil   25

The whole Yggdrasill.
Out of coming-in
Into having been!
So the picture's caught
Almost next to naught   30
But the force of thought.

[FORGIVE, O LORD . . .]

Forgive, O Lord, my little jokes on Thee
And I'll forgive Thy great big one on me.

THE DRAFT HORSE

With a lantern that wouldn't burn
In too frail a buggy we drove
Behind too heavy a horse
Through a pitch-dark limitless grove.

And a man came out of the trees   5
And took our horse by the head
And reaching back to his ribs
Deliberately stabbed him dead.

The ponderous beast went down
With a crack of a broken shaft.   10
And the night drew through the trees
In one long invidious draft.

The most unquestioning pair
That ever accepted fate
And the least disposed to ascribe   15
Any more than we had to to hate,

We assumed that the man himself
Or someone he had to obey

(198)

Wanted us to get down
And walk the rest of the way. 20

ENDS

Loud talk in the overlighted house
That made us stumble past.
Oh, there had once been night the first,
But this was night the last.

Of all the things he might have said, 5
Sincere or insincere,
He never said she wasn't young,
And hadn't been his dear.

Oh, some as soon would throw it all
As throw a part away. 10
And some will say all sorts of things,
But some mean what they say.

PERIL OF HOPE

It is right in there
Betwixt and between
The orchard bare
And the orchard green,

When the boughs are right 5
In a flowery burst
Of pink and white,
That we fear the worst.

For there's not a clime
But at any cost 10
Will take that time
For a night of frost.

LINES WRITTEN IN DEJECTION ON THE EVE OF GREAT SUCCESS

I once had a cow that jumped over the moon,
Not onto the moon but over.
I don't know what made her so lunar a loon;
All she'd been having was clover.

That was back in the days of my godmother Goose. 5
But though we are goosier now,
And all tanked up with mineral juice
We haven't caught up with my cow.

POSTSCRIPT

But if over the moon I had wanted to go
And had caught my cow by the tail, 10
I'll bet she'd have made a melodious low
And put her foot in the pail;

Than which there is no indignity worse.
A cow did that once to a fellow
Who rose from the milking stool with a curse 15
And cried, "I'll larn you to bellow."

He couldn't lay hands on a pitchfork to hit her
Or give her a stab of the tine,
So he leapt on her hairy back and bit her
Clear into her marrow spine. 20

(200)

No doubt she would have preferred the fork.
She let out a howl of rage
That was heard as far away as New York
And made the papers' front page.

He answered her back, "Well, who begun it?"   25
That's what at the end of a war
We always say—not who won it,
Or what it was foughten for.

IN A GLASS OF CIDER

It seemed I was a mite of sediment
That waited for the bottom to ferment
So I could catch a bubble in ascent.
I rode up on one till the bubble burst,
And when that left me to sink back reversed   5
I was no worse off than I was at first.
I'd catch another bubble if I waited.
The thing was to get now and then elated.

FROM IRON

TOOLS AND WEAPONS

To Ahmed S. Bokhari

Nature within her inmost self divides
To trouble men with having to take sides.

[FOUR-ROOM SHACK . . .]

Four-room shack aspiring high
With an arm of scrawny mast
For the visions in the sky

That go blindly pouring past.
In the ear and in the eye   5
What you get is what to buy.
Hope you're satisfied to last.

[IT TAKES ALL SORTS . . .]

It takes all sorts of in- and outdoor schooling
To get adapted to my kind of fooling.

[IN WINTER IN THE WOODS . . .]

In winter in the woods alone
Against the trees I go.
I mark a maple for my own
And lay the maple low.

At four o'clock I shoulder ax,   5
And in the afterglow
I link a line of shadowy tracks
Across the tinted snow.

I see for Nature no defeat
In one tree's overthrow   10
Or for myself in my retreat
For yet another blow.

A Masque of Reason   1945
A Masque of Mercy   1947

Robert Frost repeatedly explained why it was he chose to
place in a climactic position at the end of his *Complete
Poems* (1949) his one-act plays entitled *A Masque of Reason*
and *A Masque of Mercy,* which had been published in 1945
and 1947, respectively. It seemed to him that these two
masques contained, and even summarized, themes hinted
at in so many of his shorter poems.

A Masque of Reason may be viewed as Frost's attempt to
write, in dramatic blank verse, an additional chapter to the
Bible's Book of Job. Its setting is a "fair oasis" in Heaven,
and the central situation develops when Job and his wife are
able to ask God what His reasons were for torturing Job,
approximately one thousand years earlier.

In striking contrast, the setting of *A Masque of Mercy* is a
small bookstore in the vicinity of New York City, at closing
time in the evening. The "Keeper" of the store, together with
his wife, Jesse Bel, and their only immediate customer,
named Paul, would seem about ready to leave. They are
detained, however, by the arrival of a "fugitive," Jonah.
Through various analogies, the biblical story is invoked about
Jonah's impatience with God over His refusal to destroy
Nineveh, and the main action is a discourse among these
four characters, centering upon the subject of justice versus
mercy. (For background on this same theme, see Frost's
interpretation of a mercy-justice passage in *Paradise Lost,* on
pages 436–438 of this volume.)

The following extracts provide a sampling of the flavor and tone of the two *Masques*.

From A MASQUE OF REASON

GOD. Oh, I remember well: you're Job, my Patient.
How are you now? I trust you're quite recovered,
And feel no ill effects from what I gave you.

JOB. Gave me in truth: I like the frank admission.
I am a name for being put upon.

—lines 34–38

[GOD, addressing JOB.]
I've had you on my mind a thousand years
To thank you someday for the way you helped me
Establish once for all the principle
There's no connection man can reason out
Between his just deserts and what he gets.

* * *

Too long I've owed you this apology
For the apparently unmeaning sorrow
You were afflicted with in those old days.
But it was of the essence of the trial
You shouldn't understand it at the time.
It had to seem unmeaning to have meaning.
And it came out all right. I have no doubt
You realize by now the part you played
To stultify the Deuteronomist
And change the tenor of religious thought.
My thanks are to you for releasing me
From moral bondage to the human race.

(204)

The only free will there at first was man's,
Who could do good or evil as he chose.
I had no choice but I must follow him
With forfeits and rewards he understood—
Unless I liked to suffer loss of worship.
I had to prosper good and punish evil.
You changed all that. You set me free to reign.
You are the Emancipator of your God,
And as such I promote you to a saint.

—lines 47–51 and 59–79

[JOB'S WIFE, addressing GOD.]
I stood by Job. I may have turned on You.
Job scratched his boils and tried to think what he
Had done or not done to or for the poor.
The test is always how we treat the poor.
It's time the poor were treated by the state
In some way not so penal as the poorhouse.
That's one thing more to put on Your agenda.

*   *   *

All You can seem to do is lose Your temper
When reason-hungry mortals ask for reasons.
Of course, in the abstract high singular
There isn't any universal reason;
And no one but a man would think there was.
You don't catch women trying to be Plato.
Still there must be lots of unsystematic
Stray scraps of palliative reason
It wouldn't hurt You to vouchsafe the faithful.

—lines 120–126 and 135–143

[JOB, addressing GOD and referring to JOB'S WIFE.]
You have it in for women, she believes.
Kipling invokes You as Lord God of Hosts.
She'd like to know how You would take a prayer
That started off Lord God of Hostesses.

—lines 178–181

[GOD, addressing JOB.]
It would be too bad if Columbus-like
You failed to see the worth of your achievement.

—lines 186–187

[JOB, addressing GOD.]
'Twas a great demonstration if You say so.
Though incidentally I sometimes wonder
Why it had had to be at my expense.

GOD.   It had to be at somebody's expense.
Society can never think things out:
It has to see them acted out by actors,
Devoted actors at a sacrifice—
The ablest actors I can lay my hands on.

—lines 219–226

[JOB, addressing GOD.]
              [. . .] We disparage reason.
But all the time it's what we're most concerned with.
There's will as motor and there's will as brakes.
Reason is, I suppose, the steering gear.
The will as brakes can't stop the will as motor
For very long. We're plainly made to go.

(206)

We're going anyway and may as well
Have some say as to where we're headed for;
Just as we will be talking anyway
And may as well throw in a little sense.

*   *   *

I fail to see what fun, what satisfaction
A God can find in laughing at how badly
Men fumble at the possibilities
When left to guess forever for themselves.
The chances are when there's so much pretense
Of metaphysical profundity
The obscurity's a fraud to cover nothing.
I've come to think no so-called hidden value's
Worth going after. Get down into things,
It will be found there's no more given there
Than on the surface. If there ever was,
The crypt was long since rifled by the Greeks.
We don't know where we are, or who we are.
We don't know one another; don't know You;
Don't know what time it is. We don't know, don't we?
Who says we don't? Who got up these misgivings?
Oh, we know well enough to go ahead with.
I mean we seem to know enough to act on.

—lines 228–237 and 273–290

[JOB'S WIFE, addressing GOD.]
Job says there's no such thing as Earth's becoming
An easier place for man to save his soul in.
Except as a hard place to save his soul in,
A trial ground where he can try himself

(207)

And find out whether he is any good,
It would be meaningless. It might as well
Be Heaven at once and have it over with.

—lines 316–322

[GOD, addressing JOB and JOB'S WIFE.]
One at a time, please. I will answer Job first.
I'm going to tell Job why I tortured him,
And trust it won't be adding to the torture.

—lines 324–326

[JOB, addressing GOD and referring to God's "reason."]
      [. . .] I expected more
Than I could understand and what I get
Is almost less than I can understand.
But I don't mind. Let's leave it as it stood.
The point was it was none of my concern.
I stick to that. But talk about confusion!—
How is that for a mix-up, Thyatira?—
Yet I suppose what seems to us confusion
Is not confusion, but the form of forms,
The serpent's tail stuck down the serpent's throat,
Which is the symbol of eternity
And also of the way all things come round,
Or of how rays return upon themselves,
To quote the greatest Western poem yet.
Though I hold rays deteriorate to nothing:
First white, then red, then ultrared, then out.

—lines 331–346

From A MASQUE OF MERCY

PAUL.   Now if we've had enough of sacrilege,
We can go back to where we started from.
Let me repeat: I'm glad to hear you say
You can't trust God to be unmerciful.
What would you have God if not merciful?

JONAH.   Just, I would have Him just before all else,
To see that the fair fight is really fair.
Then he could enter on the stricken field
After the fight's so definitely done
There can be no disputing who has won—
Then he could enter on the stricken field
As Red Cross Ambulance Commander-in-Chief
To ease the more extremely wounded out
And mend the others up to go again.

PAUL.   I thought as much. You have it all arranged,
Only to see it shattered every day.
You should be an authority on Mercy.
That book of yours in the Old Testament
Is the first place in literature, I think,
Where Mercy is explicitly the subject.
I say you should be proud of having beaten
The Gospels to it. After doing Justice justice
Milton's pentameters go on to say,
But Mercy first and last shall brightest shine—
Not only last, but first, you will observe;
Which spoils your figure of the ambulance.

KEEPER.   Paul only means you make too much of justice.
There's some such thing and no one will deny it—
Enough to bait the trap of the ideal

From which there can be no escape for us
But by our biting off our adolescence
And leaving it behind us in the trap.

—lines 358–389

[PAUL.]   The rich in seeing nothing but injustice
In their impoverishment by revolution
Are right. But 'twas intentional injustice.
It was their justice being mercy-crossed.
The revolution Keeper's bringing on
Is nothing but an outbreak of mass mercy,
Too long pent up in rigorous convention—
A holy impulse towards redistribution.
To set out to homogenize mankind
So that the cream could never rise again
Required someone who laughingly could play
With the idea of justice in the courts,
Could mock at riches in the right it claims
To count on justice to be merely just.
But we are talking over Jonah's head,
Or clear off what we know his interests are.
Still, not so far off, come to think of it.
There is some justice, even as Keeper says.
The thing that really counts, though, is the form
Of outrage—violence—that breaks across it.
The very sleep we sleep is an example.
So that because we're always starting fresh
The best minds are the best at premises.
And the most sacred thing of all's abruption.
And if you've got to see your justice crossed
(And you've got to), which will you prefer
To see it, evil-crossed or mercy-crossed?

KEEPER.   We poets offer you another: star-crossed.
Of star-crossed, mercy-crossed, or evil-crossed
I choose the star-crossed as a star-crossed lover.

JONAH.   I think my trouble's with the crisises
Where mercy-crossed to me seemed evil-crossed.
                                                          —*lines 412–443*

[PAUL.]   Mercy is only to the undeserving.
But such we all are made in the sight of God.

  "Oh, what is a king here,
  And what is a boor?
  Here all starve together,
  All dwarfed and poor."

Here we all fail together, dwarfed and poor.
Failure is failure, but success is failure.
There is no better way of having it.
An end you can't by any means achieve,
And yet can't turn your back on or ignore,
That is the mystery you must accept.—
                                                          —*lines 500–511*

JONAH.   If what you say is true, if winning ranks
The same with God as losing, how explain
Our making all this effort mortals make?

                    *   *   *

I think I may have got God wrong entirely.

                    *   *   *

I should have warned you, though, my sense of justice
Was about all there ever was to me.

(211)

When that fades I fade—every time I fade.
Mercy on me for having thought I knew.
                    —*lines 633–635, 654, and 657–660*

[KEEPER, addressing PAUL.]
I'm no more governed by the fear of Hell
Than by the fear of the asylum, jail, or poorhouse,
The basic three the state is founded on.
But I'm too much afraid of God to claim
I have been fighting on the angels' side.
That is for Him and not for me to say.
For me to say it would be irreligious.
(Sometimes I think you are too sure you have been.)
And I can see that the uncertainty
In which we act is a severity,
A cruelty, amounting to injustice
That nothing but God's mercy can assuage.
I can see that, if that is what you mean.
Give me a hand up, if we are agreed.

PAUL.   Yes, there you have it at the root of things.
We have to stay afraid deep in our souls
Our sacrifice—the best we have to offer,
And not our worst nor second best, our best,
Our very best, our lives laid down like Jonah's,
Our lives laid down in war and peace—may not
Be found acceptable in Heaven's sight.
And that they may be is the only prayer
Worth praying. May my sacrifice
Be found acceptable in Heaven's sight.
                    —*lines 702–725*

II
OTHER SAMPLINGS

OF VARIOUS PERIODS AND KINDS

The poems that Robert Frost chose to include in his eleven volumes of new verse, published during nearly half a century, in the years 1913 to 1962, constituted what has been called his "formal statement." Supplementing the selections from that major body of poetry which are given in the preceding section, the following pages contain (arranged in a generally chronological order) certain further, and mostly but little-known, examples of Frost's verse writings, together with a substantial, varied representation of his prose.

"From your loving Rob."

CHILDHOOD LETTERS

> The earliest known writings of Robert Frost are these four
> notes, sent during the autumn of 1886 to his schoolmate
> Sabra Peabody. Twelve years old and in the throes of his first
> love, Frost was then attending a grammar school conducted
> by his mother in the little community of Salem, New
> Hampshire.
>
> The letters, saved over the years in their recipient's cast-off
> pencil box, among attic clutter, were given in 1947 to The
> Jones Library at Amherst, Massachusetts, where they are
> now preserved. They were first published in *Selected Letters
> of Robert Frost.*

DEAR SABE; I read your letter with great pleasure and will try and
answer it in a very few lines. I liked those leavs you gave me and put
them in my speller to press. I have got [to] read a compsition after
recess and I hate to offaly. I have got to stop now so as to learn my
Geography.

FROM YOUR LOVING ROB.

love /   Dont show this.
DEAR SABE; I enjoyed reading your letter very much. You need not
excuse yourself about writing for mine is as bad. Those nuts I gave you
were not as good as I expected but I am glad you liked them. As usual I
cant think of much to write. I wish you were at the supper last night but
we did not have much fun because their were not enough there. I sup-

pose Eva hasnt gotten back yet. Are you going to the Hall to-morrow night. I must stop now and remember and write soon.

FROM YOUR LOVING ROB

DEAR SABE,—I read your loving letter with great pleasure as I alway[s] do. As you could not think of much to say neither can I. I hope you will have a good time tonight and I guess you will and I would like to go if I didnt have to go some where else.

EVER YOUR FAITHFUL LOVER. ROB

love.   write soon

DEAR SABE; I will ansyer your letter to let you know that I am well and hope you are the same. About me liking Lida better than you you are all wrong because I like you twice as much as I do her and always have thought more of you than any other girl I know of. I thought you were going to the entertainment the other night but I didnt see you there. I saw Eva Hattie and your mother there. There is no fun in getting mad every so [often so] lets see if we cant keep friends Im sure I am willing. I know I have not treated you as I ought to sometimes and sometimes I dont know wheather you are mad or not and we have gotten mad and then we would get friends again ever since Westons party when I first came here. There are not many girls I like but when I like them I fall dead In love with them and there are not many I like just because I can have some fun with them like I can Lida but I like you because I cant help myself and when I get mad at you I feel mad at myself to.

FROM YOUR LOVEING ROB.

"Changed is the scene. . . ."

EARLY VERSE

According to Robert Frost, the first poem he ever wrote was
the first poem he published. Sixteen years old and a
sophomore in the high school at Lawrence, Massachusetts,
he derived his poetic inspiration from a story he had found in
William Hickling Prescott's *The Conquest of Mexico*. It was an
account of the night made terrible and sad for the Spanish by
the Aztec Indians during the Spaniards' disastrous retreat
across the causeway connecting the mainland and the island
city of Tenochtitlan. The schoolboy composed a ballad based
on the event, added an unrhymed prologue, and entitled the
whole "La Noche Triste." The morning after he finished the
poem, Rob Frost placed a copy of it on the desk of the editor
of the school's literary magazine, the *High School Bulletin,*
and was secretly ecstatic when told, later, that his offering
had been accepted for publication. "La Noche Triste" was
featured on the first page of the *Bulletin* for April 1890.

In addition to "La Noche Triste," six other examples of
Frost's early verse are given here, revealing the range of the
young poet's experimentation with tone and rhythm during
this beginning phase of his literary career: "Song of the
Wave" and "A Dream of Julius Caesar," which appeared,
respectively, in the May 1890 and May 1891 numbers of the
High School Bulletin; "Caesar's Lost Transport Ships,"
published in *The Independent* [New York] for January 14,
1897, but written, according to Frost himself, during his
senior year in Lawrence High School; "The Traitor," from the

June 1892 *Mirror,* the students' literary publication of
Phillips Academy at Andover, Massachusetts; "Clear and
Colder—Boston Common," which Frost indicated he wrote
"in about 1891," but which was first published in Lawrance
Thompson's biographical volume entitled *Robert Frost: The
Early Years;* and "Warning," dated by its author's subsequent
testimony as written in 1895, with publication in *The
Independent* for September 9, 1897.

LA NOCHE TRISTE

TENOCHTITLAN

Changed is the scene: the peace
And regal splendor which
Once that city knew are gone,
And war now reigns upon
That throng, who but
A week ago were all
Intent on joy supreme.
Cries of the wounded break
The stillness of the night,
Or challenge of the guard.
The Spaniard many days
Beseiged within the place,
Where kings did rule of old,
Now pressed by hunger by
The all-relentless foe,
Looks for some channel of
Escape. The night is dark;
Black clouds obscure the sky—
A dead calm lies o'er all.

The heart of one is firm,
His mind is constant still,
To all, his word is law.
Cortes his plan hath made,
The time hath come. Each one
His chosen place now takes,
There waits the signal, that
Will start the long retreat.

THE FLIGHT

Anon the cry comes down the line,
The portals wide are swung,
A long dark line moves out the gate,
And now the flight's begun.

Aye, cautiously it moves at first,
As ship steered o'er the reef,
Looking for danger all unseen,
But which may bring to grief.

Straight for the causeway now they make,
The bridge is borne before,
'Tis ta'en and placed across the flood,
And all go trooping o'er.

Yet e'er the other side is reached,
Wafted along the wind,
The rolling of the snake-skin drum
Comes floating from behind.

And scarcely has its rolling ceased,
Than out upon the lake,
Where all was silence just before,
A conch the calm doth break.

What terror to each heart it bears,
That sound of ill portent,
Each gunner to escape now looks,
On safety all are bent.

Forward they press in wild despair,
On to the next canal,
Held on all sides by foe and sea,
Like deer within corral.

Now surging this way, now in that,
The mass sways to and fro,
The infidel around it sweeps—
Slowly the night doth go.

A war cry soundeth through the night,
The 'tzin! the 'tzin! is there,
His plume nods wildly o'er the scene,
Oh, Spaniard, now beware!

With gaping jaws the cannon stands,
Points it among the horde;
The valiant Leon waits beside,
Ready with match and sword.

The 'tzin quick springeth to his side,
His mace he hurls on high,
It crasheth through the Spanish steel,
And Leon prone doth lie.

Falling, he died beneath his gun,—
He died at duty's call,
And many falling on that night,
Dying, so died they all.

The faithful guarders at the bridge,
Have worked with might and main,
Nor can they move it from its place,
Swollen by damp of rain.

On through the darkness comes the cry,
The cry that all is lost;
Then e'en Cortes takes up the shout,
And o'er the host 'tis tossed.

Some place their safety in the stream,
But sink beneath the tide,
E'en others crossing on the dead,
Thus reach the other side.

Surrounded and alone he sits,
Upon his faithful steed;
Here Alvarado clears a space,
But none might share the deed—

For darkness of that murky night
Hides deeds of brightest fame,
Which in the ages yet to come,
Would light the hero's name.

His faithful charger now hath fall'n,
Pierced to the very heart.
Quick steps he back, his war cry shouts,
Then onward doth he dart.

Runs he, and leaping high in air,
Fixed does he seem a space,
One instant and the deed is done,
He standeth face to face—

With those who on the other side
Their safety now have found.
The thirst for vengeance satisfied,
The Aztec wheels around.

So, as the sun climbs up the sky,
And shoots his dawning rays,
The foe, as parted by his dart,
Each go their sep'rate ways.

Upon the ground the dead men lie,
Trampled midst gold and gore,
The Aztec toward his temple goes,
For now the fight is o'er.

Follow we not the Spaniard more,
Wending o'er hill and plain,
Suffice to say he reached the coast,
Lost Fortune to regain.

The flame shines brightest e'er goes out,
Thus with the Aztec throne,
On that dark night before the end,
So o'er the fight it shone.

The Montezumas are no more,
Gone is their regal throne,
And freemen live, and rule, and die,
Where they have ruled alone.

SONG OF THE WAVE

"Rolling, rolling, o'er the deep,
Sunken treasures neath me sleep
As I shoreward slowly sweep.

Onward peacefully I roll,
Ever thoughtless of the goal,
Sea-bells round me chime and toll.

There is peace above, below,
Far beneath me sea-weeds grow,
Tiny fish glide to and fro,

Now in sunlight, now in shade,
Lost within some ocean glade
By the restless waters made.

Pushing onward as before,
Now descry the distant shore,
Hear the breakers sullen roar;

Quicken then my rolling pace,
With glad heart I join the race
O'er the white-capp'd glittering space,

Thinking naught of woe or grief,
Dancing, prancing, like a leaf,
Caring not for cliff or reef.

Lo! black cliffs above me loom,
Casting o'er me awful gloom,
And fortell my coming doom.

O! that I might reach the land,
Reach and lave the sunny sand,
But these rocks on every hand—

Seem my joyous course to stay,
Rise and bar my happy way,
Shutting out the sun's bright ray.

I must now my proud crest lower
And the wild sea roam no more."
Hark! the crash and mighty roar,
Then the wave's sport life is o'er.

A DREAM OF JULIUS CÆSAR

A dreamy day; a gentle western breeze
That murmurs softly 'midst the sylvan shades;
Above, the fleecy clouds glide slowly on
To sink from view; within the forest's depth,
A thrush's drowsy note starts echoes through
The vistas of the over-hanging trees.
All nature seems to weave a circle of
Enchantment round the mind, and give full sway
To flitting thoughts and dreams of bygone years.
Thus, as the summer afternoon wears on,
In Nature's cradle lulled to calm repose,
I watch the shifting of a purling rill,
As visions of a busy throng, of life,
Of passing days that come not back again,
Rush in confusion through my weary brain;
Till rumblings wafted o'er the distant hills,
Proclaim a timely warning to the one
Who, wandering far from shelter and from home,
Forgets that space exists, that still he lives:—
But, wrapped in Nature's all entrancing shroud,
Is lured to seek her wildest inmost realms.
The dying cadences are tossed from vale
To vale, but fall unheeded on my ear.
Anon, the winds burst on the silent scene,
And cause the leaves to dance and sing for joy.

Then clouds with bosoms darker than the night,
Rise up along the whole horizon's brink,
And all the sky is flecked with hurrying forms.
Thus, ever as the storm comes on, led by
The heralds of its wrathful power, between
The foremost rifts, like ladders long, by which
From earth to heaven the woodland nymphs may pass
Beyond the clouds, bright rays of light stretch down
Upon each grove and mead.
                              So, far and wide
A charm of magic breathes its spell around:
For at my feet a far upreaching ladder rests,
And as I gaze, a form, scarce seen at first,
Glides down; a moment, and before me stands,
With stately mien and noble wreathéd brow,
His toga streaming to the western wind,
The restless fire still gleaming in those eyes,
Just as before the Roman Senate, years
Agone, he stood and ruled a people with
His mighty will, Cæsar, first conqueror of
The Roman World. Within his hand the bolt
Of Jove gleams forth with frequent flash. Clasping
The toga's waving folds, a gem of ray
Most pure, that nigh outshines the sun, rests like
The dew of heaven. I gaze in awe, a space;
Then, with majestic mien, he points me toward
A bridge, an ancient moss-grown trunk that fell
In some fierce storm to join the brook's green banks,
And speaks: "Be gone! from Jupiter I come
To rule with storm and darkness o'er the world,"
Then with uplifted arm: "Look up, behold
My might, my legions. Conquest still is the

(2 2 5)

One passion of this fiery breast. Speak thy
Farewell to all this scene of quietude
And peace; ere from this hand I launch the fire
Of Jove, and pierce the darkness with its gleam;
Ere yonder cohorts with resistless march
Spread terror in the air and vanquish light."
He speaks and vanishes from sight. The roar
Of chariot wheels breaks on my ear. The fight
Is on, for blood in torrents falls around,
Not crimson, but a lighter hue, such as
The fairy hosts of silvery light might shed.

CÆSAR'S LOST TRANSPORT SHIPS

Some fell away to westward with the wind,
And one full darkly figured on the sun
At sunset; but the fight on Briton's beach
Got us a shelter under Dover cliff,
And all night long a voice made wild lament
Circling the confines of the restless camp;
So that we had sad thoughts of those at sea.
There would no messenger come back from them!
Each one alone went leaping down the world
With no sail set, deserted on the deck,
And in the hull a tremor of low speech.
And overhead the petrel wafted wide.

THE TRAITOR

Sea-bird of the battle surf,
      Lorna is dead.
Black on Colla's castled hill
      Ruin is spread.

Weep for Lorna who rode forth
With his king against the North.

Lorna came again at morn,
   Riding from war.
Messenger of battle won,
   Tidings he bore:—
"Quenchless was the charge he made,
Low the insurgent walls were laid."

And while revelry was rife
   Through Colla's halls,
Then the lonely warder saw,
   Pacing the walls,
Eastward in the morning's greys,
Serried spears in the sunrise blaze.

By an altar in a vault—
   Night dripping dew—
Lorna's muffled cry arose;
   Bat-like it flew:—
"Sacrifice for victory!
Priest and victim find in me!"

Sea-bird of the battle surf,
   Lorna is dead.
Black on Colla's castled hill
   Ruin is spread.
Royal seal upon the tomb
Where he sleeps in endless gloom.

CLEAR AND COLDER—BOSTON COMMON

As I went down through the common,
 It was bright with the light of day,

For the wind and rain had swept the leaves
   And the shadow of summer away.
The walks were all fresh-blacked with rain
   As I went briskly down:—
I felt my own quick step begin
   The pace of the winter town.

As I went down through the common,
   The sky was wild and pale;
I saw one tree with a jib of leaves
   In the stress of the aftergale;
But the others rattled naked poles
   As I went briskly down.
I felt my own quick step begin
   The pace of the winter town.

As I went down through the common
   In the crisp October dawn,
Benches were wet and stuck with leaves
   And the idle ones were gone.
The folk abroad raced on with me
   As I went briskly down.
I felt my own quick step begin
   The pace of the winter town.

As I went down through the common,
   Then felt I first delight
Of the city's thronging winter days
   And dazzling winter night,
Of the life and revelry to be—
   As I went briskly down.
I felt my own quick step begin
   The pace of the winter town.

WARNING

The days will come when you will cease to know,
  The heart will cease to tell you; sadder yet,
Tho you say o'er and o'er what once you knew,
      You will forget, you will forget.

There is no memory for what is true,
  The heart once silent. Well may you regret,
Cry out upon it, that you have known all
      But to forget, but to forget.

Blame no one but yourself for this, lost soul!
  I feared it would be so that day we met
    Long since, and you were changed. And I said then,
      He will forget, he will forget.

"The only thing that can back-bone an essay is thought."

HIGH SCHOOL PROSE

The following examples of Robert Frost's early prose were written while he was attending Lawrence High School, and all three were published in the *High School Bulletin*. "Petra and Its Surroundings" (which appeared in the issue for December of 1891) may actually have been done, initially, to fulfill an assignment in a history course. The "Editorial" (May 1892) is one of many Frost wrote during and shortly after he served as editor in chief of the *High School Bulletin*. "A Monument to After-Thought Unveiled" was delivered by Frost as his valedictory address at the graduation exercises for his high school class, and it was published in the *Bulletin* for June 1892.

PETRA AND ITS SURROUNDINGS

On the summit of Mt. Hor, nestles a shrine beneath which, the Arabians say, lie the bones of the priest, Aaron. It is a place of the wildest grandeur—one worthy the last resting place of the Israelitish orator, overlooking as it does the mountain fastnesses of the warlike sons of Esau, through whose country the Jews strove so long in vain to force a passage.

Mountains rise on every hand; to the north, to the west as far as the great desert, and south and east as far as the eye can reach.

From Mt. Hor the view is one of magnificent sameness; but not until the cliffs have towered above, not until the storm has crowded its over-whelming torrents down the ravines, can the grand sublimity of the situation be felt. In its unstability, the region is like an ice-flow. Every-thing is constantly changing; mountains are torn away in storm, and mountains totter and threaten in calm.

But the centre of all, once the busy capital of a thriving nation, now the "City of Tombs," the capital of ruin and decay, is in the sublimest situation of the wilderness. To reach it a detour must be made to the south and east to the city's ancient entrance, now called the Sik, which led up to the old mart.

From the confusing accounts of many travelers, one might suppose that Petra was a city, honey-combed with tombs, rising perpendicularly from the plain to the height of a thousand feet; but Petra of the Edomites, Jews, Greeks and Romans, is in a far wilder and romantic location. It lies couched down among the peaks south of Mt. Hor. To it the Sik winds down between mighty red cliffs that tower seven hun-dred feet above, closing in here and there where the rocks have cracked and slid forward, leaving nothing but a streaking of blue where the cliffs seem to meet.

It is summer; a dim light falls down into the chasm. The torrent bed that follows the gorge is parched and almost buried in tamarisk and thickets of oleanders in full bloom. The cliffs are festooned with pale fern; ivy climbs everywhere; and the searching roots of the fig-tree cling to the ravine's walls.

As one wanders on over the few chariot-worn flags which once com-pletely paved the way, how strange must be the feeling, as the mind reverts to the cave dwellers whose homes are now mere black squares upon the red crags, and then comes down to the time of the Roman, and sees the chariot hurrying down its last stadia after a weary moun-tain and desert journey, starting with its echo the eagle from his eerie in the crags above.

How dreary must seem this present desolation of which the Hebrew prophet so often prophesied.

Here the way narrows again, and over it sweeps a great arch, perhaps the city gate, perhaps triumphal.

The Sik winds on, its sides excavated, and marked with Se[m]itic and Latin inscriptions. Suddenly it widens, turns, and there stand a row of pink columns. It is this strange mixture of decay and preservation,—for these columns which front a Roman structure, or rather excavation, are nearly perfect, while but one other building in the city is standing—barbarism and debased civilization, that give Petra its great, strange wildness.

When the road unexpectedly fronts the old theatre, a new characteristic of the city is presented. The seats are of stone alternately red and purple. We have noticed the pink of the columns; the mountains in the distance are white.

The colors around are almost countless; there are maroon, scarlet, yellow, purple, pale rose, blue, grey, and many mixtures, for one traveler compares certain cliffs to mahogany, another, the same cliffs to watered silk.

So varied are the hues of the city that one wonders that the natives did not call it the Rainbow City instead of the "Red City."

Beyond the theatre, which is said to be like that of Tusculum, the road widens, and the city proper spreads out deep in among the mountains. The open ground, whose small rolling hills are covered with ruined foundations, is walled for the most part by sheer precipices, falling for hundreds of feet into the city.

What little is known of the history of Petra is of the wildest interest. Never has there been a stronghold as impregnable. What a place for romance where everything is as vague as a rainbow half faded in midair. In our society novels the imagination displayed is as it were a flying squirrel's flight from a tree-top downward; here it might take its flight as a bird from a fountain of youth.

In the city there are traces of four distinct races. For hundreds of years the Edomites held the city, *in* which they were never really conquered. The Jews were sculptors at the time of their conquest, but their chisel was the sword, and they carved naught but destruction. The Pharos, under Rome, made Petra their capital, and by them were built the pillars in the pass and the one building that still stands in the city. Since those days the Mohammedans have built shrines in the cliff niches and on the summits to which the stone-cut stairways lead.

To-day, all is ruin but the tombs that honey-comb the cliffs, and the city is a city of the dead.

[EDITORIAL]

QUESTION: Can we review an author's thought, retell his story? Yes, if you praise while so doing. Can we review a narrative of travel! No, because that would be a re-review—the traveller reviews God's thoughts (nature) and praises them. Twice told is new—thrice told is old. Herein is a definition of originality (school criterion.) We have, nevertheless, found some difficulty in persuading ourselves to this. If we agree on a definition for imagination, evidently, we can still find praise for nature beyond the first writer's. The only true praise is thought. The only thing that can back-bone an essay is thought. We then have one way of getting an essay. The trouble in the school is that in the dim past essays were entirely statistical. It came about that such were confused with those re-reviews spoken of above. And now when we criticize, we always think the following paragraph over to ourselves, fearful of the second class:

A custom has its unquestioning followers, its radical enemies, and a class who have generally gone through both these to return to the first in a limited sense,—to follow custom,—not without question, but where it does not conflict with the broader habits of life gained by wanderers among ideas. The second class makes one of the first and third.

This is best exemplified in religious thought and controversy. It is the second class that would have "an inquisition to compel liberality."

A MONUMENT TO AFTER-THOUGHT UNVEILED

A tribute to the living! We are away beneath the sombre pines, amid a solitude that dreams to the ceaseless monotone of the west wind, the blue sky looking sleepily between the slowly bending boughs, and to, its veil of morning mist, uplifted by the morning breeze, white as pure thought, the monument of monuments.

From sun-beat dizzy marts, from grassy lawns, from surging summer trees, rise countless marble columns, wrought as noiselessly as if from snow, and all by the one hand here honored alone in loneliness.

Well might this marble be a shrine, this grove, a temple whence devotees might seek the world again, and fame!

The God—but wait, that carven silence kneeling at its base, whence it tapers away into the boughs above, writes, and this is what she writes:—

There are men—that poet who has left us uniting the battered harp the sea storm cast for him upon the shore, was one of these—who go to death with such grey grandeur that we look back upon their past for some strange sorrow, such as does not fall to others, even though we know sorrow to be the same through all time. They seem like Merlins looking ages from their deep calm eyes. With what awe we stand before the mystery of their persons. Such lives are the growth of the after-thought of the soul—the serene rest after toil, in questioning and answering whence and why misfortune is.

This nobility distinguishes personality only in the degree of its development, and the broader future, will give to every soul the opportunity to come into the possession of this, its divine right. Then, when no man's life is a strife from day to day, from year to year, with poverty, will it be an attribute commonality of the world.

Aggressive life is two-fold: theory, practice; thought, action: and concretely, poetry, statesmanship; philosophy, socialism—infinitely.

Not in the strife of action, is the leader made, nor in the face of crisis, but when all is over, when the mind is swift with keen regret, in the long after-thought. The after-thought of one action is the forethought of the next.

It is when alone, in converse with their own thoughts so much that they live their conventionalities, forgetful of the world's, that men form those habits called the heroism of genius, and lead the progress of the race. This, the supreme rise of the individual—not a conflict of consciousness, an effort to oppose, but bland forgetfulness, a life from self for the world—is the aim of existence.

All this is doubly so of the theoretical. In it the after-thought of long nights beneath the universe, of soul stirrings, of the act of thought itself, is more clearly a part of the next action—its expression. Events influence the first class, the limits of language alone the second.

The poet's insight is his after-thought. It is of varied heart-beats and converse with nature. And the grandest of his ideas come when the last line is written.

Life is an after-thought: how wonderful shall be the world? that is the after-thought of life.

But look again, all this is mere shadow sheen upon the white marble. The one word there is: After-thought.

Now this dark pool beneath the trees is still. There is a white finger on its lips. Let ripples whisper here no more.

And now a last afterthought.

To those who fix today a point through which from earlier years they draw a line of life projected far into the future, this hour is of a deep significance. But there is no change here, and he who thinks to rest will rest as in a winter storm, to die.

Unbounded full ambition for the greatest heights yet unattained is not too noble for one human mind. Who or what can bound our aspirations? Will courage fail before a thousand unfavorable comparisons? There is a space of time when meteor and rain drop falling side by side may touch the yielding earth with equal force. The lighter outspeeding weight may see[m] in a space to strike with greater force. But who at last can tell which has the greater influence [on] the world, the one that bore, as scientist[s] have said, plant life or that which makes it live.

Strength and all the personality that we can crowd upon the world are ours to give in obligation. Let hope be limitless for all and let each follow hope as best he may.

To all old school associations here we show our purposed way in one bell-toned Farewell!

"The gray grass is scarce dappled with the snow. . . ."

MY BUTTERFLY

Late in life Robert Frost repeatedly spoke of the special importance he attached to that winter night in 1894 when he carried to satisfactory conclusion the writing of his poem "My Butterfly." Despite the presence of certain outmoded words and other signs of apprentice effort, "My Butterfly" remained for him the poem wherein he discovered his personal poetic idiom. Particularly, as he told a correspondent over half a century later (*Selected Letters of Robert Frost,* pp. 526–527), he valued it "for the eight lines or so beginning 'The gray grass is scarce dappled with snow' which was when I first struck the note that was to be mine."

Here is the text as submitted for publication, represented by a manuscript now preserved among the collections of the Henry E. Huntington Library, San Marino, California. "My Butterfly" appeared, with slight textual revisions, in *The Independent* for November 8, 1894. It was subsequently to be revised for its appearances within Frost's own volumes of poetry.

MY BUTTERFLY

An Elegy

Thine emulous fond flowers are dead too,
And the daft sun-assaulter, he

That frighted thee so oft, is fled or dead;
        Save only me—
    Nor is it sad to thee—
        Save only me,
    There is no one to mourn thee in the fields.

        The grey grass is scarce dappled with the snow,
Its two banks have not shut upon the river,
        But it is long ago,
        It seems forever,
    Since first I saw thee glance
    With all the dazzling other ones,
        In airy dalliance,
        Precipitate in love,
    Tossed up, tossed up, and tangling, above,
Like a limp rose-wreath in a fairy dance.
When that was, the soft mist
Of my two tears hung not on all the fields;
        And I was glad for thee,
            And glad for me,
                I wist.
And didst thou think who tottered maundering on high
Fate had not made thee for the pleasure of the wind,
            With those great careless wings?
            'Twas happier to die
            And let the days blow by,—
            These were the unlearned things.
It seemed God let thee flutter from his gentle clasp,
        Then fearful he had let thee win
        Too far beyond him to be gathered in,
    Snatched thee, o'er-eager, with ungentle grasp,
        Jealous of immortality
        (In one so fair, howe'er.)

O I remember me
How once conspiracy was rife
Against my life,
(The languor of it) and
Surging, the grasses dizzied me of thought,
The breeze three odors brought,
And a gem-flower waved in a wand.
Then when I was distraught
And could not speak,
Sidelong, full on my cheek,
What should that reckless zephyr fling
But the wild touch of your dye-dusty wing.
I found that wing withered today,—
For you are dead, I said,
And the strange birds say,—
I found it with the withered leaves
Under the eaves.

"... the astonishing magnitude of my ambition."

LETTERS ABOUT "MY BUTTERFLY"

Almost as soon as Robert Frost had finished writing "My Butterfly," he made a fair copy of it and mailed the poem to the editor of *The Independent* in New York. Heretofore his submissions to magazines had been rewarded with nothing but rejection slips. This time, however, he was more hopeful, and to the young poet's delight the editor did respond quickly. He praised "My Butterfly," enclosed a check for fifteen dollars, and asked for information about the author. Frost replied on March 28, 1894 (*Selected Letters of Robert Frost,* p. 19).

Editor of the Independant,

DEAR SIR:- The memory of your note will be a fresh pleasure to me when I awaken for a good many mornings to come; which may as well confirm you in the belief that I am still young. I am. The poem you have is the first of mine that any publication has accepted. At about the same time however that I sent you this, I disposed of three others in a similar way in other quarters. As yet they are not returned. As for submitting more of my work, you may imagine I shall be only too glad to avail myself of your kindly interest. Nevertheless since I have but recently discovered my powers, I have, of course, no great amount of verses in store and furthermore, being still inexperienced of myself, I cannot easily tell when I will have. But I shall not forget my obligations.

If you mean what might be called the legitimate education I have received when you speak of "training" and "line of study," I hope that the quality of my poem would seem to account for far more of this than I have really had. I am only graduated of a public high school. Besides this, a while ago, I was at Dartmouth College for a few months until recalled by necessity. But this inflexible ambition trains us best, and to love poetry is to study it. Specifically speaking, the few rules I know in this art are my own afterthoughts, or else directly formulated from the masterpieces I reread.

I sincerely hope I have done nothing to make you overestimate me. It cannot be, though, for rather than equal what I have written and be satisfied, I will idle away an age accumulating a greater inspiration.

There is no objection to using my name with the poem.

YOURS ROBERT LEE FROST.

TREMONT ST., LAWRENCE, MASS.

The editor of *The Independent* (the Reverend William Hayes Ward) replied somewhat coldly that he would be interested in examining further poetic offerings which Robert Lee Frost might send, but that he did hope the young poet would soon learn to spell *Independent* correctly. Shortly thereafter Frost received another letter about his poem, this time from Susan Hayes Ward, the actual literary editor of *The Independent* and a sister of the magazine's editor in chief. After expressing her delight in "My Butterfly," she urged its author to alter a few lines in the poem which she believed to be weak. She also invited Frost to say more about his literary interests. Thus began a long correspondence, here represented by three of the poet's earliest letters to Miss Ward (*Selected Letters of Robert Frost,* pp. 20–21, 23–25).

DEAR MISS WARD, It is just such a letter as you wrote me that I have been awaiting for two years. Hitherto all the praise I have received has been ill-advised and unintelligent; all the criticism, this general one upon the rueful fact that I, once the friend of so and so, should have at last turned poetaster. So that something definite and discriminating is very welcome. My thanks unlimited! Yet the consideration is hardly due me. Take my word for it that poem ["My Butterfly"] exaggerates my ability. You must spare my feelings when you come to read these others, for I haven't the courage to be a disappointment to anyone. Do not think this artifice or excess of modesty, though, for to betray myself utterly, such an one am I that even in my failures I find all the promise I require to justify the astonishing magnitude of my ambition.

You ask to know more of me. This is certainly very tempting. It might well throw one into a talking trance which nothing could dispell but a reversal of the charm. I am inclined to think, too, that I have several attributes akin to those of that Franco-Russian introspectionist (whose name I dare not attempt in writing.) But whatever the inducements to the contrary I must promise to content myself with but a slight sketch.

When I am well I read a great deal and like a nearsighted person follow the text closely. I read novels in the hope of strengthening my executive faculties. The Polish triology "With Fire and Sword," "The Deluge" and "Pan Michael" are engaging me at present. Thomas Hardy has taught me the good use of a few words and, referring still to me, "struck the simple solemn." And as opposed to this man, Scott and Stevenson inspire me, by their prose, with the thought that we Scotchmen are bound to be romanticists—poets. Then as for poems my favorites are and have been these: Keats' "Hyperion," Shelley's "Prometheus," Tenneson's "Morte D'Arthur," and Browning's "Saul"—all of them about the giants. Besides these I am fond of the whole collection of Palgrave's. So far everything looks auspicious. But it is necessary to admit that I teach "orthography" in a district school: and that in the fitness of things, the association of Eugene Aram with children in this capacity seems no more incongruous than my own. In fact so wholly uncongenial is the work that it has become for me a mere test of physical endurance. For several weeks now when not teaching I have spent my time lying around either consciously sleeping or unconsciously waking and in both cases irresponsibly iratable to the last degree. It is due to my nerves—they are susceptible to sound. Consequently the prospect is not bright—for the immediate future at least. When in this condition I can neither read nor write: nevertheless I find a few hours for study and, as I say, always entertain great hopes.

I have never read Lanier's poetry nor the volume of his you mention. I have read no technical works. The extent of my studying now is a little Greek and, for relaxation, French. Of course I have a great desire to master the former for reasons that would be commonly given. Homer is very difficult for me as yet, though, and I am often entirely discouraged. But I assure you, some time, money or no money, I shall prove myself able to do everything but spell.

I have not succeeded in revising the poem ["My Butterfly"] as you requested. That Aztec consonant syllable of mine, "l", spoils a word I am very sorry to dispense with. The only one I think of to substitute for it is "eddying" which of course weakens the impression—although I am not sure but that it merely changes it. The would-be cadence howe'er may be incorrect also, but I did not suspect it at the time. It is used in the same sense as "at any rate" would be in that case. But I cannot sustain the usage by any example I have in mind: and when once I doubt an idiom my ear hesitates to vouch for it thereafter. The line, "These were the unlearned things," is wretched. It refers directly to the two lines preceding and indirectly to the answer inevitable to that question "And did you think etc." which answer would be, God did nevertheless! Yet the line is manifestly redundant as well as retruse and I must invent one to supplant it. I shall prefer to hear from you again, if it is not asking too much, before I return the copy, not only so that I may gain time but also that I may have the benefit of your further advice.

YOURS BY RIGHT OF DISCOVERY R. L. FROST.

Miss Ward, undoubtedly troubled by some overtones or undertones of meaning in certain passages of the poem,

evidently tried to arrange a meeting in Boston with the
neophyte author, so that they might discuss some of her
suggestions for revision. It would seem, however, that Frost
did not appear at the time and place suggested and that he
wrote the following letter, dated August 22, 1894, after Miss
Ward had somehow expressed her disappointment, perhaps
by merely not writing him.

DEAR MISS WARD:- Surely you have not received my last letter. I shall be
sorry if it is too late to arrange to meet you. Write to me at least.

For I percieve that my childishness in regard to poem (said poem)
may have become wearisome. It is very trying to be noticed, you know.
But give me another chance: I may have disqualified myself for a polit-
ical career by one foolish act but I cannot have for a literary one:- all the
cannonized afford me consolation.

I am learning to spell.

I am writing better poetry.

It is only a matter of time now when I shall throw off the mask and
declare for literateur mean it poverty or riches.

You are amid real poetry, I presume; and I can imagine that a con-
ventional verse or stanza and the familiar see-saw of phrases in antithe-
sis, would distemper you.

SINCERELY ROBERT L. FROST

The Boston meeting finally did take place and the textual
revisions were completed. But when "My Butterfly" appeared
in *The Independent,* on November 8, 1894, Robert Frost was
in no position to see a copy of his poem in print: he was
more or less lost in the Dismal Swamp, somewhere near the
boundary between Virginia and North Carolina. Soon after he
found his way home, however, he wrote to Miss Ward (on
December 4, 1894).

Dear Miss Ward,- Now that you have ceased expecting to is the time you hear from me. The occasion is, or was, the appearance in print under your supervision of my first poem. I am going to thank you. Four weeks ago and until Friday last I was in Virginia, North Carolina, and Maryland, very liberally and without address, so that I have not been aware of my own doings as expressed in the phrase I "published a poem." That is the point of points:- I thank you tardily because I for my part have been out of time a little while, and thank you because you and not I published a poem, a work that certainly requires qualities I lack. And the poem does look well—don't you think it does?

Before proceeding further I percieve I must assume an attitude, or else endanger the coherency of my remarks,—for my natural attitude is one of enthusiasm verging on egotism and thus I always confuse myself trying to be modest. It is my rule to be despondent to be dignified (or coherent) and I might be cynical for the same purpose, but really unless it be enthusiastically I am at a loss to know how to comport myself on the present occasion. You see I am just returned from experiences so desperately absorbing that I am nothing morbid now and can enjoy the poem as freshly as if it were but lately written and I had not since wasted eight months in ineffectual aspiration.

Yes, I think sound is an element of poetry, one but for which imagination would become reason. I justify the use of dialect in this way: it contributes to the illusion (perhaps) and gives the artist the courage of his imaginings. Kipling says nearly all he says under the influence of sound. I am so fond of sound that I was wishing the other day he would write some more poetry. Listen to that!—when we generally read poetry because we are in the business and it is written.

I have one or two poems to send you when I find time to revise them.

Sincerely Robert L. Frost.

". . . one day two little fairies peeped over the pasture wall. . . ."

STORIES FOR HIS CHILDREN

While Robert Frost and his family were living on their farm in Derry, New Hampshire, he frequently entertained his four children—Lesley, Carol, Irma, and Marjorie—by telling them stories he imaginatively fashioned around their own experiences on the farm. Perhaps with a view to publishing these stories sometime, he wrote out sixteen of them, creating a manuscript volume now within the C. Waller Barrett Collection of the University of Virginia Library. Three of these sixteen prose pieces are included here, published for the first time. Needed punctuation has been supplied by the editors. (The quotation used as a title for this section occurs in one of the opening sentences of another of the narratives in this overall group.) The little story told in rhymed couplets, "The Blue Bird to Lesley," is quoted from a manuscript preserved in the Henry E. Huntington Library; a later and shorter version of the poem appears in *The Poetry of Robert Frost*, pp. 135–136, under the title "The Last Word of a Bluebird."

OLD STICK-IN-THE-MUD

Irma went wagging her dress out into the big pasture. And one of the fenceposts down in the low ground saw her and asked her what she was after.

"Checkerberries!"

"Are you sure it isn't cranberries? I know where there are some of those, or were last fall."

"No, checkerberries!"

"Well, I guess I can direct you to some of those. Just ahead of you."

"I don't see any."

"Not there; to your right, to your right. Oh no no no no. Here, you come here and hold this wire, and I'll go and find some for you."

So Irma went and unbuttoned the barbed wires from him—there were three of them—and he showed her how she would have to hold them to keep them just the right distance apart so that the cow couldn't get out: one in her mouth and one in each hand. She had to take a very awkward position, and the wire in her mouth made it hard for her to talk.

The fencepost pulled himself out of his hole and set off. He didn't seem to know as well where the checkerberries were as he thought or pretended he did, for he went zigzagging here and there, brushing the grass with his foot without once stooping to pick any. Finally he came back to Irma and said,

"I just thought: what would I pick into if I happened to find berries?"

"If you *happened* to find berries!" Irma sputtered on account of the wire in her mouth. "I thought you said you knew where the berries were. Pick them into your hands. But hurry up. I can't keep these wires spaced right much longer."

"But I haven't any hands. Perhaps I'd better go up to the house for a can."

"If *you* do!" Irma spluttered. "I'll just drop everything and let the fence fall."

"Don't do that. The cow will get out."

"I will!—now!"

"Oh don't, little girl. Well, go ahead. I don't care. Drop 'em. It won't be my loss. The cow's yours. And you know how it will be if she gets a taste of apples; she'll simply go apple crazy and then she'll have to go into the barn for the rest of the season."

Irma squeezed a tear out of each eye as the fencepost stumped off.

On his way to the house he came to a hole in the pine grove where long ago someone had taken out a few loads of dirt and had afterwards dumped rubbish there. In it he spied a very rusty old tomato can (but not much rustier than the wire Irma held in her mouth so faithfully through all) which he thought would do well enough. He waved it at Irma as he came hurrying back with it.

"Just you hold on a minute or two longer in all three places," he laughed.

Irma had made up her mind to tell Papa.

There were berries, as Irma knew very well from having been there before with the other children, and presently the fencepost found them. He picked and picked, and if he had had a corn can instead of a tomato can I believe he would have filled it; as it was he must have picked a pint. Irma began to be afraid that he was tricky and might be planning to go off when he got through and leave her to hold up the fence forever. But presently he came and let her look down into the can at the berries.

"Oo!" she exclaimed.

"Now button the wires on to me," he said, "and go home to Papa." He dropped into his watery hole with a splash.

She did as she was told, wiped her mouth on her sleeve, picked up her berries and was about to run for it, when suddenly she remembered that she wasn't going to forgive the fencepost no matter how han[d]somely he treated her in the end. So she put her head on one side, wagged her dress, and said big-lady-silly-ways,

"What's your cutey little name, please?"

"What, mine? Why, my name's Old Stick-In-The-Mud,"

That was all she wanted, and she ran home to tell Papa on him.

First she bragged a little about her berries, and then she settled down to cry so that someone would ask her what was the matter. That gave her a chance to tell her story. She told the whole thing, not leaving out the place where the fencepost laughed at her.

"What fencepost was it, dear?" Mama asked.

"It was Old Stick-In-The-Mud. I got it out of him."

"Oh! Old Stick-In-The-Mud," laughed Papa. "He's a nice old fellow. He wouldn't do anything to hurt you. That's just his funny way. He's awfully old—oldest one on the farm—stands in an awfully wet hole too—sort of leans forward. But, goodness, he likes little girls, likes everybody. He's knotty but not naughty. Remember to say 'thank you' to him next time you're down that way."

THE BLUE BIRD TO LESLEY

As I went out, a crow
In the dooryard said, 'Oh,
I was looking for you!
How do you do?
Well, I just came to tell you
To tell Lesley,—will you?—
That her little blue bird
Wanted me to bring word
That the north wind last night
That made the stars bright
And made ice on the trough
Almost made him cough
His little tail off.
He wanted to see her,
But winter's so near—
He just had to fly!
But he sent her, Good-bye,
And said to be good,
And bring in the wood,
And wear her red hood,
And look for fox tracks

In the snow with an ax,
(But not catch a cold,)
And get five years old,
And do everything,
And perhaps in the spring
He'll come back and sing.
He felt you don't know
How sorry to go
And leave the poor baby
Her ribbon off maybe,
As wild as a bear,
And no one to care
And give her her supper
But mama and papa.
But he told me to say
He would think every day—
Every time he began a
Coconut or banana—
And wonder about her
And cry some without her.[']

[A CONVERSATION]

One day Schneider chased a woodchuck down his hole and began digging after him like everything.

But the woodchuck had two holes, and he came up out of the other one and sat up and said,

"I see your tail, Schneider, I see your tail."

Schneider ran over and chased him down that hole and began digging there.

Then the woodchuck came up out of the first hole and sat up and called again,

"I see your tail, Schneider, I see your tail."
Schneider was so mad that he gave up and went home.
The woodchuck laughed and said,
"Good-bye, Schneider. Come again."
Schneider said,
"Oh, stop talking. Woodchucks can't talk."
And the woodchuck said,
"Neither can dogs."
That's so, they can't.

THE WISE MEN

Carol kissed us all good-by and climbed up into the nut tree, going quickly round and round the trunk, where the branches were best, until he was out of sight. He was out of hearing too before any of us thought to ask him when he would be back, so there was nothing to do but wait and see. He was so long gone, with no sign of him—not a falling twig or nut—that we began to wonder, especially as it grew dark. We were afraid that he would not risk climbing down by starlight and we would have to stay under the tree all night.

That was the way it turned out. We took turns watching for him, and morning came and there was no Carol. The night was perfectly quiet and the leaves were still in the whole great tree and each of us as he sat alone listened intently for any sound of the little boy. We thought he might have shouted to us some word of what was keeping him. But he seemed to have forgotten us.

It was the same all day, for the tree seemed as deserted as if it hadn't held so much as a bird's nest. We let everything else go on the farm; the cow unmilked, the weeds unhoed while we stood and talked about the strange thing that had happened to us. The day passed and another night.

But toward evening the next day there was the cry,

"Here he comes."

Margy had seen him or seen the nails of his bootheels feeling for a footing away among the branches. How strange he looked. He looked changed. First we all ran forward: then we all ran back—three steps. He had touched ground, and now he turned toward us blinking—an old grey man. His beard was long and white and pointed, and his hat was long and red and pointed and all covered with stars and new moons. He wore a long cloak clear to his feet and carried a big book under his arm. He turned three times round and round as if he wished to make himself dizzy, but it was only to get his bearings. Then without a look to show that he knew we were there, he walked straight past us up the little hill into the sweet ferns and tramp tramping away into the woods. Well!

We hadn't said a word, we hadn't moved, until he was gone. Now we started chattering. Irma said he was as small as Carol, but too old. Lesley said to get as old as that he would first have to grow to the size of a man, and that might take five years if he [. . . ate] well, and then he would have to shrink back to his own size, and that would take five hundred years because it takes longer to grow small than it does to grow large.

Margy was for going after him.

Lesley said,

"The way he's headed, he'll come out in the village if he goes far enough and doesn't climb another tree; and the people will bring him back to us—if they can tell who he is. That's so: they can't, can they?"

Suddenly, Margy and Irma cried out at the same time,

"Here he comes again" and "Here comes another."

We didn't know which was right.

This one was exactly like the other, beard hat cloak book and all. He went through the same movements, turning slowly three times to get his bearings, and then set out for the ferns and the woods in the footsteps of the other. But we were not so surprised as before. We got our voices and managed to speak. We even tried to stop him by putting ourselves in his way, though we didn't dare to lay hands on him, he was so queer. He brushed past us and out of sight.

We all gathered under the tree to look up for the appearance of another one. As we were standing so, along came Smith and pulled up his horse to talk about the weather. But you may imagine that we didn't want him there when another of those old men might come down at any minute—and then what would people think of our farm? So we tried not to encourage him to talk, answering him only with yes or no and not saying anything new ourselves. We got rid of him just in time. If he had looked back as he drove away he might have seen as it was, but I think he was a little cross at our bad manners. It was the third of the old men, and exactly like the other two. I am sure you would have found the number of stars and new moons on the hats of all three precisely the same. He left us like the others.

The question was, were they Carol? How could they be? It was a great puzzle.

But not for long, for hardly had we lifted our eyes to the tree again when we saw the real Carol coming down in the same clothes he went up in. He came to the ground with a thud.

"Have you seen my cap down here?" he said.

"No, but we saw three old men," we said.

"It ought to have come down. I dropped it. Are you sure you didn't see it?"

"No, but we saw three old men," we said.

"Oh, those fellows."

"Who were they?"

"Three old know-it-alls I got acquainted with up there. How long have I been gone? Say, it's the strangest thing about that hat. I dropped it for you so you'd know I was all right. It must have been day before yesterday. I don't want to lose that. I'll tell you about the old men some other time. Let's hunt for the hat."

"No, tell us now. What were they doing in our Nut Tree?"

"Trying to find out how high the sky is. When I arrived on top, there they sat in a ring, looking up in the sky, with their hats sticking out behind and their beards in front. Each had a book open in his lap and his finger marking a place on a page. I said Hello to them, but they were to[o] solemn to notice anything like that, so I tried again with a question:

"'What are you doing?'

"Everyone looked suddenly at me as if I was new, rounding his eyes terribly and opening his mouth. Then they looked at each other. No one spoke.

"'What are you doing?' I said again.

"'Trying to find out something.' They answered in one voice and tipped their heads back again.

"'What?'

"No answer.

"'I should think such old men as you would know everything,' I said, to tease them.

"'We do, we do, we do. Everything but just one thing, and if you had[n't] come and interrupted us we'd have known that in a few minutes.'

"'What is it?'

"'How high the sky is.'

"'Oh, I'll give you something you can tell me if you know everything. What's it going to do tomorrow?'

"They all tipped up their faces again.

"'What's it going to do tomorrow, if you know everything? That's what I'm up here to find out.'

"'We don't want to talk to you,' they mumbled without taking their eyes off the sky.

"But I stuck to it:

"'Tell me what it's going to do tomorrow.'

"That was too much for one of them. I don't know which one, for there was no way of telling them apart. He slapped his book shut, got up and went down the tree.

"So I bothered the other two for a while without getting a word out of them, though I could tell by the shaking of the little tassle away out on the end of their hats that they were disturbed; until one after the other they left me in a rage. Then I came down. But the funniest is about that cap."

Among the Poems He Left Behind

GROUP ONE

"Someone in Chicago asks to republish," Robert Frost complained to a friend in 1947, "a poem I left behind in the Saturday Review and as it might be assumed intentionally" (*Selected Letters of Robert Frost,* p. 526). For various reasons, Frost "left behind" over the years a number of his poems, some existing only in manuscript and never published, and some which had been printed in magazines or elsewhere but which he never chose to bring forward into his own books.

All three of the poems in the present group—the first of five such units within this volume—remained in manuscript at the time of Robert Frost's death, yet each is a relatively early poem. "When the Speed Comes," based on his experiences while working in a textile mill at Lawrence, Massachusetts, in 1893–1894, was written some dozen years later while he was living on his farm at Derry, New Hampshire. "Despair," also written at Derry, reflects a suicidal mood of the poet, which lasted for some time during 1900–1901. "My Giving" was sent to Susan Hayes Ward at Christmastime in 1911. Each of these poems was first published in *Robert Frost: The Early Years,* pp. 158, 267, and 380.

WHEN THE SPEED COMES

When the speed comes a-creeping overhead
And belts begin to snap and shafts to creak,

And the sound dies away of them that speak,
And on the glassy floor the tapping tread;
When dusty globes on all a pallor shed,
And breaths of many wheels are on the cheek;
Unwilling is the flesh, the spirit weak,
All effort like arising from the dead.

But the task ne'er could wait the mood to come,
The music of the iron is a law:
And as upon the heavy spools that pay
Their slow white thread, so ruthlessly the hum
Of countless whirling spindles seems to draw
Upon the soul, still sore from yesterday.

DESPAIR

I am like a dead diver after all's
Done, still held fast in the weeds' snare below,
Where in the gloom his limbs begin to glow
Swaying at his moorings as the roiled bottom falls.
There was a moment when with vainest calls
He drank the water, saying, "Oh let me go—
God let me go!"—for then he could not know
As in the sun's warm light on earth and walls.

I am like a dead diver in this place.
I was alive here too one desperate space,
And near prayer in the one whom I invoked.
I tore the muscles from my limbs and choked.
My sudden struggle may have dragged down some
White lily from the air—and now the fishes come.

MY GIVING

I ask no merrier Christmas
Than the hungry bereft and cold shall know
      That night.
This is all I can give so that none shall want—
My heart and soul to share their depth of woe.
I will not bribe their misery not to haunt
My merrymaking by proffer of boon
That should only mock the grief that is rightly theirs.
Here I shall sit, the fire out, and croon
All the dismal and joy-forsaken airs,
Sole alone, and thirsty with them that thirst,
Hungry with them that hunger and are accurst.
No storm that night can be too untamed for me,
If it is woe on earth, woe let it be!
Am I a child that I should refuse to see?
What could I plead asking them to be glad
      That night?
      My right?
Nay it is theirs that I with them should be sad
      That night.

Stories for Chicken Farmers

From the very outset of Robert Frost's attempt to support himself and his family on his Derry, New Hampshire, farm, he was a genuine poultryman. The brief item in *The Derry News* announcing his arrival in town during the autumn of 1900 read: "R. Frost has moved upon the Magoon place which he recently bought. He has a flock of nearly 300 Wyandotte fowls." With the passage of time Frost was even to derive literary stimulus from this particular farming activity, and in the interval 1903–1905 he published at least eleven prose contributions in two different poultry magazines. All except one of these pieces were short stories or sketches, and three of them are presented here. The first, "A Just Judge," originally appeared in the March 1903 number of *The Eastern Poultryman.* The other two, "Old Welch Goes to the Show" and "Dalkins' Little Indulgence," were printed, respectively, in the August 15, 1903, and December 15, 1905, issues of *Farm-Poultry.* (Reprinted from *Robert Frost: Farm-Poultryman,* pp. 37–44, 60–66, and 98–106.)

A JUST JUDGE

There was once a ninety-six point hen, and she was a ninety-six point hen, and she really existed, and this story recounts only facts. The judge that first scored her said to the man beside him who footed up the cuts, "Well, that is the least I can give her." He might have been pardoned for saying, "Well, that is the most I can give her," but that was not that judge's style.

She was what is called a chance bird. Not that she did not come of good stock. Her parentage was not altogether obscure. Only there was nothing in her ancestry that quite accounted for her, and she outclassed all her sisters and her cousins and her aunts, some of whom were on exhibition with her at her first show.

That judge said privately that he would have been glad to score her a hundred, and it seemed foolish not to, but he had to think of himself. "I made that score card in the sweat of my brow," he was reported as saying.

"Well, what were her defects?" some one asked him.

"You will have to consult the score card; I don't pretend to remember; the impression she left on me was one of perfection." Which was the making of that pullet.

From the time they hung the blue ribbon on her coop, she always had an audience to the end of the show. She was well trained and took it all as a matter of course. She showed herself front, three-quarters, profile, back, almost as regularly as a revolving show case. But she listened to the praise on every hand with composure, the more so as much of it would have made her of another breed entirely.

This story is about the confirmation of the first judge's judgment by that of judges that came after him. For No. 1 so to call her did not go home to the breeding pens of the man that raised her. She was bought, as it proved, for showing until used up, and sent on her travels. She had a cold winter. She made her debut early in the season, when the important shows were all to come. She went to them all by express in a draughty shipping coop, and at all of them she won first place, always with special mention from her judges.

But if she was worth anything as a breeder or to keep this was not the kind of treatment she was entitled to, and if she liked it herself at first, she soon tired of it. It ceased to console her that she was making one man's reputation. She became a bird acquainted with depot platforms in all sorts of weather. She learned to judge humanity at large by the treatment she had received at the hands of expressmen. She suffered a disillusionment that manifested itself in a change in the carriage of her tail.

That was the beginning of the end. Next it was her face paled; then her legs lost their color; her eyes dimmed. And just in time to save herself from being ridiculed as a bird greatly over-estimated at the lesser shows, on the eve of the greatest show of all she collapsed entirely. She lay in her pen a heap of ruffled feathers, such a sorry spectacle as invited only pity. She had made a glorious campaign and this was the upshot. It would have been kinder to her reputation to have spared her a little and given her a chance to win at the only show really worth while.

But though she was plainly marked for death, she was not forgotten in her last hours. Experts told her story again over her prostrate form. She had more victories to her credit than any other bird of the season, and what a pity that she should not have been allowed to put the finishing touch to her record by winning here. She must have won, some said. It was doubted and argued. Judges present who had known and scored her were appealed to. With them it was a personal matter. They defended her with spirit. One said, "I firmly believe that pullet was sent into this world especially for this show—and look at her. It's a shame!"

A life-sized photograph of her was produced from somewhere, taken when at her best by a committee of some club appointed to revise the standard. Someone had written under it, "Real Perfection as distinguished from Ideal Perfection."

All this was vindication enough and more than enough for the opinion of the judge that had brought her out of the obscurity of her first show. But the remarkable part was to follow.

It was not generally known that even at the point of death the famous No. 1 found a buyer. In the excitement of the close of the show she was not thought of. By those that knew of her sale it was assumed that she was destined for stuffing and mounting. No one ever expected to see her again or hear of her either, after the echoes of her first season's achievements had died away.

But that was not the kind of pullet she was. She was bought at a risk by a man that knew his business and intended to give her a fighting chance—which was all she asked. She was carried far, far from shows and the fear of shows, to a settled life and natural conditions. And she amply repaid everything that was done for her, and came straight back to life, and before spring was well advanced was laying precious eggs, though considering her antecedents, they were probably not nearly as precious as herself.

She was lost to the world in the mountains of northern Vermont, where hens being known by the amount of noise and dirt they make, are not distinguished one from another. Her owner was of the quiet kind that prefer to let their belongings as well as their actions speak for themselves. She was not advertised and she had no visitors. She bucked the trap nest at least thrice a week, and as her eggs proved fertile in spite of what she had been through, by the end of the summer a good proportion of the chickens about the place bore the toe marks that related them to her. She tended strictly to business and her work showed that she had two at least of the requisites of a good breeder, she was prolific and fertile. Whether it would turn out that she could transmit her superior qualities was another matter.

But it was not merely as a breeder that her owner valued her. He had built somewhat on his hope of winning with her another year; but he did not under-estimate the chances he took when he bought her with this in view. The chances were there: first and foremost, she might never recover; then if she recovered, she might never recover her original form; and there was always the chance that like many another wonder, she might not be able to hold her own through the breeding season and the moult. She soon disappointed his fears as to her recovery and her recovery of form, and with the care she had, she approached the moult with everything in her favor.

The moult is a trying time to the poultryman. He would gladly cut it out. There is not an object in sight to keep his courage up. The hens are a disgrace, and as for the growing stock, for all that one can tell, they may be all culls. It will be Christmas, it seems, before the youngsters throw the red or the oldsters reclothe themselves against the cold. One poultryman who always displayed the sign "No Admittance" on his houses during the last moult, in a moment of exasperation went and superadded the word "Positively" with his own hand.

No. 1 was as disheartening as the rest of them in the doldrums. She went to pieces all in one day like a smitten thistle head. She was as ready for a swim as anyone could be without the inclination, and she didn't seem to care how long she stayed so or who saw her. At length she began to grow short quills as if in her second year she intended to be a porcupine, but she took her own time about this even. "Better a porcupine," her owner said, "than that sort of an undrawn carcass." But finally his patience (what there was of it) was rewarded, and No. 1 was in feathers again.

And he swore that she was the same old bird. It often happens that fowl are so changed by the moult that their owners do not know them, nor they their owners. But No. 1 was the identical bird, or his eyes deceived him. Of course he might be partial—and then again he mightn't be. At any rate he was ready to back her.

The shows began. Poor No. 1, if she had known what was in store for her, would perhaps have contrived not to clothe her nakedness. She found out when it was too late that she was in for another strenuous winter. She made her first appearance near home; it was a small show but it was bad enough. The babel of roosters in the large hall, the smell of cats, and the uniformity of the coops made her deathly sick. It was like reopening an old wound. She was expected to win there hands down, and she did, and this was the manner of it.

It was scoring time, and a group halted before her coop, among them her owner: but the one she noticed particularly, or should have noticed, since if she had but known it, she owed him a grudge, was the judge who had discovered her in the first place. There he was again with the same hypercritical look in his eyes or eyebrows. He began an inventory of her faults carelessly enough, but as he proceeded his expression changed. Suddenly he looked up and around him as if for an explanation in the faces of his audience. Finding none, he resumed his task, but with more and more perplexity.

"What do you make it?" he said at last.

"Four," said his attendant.

He took the card and regarded it with open mouth. "I wonder," he said. Then he crumpled it and thrust it into his pocket. "Try again! I must be getting old that I cannot find faults as I used to. Two in two years."

The result was the same. "Gentlemen," he said to the company, "who owns this bird and where is he? Unless I am greatly mistaken, she and I have met before. I scored a bird 96 points once and I never intended to score another that, if I could help it, and I don't believe I have, for I think she's the same one. Does anyone know if her owner is in the hall?"

"Here," said the individual in question.

"Do you happen to have any of the score cards this fowl made last year?"

"All of them, I think," was the answer. "Right here in my pocket. I bought them with the bird."

"Well, the first one has my name on it and I should like to see, and have the rest of you see, how it compares with the one I have just signed. She is the only bird I ever scored ninety-six."

The cards were held side by side. The judge beamed. "I said once that I should be glad to score her 100, because I wasn't sure I saw the faults I gave her, but I have found the same ones again, so they must be there, but, by cracky, they were hard to find—they were hard to find."

With the rest of her story we are not concerned. She was mercifully preserved from a repetition of her experience of the previous winter by the interference of the judge to secure her for himself. He bought her at a fabulous price, and kept her as a living witness to his own consistency as a judge.

OLD WELCH GOES TO THE SHOW

After Getting Ready—Good and Ready

Old Welch did not care about having his neighbors in when he was getting ready for the show, because, as he said, "The laity don't understand, and can't be expected to."

Still, he did not admit that there was anything to conceal. He used to say, "I guess 'tis fair enough to groom and tame the birds a little before showing." He scorned the defence that if he was bad others were worse. Others might be worse, he was not bad. He was an honest man.

His saying about grooming and taming the birds obtained wide currency. He was asked, when caught in the act, which he called going over the birds for black feathers,—grooming or taming. "Taming," he answered, with the suggestion of a wink.

Of course that made the uninitiated laugh. But as long as the gossip was confined to the neighborhood, Welch did not care, and he knew that as long as he showed that he did not care, it would go no further and do no harm.

There is something fascinating about the like of Welch that peculiarly fits them for corrupters of youth. Welch always had one or more boys around him; and the boys seemed never to tire of asking about the black feathers—whether they were a defect or not, and never to tire either of the old man's unvarying answer: "I calculate the judges would full rather not see any."

Welch loved to please the judges. One of their peculiarities was a passion for featherless legs, and Welch did what he could to see that they got them. There must have been a Brahma cross for blockiness somewhere back in his strain, for he often had legs as fringed as a cowboy's. But that was one of the easiest things remedied—according to the boys.

Old Welch's were White Wyandottes, and he was reported as saying that all he asked of nature was the Wyandotte, and he could supply the rest. "You just put a little of this here chloride of lime in the water on washing day, and—yes, it deadens the feathers, but a dead white is what you're after."

He revealed these trade secrets to the boys that sought him for their first taste of the fruit of the tree of the knowledge of good and evil. And the boys retailed them at the village store, where it was simply opined that Welch probably hated to win.

Welch usually had his chickens out early, and the showing season seldom found him unprepared. But one year his first hatches were so exceptionally fine that the gods fell in love with them, and they died young. His later ones were quite as good, but as they were too late to be of any use to him, he was allowed to keep them. Welch was eloquent in his racy way. His favorites among the boys sought his society every day, and he got all his dirty work done for nothing.

"What are you going to do about it?" one of them asked him.

"Do? I ain't got nothing to do with." For an artist like Mr. Welch this was a confession indeed.

"Can't you show yearlings?"

"This strain ain't bred for yearlings, sonny." By which he was understood to mean that his strain did not hold up well—were good for one year only.

"But can't you doctor yearlings?"

"Doctor, doctor. Don't use that word to me, son."

The boy was too old to be easily cowed, so he only said, "Well, groom and tame them, then."

This appealed to the sport in the old man, and he was mollified.

"Let's see how many we have got of that first lot," he said. "All I ask is maturity. They must have maturity. I can't furnish that. I suppose now a woman could—at least she could make them look younger than they are. But there's no use in my trying. I'm a man, and a plain one. I want 'em old enough, and surely that ain't asking much. I must get to the shows with something, or I shan't know 'tis winter, except by the cold."

"What's the matter with that fellow?" said the youngster, with something of the real air.

"Haven't I learned you no better than that? Why, there's pretty nearly everything the matter with him. His comb don't fit, his eyes ain't mates. He's yellow, and his legs ain't. He's too high posted. He's whale backed and hollow chested. But just to show you what I can do, I'm going to take that dog shaped specimen, and renovate him—renovate him."

"His eyes ain't mates, come to look at them. How will you fix that?"

"I've thought of a way. The hardest will be to make him throw a chest."

What follows rests on the authority of boys, and not particularly good boys. It received a partial confirmation from chance witnesses, and from the established fact that when the time came old Welch went to the show.

One day a visitor came upon Welch by the kitchen stove, with a cockerel between his knees, and a hot wire in his hand. "Taming that one?" was the ready question.

Welch was in a serious mood. "This is the way the pick of the comb is brought down to conformity with the head—by searing underneath." You would have thought it was the regular thing. The visitor's levity was rebuked.

Someone else was a witness to the finishing touches on the bird. Welch was polishing its legs, "just as you polish your shoes when you're out to be looked at," he explained. "That? Oh, that's butter color; brings out the yellow a little, maybe—but that's what the judges seem to like."

"Call it grooming or taming?" the other wanted to know.

Welch had heard this too often to resent it for anything but its age. "Speaking of taming," he answered patiently, "I never had a bird as tame as this one, especially on one side, where he's absolutely tame." He proved it by making sudden passes at the left eye, which never blinked. "He's tame on the other side, too, but not *as* tame."

There was only the boys' word for it, but it was believed that Welch had employed the services of an oculist in renovating the bird. One of the bird's eyes had been yellow; after the encounter with the oculist it was red like the other, but he did not seem to notice anything with it.

The boys said "glass." The boys said almost anything. They told about what might be called a pneumatic front. Welch had got the idea from the Asiatics who, he had read, practiced inflating the skin of camels with air to make them salable. It was a delicate operation, almost requiring the services of a veterinary. His instruments were a sharp knife, a bicycle pump, and needle and thread. Of course this was left to the last moment for fear of mortification.

Now everything was accounted for but the bird's general shape. Let what follows be spoken with reserve. You are not asked to believe it. The poor, the much enduring bird's lines were corrected, it was said, with a pair of Wyandotte shaped corsets designed by Welch, and made to order. You may say that you never heard of such a thing. You never did hear of such a thing, because no such thing ever existed until Welch devised it (if he did devise it). Therein lay his originality as a breeder. He literally recast that cockerel. It took two weeks of the tightest lacing known to fashion to satisfy the old man. Once or twice the lifelike glass eye was actually squeezed out in the process, and had to be searched for and put back. But in the end science triumphed.

Old Welch was a proud man when he surveyed the finished product. " 'Tis the best job I ever did," he said, "all things considered. What's the use of breeding in for a term of years, when you can make all the wonders you want practically out of mud, at trifling cost?"

"But," said one of the boys, doubtfully, "I should think a good deal would depend on the judge when you showed a bird like that."

"It does—it does. You have to be extra careful in choosing your judge. 'Tis with judges, as with other folks, there ain't only now and then one that's suited to your purpose. Now I only know one judge this year that that bird'll do to show to."

The old reprobate was so pleased with himself that he must take a boy to the show with him, and introduce him to the old timers as a natural born breeder.

The cockerel was Welch's only entry, and it had a red ribbon on its cage. The boy who told the story might as well have made it blue while he was about it, but he said red, and red we must keep it. Red was satisfactory to Welch.

Welch might easily have sold the bird, but when it came to that his conscience smote him. He had a code of his own. If the right person had made him an offer he might not have been so virtuous, but he could not bring himself to palm his work off on a green-horn, especially one that did not pretend to be anything else.

The greenhorn had picked up some of the technicalities, and he was particular to ask Welch, as a friend, if the bird was not a "chance bird."

"Chance bird," said Welch, with a twitch of the lips, "better say design. I designed him, made him out of whole cloth. I can talk this to you, because you won't understand. The fact is, he owes just the leastest leetle mite too much to the way he was groomed. I shouldn't want to recommend him to you, because I ain't quite sure that he'd breed true, and you may know that I wouldn't say so unless there was reason."

DALKINS' LITTLE INDULGENCE

A Christmas Story

It is no matter how much Dalkins paid for the bird; the point is that the man who sold it to him somehow got the impression that he did not pay enough—that he would have paid more. He could not have denied that Dalkins paid him all he asked. So that he had himself to blame if it was not enough. But he got to talking as if he had been cheated—and badly cheated. He enlarged upon the bird until he said he shouldn't wonder if Dalkins would get a cool fifty for it. He groomed it, so to speak, as he thought of it. He made it a little whiter than white, a little more symmetrical than symmetry.

As a matter of fact it was the kind of bird that is worth what one can get for it. It transcended scoring, as it was better than any score reputable judges are willing to sign. It was a bird framed by nature for comparison judging.

If the man who sold it to Dalkins made the mistake of parting with it for a cent less than fifty dollars, he deserved sympathy, but he was the only one who could see that Dalkins deserved blame. He showed himself a poor loser. He talked early and late to all comers about his misfortune that was another man's fault. But almost all comers had been in the same fix themselves, and knew how to make allowances. They did not believe too heartily in the pricelessness of his bird—a suspicion of which made him but talk the more.

The wonderful part of this story is that this fellow had picked the bird up away over back in Peacham, Vt., for one dollar and fifty cents. These figures I am willing to vouch for. In that case he did fairly well if he got a five for it. Mind you, I don't say what he got. At the time I heard various rumors. This part of the story must remain shrouded in mystery—men are such liars. I vouch for nothing that you cannot safely believe.

Though he was far enough away from this man and his troubles, the facts here stated somehow or other reached Dalkins. He had come by the bird through an agent of his who had spotted it by the merest accident from his carriage in passing. He had not been too curious about its history and antecedents at the outset; with him the bird in the hand was the thing. But a certain letter aroused his interest. It was anonymous, doubtless from someone in no way concerned, but bent on mischief making, and informed him that the remarkable bird had been raised by the writer's next door neighbor, and had been started on its career for one dollar and fifty cents. He questioned his agent about it. The agent had heard some such tale. Evidently gossip had been buzzing in the hill town of Peacham. He had heard also that the bird was of the Dalkins strain direct. That was calculated to please Dalkins. He wondered if they couldn't find out who raised it. He would have liked the poor benighted fellow who would part with such a jewel for one fifty to know by its fruits what a thing the Dalkins strain was.

"He didn't suspect what he was doing," he said.

"It isn't likely," said the agent.

"And the fellow who sold him to you?"

"He had some idea, because he's kicking himself for having sold it. I have seen him since. He is talking at a great rate."

"The bird has made some stir already, then; that's what they call the fatal gift of beauty, isn't it?"

The agent was duly embarrassed. Dalkins was thinking.

"Say," he said at last, "I want you to find that original owner and bring him to the New York show on me. And bring the other fellow too—both of them. I guess I'm good for it. Tell them 'tis a Christmas notion of mine—the show is near enough to Christmas for that. It'll make it easier for you. We'll show them a thing or two, and we'll show the kicker that he only knows a little bit more than the other fellow. And I think I'll show you something. Not a word of this to anyone outside, and not too many words to them. Just say 'tis my treat—consolation treat. 'Tis an order."

Dalkins' agent found the original owner away over in Peacham one bitter cold morning a day or two after Christmas. Peacham is a New England street town, that is to say, it consists of but one street, which runs north and south along a sharp ridge that looks like the back of a razor backed world. The railroad, when it was built, missed it by about eight miles on the right, and that seemed to send it into a decline—such a close call; no doubt. Many of its fine old houses are going to ruin, and there is never a new one to take their place. The age and size of its shade trees suggested that it might do very well in summer; but on such a day in winter it made the agent fairly groan at the patience of the people who could abide there. He inquired at the postoffice store for his man, and was sent to the woods for him. He came upon him snaking out logs in a grove recently laid waste, as seriously at work as if he had entirely given up seeing Santa Claus that year. He laid before him his invitation, and while not persuading him on the spot to accept it, succeeded in making him regard it as worth considering. At any rate, he carried him away in triumph from his toil like a Cincinnatus, a Putnam, or a Parker. He left his ox team standing in a brush pile in the care of his fellow workmen.

Before he left he had dinner with him, and it was all arranged. The fellow was a little sheepish at first, as one accused of deliberately circulating counterfeit money—only in this case it would have been a counterfeit bird. He suspected that his punishment was going to take the form of a practical joke. But he decided he was equal to it if only it wasn't to cost him anything, and the return ticket the agent laid down for him set at rest his fears on that score.

The agent had less trouble with the other fellow—Durgin, if the name must out. He considered the invitation his due. "Aw yes," he yawped, "he knew how it all was. Nobody probably intended to do him. It was business, just business. Only he thought," etc. Of course he wasn't a fool. He knew a good bird when he saw one. Only sometimes his mind didn't work quick enough, etc. Yes, he'd be glad to meet Mr. Dalkins. He bore no grudge. He wasn't that kind. Only he thought, etc. The main thing was that he accepted the ticket.

Scene, the New York show. Mr. Dalkins is doing the honors. When I say doing, I mean doing. He never let those two importations of his out of his sight for three days, and he never gave them a restful half hour. And it was not all inside the Garden. But let us draw a veil over anything that was irrelevant to the show proper. What have I to do with the Rialto and the Bowery? Suffice it to say that he gave two simple souls the time of their lives, and beat them out in his own enjoyment of it, in spite of the fact that it was on him and it came high.

The grand finale Mr. Dalkins had all prearranged, and he looked forward to it with the anticipation of a boy. No one had an inkling of what was coming, unless it was his agent to whom he once said in an aside: "The bird *the* bird, was sold, I suppose you didn't know, before anything was placed, but he's not to change hands till the last day of the show. I want you to be there when he does."

And once he had said to the second in line of possession, "So it sticks in your crop that you should have had fifty for your trade. Well, we won't let that spectre intrude on our festivities. Time enough for discussion afterward. There's always a way to settle such matters between gentlemen."

But the victim, though disliking the tone of banter in this, smelt not a rat. He and the original owner came to the final catastrophe as unprepared as the babe new born. They were so absorbed in the pleasure of the hour that it never occurred to either that he might be destined in the mind of the master to point a moral or adorn a tale. When it suited Dalkins' sense of dramatic fitness, they were led like lambs to the slaughter.

He towed the brace of them round to a certain much beribboned coop in the last hours of the show. He had made it a point to take them there several times a day during their stay to punctuate their experiences and keep them from forgetting to whom they were indebted for their popularity. He had never said much in the feathery presence. He found it more impressive to look in silence. His charges divided their hushed regard between him and the bird, awed by the thought of what great things might be passing in the mind of such a man at such a moment.

Now he led them there for the last time. Tomorrow it was good bye. The tumult and the crowing would die away. He told them that they must have a last look at the prize they had let slip through their fingers. Might it be a lesson to them!

As it happened they found someone there before them. He showed himself more than usually interested, and they hung back until he should have completed his scrutiny. Upon lifting his head from the note book he employed, he recognized Dalkins. He had been about to move off. He stood still. There may have been a momentary gleam of fun in his eye. It passed unnoticed.

"Splendid," he said, with an indicative wave of the hand, "I want him."

"I thought of you, Wilson, when I put him in here. Isn't he what you were looking for in the fall? I thought you would want him."

"I do. Your price?"

Dalkins made a movement with his fingers as if he despaired of having enough to give the sign. He ended by holding up, side by side, and far forward, one finger on each hand.

The agent, Durgin, and the original owner, turned pale. The first thought he was insane, the second that he was making a fake sale, the third that he hadn't been so far wrong in his estimate of the bird. To these three the two fingers meant two dollars.

"Shade it," said Mr. Wilson.

"Will you give me a dollar fifty?" laughed Dalkins.

"What are a few dollars here or there when it is a question of such a bird?" said Wilson as he went down for his wad.

"This is the payee." Dalkins obtruded the original owner.

"His bird, is it?"

"In a way, yes. He raised it up back here a few hundred miles, and I don't consider that he was ever honestly separated from it." This with a withering eye to Durgin.

"It wasn't stolen?"

"It comes to that. He was induced to sell it for one dollar and fifty cents."

For a moment Wilson hesitated and drew back, but it was only a moment. He looked at the bird again. "Well," he said, "I'm not supposed to know that. A bargain's a bargain."

(2 7 4)

At the moment of being thrust into prominence by the collar, the original owner, somewhat taken by surprise, had mechanically turned up a hand. Now Dalkins seized upon this and held it as in a vice, while Wilson heaped bills upon it till the count should have been lost, though it wasn't. The sum total was two hundred dollars. All the time Durgin had been opening wider and wider at the mouth.

"If I let go," said Dalkins to the original owner, "can I trust you to put that money where it belongs, and not bother me with arguments? Remember it is Christmas, or was a week or so since."

The original owner smiled weakly, but made no remonstrance.

"Where do I come in?" piped up poor Durgin.

"For a good time, and a valuable lesson," snapped Dalkins. "If there's anything else you want but can't seem to lay your hands on, just take it out in kicking."

Then Dalkins gently but forcibly closed the original's fingers over the paper in his hand, and headed him down the aisle. Durgin followed with a rattling in his throat that suggested roup, but merely indicated the impulse to speak without the ability.

Everybody followed, the little procession attracting considerable attention in the hall. It was thought someone had been arrested by a plain clothes man for stealing ribbons from the cages. The original had almost lost consciousness of what was going on around him. He heard as in a dream amid the uproar of roosters, that sounded like a dying yell that wouldn't die, the voice of Dalkins saying, "Go tell that up in the hills, and make them stop breeding mongrel stock."

"... *the beginning of a book's career.*"

LETTERS ABOUT *A BOY'S WILL* AND ABOUT WRITING

Living in England when *A Boy's Will* was issued there in
1913, Robert Frost yearned to share with a few friends back
home his great excitement over having a book of his poems
published—at the age of thirty-nine. The first with whom he
chose to share the news of his good fortune was John T.
Bartlett, who had been one of Frost's favorite students
during his years of teaching at Pinkerton Academy in Derry,
New Hampshire. Bartlett had under Frost's influence become
a journalist, and in 1913 he was engaged as a newspaper
reporter in Vancouver, British Columbia. The letters that
follow are drawn from *Selected Letters of Robert Frost* (pp.
65ff) and relate not only to the poet's book but, also, to
certain of his theories of writing, generally.

DEAR JOHN:- About now you are in receipt of my coverless book[*].
Now you are reading it upside down in your excitement. What's the
matter? You look pale. I see it all as true to life as in a melodrama. Your
wife gathers around the table. The dog gets stepped on—the Indian
Runner Dog. And Ruksh the dog utters a fearful cry. No canine cry is
that, etc. It curdles the Annie Frazier River. A chair goes over.

"Wait," you say.

"Wait a minute!"

"Hold on!"

*Unbound page proofs stamped, "FIRST REVISE / 30 JAN. 1913." Now in the Barrett Collection, University of Virginia Library.

"Give me time!"

"I tell you I can understand this if you give me time and dont hurry me!"

"In fact it isnt that I cant understand it."

"I can understand it all right."

"But I cant believe it."

"It is what I may call the startlingness of the intelligence."

"Suppose I were to telegraph you from Raymond [the New Hampshire birthplace of John Bartlett] or some other center where things happen and news is manufactured that Sir Peg a Ramsey had demonstrated on the zylophone that there was more radium than neon and helium than yes than in no."

"You would be excited, wouldn't you?"

"Come own up. Of course you'd be."

"It would make all the difference in the world."

"You'd feature it—you'd call attention to it in a leader."

"Well it's like that—only—what shall I say?"

"Only more serious, more momentous."

"So unlike poetry—except Masefield's."

"If a man has anything he wants to break to us let him use prose—prose is his vehicle."

"Listen to this—it comes with too great a shock in verse."

"Get ready:"

"eurt saw thguoht I lla fo erus erom ylnO"

"It is too, too much."

And so you run on till Mrs. Margaret interposes with a woman's good sense:

"Perhaps if you read it right side up it wouldn't mean so much."

"It might not mean anything."

Still I think you will treat the book kindly for my sake. It comes pretty near being the story of five years of my life. In the first poem I went away from people (and college); in the one called A Tuft of Flowers I came back to them actually as well as verbally for I wrote that poem to get my job in Pinkerton as little Tommy Tucker sang for his supper, and Brer Merriam read it for me at a Men's League Banquet in Derry Village because I was too timid to read it myself. [. . .]

R.F.

DEAR JOHN, - I have nothing to write about except our anxieties for you and Margaret and my anxieties for the success of my book which are two so incommensurable things that they ought not of right to be brought together in one letter. However one must write something, for you will be wanting to hear. A letter now and then even if it seems an answer to nothing in particular can't come amiss. I know I could bear to get one from you oftener than I do. I have no regular correspondent on the other side either in Derry or in Plymouth. I cut myself off from the Derry crowd in disgust [. . .]. I rather deliberately queered myself with Silver and the Plymouth crowd by laying it on pretty thick though with studied modesty, about my little achievements here in answer to their clamor for something literary from the neighborhood of Westminster Abbey. You see I could talk about myself on that for a joke and call it highly literary. Instead of lingering over the tombs and busts in the Abbey (where I have never been) I talked in simple truth about my book. I had it in for them. Silver asked three times for something literary. Then he got it. He hasn't yipped since. The Lord do so to me and more also if I could help it. And I was artful enough to leave something untold that I could send around and make sure of his getting as if by accident by way of Mrs Frost and some of the ladies. He's an awfully mild master, is Silver, when he has you where he can pay what he wants to. But he's jealous to a fault. I know where he lives. The story when pieced together amounted to just this—I don't know whether I have bothered you with it before. I found a publisher for my book in the first office I walked into. The firm pays all expenses of publication which is a very unusual thing in the case of a first book. I am under contract to let the same firm have my next four books if I ever write any more. I had hardly signed this contract when I had requests for a book from two American publishers, one a most flattering thing from Mosher of Portland, whose letterpress is considered perhaps the most beautiful in the States. I seem to have found a friend in Mosher. Some time when you are happy and feeling flush I wish you would send him a dollar for a year of his little magazine of reprints called The Bibelot. His address is Portland, Maine. You will like the magazine.

I have got off the track a little bit. But I think I have told you about the whole story as Silver had it. Where the anxieties come in? Bless you, all that hit my Plymouth friends so hard is just the beginning of a book's career. I am in mortal fear now lest the reviewers should fail to take any notice of it. Such a work isn't sold in the bookstores but through the notices in the papers entirely. It is going the rounds now and it remains to be seen whether it will fall flat or not. Something however it has already done for me in ways too mysterious to go into. It has brought me several interesting friendships which I can tell you about without exciting any jealousy in your breast because you know that I care more for you and your opinion of me (formed when I was fifteenth in command at Pinkerton) than for the opinion of all the rest of them put together. Yeats has asked me to make one of his circle at his Monday Nights when he is in London (and not in Dublin). And he told my dazzling friend Ezra Pound that my book was the best thing that has come out of America for some time. Of course we needn't believe that. I spent the evening with Yeats in his dark-curtained candlelit room last week. We talked about The Land of Heart's Desire among other things. He is the big man here in poetry of course, though his activity is largely dramatic in late years. I have met Maurice Hewlett within a day or two. Hewlett not very intimately. You know him for his novels. He himself cares only for his poetry. And then there is May Sinclair the author of The Divine Fire etc. etc. I took tea with her yesterday and expect to go there again shortly. She professes to see something unusual in my book. I like that of course because she is known as an expert in new poetry. She is the lady who made the reputation of Vaughn Moody, Torrence and Edwin Arnold [Arlington] Robinson by naming them as the principal poets in the States. And Ezra Pound, the stormy petrel, I must tell you more about him when I have more time. He has found me and sent a fierce article to Chicago denouncing a country that neglects fellows like me. I am afraid he over did it and it may be a mercy all round if it isn't printed. It is likely to be though as he always seems to have his way with the magazine it has gone to [*Poetry*]. All this ought to be enough to satisfy me for the time being you will think. But dear dear. The boom is not started yet. And then there is the money question. I am going to run short and have to go to the American Consulate for assisted passage home. There is little money ahead. Hewlett was boasting that he had three pounds, his first royalty on a book of poems published four years ago. Gosh.

I hope this letter will pass two or three coming the other way and bringing good news of Margaret and of you.

Affectionately R.F.

Dear John: I have to be chary of my favors to get anything out of you. The book [*A Boy's Will*] goes with this as per your kick of recent date. You are now supposed to order of your own motion and without undue pressure from me not less than fifteen nor more than twenty copies at forty cents (inclusive of post) the copy. You must do this of the publisher and not of me so as to make it look as if I had taken hold in the far west (why, God only knows). Then you must get me a notice in the most literary of the Vancouver dailies or weeklies. Make it personal if you like, a sort of news item. Like this: Jaunty Bart., the popular and ever censorious fakeer of the Sun staff is in receipt of etc etc. till you get to "allow me to sell you a couple" (quoting from Alice). You know the sort of thing. Be sure to say, This is hot stuff. A few choice copies left. Call it a farm product without fear of contradiction. It is inevitable (that's the word) as inevitable as a cabbage or a cucumber (if the cut worms don't get it.) Funny how you and I both go in for farming. I am looked on as someone who has got the poetry of the farm. Can't you ring me into one of your columns in the Montreal Star? In a word do your dambdest and hang the consequences. I am mes enfants

LIVING IN YOU MORE THAN YOU CAN IMAGINE. R.F.

DEAR JOHN: What do you say if we cook up something to bother the enemies we left behind in Derry? It won't take much cooking, but what it does will come on you. You have two of my reviews now. If you haven't I will see that you have others to take their place. One is good for one reason; the other for another. Pound's [*Poetry: A Magazine of Verse*, May 1913] is a little too personal. I don't mind his calling me raw. He is reckoned raw himself and at the same time perhaps the most prominent of the younger poets here. I object chiefly to what he says about the great American editors. Not that I have any love for the two or three he has in mind. But they are better ignored—at any rate they are better not offended. We may want to use them some time. The other I value chiefly for its source, The English Review, the magazine that found Masefield and Conrad. The editor himself [Norman Douglas] wrote that particular notice.

I am sending you one more review which you can hold on to for a while. One more still and we shall have the ingredients of our Bouill-abais[s]e (sp.) assembled. If nothing slips up we will get that in the August number of The Bookman (English). The editor has asked me for my photograph and a personal note to accompany the review. I suppose everything depends on whether I look young enough in my photograph to grace the ballet. Why did you wear me out teaching you things you knew already?

Well then in August, say, as soon as you get The Bookman you can begin a little article for Morse-back of The News and Enterprise like this:

Former pupils of R. F. at Pink may be interested to learn of the success of his first book published in London. A recent number of The Bookman (Eng.) contains etc.—You are not to get the least bit enthusiastic—I know you my child. Keep strictly to the manner of the disinterested reporter. Make the article out of the reviews almost entirely. In mentioning The English Review you might mention the fact that it is a leading literary monthly here.

All this is if you have time and inclination. It will necessitate some typewriting. I would copy Ezra Pound's article so as to get rid of the break about the editors. Leave in any derogatory remarks. We like those. I fancy I should leave out the quotation from "My November Guest" which mangles a poem that needs to be taken as a whole and they quote it as a whole in the Poetry and Drama review I am enclosing. You see the scheme is to make The Bookman affair the occasion for your article and then drag the rest in by the ears. Say simply "The following is taken from—" Or if you see some other way to go about it, all right. You might do it in the form of a letter to the News, beginning, "I thought former pupils of R F at Pink etc" and sign yourself J. T. B. Anything to make Mrs Superior Sheppard and Lil' Art' Reynolds unhappy. (You put these people into my head.) But I suppose I care less about teasing my out-and-out enemies than my half friends like John C. Chase. I told you how I charged John C. forty dollars for the catalogue and when he winced told him that I didn't get it often but when I did I got about that much for my poetry. He never quite got over that. He clipped a cheap joke on poets one day and sent it to me by Miss Bartley so that she would share in my discomfiture. I only stood it tolerably well. I didn't mind it at first as much. I got tired of it.

AFFECTIONATELY, MES ENFANTS R.F.

DEAR JOHN: - Those initials you quote from T. P.'s belong to a fellow named Buckley and the explanation of Buckley is this that he has recently issued a book with David Nutt, but at his own expense, whereas in my case David Nutt assumed the risks. *And* those other people Buckley reviewed are his personal friends or friends of his friends or if not that simply examples of the kind of wrong horse most fools put their money on. You will be sorry to hear me say so but they are not even craftsmen. Of course there are two ways of using that word the good and the bad one. To be on the safe side it is best to call such dubs mechanics. To be perfectly frank with you I am one of the most notable craftsmen of my time. That will transpire presently. I am possibly the only person going who works on any but a worn out theory (principle I had better say) of versification. You see the great successes in recent poetry have been made on the assumption that the music of words was a matter of harmonised vowels and consonants. Both Swinburne and Tennyson arrived largely at effects in assonation. But they were on the wrong track or at any rate on a short track. They went the length of it. Any one else who goes that way must go after them. And that's where most are going. I alone of English writers have consciously set myself to make music out of what I may call the sound of sense. Now it is possible to have sense without the sound of sense (as in much prose that is supposed to pass muster but makes very dull reading) and the sound of sense without sense (as in Alice in Wonderland which makes anything but dull reading). The best place to get the abstract sound of sense is from voices behind a door that cuts off the words. Ask yourself how these sentences would sound without the words in which they are embodied:

> You mean to tell me you can't read?
> I said no such thing.
> Well read then.
> You're not my teacher.

———

He says it's too late.

Oh, say!

Damn an Ingersoll watch anyway.

———

One-two-three—go!

No good! Come back—come back.

Haslam go down there and make those kids get out of the track.

———

Those sounds are summoned by the audile [audial] imagination and they must be positive, strong, and definitely and unmistakably indicated by the context. The reader must be at no loss to give his voice the posture proper to the sentence. The simple declarative sentence used in making a plain statement is one sound. But Lord love ye it mustn't be worked to death. It is against the law of nature that whole poems should be written in it. If they are written they won't be read. The sound of sense, then. You get that. It is the abstract vitality of our speech. It is pure sound—pure form. One who concerns himself with it more than the subject is an artist. But remember we are still talking merely of the raw material of poetry. An ear and an appetite for these sounds of sense is the first qualification of a writer, be it of prose or verse. But if one is to be a poet he must learn to get cadences by skillfully breaking the sounds of sense with all their irregularity of accent across the regular beat of the metre. Verse in which there is nothing but the beat of the metre furnished by the accents of the pollysyllabic words we call doggerel. Verse is not that. Neither is it the sound of sense alone. It is a resultant from those two. There are only two or three metres that are worth anything. We depend for variety on the infinite play of accents in the sound of sense. The high possibility of emotional expression all lets in this mingling of sense-sound and word-accent. A curious thing. And all this has its bearing on your prose me boy. Never if you can help it write down a sentence in which the voice will not know how to posture *specially*.

That letter head shows how far we have come since we left Pink.

Editorial correspondent of the Montreal Star sounds to me. Gad, we get little mail from you.

Affectionately R.F.

Maybe you'll keep this discourse on the sound of sense till I can say more on it.

Dear John: [. . .] I set a good deal of store by the magazine work you are doing or going to do. That is your way out of bondage. You can— must write better for a magazine than there is any inducement to do for a daily.

My notion is that your work is coming on. Your style tightens up. What you will have to guard against is the lingo of the newspaper, words that nobody but a journalist uses, and worse still, phrases. John Cournos who learned his trade on the Philadelphia Record, where he went by the nickname of Gorky, has come over here to write short stories. He is thirty. His worst enemy is going to be his habit of saying cuticle for skin.

I really liked what you wrote about me. Your sentences go their distance, straight and sure and they relay each other well. You always had ideas and apprehended ideas. You mustnt lose that merit. You must find some way to show people that you have initiative and judgment. You must "get up" new things as new even as a brand new department for some paper.

[. . .] I want to write down here two or three cardinal principles that I wish you would think over and turn over now and again till we *can* protract talk.

I give you a new definition of a sentence:

A sentence is a sound in itself on which other sounds called words may be strung.

You may string words together without a sentence-sound to string them on just as you may tie clothes together by the sleeves and stretch them without a clothes line between two trees, but—it is bad for the clothes.

The number of words you may string on one sentence-sound is not fixed but there is always danger of over loading.

The sentence-sounds are very definite entities. (This is no literary mysticism I am preaching.) They are as definite as words. It is not impossible that they could be collected in a book though I don't at present see on what system they would be catalogued.

They are apprehended by the ear. They are gathered by the ear from the vernacular and brought into books. Many of them are already familiar to us in books. I think no writer invents them. The most original writer only catches them fresh from talk, where they grow spontaneously.

A man is all a writer if *all* his words are strung on definite recognizable sentence sounds. The voice of the imagination, the speaking voice must know certainly how to behave how to posture in every sentence he offers.

A man is a marked writer if his words are largely strung on the more striking sentence sounds.

A word about recognition: In literature it is our business to give people the thing that will make them say, "Oh yes I know what you mean." It is never to tell them something they dont know, but something they know and hadnt thought of saying. It must be something they recognize.

A Patch of Old Snow

In the corner of the wall where the bushes haven't been trimmed, there is a patch of old snow like a blow-away newspaper that has come to rest there. And it is dirty as with the print and news of a day I have forgotten, if I ever read it.

Now that is no good except for what I may call certain points of recognition in it: patch of old snow in a corner of the wall,—you know what that is. You know what a blow-away newspaper is. You know the curious dirt on old snow and last of all you know how easily you forget what you read in papers.

Now for the sentence sounds. We will look for the marked ones because they are easiest to discuss. The first sentence sound will do but it is merely ordinary and bookish: it is entirely subordinate in interest to the meaning of the words strung on it. But half the effectiveness of the second sentence is in the very special tone with which you must say—news of a day I have forgotten—if I ever read it. You must be able to say Oh yes one knows how that goes. (There is some adjective to describe the intonation or cadence, but I won't hunt for it.)

One of the least successful of the poems in my book is almost saved by a final striking sentence-sound (Asking for Roses.)

Not caring so very much *what* she supposes.

Take My November Guest. Did you know at once how we say such sentences as these when we talk?

She thinks I have no eye for these.

———

Not yesterday I learned etc.

———

But it were vain to tell her so

———

Get away from the sing-song. You must hear and recognize in the last line the sentence sound that supports, No use in telling him so.

Let's have some examples pell-mell in prose and verse because I don't want you to think I am setting up as an authority on verse alone.

My father used to say—
You're a liar!
If a hen and a half lay an egg and a half etc.
A long long time ago—
Put it there, old man! (Offering your hand)
I aint a going [to] hurt you, so you needn't be scared.

Suppose Henry Horne says something offensive to a young lady named Rita when her brother Charles is by to protect her. Can you hear the two different tones in which she says their respective names. "Henry Horne! Charles!" I can hear it better than I can say it. And by oral practice I get further and further away from it.

Never you say a thing like that to a man!
And such they are and such they will be found.
Well I swan!
Unless I'm greatly mistaken—
Hence with denial vain and coy excuse
A soldier and afraid (afeared)
Come, child, come home.
The thing for me to do is to get right out of here while I am able.
No fool like an old fool.

It is so and not otherwise that we get the variety that makes it fun to write and read. *The ear does it.* The ear is the only true writer and the only true reader. I have known people who could read without hearing the sentence sounds and they were the fastest readers. Eye readers we call them. They can get the meaning by glances. But they are bad readers because they miss the best part of what a good writer puts into his work.

Remember that the sentence sound often says more than the words. It may even as in irony convey a meaning opposite to the words.

(288)

I wouldn't be writing all this if I didn't think it the most important thing I know. I write it partly for my own benefit, to clarify my ideas for an essay or two I am going to write some fine day (not far distant.)

To judge a poem or piece of prose you go the same way to work—apply the one test—greatest test. You listen for the sentence sounds. If you find some of those not bookish, caught fresh from the mouths of people, some of them striking, all of them definite and recognizable, so recognizable that with a little trouble you can place them and even name them, you know you have found a writer.

Before I ring off you may want to hear the facts in the case of us.

We are still in Beaconsfield but trying hard to get rid of our house six months before our lease is out in order to get away into Gloucester with Wilfrid Gibson and Lascelles Abercrombie (see Victorian anthology for both of them).

Book II, North of Boston, should be out now. The publisher is dilatory. [. . .]

Affectionately Rob

It was during this same interval that Frost discussed further his theories of poetry in letters to his American friend Sidney Cox. The following excerpts are quoted from Cox's volume entitled *A Swinger of Birches: A Portrait of Robert Frost,* pp. 110–113, wherein these passages from two letters of 1914 are included.

The living part of a poem is the intonation entangled somehow in the syntax idiom and meaning of a sentence. It is only there for those who have heard it previously in conversation. . . . It is the most volatile and at the same time important part of poetry. It goes and the language becomes dead language, the poetry dead poetry. With it go the accents, the stresses, the delays that are not the property of vowels and syllables but that are shifted at will with the sense. Vowels have length there is no denying. But the accent of sense supersedes all other accent, overrides it and sweeps it away. I will find you the word 'come' variously used in various passages, a whole, half, third, fourth, fifth and sixth note. It is as long as the sense makes it. When men no longer know the intonations on which we string our words they will fall back on what I may call the absolute length of our syllables, which is the length we would give them in passages that meant nothing. . . . I say you can't read a single good sentence with the salt in it unless you have previously heard it spoken. Neither can you with the help of all the characters and diacritical marks pronounce a single word unless you have previously heard it actually pronounced. Words exist in the mouth not books.

It may take some time to make people see—they are so accustomed to look at the sentence as a grammatical cluster of words. The question is where to begin the assault on their prejudice. For my part I have about decided to begin by demonstrating by examples that the sentence as a sound in itself apart from the word sounds is no mere figure of speech. I shall show the sentence sound saying all the sentence conveys with little or no help from the meaning of the words. I shall show the sentence sound opposing the sense of the words, as in irony. And so till I establish the distinction between the grammatical sentence and the vital sentence. The grammatical sentence is merely accessory to the other and chiefly valuable as furnishing a clue to the other. You recognize the sentence sound in this: You, you . . . ! It is so strong that if you hear it as I do you have to pronounce the two yous differently. Just so many sentence sounds belong to man as just so many vocal runs belong to one kind of bird. We come into the world with them and create none of them. What we feel as creation is only selection and grouping. We summon them from Heaven knows where under excitement with the audile [audial] imagination. And unless we are in an imaginative mood it is no use trying to make them, they will not rise. We can only write the dreary kind of grammatical prose known as professorial.

A word more. We value the seeing eye already. Time we said something about the hearing ear—the ear that calls up vivid sentence forms.

We write of things we see and we write in accents we hear. Thus we gather both our material and our technique with the imagination from life; and our technique becomes as much material as material itself. . . .

You aren't influenced by that Beauty is Truth claptrap. In poetry and under emotion every word is "moved" a little or much—moved from its old place, heightened, made, made new. . . . I want the unmade words to work with, not the familiar made ones that everybody exclaims Poetry! at. Of course the great fight of any poet is against the people who want him to write in a special language that has gradually separated from the spoken language by this "making" process. His pleasure must always be to make his own words as he goes and never to depend for effect on words already made, even if they be his own.

". . . getting the sound of sense."

AN INTERVIEW

While he was articulating his theory of poetry in 1913, following the publication of his first book, *A Boy's Will,* Robert Frost had written to his friend John Bartlett, "I alone of English writers have consciously set myself to make music out of what I may call the sound of sense." In 1915, shortly after returning to the United States from England, Frost provided one of his best statements of this theory in an interview with William Stanley Braithwaite. Originally published in the *Boston Evening Transcript* for May 8, 1915, it is here reprinted from *Interviews with Robert Frost,* pp. 3–8.

The success which has immediately come to the poetry of Robert Frost is unique. It has no exact parallel in the experience of the art in this country during the present generation. [. . .]

To appreciate Mr. Frost's poetry perfectly one has got to regard carefully the two backgrounds from which it is projected; fully under the influence of his art these two backgrounds merge into one, though each has its special distinction. There is the background of his material, the environment and character which belong to a special community; and there is the background of art in which the fidelity of speech is artistically brought into literature. This latter is a practice that brings up large and important questions of language and meaning in relation to life on the one hand and to literature on the other.

Mr. Frost has been through the longest period of experimentation in mastering the technique of his art of any other American poet. What he finally arrived at in poetic expression he finds as the highest accomplishment in the greatest English poets and asserts that the American poets who have shown unquestionable genius, especially a man like Edwin Arlington Robinson, have in a large measure the same quality of speech which is at once both artistic and the literal tone of human talk. But no poet in either England or America, except this newly arrived New England poet, has consciously developed and practiced this essential and vital quality of poetry which he characterizes as sound-posturing.

The poet was in his twentieth year when he realized that the speech of books and the speech of life were far more fundamentally different than was supposed. His models up to this period, as with all youthful poets and writers, had been literary models. But he found quite by accident that real artistic speech was only to be copied from life. On his New Hampshire farm he discovered this in the character of a man with whom he used to drive along the country roads. Having discovered this speech he set about copying it in poetry, getting the principles down by rigorous observation and reproduction through the long years which intervened to the publication of his books.

He also discovered that where English poetry was greatest it was by virtue of this same method in the poet, and, as I shall show, in his talk with me he illustrated it in Shakespeare, Shelley, Wordsworth, and Emerson. That these poets did not formulate the principles by which they obtained these subtle artistic effects, but accomplished it wholly unconscious of its exact importance, he also suggested. But with a deliberate recognition of it as a poetic value in the poets to come, he sees an entirely new development in the art of verse.

The invitation which brought Mr. Frost to Boston to read the Phi Beta Kappa poem on Wednesday at Tufts College gave me the opportunity to get from the poet his views on the principles of sound-posturing in verse and some reflections on contemporary poets and poetry in England and America.

Before returning home, it will be interesting to note, the publication of Mr. Frost's books in England awakened a critical sympathy and acceptance, among English writers, of his ideas. His work won over, by its sheer poetic achievement, critics and poets, who had not realized before the possibilities of reproducing the exact tone of meaning in human speech in literary form. Where the poet's work is not fully appreciated in this country is where this principle is not understood. The substance of New England farm life of which his poetry is made has attracted immense interest, but in some quarters the appreciation of this substance is a little modified because the reader has only partially grasped the significance of the form. So it was this I wished the poet to explain in my very first question.

"First," he said, "let me find a name for this principle which will convey to the mind what I mean by this effect which I try to put into my poetry. And secondly, do not let your readers be deceived that this is anything new. Before I give you the details in proof of its importance, in fact of its essential place in the writing of the highest poetry, let me quote these lines from Emerson's 'Monadnoc,' where, in almost a particular manner, he sets forth unmistakably what I mean:

> Now in sordid weeds they sleep,
> In dulness now their secret keep;
> Yet, will you learn our ancient speech,
> These the masters who can teach.
> Fourscore or a hundred words
> All their vocal muse affords;
> But they turn them in a fashion
> Past clerks' or statesmen's art or passion.
> I can spare the college bell,
> And the learned lecture, well;
> Spare the clergy and libraries,
> Institutes and dictionaries,
> For that hearty English root

Thrives here, unvalued, underfoot.
Rude poets of the tavern hearth,
Squandering your unquoted mirth,
Which keeps the ground and never soars,
While Jake retorts and Reuben roars;
Scoff of yeoman strong and stark,
Goes like bullet to its mark;
While the solid curse and jeer
Never balk the waiting ear.

"Understand these lines perfectly and you will understand what I mean when I call this principle 'sound-posturing' or, more literally, getting the sound of sense.

"What we do get in life and miss so often in literature is the sentence sounds that underlie the words. Words in themselves do not convey meaning, and to [. . . prove] this, which may seem entirely unreasonable to any one who does not understand the psychology of sound, let us take the example of two people who are talking on the other side of a closed door, whose voices can be heard but whose words cannot be distinguished. Even though the words do not carry, the sound of them does, and the listener can catch the meaning of the conversation. This is because every meaning has a particular sound-posture; or, to put it in another way, the sense of every meaning has a particular sound which each individual is instinctively familiar with and without at all being conscious of the exact words that are being used is able to understand the thought, idea, or emotion that is being conveyed.

"What I am most interested in emphasizing in the application of this belief to art is the sentence of sound, because to me a sentence is not interesting merely in conveying a meaning of words. It must do something more; it must convey a meaning by sound."

"But," I queried, "do you not come into conflict with metrical sounds to which the laws of poetry conform in creating rhythm?"

"No," the poet replied, "because you must understand this sound of which I speak has principally to do with tone. It is what Mr. Bridges, the Poet Laureate, characterized as speech-rhythm. Meter has to do with beat, and sound-posture has a definite relation as an alternate tone between the beats. The two are one in creation but separate in analysis.

"If we go back far enough we will discover that the sound of sense existed before words, that something in the voice or vocal gesture made primitive man convey a meaning to his fellow before the race developed a more elaborate and concrete symbol of communication in language. I have even read that our American Indians possessed, besides a picture-language, a means of communication (though it was not said how far it was developed) by the sound of sense. And what is this but calling up with the imagination, and recognizing, the images of sound?

"When Wordsworth said, 'Write with your eye on the object,' or (in another sense) it was important to visualize, he really meant something more. That something carries out what I mean by writing with your ear to the voice.

"This is what Wordsworth did himself in all his best poetry, proving that there can be no creative imagination unless there is a summoning up of experience, fresh from life, which has not hitherto been evoked. The power, however, to do this does not last very long in the life of a poet. After ten years Wordsworth had very nearly exhausted his, giving us only flashes of it now and then. As language only really exists in the mouths of men, here again Wordsworth was right in trying to reproduce in his poetry not only the words—and in their limited range, too, actually used in common speech—but their sound.

"To carry this idea a little further it does not seem possible to me that a man can read on the printed page what he has never heard. Nobody today knows how to read Homer and Virgil perfectly, because the people who spoke Homer's Greek and Virgil's Latin are as dead as the sound of their language.

"On the other hand, to further emphasize the impossibility of words rather than sound conveying the sense of meaning, take the matter of translation. Really to understand and catch all that is embodied in a foreign masterpiece it must be read in the original, because while the words may be brought over, the tone cannot be.

"In the matter of poetry," the poet continued, "there is a subtle differentiation between sound and the sound of sense, which ought to be perfectly understood before I can make clear my position.

"For a second let me turn aside and say that the beginning of literary form is in some turn given to the sentence in folk speech. Art is the amplification and sophistication of the proverbial turns of speech.

"All folk speech is musical. In primitive conditions man has not at his aid reactions by which he can quickly and easily convey his ideas and emotions. Consequently, he has to think more deeply to call up the image for the communication of his meaning. It was the actuality he sought; and thinking more deeply, not in the speculative sense of science or scholarship, he carried out Carlyle's assertion that if you 'think deep enough you think musically.'

"Poetry has seized on this sound of speech and carried it to artificial and meaningless lengths. We have it exemplified in Sidney Lanier's musical notation of verse, where all the tones of the human voice in natural speech are entirely eliminated, leaving the sound of sense without root in experience."

"*I am going to tell you something. . . .*"

EARLY LETTERS TO UNTERMEYER

In his long correspondence with poet-critic-editor Louis Untermeyer, ranging over a period of nearly half a century, Robert Frost was far more self-revealing than he was in any other single group of his letters. Quoted here are four samples, written in 1916 and 1917, drawn from *The Letters of Robert Frost to Louis Untermeyer,* pp. 28–63, letters which contain particular references to both Edgar Lee Masters and Amy Lowell.

DEAR OLD LOUIS When I have borne in memory what has tamed Great Poets, hey? Am I to be blamed etc? No you ain't. Or as Browning (masc.) has it:

> That was I that died last night
> When there shone no moon at all
> Nor to pierce the strained and tight
> Tent of heaven one planet small.
> Might was dead and so was Right.

Not to be any more obvious than I have to be to set at rest your brotherly fears for my future which I have no doubt you assume to be somehow or other wrapped up in me, I am going to tell you something I never but once let out of the bag before and that was just after I reached London and before I had begun to value myself for what I was worth. It is a very damaging secret and you may not thank me for taking you into it when I tell you that I have often wished I could be sure that the other sharer of it had perished in the war. It is this: The poet in me died nearly ten years ago. Fortunately he had run through several phases, four to be exact, all well-defined, before he went. The calf I was in the nineties I merely take to market. I am become my own salesman. Two of my phases you have been so—what shall I say—as to like. Take care that you don't get your mouth set to declare the other two (as I release them) a falling off of power, for that is what they can't be whatever else they may be, since they were almost inextricably mixed with the first two in the writing and only my sagacity has separated or sorted them in the afterthought for putting on the market. Did you ever hear of quite such a case of Scotch-Yankee calculation? You should have seen the look on the face of the Englishman I first confessed this to! I won't name him lest it should bring you two together. While he has never actually betrayed me, he has made himself an enemy of me and all my works. He regards me as a little heinous. As you look back don't you see how a lot of things I have said begin to take meaning from this? Well . . .

But anyway you are freed from anxiety about my running all to philosophy. It makes no difference what I run to now. I needn't be the least bit tender of myself. Of course I'm glad it's all up with Masters, my hated rival. He wasn't foresighted enough, I'll bet, to provide against the evil day that is come to him. He failed to take warning from the example of Shelley who philosophized and died young. But me, the day I did The Trial by Existence (*Boy's Will*) says I to myself, this is the way of all flesh. I was not much over twenty, but I was wise for my years. I knew then that it was a race between me the poet and that in me that would be flirting with the entelechies or the coming on of that in me. I must get as much done as possible before thirty. I tell you, Louis, it's all over at thirty. People expect us to keep right on and it is as well to have something to show for our time on earth. Anyway that was the way I thought I might feel. And I took measures accordingly. And now my time is my own. I have myself all in a strong box where I can unfold as a personality at discretion. Someone asks with a teasing eye, "Have you done that Phi Beta Kappa poem yet?" "No, I don't know that I have, as you may say." "You seem not to be particularly uneasy about it." "Oh, that's because I know where it's coming from, don't you know." Great effect of strength and mastery!

Now you know more about me than anyone else knows except that Londoner we won't count because he may be dead of a lachrymous.

And don't think mention of the war is anything to go by. I could give you proof that twenty years ago in a small book I did on Boeme and the Technique of Sincerity I was saying "The heroic emotions, like all the rest of the emotions, never know when they ought to be felt after the first time. Either they will be felt too soon or too late from fear of being felt too soon."

Ever thine R.F.

I must give you a sample from the fourth book, "Pitchblende." As a matter of fact and to be perfectly honest with you there is a fifth unnamed as yet, the only one unnamed (the third has been long known as "Mountain Interval") and I think the most surprising of the lot (circa 1903). But none of that now.

OLD AGE

My old uncle is long and narrow.
And when he starts to rise
After his after-dinner nap
I think to myself
He may do it this once more
But this is the last time.
He lets one leg slip off the lounge
And fall to the floor.
But still he lies
And looks to God through the ceiling.
The next thing is to get to his outside elbow
And so to a sitting posture

And so to his feet.
I avert my eyes for him till he does it.
Once I said from the heart,
"What is it, Uncle?—
Pain or just weakness?
Can't we do anything for it?"
He said "It's Specific Gravity"
"Do you mean by that that it's grave?"
"No, not as bad as that yet, child,
But it's the Grave coming on."
Then I knew he didn't mean Seriousness
When he said Gravity.
Old age may not be kittenish
But it is not necessarily serious.

R.F.

Someone writes to tell me that the Poetry Society had one of my poems to abuse in manuscript the other night. Absolutely without my knowledge and consent. I don't mind their abuse, but I do mind their trying to make it look as if I was fool enough to come before them for judgment except with something I had cooked up for their limitations. Protest for me, will you? I wonder how in the world they got the manuscript.

DEAR OLD LOUIS: Seriously I am fooling. And so are you with your crocodile you'llyou'llations. Come off. I thought you and we was going to be rebels together. And being rebels doesn't mean being radical; it means being reckless like Eva Tanguay. It means busting something just when everybody begins to think it so sacred it's safe. (See Rheims Cathedral—next time you're in France.)

These folks that get on by logical steps like a fly that's climbed out of the molasses a little way up the side of the cup—them I have no use for. I'm all for abruption. There is no gift like that of suddenly turning up somewhere else. I like a young fellow as says, "My father's generation thought that, did they? Well that was the Hell of a way to think, wasn't it? Let's think something else for a change." A disconnective young fellow with a plenty of extrication in his make-up. You bet your sweet life. What *would* the editors of the Masses say to such onprincipled—what shall I call it?

The only sorrow is that I ain't as reckless as I used to be. That is to say not in as many departments.

The sacred theory that you may not have theories is one I might not hesitate to lay hands on. But dear me it will have to wait till I have a day off. There's the planting to think of and the Phibetakappa poem and I can't tell you what all.

Meanwhile and till I can go to join him here's a sigh and a tear for poor old Masters. That stuff on the outside of Sandburg's book is enough to prove my original suspicion, not that Masters is just dead but that he was never very much alive. A fellow that's that way can't ever have been any other way. But we won't labor that. We won't labor or belabor anything and so we shall save ourselves from all things dire. Nothing but what I am "forced to think," forced to feel, forced to say, so help me, my contempt for everything and everybody but a few real friends.

You are of the realest of these. Who else has struck for me so often in swift succession. I had seen what you wrote in Masses. The devil of it is I am getting so I rather expect it of you. Don't fail me!

ALWAYS YOURS R.

DEAR LOUIS: Under separate cover I have told you why I ain't got no sympathy for your total loss of all the arts. You tried to have too many at the present price of certified milk. Why would you be a pig instead of something like a horse or a cow that only has one in a litter, albeit with six legs sometimes, for I have seen such in my old mad glad circus-going days. But that's all put behind me since I discovered that do or say my damndest I can't be other than orthodox in politics love and religion: I can't escape salvation: I can't burn if I was born into this world to shine without heat. And I try not to think of it as often as I can lest in the general deliquescence I should find myself a party to the literature of irresponsible, boy-again, freedom. No, I can promise you that whatever else I write or may have been writing for the last twenty-five years to disprove Amy's theory that I never got anything except out of the soil of New England, there's one thing I shan't write in the past, present, or future, and that is glad mad stuff or mad glad stuff. The conviction closes in on me that I was cast for gloom as the sparks fly upward, I was about to say: I am of deep shadow all compact like onion within onion and the savor of me is oil of tears. I have heard laughter by daylight when I thought it was my own because at that moment when it broke I had parted my lips to take food. Just so I have been afraid of myself and caught at my throat when I thought I was making some terrible din of a mill whistle that happened to come on the same instant with the opening of my mouth to yawn. But I have not laughed. No man can tell you the sound or the way of my laughter. I have neighed at night in the woods behind a house like vampires. But there are no vampires, there are no ghouls, there no demons, there is nothing but me. And I have all the dead New England things held back by one hand as by a dam in the long deep wooded valley of Whippoorwill, where, many as they are, though, they do not flow together by their own weight more than so many piled-up chairs—(and, by the way, your two chairs have come). I hold them easily—too easily for assurance that they will go with a rush when I let them go. I may have to extricate them one by one and throw them. If so I shall throw them with what imaginative excess I am capable of, already past the height of my powers (see Amy the next time you are in Boston).

I suppose it's a safe bet that the form your pacifism, your Protean pacifism, takes at this moment is "Down with Mitchel." Next it will be—you say! Do you see these transmogrifications more than one or two ahead? Aw say, be a nationalist. By the love you bear Teddy!

Yours while you're still bad enough to need me, Robert Frost

Dear Louis: Do you want to be the repository of one or two facts that Amy leaves out of account?

For twenty-five out of the first forty years of my life I lived in San Francisco, Lawrence, Mass., Boston, Cambridge, Mass., New York, and Beaconsfield, a suburb of London.

For seven I lived in the villages of Salem, Derry, and Plymouth, New Hampshire.

For eight I lived on a farm at Derry though part of that time I was teaching in the Academy there.

I began to read to myself at thirteen. Before that time I had been a poor scholar and had staid out of school all I could. At about that time I began to take first place in my classes.

I read my first poem at 15, wrote my first poem at 16, wrote My Butterfly at eighteen. That was my first poem published.

With Elinor I shared the valedictory honor when I graduated from the High School at Lawrence, Mass.

I was among the first men at Amy's brother's old college during my two years there, winning a considerable scholarship. In those days I used to suspect I was looked on as more or less of a grind—though as a matter of fact I was always rather athletic. I ran well. I played on town school ball teams and on the High School football team. I had my share of fights, the last a rather public one in Lawrence in 1896 that cost me the humiliation of going into court and a ten dollar fine.

It is not fair to farmers to make me out a very good or laborious farmer. I have known hard times, but no special shovel-slavery. I dreamed my way through all sorts of fortunes without any realizing sense of what I was enduring. You should have seen me, I wish I could have seen myself, when I was working in the Arlington Mills at Lawrence, working in the shoe shop in Salem N.H., tramping and beating my way on trains down South, reporting on a Lawrence paper, promoting for a Shakespearean reader (whom I abandoned because, after trying him on a distinguished audience I got him in Boston, I decided he wasn't *truly great!*) Nothing seemed to come within a row of apple trees of where I really lived. I was so far from being discouraged by my failure to get anywhere that I only dimly realized that anyone else was discouraged by it. This is where the countryman came in: I would work at almost anything rather well for a while, but every once in so often I had to run off for a walk in the woods or for a term's teaching in a lonely district school or a summer's work haying or picking fruit on a farm or cutting heels in a shed by the woods in Salem. Gee Whiz, I should say I was just the most everyday sort of person except for the way I didn't mind looking unambitious as much as you would mind, for example. Of course it's no credit to me. I knew what I was about well enough and was pretty sure where I would come out.

Amy is welcome to make me out anything she pleases. I have decided I like her and, since she likes me, anything she says will do so long as it is entertaining. She has been trying to lay at my door all the little slips she has made in the paper on me. She gets it all wrong about me and Gibson and Abercrombie for example. I knew neither of those fellows till North of Boston was all written. All I wrote in the neighborhood of those two was part of Mountain Interval. I doubt if she is right in making me so grim, not to say morbid. I may not be funny enough for Life or Punch, but I have sense of humor enough, I must believe, to laugh when the joke is on me as it is in some of this book of Amy's.

I really like least her mistake about Elinor. That's an unpardonable attempt to do her as the conventional helpmeet of genius. Elinor has never been of any earthly use to me. She hasn't cared whether I went to school or worked or earned anything. She has resisted every inch of the way my efforts to get money. She is not too sure that she cares about my reputation. She wouldn't lift a hand or have me lift a hand to increase my reputation or even save it. And this isn't all from devotion to my art at its highest. She seems to have the same weakness I have for a life that goes rather poetically; only I should say she is worse than I. It isn't what might be expected to come from such a life—poetry that she is after. And it isn't that she doesn't think I am a good poet either. She always knew I was a good poet, but that was between her and me, and there I think she would have liked it if it had remained at least until we were dead. I don't know that I can make you understand the kind of person. Catch her getting any satisfaction out of what her housekeeping may have done to feed a poet! Rats! She hates housekeeping. She has worked because the work has piled on top of her. But she hasn't pretended to like house-work even for my sake. If she has liked anything it has been what I may call living it on the high. She's especially wary of honors that derogate from the poetic life she fancies us living. What a cheap common unindividualized picture Amy makes of her. But, as I say, never mind. Amy means well and perhaps you will come to our rescue without coming in conflict with Amy or contradicting her to her face.

I wish for a joke I could do myself, shifting the trees entirely from the Yankee realist to the Scotch symbolist.

Burn this if you think you ought for my protection.

Always yours R.

A Way Out

A ONE-ACT PLAY

Having based so large a part of his poetic theory on "the sound of sense" in the dramatic tones of the human voice, Robert Frost quite naturally developed and maintained a lasting wish that someday he himself might achieve success as a dramatist. An early evidence of his leaning toward drama is found in his one-act play, *A Way Out,* first published in 1917 and subsequently produced by Amherst College students in 1919. In 1929, with a preface by Frost, *A Way Out* was reprinted at New York by the Harbor Press as a separate volume.

Preface

Everything written is as good as it is dramatic. It need not declare itself in form, but it is drama or nothing. A least lyric alone may have a hard time, but it can make a beginning, and lyric will be piled on lyric till all are easily heard as sung or spoken by a person in a scene—in character, in a setting. By whom, where and when is the question. By a dreamer of the better world out in a storm in autumn; by a lover under a window at night. It is the same with the essay. It may manage alone or it may take unto itself other essays for help, but it must make itself heard as by Stevenson on an island, or Lamb in London.

A dramatic necessity goes deep into the nature of the sentence. Sentences are not different enough to hold the attention unless they are dramatic. No ingenuity of varying structure will do. All that can save them is the speaking tone of voice somehow entangled in the words and fastened to the page for the ear of the imagination. That is all that can save poetry from sing-song, all that can save prose from itself.

I have always come as near the dramatic as I could this side of actually writing a play. Here for once I have written a play without (as I should like to believe) having gone very far from where I have spent my life.

A WAY OUT

Characters: ASA GORRILL

A STRANGER

Scene: A bachelor's kitchen bedroom in a farmhouse with a table spread for supper. Someone rattles the door-latch from outside. ASA GORRILL, *in loose slippers, shuffles directly to the door and unbolts it. A stranger opens the door for himself and walks in.*

STRANGER [*after a survey*]. Huh! So this is what it's like. Seems to me you lock up early. What you afraid of?

ASA [*in a piping drawl*]. 'Fraid of nothing, because I ain't got nothing—nothing't anybody wants.

STRANGER. I want some of your supper.

ASA. Have it and welcome if it tempts your appetite. You see what it is.

STRANGER [*after looking*]. What is it?

ASA. Well, it's some scrapings of potatoes and string beans from other meals I was warming over. They've got kind of mixed together.

STRANGER. Should think so. What else you got in the house? What you got in here?

ASA. That door's closed with nails. You can't get in there. This is all the room I live in. Here's the cupboard, if you're looking for it. It's bare.

STRANGER [*knocks over a chair as he goes about*]. Got any bread?

ASA [*trembling*]. I don't know what you mean by coming into a person's house as if you owned it. I never was subject to anything like it. If I had some bread, you don't go the right way about to get any.

STRANGER. Cut that. I'm here for business. You're supposed to be poor then?

ASA [*with dignity*]. I am poor.

STRANGER. Sure there's nothing hidden in the mattress—or in that nailed-up room? Oh, I haven't come to kill you for it. I shan't kill you anyway till I have something to go on. You needn't be scared till you're hurt. I only meant your being poor was part of the job if anybody was going to undertake it.

ASA. See here, it's time you told me what your business is in my house or go out. I don't understand a word you say. I ain't been subject to anything like it all these years since Orin died.

STRANGER. Aw, don't whine to me about it. I've heard of you and your brother keeping old-maid's hall over here in this neck of the woods, patching each other's trousers and doing up each other's back hair. Look ahere, old boy, I ain't going to be a mite harder on you than I have to be for my own good. I was passing this way and in trouble and I just thought I'd look in on you and look you over as a possible way out.

ASA. As to that I don't know. I don't know what I might or mightn't do to help a person that didn't come at me wrong and spoke me civil. I think you can't pass this way very often—who does for the matter of that? I don't remember of ever seeing you before. You know me though?

STRANGER. Better than you know me. I only just came to the shoeshop down at the Falls last winter. But I've heard of you times enough. As a matter of fact I wasn't exactly passing: your reputation brought me somewhat off my road. You popped into my head like an idea.

ASA. I'm going to give you some tea before it gets cold and have some myself to steady me. Another time see to it you make a civiler beginning with anybody you're expecting favors of. . . . You take it without milk? Brother and I ain't had no cow since the barn burned down in '98. Brother Orin died the year after that.

STRANGER. For God's sake, what do you live on—nothing but potato mash?

ASA. There again! Criticising! I don't see what there is in that to make you take it the way you do. Where does it pinch you? Shall I give you some?

STRANGER [*pausing as he walks back and forth in perplexity*]. Mash! Don't. Is it pretty generally known you live on potato mash?

ASA. Generally known—

STRANGER. I mean, would it excite suspicion if you gave it up and took to eating mince pie, damn it?

ASA. Excite—

STRANGER. Do you ever have bread?

ASA. When I bake, when I happen to have flour in the house.

STRANGER. Where do you get money to buy flour?

ASA. I sell eggs.

STRANGER. Oh, eggs are at the bottom of it. Nothing unless eggs. God, it's worse than I thought, worse than I bargained for after twenty dollars a week and nobody to take care of but myself. But there's one thing I noticed there: you do go into the village shopping now and then when the hens are laying—when there are eggs. It's not just as if you never bought a thing, nor spoke to a soul.

ASA. You ain't pitying me, be you, mister?

STRANGER. Pitying you! No, I'm pitying myself. You like it all and I shan't. Sit down and let me tell you. I can see you haven't heard. As you see me here, I'm—well, I'm in no position to waste pity on anybody else, or think of anybody else and I'm not going to. You can bank on that. I'm running away from a murder I'm accused of having committed. [ASA *drops his face into his hands on the table and groans.*] And I've turned in here to you for help.

ASA. Oh, I can't have anything to do with this. I never have had no trouble and I ain't a-going to begin now. I'm a peaceable man.

STRANGER. I wasn't intending to give you much choice in the business.

ASA. Oh, but you won't drag me into your crime. After all I've done to keep out of things!

STRANGER. It just shows you—

ASA. You want me to hide you here. Think of it!

STRANGER. I haven't quite decided what I want you to do yet. All is, I've done the deed, they're out after me, I've been zigzagging 'cross country (not daring to use the trains) for three days and now I've hit on you as my only salvation. And I'm going to use you one way or another; so you might as well pick your head up off the table and be a man about it—not a wet dishrag. The cuss of it is I was seen at least once today, walked right out of the woods onto a team full of women and hadn't sense enough to keep to the road as if nothing was up, but dodged back into the woods where I came from. That'll tell 'em I haven't got far off. I've got to think quick, but not too quick. No use losing my head.

ASA. I don't see that there's so very much to think of except a hiding place. I'll hide you for tonight. If I must, I must.

STRANGER. Yes, you must, old boy, or I might kill you. It wouldn't amount to another crime to kill a half man like you. Throw you in extra and call it one crime. Does anyone know for certain you're not a woman in man's clothing anyway? . . . But it's not so simple. Tonight's not all I have to consider. There's other nights coming. Where will I be tomorrow night and the night after that? I'll leave it to you if it's not a puzzler.

ASA. Just as fur as you can get from here, I should think.

STRANGER. I don't know that you know, but it's the fashion nowadays to hide just as near the scene of the crime as you can stay.

ASA. Oh, dear, you don't mean you're thinking of fastening onto me for good and living the rest of your nat'ral life in any concealment I can give you.

STRANGER. Maybe, maybe. I'm out of a good job in the cutting room, anyway. I can't go back there, can I? I'm willing to let you advise me up to any reasonable point. I was thinking how it would be to be you if worst came to worst as it may yet. We might agree to be you turn and turn about, one of us lying up in hiding while the other was out stretching his legs and satisfying the hanker to see folks. The danger there, is that there would be always an extra one around to be discovered. And there are a lot of dangers. It would never do. I should have to trust you too much not to give me away. And we might quarrel as to who had the lion's share of the time out. And then appearing in turn might be almost as risky as side by side. People might be led to see differences that they could only explain on the assumption that you were two instead of one.

ASA. If you're expecting followers, the less noise we make talking the better. What's to hender their being all round the house now and looking in the window? That curtain's no more than a piece of cotton sheet. You can see right through it when the balance of light is on this side from the fire. [*He tucks the sheet in at the edges and corners.*] But say, it comes to me if you could tell me you didn't do this murder— then I shouldn't be doing anything wrong.

STRANGER. I did it fast enough.

ASA. How—how—how— Don't tell me though. I'd best not hear. Do you mean by the cutting room the place where you done it?

STRANGER. Queer codger, aren't you?

ASA. Guess I am.

STRANGER. Say, I've been getting it through my head you must have been the one meant by that hermit article in one of the Boston papers here awhile back—before I came to the Falls. Recollect any one's calling on you with a pencil and a piece of paper held out in front of him so-fashion? Or did he write you up from a safe distance the way Whoses did the North Pole? Great talk he put in your mouth about hermiting—if you were the one. Let's see, what did he say was the matter with you?—crossed in love?

ASA. You've heard that, most like.

STRANGER. I've heard something.

ASA. No, it was Orin that was crossed in love in a manner of speaking. He was promised to a gal who kept him waiting more than fifteen years and then married someone else because she wouldn't come to live in this house till he divided the property with me or bought me out and got rid of me. Orin stood by me; so I stood by him.

STRANGER. You haven't got any real prejudices in favor of this way of living then? I mean you didn't take it up as a man goes into the Methodist Church in preference to the Baptist or the Orthodox?

ASA. Dunno's I did.

STRANGER. What I'm trying to get at is how you look at things—if you look at them.

ASA. As f'r instance?

STRANGER. Well, what do you say about women when they come up in conversation? Supposed to hate 'em?

ASA. I so seldom have occasion to speak of 'em.

STRANGER. Then what do you do when you see 'em? Run? Same as I did today from that carriage-load of 'em.

ASA. Don't know's I run exactly. I'd a leetle rather not meet 'em face to face.

STRANGER. All right, we've got that then. Think the world's a bad place and all that nonsense?

ASA. Sholy it ain't any better'n it ought to be, what with all the killing and the murdering and the whatnot. Now is it? Come.

STRANGER. I was reading where a man living on a farm back like this had a queer religion about inhaling from your own shoes when you took them off to go to bed so's to get back the strength lost by settling in the daytime. And there was something about not having the cow calf when the sun was "in his legs." "Awlmanick" expression—"in his legs." Ain't that right? You see I'm up on some of this already. There were three cities the man could see throwing light on the sky at night, which, being a God-fearing man, he called "the cities of the plain."

According to him they kept getting brighter and brighter attempting like to turn night into day in the face of nature. You could judge how the Lord took it from the way the thunder storms kept increasing in number and destructiveness owing to the attraction of the electricity and the wiring. Stood to reason. Anyway the old man expected nothing but that some night the Lord would fetch up a storm that would wipe out those cities in a blue blaze.

ASA. Wasn't it awful!

STRANGER. It hasn't happened yet. I suppose you've a notion or two like that. But *you* wouldn't know it if you had.

ASA. I don't hold with no such doctrine as that of inhaling from your own shoes, certain.

STRANGER. Ever been heard to say you like the innocent woods and fields and flowers like a poem in print?

ASA. Dunno's I have.

STRANGER. I guess it's just a case of plain damn fool; which ought not to be hard to give an imitation of. I supposed people that lived alone had to have something to say for themselves. But that's what comes of my being all bothered up with literary reading. You haven't got ideas enough to make a hermit's life interesting. And the reporter lied when he said you had. I'll bet he never came nearer than five miles of you. Afraid you'd spoil the story if he came too near. But what gets me is what you say to people in self-defense, ministers for instance, when they tell you you've no right to keep yourself to yourself the way you do. How do you fend 'em off?

ASA. It's so long since I was bothered by anybody I've most forgotten.

STRANGER. I bet you have.

ASA. Orin knew how to send 'em about their business.

STRANGER. Orin by the side of you must have been someone. . . . I guess if I can get the outside appearances right—Oh, one thing more: Neighbor with anyone?

ASA. No, as you may say, no.

STRANGER. Write any letters?—And your handwriting! I'll be sure to forget something in all this rush. Got a pencil? Here's a stub. On that pasteboard box cover. Anywhere. Just your name. Write it two or three times—will you?—as long as it don't cost any more. What— what's that? Asie Gorrill. So it was: seems to me I remember it was Asie. [*After a considering pause, he goes to the window, draws aside the curtain, and looks out.*] Those your pine woods?

ASA. It ain't right, mister, examining into me further and further. You ain't got time to plague me so—not if you're going to save your own skin—not if you're what you are by your own telling.

STRANGER. Never you mind me. You're rich, you old skivins. You own all that timber, and you won't touch it. Pretending to be poor! You're just as two-faced as the next man. I knew I could get something against you to work me up if I tried hard enough. Who are you saving the woods for? Any heirs? Me?

ASA. What does that mean?

STRANGER. It means I ought to kill you and skip the country with it under my arm.

ASA. I shouldn't think you'd feel [*he gulps aloud*] as much like joking as you appear to. Hee, hee.

STRANGER. Asie, I believe you're a bad lot and entitled to no more consideration than any other grown-up man. . . . About my age, though. About my build. All I'd have to do is cave in a little, slump— let my mouth and eyes hang open. Say, push the table back and walk up and down the way you've seen me doing. Them's orders. I'm not inviting you. Do it! . . . I'll thank you for what you have on your feet— slippers is it? How do I know they aren't some I made? Make you a present of my shoes.

ASA. Oh, I shan't need 'em. I mostly go barefoot anyway. I only slipped these on to haul wood.

STRANGER. Oh, wood. How do you haul wood? Wheelbarrow?

ASA. No, I drag it in, in poles two at a time, one under each arm. I take what's died standing—

STRANGER [*going to a bed-post*]. What's all this? Extra togs? Jumper? [*Comparing it with what* ASA *has on.*] Overalls? [*Comparing.*] Watch me! [*Putting on jumper and overalls.*] Light a light, why don't you?

ASA. Oh, I don't allow myself no lamp! I'll throw the stove door open. I can put on some more wood. It's about my bedtime anyway.

STRANGER. I'm putting you to bed tonight. I'm going to let you stay up later than usual on account of company. Now watch me. [*He takes a turn up and down the room.* ASA *stumbles getting out of his way.*] No trouble about the thin voice. [*He speaks more or less in* ASA'S *piping drawl from here on.*] Now I want you should let me show you some- thing that'll amuse and maybe bother you. I'm going to mix us up like your potato and string beans, and then see if even you can tell us apart. The way I propose to do is to take both your hands like this and then whirl round and round with you till we're both so dizzy we'll fall down when we let go. Don't you resist or holler! I ain't a-going to hurt ye—*yet.* Only I've got to get up some sort of excitement to make it easier for both of us. And then when we're down, I want you should wait till you can see straight before you speak and try to tell which is which and which is t'other. Wait some time.

ASA. Let go of me. I know what you be; you're a crazy man from a madhouse.

STRANGER. You'd best humor me then. [*He lifts* ASA'S *hands still higher and stands looking at him. The fire burns brighter and lights them unevenly.*] Old boy!

ASA. What is it?

STRANGER. I'm thinking—

ASA. What?

STRANGER. Old boy, are you happy?

ASA. Oh!

STRANGER. Are you happy? Have you anything to live for? Lord, didn't you ever ask yourself a question like that—with so much time on your hands? I ought not to expect it of you. It will take me to do this thing right when I come into office. Oh, well.

ASA [*looking wildly behind him toward the door*]. I wouldn't have believed it.

STRANGER. What was I telling you! It just shows that if you won't go to life, why life will come to you. I should think a man in your position would have to think such thoughts. I know I should. And you would if you'd ever read so much as a Sunday paper to set you going on them. But I musn't be any longer with you. Come! One, two, three, swing! Swing, damn you! Don't hold back. Faster! . . . Faster! [ASA *moans as he circles. The* STRANGER *moans too. The slippers fly off his feet. After some time they break apart and go to the floor, where they lie, both moaning.*]

FIRST TO SPEAK. I know. I ain't lost track. It's you that done the crime!

SECOND [*screaming*]. It's not! [*He half rises and falls back.*]

FIRST. It is! And I'm not afraid of you any more. You've got to go. God will give me strength to wrastle with a rascal. [*The* SECOND *snarls, throws himself backward, and faints. The* FIRST *strikes him a blow with his fist on the head and drags him across the floor and out of the house. The room is left empty for some time. . . . A loud knock. Another. The door is thrown open. Heads appear in the doorway.*]

A VOICE. Gone to bed, Asie? His fire's lit. He can't be far off. Here he is now. [*The* HERMIT *pushes in past them, breathless, and faces them from the table.*] We're after a man, Asie. You haven't seen him?

ASA. Ain't I, though? He's been and gone.

A VOICE. How long since? Which way?

ASA. Not five minutes. Through the woods. He was dragging me off to kill when he heard you coming and run. I was going to follow, but I gave it up and came back. What's he been up to?

A VOICE. You're no good, Asie.

ANOTHER VOICE. What had you done to him to get him against you?

ASA. You'd better hurry. [*He beats the table with his fist.*]

A VOICE. Someone had better be not too far off so as to take care of Asie. [*They confer, gradually closing the door. The minute they are gone the* HERMIT *snatches the socks off his feet and throws them into the fire. He picks up the pair of shoes on the floor and sends them the same way. He bolts the door softly. He stands listening.*]

SOMEONE [*later, as if repassing, sings out*]. Good-night, Asie!

THE HERMIT [*getting into bed so as to answer with his face in the pillow*]. Good-night.

[CURTAIN.]

Among the Poems He Left Behind

GROUP TWO

Of these three uncollected poems, "The Parlor Joke" is the earliest. Inspired by labor troubles at Lawrence, Massachusetts, during 1909 and 1910, it was first published in *A Miscellany of American Poetry, 1920*. The weather joke entitled "A Correction" is an example of Frost's casual and playful rhyming. It was initially written to serve as a postscript to a letter sent from Franconia, New Hampshire, to George F. Whicher, during the winter of 1920. With Frost's permission, it was first printed in a volume edited by the poet David McCord called *What Cheer: An Anthology of American and British Humorous and Witty Verse . . .* (New York, 1945). "The Middletown Murder" first appeared in *The Saturday Review of Literature* for October 13, 1928.

THE PARLOR JOKE

You won't hear unless I tell you
How the few to turn a penny
Built complete a modern city
Where there shouldn't have been any,
And then conspired to fill it
With the miserable many.

They drew on Ellis Island.
They had but to raise a hand
To let the living deluge
On the basin of the land.

They did it just like nothing
In smiling self-command.

If you asked them *their* opinion,
They declared the job as good
As when, to fill the sluices,
They turned the river flood;
Only then they dealt with water
And now with human blood.

Then the few withdrew in order
To their villas on the hill,
Where they watched from easy couches
The uneasy city fill.
"If it *isn't* good," they ventured,
"At least it isn't ill."

But with child and wife to think of,
They weren't taking any chance.
So they fortified their windows
With a screen of potted plants,
And armed themselves from somewhere
With a manner and a glance.

You know how a bog of sphagnum
Beginning with a scum
Will climb the side of a mountain,
So the poor began to come,
Climbing the hillside suburb
From the alley and the slum.

As their tenements crept nearer,
It pleased the rich to assume,
In humorous self-pity,

The mockery of gloom
Because the poor insisted
On wanting all the room.

And there it might have ended
In a feeble parlor joke,
Where a gentle retribution
Overtook the gentlefolk;
But that some beheld a vision:
Out of stench and steam and smoke,

Out of vapor of sweat and breathing,
They saw materialize
Above the darkened city
Where the murmur never dies,
A shape that had to cower
Not to knock against the skies.

They could see it through a curtain,
They could see it through a wall,
A lambent swaying presence
In wind and rain and all,
With its arms abroad in heaven
Like a scarecrow in a shawl.

There were some who thought they heard it
When it seemed to try to talk
But missed articulation
With a little hollow squawk,
Up indistinct in the zenith,
Like the note of the evening hawk.

Of things about the future
Its hollow chest was full,

(323)

Something about rebellion
And blood a dye for wool,
And how you may pull the world down
If you know the prop to pull.

What to say to the wisdom
That could tempt a nation's fate
By invoking such a spirit
To reduce the labor-rate!
Some people don't mind trouble
If it's trouble up-to-date.

A CORRECTION

When we told you minus twenty
Here this morning, that seemed plenty.
We were trying to be modest
(Said he spitting in the sawdust),
And moreover did our guessing
By the kitchen stove while dressing.
Come to dress and make a sortie,
What we found was minus forty.

THE MIDDLETOWN MURDER

Jack hitched into his sky blue bob
And drove away to the lumber job.

A week was what he had aimed to stay,
And here he was back inside of a day.

Kate came to the door to ask him why.
"To give you another kiss goodbye."

The gun he took to the woods for meat
Came out from under his blanket seat.

Kate tried to laugh at him. "You go long,
And don't be silly. Is something wrong?"

They stood and looked at each other hard,
Kate plainly blocking the door on guard.

Suddenly Jack began to shout:
"I know who's in there. So come on out!"

If someone extra was there with Kate.
He wasn't to be brought out by hate.

(Some people are best brought out by love.
The others you have to drag or shove.)

Then suddenly something frightened Jack,
And sent him shouting around in back.

"Hey, no you don't you goddam snide,
None of your tricks on me," he cried.

Kate cut across the house inside,
Leaving the door of the kitchen wide.

Now three of them choked the door emerging;
You couldn't tell which was pulling or urging.

"In a killer's choice like this of three,
There's some can't tell which it should be;
But I'll soon show you it won't be me.

"You have been my friend; you have eaten my salt;
But this was eating my sugar, Walt.

"The joke's on me for trusting a whore.
Wouldn't it make a rifle roar?

"To pro-long life and humor Kate
I'll give you a start as far as the gate."

He looked at a button along his gun,
But kept from shooting and told him, "Run!"

The first shot fired was over Walt's head.
He still was running; he wasn't dead.

The second shot went by one arm,
The third by the other, and did no harm.

The fourth, and next to last, was low.
Walt felt it under him ploughing snow.

He thought, "I'm running in luck to-day,
I'm getting away—I'm getting away."

Just what to Jack would be meat and drink
To have the galloping bastard think.

All four misses were only art.
The fifth shot fired went through the heart.

The fifth was the bullet that stained his shirt,
And dove him into the snow and dirt.

We call that "bounding a man all round
Before locating his principal town."

"Now, back to your keeping house," Jack said.
"I guess you'd better go make the bed.

"No first you'd better put up your hair.
After that's done we'll see what's fair."

He pulled her in and shut the door,
And wouldn't let her look out any more.

Kate didn't know what the law would say
To a man for killing a man that way.

She hated to be the death of two.
But what was a woman going to do?

Be ready for when the sheriff came,
And say Jack wasn't the one to blame?

The least you could always do was lie
To hurry the day of trouble by;

And it wouldn't be long before you were glad
Of the worst young day you ever had,

It was so much better than any old.
But my, the sheriff would probably scold.

All the sheriff said was, "Cousin Kate,
You're the prettiest black haired girl in the state."

(The township numbered a couple of dozen,
And most of them called each other cousin.)

"I suppose you were born to have your fun,
But in doing to these two what you've done,

"If you wanted to get the good one jailed,
The bad one murdered, you haven't failed.

"I'll do it as gently as I can,
But cousin, I've come to take your man.

"Let it be a lesson to you for life;
Next time you marry, be a wife."

Someone lying stiff in the road
Like a cordwood stick from a farmer's load.

And over him like a frightened dunce
A guide post pointed all ways at once.

No curious crowd had gathered yet,
But a rural letter-box choir quartette

That stood in drift at the crossroads corner.
They had human names like Stark and Warner.

But more like ghouls than men they stood,
As much as singing that bad was good.

"We seem to lack the courage to be ourselves."

AN INTERVIEW

This interview by Rose C. Feld originally appeared in *The New York Times Book Review* for October 21, 1923. It is here reprinted from *Interviews with Robert Frost,* pp. 46–53.

Have you ever seen a sensitive child enter a dark room, fearful of the enveloping blackness, yet more than half ashamed of the fear? That is the way Robert Frost, poet, approached the interview arranged for him with the writer. He didn't want to come, he was half afraid of coming, and he was ashamed of the fear of meeting questions.

He was met at his publisher's office at the request of his friends there. "Come and get him, please," they said. "He is a shy person—a gentle and a sensitive person—and the idea of knocking at your doors, saying, 'Here I am, come to be interviewed,' will make him run and hide." The writer came and got him.

All the way down Fifth Avenue for ten or fifteen blocks he smiled often and talked rapidly to show that he was at ease and confident. But he was not. One could see the child telling itself not to be afraid.

Arrived at the house, he took the chair offered him and sat down rigidly. Still he smiled.

"Go ahead," he said. "Ask me the questions. Let's get at it."

"There are no questions—no specific questions. Suppose you just ramble on about American poetry, about poets, about men of the past and men of the present, about where we are drifting or where we are marching. Just talk."

He looked nonplused. The rigid smile gave way to one of relief and relaxation.

"You mean to say that you're not going to fire machine-gun questions at me and expect me to answer with skyrocketing repartee. Well, I wish I'd known. Well."

The brown hand opened up on the arms of the chair and the graying head leaned back. Robert Frost began to talk. He talked of some of the poets of the past, and in his quiet, gentle manner exploded the first bombshell. He exploded many others.

"One of the real American poets of yesterday," he said, "was Longfellow. No, I am not being sarcastic. I mean it. It is the fashion nowadays to make fun of him. I come across this pose and attitude with people I meet socially, with men and women I meet in the classrooms of colleges where I teach. They laugh at his gentleness, at his lack of worldliness, at his detachment from the world and the meaning thereof.

"When and where has it been written that a poet must be a club-swinging warrior, a teller of barroom tales, a participant of unspeakable experiences? That, today, apparently is the stamp of poetic integrity. I hear people speak of men who are writing today, and their eyes light up with a deep glow of satisfaction when they can mention some putrid bit of gossip about them. 'He writes such lovely things,' they say, and in the next breath add, half worshipfully, 'He lives such a terrible life.'

"I can't see it. I can't see that a man must needs have his feet plowing through unhealthy mud in order to appreciate more fully the glowing splendor of the clouds. I can't see that a man must fill his soul with sick and miserable experiences, self-imposed and self-inflicted, and greatly enjoyed, before he can sit down and write a lyric of strange and compelling beauty. Inspiration doesn't lie in the mud; it lies in the clean and wholesome life of the ordinary man.

"Maybe I am wrong. Maybe there is something wrong with me. Maybe I haven't the power to feel, to appreciate and live the extremes of dank living and beautiful inspiration.

"Men have told me, and perhaps they are right, that I have no 'straddle.' That is the term they use: I have no straddle. That means that I cannot spread out far enough to live in filth and write in the tree-tops. I can't. Perhaps it is because I am so ordinary. I like the middle way, as I like to talk to the man who walks the middle way with me.

"I have given thought to this business of straddling, and there's always seemed to me to be something wrong with it, something tricky. I see a man riding two horses, one foot on the back of one horse, one foot on the other. One horse pulls one way, the other a second. His straddle is wide, Heaven help him, but it seems to me that before long it's going to hurt him. It isn't the natural way, the normal way, the powerful way to ride. It's a trick."

"What is it you teach at Amherst and how?" the writer asked while Mr. Frost was speaking about his students.

"Well, I can't say that you can call it teaching. I don't teach. I don't know how. I talk and I have the boys talk. This year I'm going to have two courses, one in literature and one in philosophy. That's funny. I don't know that I know much about either. That's the reason perhaps that we get along so well.

"In the course in literature we're going to read a book a week. They're not going to be the major authors, the classics of literature, either. They're going to be the minor writers—people that aren't so well known.

"Why do I [do] that? For a reason that I think rather good. Those boys will, in the course of their education, get the first-rank people whether I give it to them or not. That's what education very largely means today—knowing the names that sound the loudest. That's what business means; that's what success means. Well, I'd like to get out of that rut for a while. I'd like to get the boys acquainted with some of the fellows who didn't blow their trumpets so loudly but who nevertheless sounded a beautiful note.

"We're not going to read the works in class; we couldn't do all of that. The boys will do their reading at home. They'll read in class the things that appeal to them most; an incident, a bit of dramatic action. I'll let them read what they wish. And then we'll have some fun in their telling me why they made their choice; why a thing called to them.

"I don't want to analyze authors. I want to enjoy them, to know them. I want the boys in the classes to enjoy their books because of what's in them.

"Here again, perhaps, I am old-fashioned. Youth, I believe, should not analyze its enjoyments. It should live. It doesn't matter what they think Hazlitt thought or tried to do in his works; what matters is the work, the story, the series of incidents. Criticism is the province of age, not of youth. They'll get to that soon enough. Let them build up a friendship with the writing world first. One can't compare until one knows.

"I hope it will work out all right. I don't know. I haven't done just this thing before. I don't like teaching the same thing year after year. You get stale doing that.

"Philosophy—that's another subject that I'm going to teach. Philosophy of what? Of life; of people about you, of course.

"What's my philosophy? That's hard to say. I was brought up a Swedenborgian. I am not a Swedenborgian now. But there's a good deal of it that's left with me. I am a mystic. I believe in symbols. I believe in change and in changing symbols. Yet that doesn't take me away from the kindly contact of human beings. No, it brings me closer to them.

"It's hard to explain this thing; it's hard to talk about it. I don't expect to talk much about it to the boys at college. But I want them to feel that a philosophy of life is something that is not formal, that means delving in books and superimposing on themselves. No, a philosophy of life is an attitude to life.

"Plato doubtless thought that he was discovering something new when he wrote his treatise. He didn't. He gave written expression to an attitude toward life that he had probably found in some of his friends. It wasn't worked out like a problem in mathematics. It grew in men. Men are the important factors to remember. They are the soil which brings forth the fruit.

"One cannot say that the real American poetry is the poetry of the soil. One cannot say it is the poetry of the city. One cannot say it is the poetry of the native as one cannot say it is the poetry of the alien. Tell me what America is and I'll tell you what its poetry is. It seems to me we worry too much about this business. Where there is life there is poetry, and just as much as our life is different from English life, so is our poetry different.

"The alien who comes here for something different, something ideal, something that is not England and not France and not Germany and finds it, knows this to be America. When he becomes articulate and raises his voice in an outburst of song, he is singing an American lyric. He is an American. His poetry is American. He could not have sung that same song in the place from where he hails; he could not have sung it in any other country to which he might have emigrated. Be grateful for the individual note he contributes and adopt it for your own as he has adopted the country.

"America means certain things to the people who come here. It means the Declaration of Independence, it means Washington, it means Lincoln, it means Emerson—never forget Emerson—it means the English language, which is not the language that is spoken in England or her provinces. Just as soon as the alien gets all that—and it may take two or three generations—he is as much an American as is the man who can boast of nine generations of American forebears. He gets the tone of America, and as soon as there is tone there is poetry.

"People do me the honor to say that I am truly a poet of America. They point to my New England background, to the fact that my paternal ancestor came here some time in the sixteen hundreds. So much is true, but what they either do not know or do not say is that my mother was an immigrant. She came to these shores from Edinburgh in an old vessel that docked at Philadelphia. But she felt the spirit of America and became part of it before she even set her foot off the boat.

"She used to tell about it when I was a child. She was sitting on the deck of the boat waiting for orders to come ashore. Near her some workmen were loading Delaware peaches on to the ship. One of them picked out one of them and dropped it into her lap.

"'Here, take that,' he said. The way he said it and the spirit in which he gave it left an indelible impression on her mind.

"'It was a bonny peach,' she used to say, 'and I didn't eat it. I kept it to show my friends.'

"Looking back would I say that she was less the American than my father? No. America meant something live and real and virile to her. He took it for granted. He was a Fourth-of-July American, by which I mean that he rarely failed to celebrate in the way considered proper and appropriate. She, however, was a year-around American.

"I had an aunt in New England who used to talk long and loud about the foreigners who were taking over this country. Across the way from her house stood a French Catholic church which the new people of the village had put up. Every Sunday my aunt would stand at her window, behind the curtain, and watch the steady stream of men and women pouring into church. Her mouth would twist in the way that seems peculiar to dried-up New Englanders, and she would say, 'My soul!' Just that: 'My soul!'

"All the disapproval and indignation and disgust were concentrated in these two words. She never could see why I laughed at her, but it did strike me very funny for her to be calling upon her soul for help when this mass of industrious people were going to church to save theirs.

"New England is constantly going through periods of change. In my own state (in Vermont, I mean) there have been three distinct changes of population. First came the Irish, then the French, and now the Poles.

"There are those among us who raise their hands in horror at this, but what does it matter? All these people are becoming, have become, Americans.

"If soil is sacred, then I would say that they are more godly in their attitude to it. The Pole today in New England gets much more out of his plot of ground than does his Yankee neighbor. He knows how to cultivate it so that each inch produces, so that each grain is alive. Today the Pole may not be aware of the beauty of the old Colonial house he buys and may in some cases desecrate it, but three generations from now, two generations, his children will be proud of it and may even boast of Yankee heritage. It has been done before; it will be done in the future.

"And if there are poets among these children, as surely there will be, theirs will be the poetry of America. They will be part of the soil of America as their cousins may be part of the city life of America.

"I am [im]patient with this jealousy of the old for the young. It is change, this constant flow of new blood, which will make America eternally young, which will make her poets sing the songs of a young country—virile songs, strong songs, individual songs. The old cannot keep them back.

"I was amused years ago by the form this jealousy of tradition will take. One of the most brilliant pupils in the class at college was the son of a Polish farmer. Everybody admitted his mental superiority. But the old New Englanders would not swallow the pill as given. They sugar-coated, by backstairs gossip, which insisted that the real father of the boy must have been a Yankee.

"We are supposed to be a broad-minded country, yet in this respect we are so very narrow. Nobody worries about foreign strains in English or French literature and politics. Nobody thinks that England has been tainted by Disraeli or Zangwill or Lord Reading. They are taken as Englishmen; their works are important as English works. The same is true of French writers of foreign strain. We seem to lack the courage to be ourselves.

"I guess that's it. We're still a bit afraid. America, for instance, was afraid to accept Walt Whitman when he first sang the songs of democracy. His influence on American poetry began to be felt only after the French had hailed him as a great writer, a literary revolutionist. Our own poet had to be imported from France before we were sure of his strength.

"Today almost every man who writes poetry confesses his debt to Whitman. Many have gone very much further than Whitman would have traveled with them. They are the people who believe in wide straddling.

"I, myself, as I said before, don't like it for myself. I do not write free verse; I write blank verse. I must have the pulse beat of rhythm, I like to hear it beating under the things I write.

"That doesn't mean I do not like to read a bit of free verse occasionally. I do. It sometimes succeeds in painting a picture that is very clear and startling. It's good as something created momentarily for its sudden startling effect; it hasn't the qualities, however, of something lastingly beautiful.

"And sometimes my objection to it is that it's a pose. It's not honest. When a man sets out consciously to tear up forms and rhythms and measures, then he is not interested in giving you poetry. He just wants to perform; he wants to show you his tricks. He will get an effect; nobody will deny that, but it is not a harmonious effect.

"Sometimes it strikes me that the free-verse people got their idea from incorrect proof sheets. I have had stuff come from the printers with lines half left out or positions changed about. I read the poems as they stood, distorted and half finished, and I confess I get a rather pleasant sensation from them. They make a sort of nightmarish half-sense."

As he rose to go, he said, "I am an ordinary man, I guess. That's what's the trouble with me. I like my school and I like my farm and I like people. Just ordinary, you see."

Some Observations on Style

"Many sensitive natures have plainly shown by their style that they took themselves lightly in self-defense," wrote Robert Frost to Untermeyer on March 10, 1924 (*The Letters of Robert Frost to Louis Untermeyer*, pp. 165–166). This observation becomes particularly illuminating if it is reconsidered within the context of the following passage which contains it.

[. . .] I have come to the conclusion that style in prose or verse is that which indicates how the writer takes himself and what he is saying. Let the sound of Stevenson go through your mind empty and you will realize that he never took himself other than as an amusement. Do the same with Swinburne and you will see that he took himself as a wonder. Many sensitive natures have plainly shown by their style that they took themselves lightly in self-defense. They are the ironists. Some fair to good writers have no style and so leave us ignorant of how they take themselves. But that is the one important thing to know: because on it depends our likes and dislikes. A novelist seems to be the only kind of writer who can make a name without a style: which is only one more reason for not bothering with the novel. I am not satisfied to let it go with the aphorism that the style is the man. The man's ideas would be some element then of his style. So would his deeds. But I would narrow the definition. His deeds are his deeds; his ideas are his ideas. His style is the way he carries himself toward his ideas and deeds. Mind you if he is down-spirited it will be all he can do to have the ideas without the carriage. The style is out of his superfluity. It is the mind skating circles round itself as it moves forward. Emerson had one of the noblest least egotistical of styles. By comparison with it Thoreau's was conceited, Whitman's bumptious. Carlyle's way of taking himself simply infuriates me. Longfellow took himself with the gentlest twinkle. I don't suppose you know his miracle play in The Golden Legend, or Birds of Killingworth, Simon Danz, or Othere.

I own any form of humor shows fear and inferiority. Irony is simply a kind of guardedness. So is a twinkle. It keeps the reader from criticism. Whittier, when he shows any style at all, is probably a greater person than Longfellow as he is lifted priestlike above consideration of the scornful. Belief is better than anything else, and it is best when rapt, above paying its respects to anybody's doubt whatsoever. At bottom the world isn't a joke. We only joke about it to avoid an issue with someone to let someone know that we know he's there with his questions: to disarm him by seeming to have heard and done justice to his side of the standing argument. Humor is the most engaging cowardice. With it myself I have been able to hold some of my enemy in play far out of gunshot. [. . .]

Education by Presence

AN INTERVIEW

This interview by Janet Mabie was first published on
December 24, 1925, in *The Christian Science Monitor,* under
the title "Robert Frost Interprets His Teaching Method." It is
now reprinted from *Interviews with Robert Frost,* pp. 67–71.

When Robert Frost read at the Institute of Modern Literature at Bowdoin College earlier in the year he suggested, in passing, a new method of instruction, employed by him at Amherst, which he would like to see in more general use in the colleges and which he has taken with him to his new post at the University of Michigan. "Education by presence," he called it, pausing then only to emphasize the obvious effects upon university students of the mere presence among them (upon the campus) of leading scholars in major lines, even if those leaders never took textbook in hand to conduct ordinary courses of classroom instruction.

Robert Frost is a poet. (He is several other things besides, but first of all he is a poet—although it is true that for some time more people knew him as school teacher, rather than poet.) It is not common for poets to have radical ideas upon a subject which has become, on the whole, as standardized as college instruction. Perhaps it is because Mr. Frost is primarily what he is that there is a poetic twist to the method he would like to see used for teaching college students.

Twenty years ago Mr. Frost was a poet. Over a considerable portion of the intervening years he was one of the few people who knew this, he says. Now, although he does not say it, a great many people know it.

In the long years before recognition warranted his choosing the field of poetry above school teaching, Mr. Frost was doubtless busy with considering this plan for education which he has now been willing to discuss with a representative of *The Christian Science Monitor.* Mr. Frost had ample experience with teaching in one way and another. He would not be arbitrary concerning the greater usefulness of the one he is now engaged in; neither is he hesitant about pointing out some advantages he feels it has for his purposes—possibly for the purposes of other teachers as well.

"The most impressive thing in a college career," said Mr. Frost, "is often having over one someone who means something, isn't it? It is hard to tell how teachers act upon a student, but part of their impress must be the effect of their reputations outside the college. Students get most from professors who have marked wide horizons.

"If a teacher is evidently a power outside, as well as inside, the college, one of whom you can hear along other highways, then that teacher is of deep potential value to the students. If the student suddenly finds that the teacher he has perchance listened to with indifferent attention, or not at all, is known all over the country for something not too bad, suddenly his communications take on luster.

"The business of the teacher is, I presume, to challenge the student's purpose. 'This is life, your career is ahead of you,' he must say. 'Now what are you going to do about it? Something large or small? Will you dabble or will you make it a real one?'

"I do not mean the challenge should be made in words. That, I should think, is nearly fruitless. It must soon begin to sound to the students like rote. Besides, a man can't, you know, be forever standing about on a campus crying out at the students, 'What are you going to do about it?' No, what I mean is that his life must say that; his own work must say that.

"My greatest inspiration, when I was a student, was a man whose classes I never attended. The book that influenced me most was *Piers the Plowman*, yet I never read it. When I realized how much the book had influenced me I felt I should read it. But after considering it I decided against reading it, fearing it might not be what I had thought when I started out to do what I have since done—what the book, unread, inspired me to do.

"Everybody knows that there is such a thing as education by presence and has benefited more or less by it. You take my own case, for instance. I never have set up to be a particularly good teacher in regular catch-as-catch-can, catch-them-off-their-guard-three-days-in-the-week classroom work. I refuse to quiz day after day, to follow boys up with questions I myself can answer. I refuse to stand up and lecture a steady stream for fear of the consequences to my character.

"Three days in the week, thirty-five weeks in the year is at least three times as much as I have it in me to lecture on any subject anyway. It is at least three times as often as I have the nerve to face the same audience in a week, and three times as often as I have the patience when I know the audience has been doing nothing to help itself in the intervals between my lectures.

"No, I am an indifferent teacher as teachers go, and it is hard to understand why I am wanted around colleges unless there is some force it is thought I can exert by merely belonging to them. It must be that what I stand for does my work.

"I am right in the middle of certain books; that is to say, I have written four of them and expect to write about four more. Well, these books, as much the unwritten as the written, are what I am to the college. If teaching is, as I say, asking rather than answering questions, my books do most of mine with very little help from me. Or so I like to think.

"What I am saying is that there are and always have been three ways of teaching, namely, by formal contact in the classroom, by informal contact, socially as it were, and by virtually no contact at all. And I am putting the last first in importance—the teaching by no contact at all.

"I have always thought a man's chief strength came from being able to say (after St. Paul and Kipling) 'Of no mean city am I'—of no mean college am I—speaking intellectually. It must mean something to the student to be aware of the distinguished research scholars around him. For my part I am helped by the thought of the artists who are my fellow citizens. It is encouraging to belong in the same circle with people who see life large.

"The teacher who has student contacts which are but informal—extra-class, say—fills a spacious place in the student's needs. Perfect informality of contact is in offering oneself as someone the student may like to show his work to. Men have come to me with paintings, because they felt my sympathy with anything they might do, even though it was frequently intrinsically something I knew little about. The college, I think, could be partly built, in the upper tier, of teachers who offered themselves or were offered thus.

"By 'upper tier' I mean a few of the teachers could be offered wholly this way and all of the teachers more or less. Every teacher should have his time arranged to permit freer informal contacts with students. Art, the various sciences, research, lend themselves to this treatment.

"You could perfectly well build an institution on informal contacts. I'd give every teacher who wanted it—who could be happy in it; who wouldn't despise it—a chance at this informal teaching. Some I'd give more; some I'd give less. Some I'd give—isn't there a phrase, 'nothing else but'?

"Half the time I don't know whether students are in my classes or not; on the other hand, I can stay with a student all night if I can get where he lives, among his realities. Courses should be a means of introduction, to give students a claim on me, so that they may come to me at any time, outside of class periods. If the student does not want to press his claim, well, for him I must give an examination. But he has already lowered his estimation. The student who does not press his claim has to that extent been found wanting. I favor the student who will convert my claim on him into his claim on me.

"I am for a wide-open educational system for the free-born. The slaves are another question. I will not refuse to treat them as slaves wherever found. 'Those who will, may,' would be my first motto; but my close second, 'Those who won't, must.' That is to say, I shouldn't disdain to provide for the slaves, if slaves they insisted on being. I shouldn't anyway unless I were too busy with the free-born.

"One mark of the free-born, however, is that he doesn't take much of your time. All he asks of his teacher is the happiness of being left to his own initiative, which is more of a tax on the teacher's egotism than on the teacher's time. Give me the high-spirited kind that hate an order to do what they were about to do of their own accord.

"It is amusing the way your best-laid plans go wrong in dealing with a class or audience. An examination often turns into an examination of the teacher's ability to ask questions clearly.

"I recently was compelled to give an examination, since such must be. In my classroom at the appointed time I said, 'Do something appropriate to this course which will please and interest me.' (It was a course in literature. There had been a wide choice of books.) I left the room.

"I thought probably three or four would get up and go home, thinking I already knew them well enough, that I already had their grades ready anyhow to hand in at the office. I thought others would come to me, a little later, and take it out in talk. I placed a limit upon them of four bluebooks, and you know perfectly well no one ever wrote four bluebooks in Amherst College; but I hoped some poor boy might write four in order to convince himself was doing everything he should.

"I went away, upstairs. Presently one after the other, 'the whole kit and caboodle,' came ambling upstairs and waited their turns to say something pleasant to me in parting. That's the way they understood the word 'please' in my leading question. You never can tell what you have said or done till you have seen it reflected in other people's minds.

"We haven't talked of formal classroom teaching. There, I suppose, it is the essence of symposiums I'm after. Heaps of ideas and the subject matter of books purely incidental. Rooms full of students who want to talk and talk and talk and spill out ideas, to suggest things to me I never thought of. It is like the heaping up of all the children's hands, all the family's hands, on the parental knee in the game we used to play by the fireside."

"It is an ancient friend of yours. . . ."

SIX RHYMED LETTERS

Occasionally, when in a playful mood, Robert Frost sent to his friends rhymed notes or letters, and six examples of such are given in this section. The first was written in 1902 or 1903 to Carl Burell whom Frost had known from high school days in Lawrence, Massachusetts, and is in the nature of an apology. It would seem that Burell, then living in Suncook, New Hampshire, had invited Robert and Elinor Frost to visit him at the time of a "flower convention"—perhaps a wild-flower exhibition in which Burell planned to participate. Apparently Frost, after failing to make a timely response, sent these humorous lines to C. B. (or "Coebee") by way of belated apology, giving to Mrs. Frost a flower name: "the Derry Gentian." The manuscript is preserved in the Dartmouth College Library, and it is now reprinted from its initial publication in *Robert Frost: The Early Years,* p. 551.

To Coebee;—
If I remember straightly
Me and the Derry Gentian
Got a formal invite lately
To attend a flower convention
('Twas the letterhead of Gately
I may casually mention)[.]
We were disappointed greatly
But the limits of our pension

And the said flower[']s backward condition
And a hatch of eggs impending

Complicated our position:
We couldn't think of attending.
There warnt no use in wishing
Nor Monstr' inform' ingend-'ing,
So with your kind permission
We staid and did fence mending.

If again you should require us
To help you make a showing
Come out openly and hire us—
At least pay our fare going.
Then if you want to fire us
You'll feel free[-]er to do the toeing.
But be sure and not desire us
When the Gentian isn't blowing.

The second rhymed letter, or draft thereof, is entirely
different in form. It was written at the Derry farm in 1907,
near the close of a particularly hard winter during which
Frost had been seriously ill with pneumonia. It is, manifestly,
a parody of Coleridge's famous "Rime," even to the provision
of shoulder notes. The text is here transcribed from the
original holograph, located within the Barrett Collection of
the University of Virginia Library.

The ancient friend
begins to explain
why he hasn't
written sooner.

It is an ancient friend of yours
And he taketh a minute or two
To tell you how the business goes
And how the family do.

A blizzard freezes
him to the
gizzard.

Down dropped the leaves the nuts dropped down
Merrily did we enter
The time of snow, until one blow
It froze us to the center.

(346)

The sink re-
gurgitates and
the apple onions
and potatoes goe.

Fur thinking caps

Zeroism kills
the time-killer
and the rain
comes down
dry.

Ineffectualness
of the makers
name and 'patent
applied for' on the
Yankee notion.

Bugs

The cow gradually
goes dry.

Winter should
be taken like
a toddy.

Three days it shook the house and it
Was tyrannous and strong
It froze the cellar it froze the sink
We had to wear fur caps to think
And for the south did long.

Alone alone all all alone
Alone on a windy hill
With water water everywhere
And never a drop to spill.
The question was would the time kill us
As we the time did kill.

A dreary time a dreary time
We drank the cider potion
As idle as the makers name
Upon a Yankee notion

And some in dreams persuaded were
And some in common séance
That the fiends that else must have gotten a hold
By naught but the utter absolute cold
Were kept in a state of abeyance.

Nine fathoms deep they were kept asleep
As deep as the frost in Siberia
And some were blobs and some were worms
But all were small for they were the germs
Of pneumonia and diptheria.

But I cannot agree with the germ theoree
And I'll take my winters hot
Un-Pasteurized by zeroic nights
A little rather than not.

Since then I have strange power of speech
That makes me prose in verses

He cannot
pray.

But when I try to speak aloud
It takes the form of curses
Plain oathes with me—with the women folk
My goodnesses and mercies.

Inelastic
currency
as much to
blame as
anything.

The Hermit good lived where he could
I would be down in the tropics
Where there are no gales of coughter more
But I cannot muster the kopecks

The third example, "For Allan . . . ," is actually a Christmas greeting to a small boy, Allan Neilson, son of President William Allan Neilson of Smith College. Obviously, the youngster had indicated a desire to know how Robert Frost wrote his poems. The text, until now unpublished, was written out by the poet, in or shortly after 1917, on a card which also bears a mounted sketch by Frost's daughter Lesley, depicting a field and grove of trees. The original is in the Dartmouth College Library.

For Allan
Who wanted to see how I wrote a poem.

Among these mountains, do you know,
I have a farm, and on it grow
A thousand lovely Christmas trees.
I'd like to send you one of these,
But it's against the laws.
A man may give a little boy

A book, a useful knife, a toy,
Or even a rhyme like this by me
(I write it just like this you see).
But nobody may give a tree
Excepting Santa Claus.

Robert Frost

Fourth is a rhymed thank-you letter written from South Shaftsbury, Vermont, on October 26, 1931, to Frost's long-time friend Louis Untermeyer, acknowledging the gift of a telescope and tripod. It is quoted from *The Letters of Robert Frost to Louis Untermeyer,* pp. 215–216.

Dear Louis:

The telescope has come and I am charmed.
I don't see how on earth I ever farmed
A day without a tool so all important.
I have to tell you though (perhaps I oughtn't)
That come to get the barrel up and pointed
I can't see Hoover as the Lord's annointed;
I can't see E. A. Robinson's last book—
As yet—I'll have to have another look.
At first I couldn't even see the moon.
And that not just because there wasn't one;
There was, according to the almanac.
One whole night I was pretty well set back.
Perhaps the object glass demanded dusting
Or the small lenses needed readjusting.
Perhaps as in the picture I'm inclosing

Some question of the day was interposing
Between me sinful and my hope of heaven.
But never mind, I didn't blaspheme even.
I had one of the two things Shakespeare wanted most.
Write on my tombstone for post-mortem boast:
I had—I had the other fellow's scope.
I need nobody else's art, I hope.

[. . .] R.F.

In a sense, the fifth example is also a letter of thanks. The
poet Robert Hillyer had defended Frost against various
critics in an article ironically titled "Robert Frost 'Lacks
Power,'" which appeared in *The New England Quarterly* for
April 1932. Frost made no immediate expression of his
gratitude, but he did ultimately send to Hillyer the following
humorous acknowledgment, the original manuscript of
which, in an envelope postmarked September 28, 1932, is
part of the C. Waller Barrett Collection at the University of
Virginia Library. It has never before been published. The
frame of reference used by Frost is Hillyer's *The Coming
Forth by Day* (1923), with direct quotes from the book,
playful allusions to gods treated therein, and special focus
on the Egyptian concept of immortality through the retention
or remembrance of one's name.

A Restoration

In the dark moment on the Eastern Stairs,
I had one of my characteristic scares.
On feeling in my soul I missed my name.
(I'd swear I had it on me when I came.)
'Twas when the gods began to brag of theirs.

Without my name in this place, I could see
I should be no one—simply nobodee.
Incontinently I became outpourous:
["]O Ra Rah Rah, Osiris and O Horus,
Oh let my name be given back to me![”]
"You're sure you didnt lose it through a hole,"
Osire suggested. "N'Osire it was stole."
A female voice piped up "What's all the crisis?
Is something missing?" I replied "Aye, Aye-sis
My name is missing. Someone's picked my soul."
On the last Staircase, my but what a row.
Someone to calm me asked me with a bow
Was this nym I was after just my pseudo.
I only shouted louder "No, my Kudo.
I want my name back and I want it now."
The Ra Rah Rah King summoned Robert Hillyer
["]Do something to abate this clamor will yer?
Find and restore this fellow's Kudonym.[”]
And Robert did it, glory be to him.
Oh what a friend to have for my familiar.

R. Frost

The final specimen is yet another letter of thanks. In 1936
Leonard Bacon published a witty, satirical volume of verse,
Rhyme and Punishment, which he dedicated to Robert Frost.
Frost's acknowledgment, dated January 24, 1937, amounts
to a light-hearted parody of the wonderfully outrageous
hyperdithyrambic meters employed by Ogden Nash, who had
playfully made the claim that he had drawn inspiration from
Julia A. Moore (1847–1920), the "Sweet Singer of
Michigan." This Frost–Bacon communication initially
appeared in *Selected Letters of Robert Frost,* pp. 439–440.

Dear Leonard Bacon:

I don't know whether you are in this world or in the Old
But I wanted to tell you before what is between us gets too cold
How much moral satisfaction not to say pleasure I took in your
                                    punishing rhymes.
I can see you feel pretty much as I do about these provocative times.
Neither of us would be driven to drink by them nor to suicide
But that we find them rather too diverting from our preferred
                                    pursuits cannot be denied.
Still we wouldn't have missed them, would we, by any of the close
                                    calls we have ever had?
For my part I have got more out of the last four years perhaps
                                    than out of any previous Olympiad.
The only exception to our almost absolute unanimity
Is the way you ride the Methodists to an extremity.
As a good Congregationalist out of Peace Dale, I take it you are
                                    willing to interpose the Episcopalian
Between our Puritan institutions and the none too sympathetic
                                    Catholic alien.
But after using the Episcopalian in their way you have him on
                                    your hands unless you are foxy
Enough to bring in Methodism to render him harmless to our
                                    Orthodoxy.
Set an Anglican to catch a Roman and a Chapel-goer to catch an
                                    Anglican
And I don't see how the good old world can ever again be stolen
                                    from the honest man.
I'd say we called a meeting and organized a party to promote our
                                    politics
But I know myself too well; I have had that idea before and it
                                    never sticks.

(352)

There may be a show-down coming, but if there is, we'll just have
to wait for the day
Before we go to Abercrombie and Fitch's to outfit for the fray.
I rely on the large number of our kind there must be in a country
like this that don't easily get worked up and excited.
They can stand no end of being left out of account and slighted
They even enjoy looking unimpressive
To the truculent and aggressive.
But there's a concentrated something in them away at the core
That I'd advise anybody to look out for if it ever comes to a war.
No there's nothing that we can do for the present except write
poems and farm
And meet in some quiet place like Franconia for a talk next
summer—that couldn't do any harm.
Don't think I got this trick of rhyme without much obvious metre
from Ogden Nash, dod rot it.
No I got it from the Sweet Singer of Michigan where he is honest
enough to acknowledge he got it.

Ever yours Robert Frost

"Still your teacher! But I must desist."

COACHING A YOUNGER WRITER

During the greater part of his life, Robert Frost devoted much energy to encouraging aspiring poets, and one might cite in this connection the Introduction he contributed to *The Arts Anthology: Dartmouth Verse 1925,* a volume of undergraduate poetry assembled and published by a group of students at Dartmouth College. His text began:

"No one given to looking under-ground in spring can have failed to notice how a bean starts its growth from the seed. Now the manner of a poet's germination is less like that of a bean in the ground than of a waterspout at sea. He has to begin as a cloud of all the other poets he ever read. That can't be helped. And first the cloud reaches down toward the water from above and then the water reaches up toward the cloud from below and finally cloud and water join together to roll as one pillar between heaven and earth. The base of water he picks up from below is of course all the life he ever lived outside of books.

"These, then, are the three figures of the waterspout and the first is about as far as the poet doomed to die young in everyone of us usually gets. He brings something down from Dowson, Yeats, Morris, Masefield, or the Imagists (often a long way down), but lifts little or nothing up. If he were absolutely certain to do as doomed and die young, he would hardly be worth getting excited over in college or elsewhere. But you can't be too careful about whom you will ignore in

this world. Cases have been known of his refusing at the
last minute to abdicate the breast in favor of the practical[,]
and living on to write lyric like Landor till ninety.

"Right in this book he will be found surviving into the second
figure of the waterspout, and, by several poems and many
scattered lines, even into the third figure. [. . .]"

An entirely different, yet thoroughly representative, set of
insights concerning Robert Frost's sympathetic attitude
toward younger writers is provided by a group of hitherto
unpublished letters (preserved at Dartmouth College) written
over a period of nearly three decades to Charles H. Foster.

When the correspondence began, Charles Foster had just
finished his junior year at the Peddie School in New Jersey.
The young man had been brave enough to enclose with his
initial letter to Frost a few of his own poems. He said,
moreover, that he hoped he might enter Amherst College in
the fall of 1932 and that he liked to imagine he might prove
to have Frost as one of his teachers. Responding under date
of July 6, 1931, the poet offered brief but genuine
encouragement.

My DEAR BOY: There is much that is imaginative in your poetry
already. Make the most of your imagination. Remember what you think
in a poem is never as important as what you imagine.

ALWAYS YOUR FRIEND ROBERT FROST

Soon after Charles H. Foster was settled as a freshman at
Amherst College in the autumn of 1932, he found the

courage to seek out Robert Frost's home, to knock on the door, and indeed to offer an original quatrain as his "calling card." Frost cordially welcomed him, and during this visit the chief subject of their conversation was the young man's own poetry. Thus began a friendship which developed steadily in the years that immediately followed.

During the summer vacation of 1933, Foster wrote Frost and said he had been reading, among other things, A. E. Housman's newly published lecture, *The Name and Nature of Poetry,* "and didn't agree with him much." Frost, familiar with the contents of Housman's little book, shared his own reservations in a reply written from South Shaftsbury, Vermont, on July 28, 1933.

DEAR FOSTER: Housman is no sage whatever else he is. His prose on poetry makes a fool book. His showy modesties are all the most arrant conceit. What he is sweating to praise in all that talk about poetry sans mind is Housman. He achieves a minimum of mind by writing his poetry as out of adolescent pessimism and for the rest staying all his life a philologist. Dont let him bother you.

You may say safely enough a poem is a mood if you carefully mean by that it begins in mood and embodies mood. But the body has to be mentioned in the specifications. The body is words phrases things ideas (metaphors) and dramatic tones of voice—not to say meter and stanza.

Walter Prichard Eaton said to me only day before yesterday that his father objected to the word crow in a poem. The bird had be a raven to be poetical. Then to my surprise he defended his father: whose reason he claimed was a good reason namely that poetry had to show loftiness.

There lurks another fallacy. Poetry has to heighten—poetry is the act of heightening not taking advantage of what has already been elevated by previous poets. How heightened? By perpetual play of every faculty of art imagination and figurativeness that heaven bestows.

You have to look out for these shallow fellows—Yes and these deep fellows. Think for yourself. Concentrate poetry. That's the word for you—concentrate. Gather yourself for effort and concentrate the product.

We are fairly quiet. You read Plato. I have read nothing but a little Gibbon. I picked five kinds of wild fruit on the place in one day lately. strawberries, red raspberries, black caps blueberries and checker-berries.

EVER YOURS ROBERT FROST

Continuing his conversations with Frost as soon as he returned to Amherst, Foster discovered that his mentor did not share in the general enthusiasm being accorded the poetry of Paul Engle, whose volume entitled *American Song: A Book of Poems* had appeared in the spring of 1934. By way of argument, Foster apparently persuaded Frost to re-read *American Song,* and the result was the following letter, postmarked September 12, 1934.

DEAR CHARLES: Forgive me for not having written you the letter I intended to write about Paul Engel when I should have read him fairly. Before we try him we have to ask ourselves how good we want him to be at his age. He strikes me as both too loud and too long. But then strength may be manifested by loudness and length. I hate to think so. Nevertheless it may be. Lets give the boy a chance. At least he is manly unaffected and unprecious. He hews the wood that someone to come after him or he himself in a later phase will carve fine. I should like to deal with him generously you may imagine for the country's sake. Another good thing about him is his love of his country. It is about time some one turned up in our literature of a disposition not to complain of whats set before him. All times all countries all people are bad. Oh yeah! So are they all good. It doesnt take rank as an idea to put it either way. And I should rather imply it than say it outright either way. But I confess I have had enough of the divine unrest and dissatisfaction habituals. I've had too much. I may like to tell myself scarey bedtime stories for the bad dreams that will result. I like sinister effects. I even like sordid effects. But you have to allow and provide for effects wearing out. They arent effects unless contrasted well and often. With me it has to be every few days or even hours. I'm the opposite with effects to what I am with friends. Friends are forever: but the one thing about artistic effects is not to get bogged down in them. Keep your extricativeness working. I have never really lived with the sordidities of my time. I havent objected to having them there to resort to for their sensation when I wanted it. But a good deal of the time I have forgotten them. I really rather dislike them for being so much on principal and professionally what they are. And I dont mind seeing them go out of style—if they are going. The rise of Paul Engle may mean that we are in for a less belly aching generation. From what I hear people say, he is being taken as part of the new gospel of American Facism. Amusing— fun—and all that—but of course entirely beside the point.

The still small voice is all I am susceptible to. Lets see what you can give us.

I have had a lot to think of this year. You must realize that. I've had to neglect friends. Pretty soon Ill be back in Amherst and we'll be seeing each other again. I'll bet you'll have become such a social worker you want to take me in hand to do me good. I was asked by one of the departments in Washington the other day what me and my fellow crafts men would like done for us. What would we? I for one would like to be improved in all my faculties.

Ever yours R.F.

The little poems are good. They are still flung too free. You must clench them. You know that in theory. Practice it. Silence used to help me—not saying a word for whole days.

Foster's own verse continued to improve. He was awarded the Collins Armstrong Poetry Prize at Amherst in both his junior and senior years (on neither occasion was Robert Frost one of the judges), and for the graduation of his class in 1936 he was honored by being designated Ivy Poet.

Foster was well aware, however, that he could not earn a living through his poetry. At first he was encouraged by Frost to resist the ordeal of undertaking graduate work in order to prepare himself for college teaching, but Frost's attitude was subsequently modified after he received a letter from Professor Norman Foerster, Director of the School of Letters at the State University of Iowa. Foerster had written to invite Robert Frost to give a public reading at Iowa City. Frost, in discussing the invitation with an Amherst colleague, learned that Foerster was in fact heading up a program that awarded advanced degrees to young writers on the basis of offerings of original poetry or prose, in lieu of a thesis. Responding, Frost declined the invitation to speak, but he took occasion to recommend Charles H. Foster as a candidate for graduate work in Iowa's School of Letters. Professor Foerster thereupon replied, "My guess is that Charles Foster is our sort. Writers with ability are allowed to substitute creative or

critical things for the conventional dissertation, both M.A. &
Ph.D. Along with study, he would probably enjoy helping with
[the newly established journal of critical and imaginative
writing] *American Prefaces*. If he will give me his address, I
will send information." Frost forwarded this letter in writing to
Foster under date of December 18, 1935.

DEAR CHARLES: Unless your other advisers are against it, I think we
have here (in the enclosed) the solution of your life problem. Thank
Roy Elliot for suggesting Norman Foerster. I described you as a poet
who would like to get his last two degrees in making poetry. It will be
very interesting to me to see you through this experiment. You may
prefer to shade the undertaking into something in prose related to
poetry. Tell Foerster your hopes. But dont mix them with your fears.
You have suffered enough indeci[s]ion[s] around Amherst without
carrying them to your new field. You might well venture to candidate in
poetry outright. You will surely in the natural course of your mind
write quantity enough. Out of quant[it]y quality. Your final collection
or rather selection would be your bid for passage I suppose. It would
be very novel. Perhaps you would be the first person in the world to take
a doctor's degree in actually writing verse. But you do as you please or
as you and Foerster agree on. Isn't it fine to have the worries over?

One word of advice in parting: you must try to go deeper and deeper
in the thought part. The great thing is to have something happen, an
event, an action in a poem. (See George Herberts The Pulley.) But
there must be a thought stiffening in it too. You've got to refrain from
saying the common places of wisdom and reason and damn yourself
back till you break out in little bits all your own—little get-ups. Make a
business for a while of having ideas. You might well have ten or a dozen
this winter Send them to me and I will tell you how relatively good they
are. Emerson built his essays out of note-book ideas like that.

I didnt get south scathless. I'm in bed with a cold here in the Webster Hotel in New York. I hope to be well enough to take the Orange Blossom Special for Coconut Grove Fla. on Friday. My address there will be 3670 Avacado Ave.

ALWAYS YOURS ROBERT FROST

Foster reacted favorably to the suggestion. Soon after he received word that he had been admitted to Iowa's unusual program, he sent some of his "little get-ups" to Frost, who responded on March 1, 1936, from Harvard, where he had just begun to serve as Charles Eliot Norton Lecturer in Poetry.

DEAR CHARLES: The poem gets better as you get it squeezed down. It looks as if you might prove a genuine case of natural facility and acquired difficulty. I dont know that I ever met a sure one before. You've got to make it harder and harder for yourself in speech and writing. You see that and you have gone about it. The pensees you sent are for you to judge as you look back at them in six months, a year, two years. You will decide some are empty, others not original, a few substantial and all your own. We must see each other this spring. I shall probably be in Amherst two or three times. Perhaps when I have got acclimated here at Cambridge you and Doris will drive down to see us. I am not feeling very fit for the job. I wasted a lot of time in Florida getting over a cold and I got an intestinal grippe bug the minute I got back to N.Y. What the Hell is the matter with me do you as a Christian suppose?

You may have noticed I have a book coming out and it is already named, whether it prove a boy or a girl, A Further Range. Dont buy a copy and you may get one given you.

Im glad it is all right with Foerster. He will be a salutary friend. But persuade him to let you write your short poems for him. The epic will come in later. I understand one of the publishers is starting an epic department. We may be in for an epic age.

EVER YOURS ROBERT FROST

> Although Foster's application for admission at Iowa had been
> accepted long before the beginning of the 1936 fall term,
> the young man began to experience misgivings and was
> ultimately quite undecided about whether he really should
> go. (Foster had by now married and was temporarily working
> at the Plimpton Press in Norwood, Massachusetts—a
> position Frost had helped him secure.) Frost, surprised by
> his young friend's uncertainty and annoyed by accounts of
> family pressures that had been brought to bear, expressed
> unrestrained impatience on July 19, 1936.

DEAR CHARLES: I'm glad you are taking your job and your medicine like a married man. Take them as seriously as you please, but learn never to take me seriously either for or against. I didnt of course mean it if I said that I depended on you to represent me at the Plympton Press. I dont depend on you for anything but friendship and dont you ever anymore depend on me for anything but reading your verse. You can always count on me to be interested in that as long as you write it. But I'm not now and I never really was interested in your way of life. You've got to brace up and take your life in your own hands. I dont care a hang whether you get two three or a dozen more degrees to satisfy your father. The more I see into your relations with him the more I see you are none of my business. You mustn't play my ideas off against his. I dont like to be used that way. As I think I must have said more than once before the fact that you have had to reason about running wild shows that you should stick to the life of reason. Dont feel condemned in the verdict of my words which are no more than the verdict of your own nature. There are poets of reason no less renowned than of unreason. It may well be the only poetry you could write would be out of the staid and academic. Why fuss and hesitate? You cant more than lose your life anyway as I used to tell myself. Most lives are meant to be lost. At least any that are found have to be lost first. You must try to get my position clear in your head. You can be anything you please for all of me. I dont want to be made at all responsible for you. You wouldnt want to make me now would you, come to think it over. And you mustnt tell me of your fathers bids against me again. He seems to be a threatener. I'm not. You lose nothing by not consulting me further about your future. You keep my friendship and my interest in your verse whether you go to college or go into business. So cheer up and dont continue to think me hard to please.

EVER YOURS RF

Foster concluded to follow through with his plan for graduate work, and he did enter Iowa in the fall of 1936. A few weeks later he wrote to Frost and, apparently, said he hoped the poet had not been worrying about him. Frost answered from Amherst on December 5, 1936.

DEAR CHARLES: You'll begin to wonder what in the world of art and education has become of me. I've been neglecting everything and everybody with great impartiality. Doctor's orders. I had bad shingles which, I'm told, you cant have except from worry. I must have worried about you without knowing it. I can think of nothing else I had to worry about. Maybe there's some mistake. I always say there are five things to do about life, laugh cry swear pray and worry; and I should have claimed that the one I did least of was worry. I don't concede that I have worried about you even. So set your conscience at rest. I'm sure that if you are going to be a poet you will be a poet. You will draw up into an attitude of your own toward things and from there strike and strike again. There must be some truth you want to have so in spite of the crowd[.] Someday you'll find that prejudice speaking out of your verse and then it will be poetry. Meanwhile be as important in your ideas as original as you can concentrate force to be. And dont worry. I wont if you wont. No one ever yet worried himself into art.

I'll bet you have a fine time with Norman Foerster. He has the large spirit. I couldn't wish you in better company. Remember me to him.

A.E's son acting for a publisher, is on the hunt for a man who is at once a farmer a character and a writer. I know people who combine the first two. I hope to find him someone who combines all three. Henry Wallace has tried and failed. I think Henry Wallace should be ashamed—to have had a farm magazine in his family three generations and not developed or discovered the right kind of man—not one case of him in sixty years. By a character we mean a philosopher moralist poet. I suppose what we are after is a rare bird. Only once in a thousand years do you get a criminal a character and a writer in one. Villon—Verlaine—Poe. Still we've got to find a farmer-character-writer or bust. Iowa is a hopeless field of research. The farmers out there all have the grievance of huge turnover and no profit. A young friend of Henry Wallace's and mine out there has a farm turnover of 32,000 and nothing to show for it. Lets see what we can do in New England. Now I wish you were a farmer. You are a character already. Yes and a writer. Im sure of it.

Our best to you and Doris.

EVER YOURS ROBERT FROST

Very soon, however, Frost began to fear that perhaps too many experts at the University were giving Foster too much advice on how to improve the poetry the young man was writing there. When Foster relayed some of the suggestions made to him and asked for comments, Frost wrote as gently as he could on this subject, in a letter dated September 11, 1937.

DEAR CHARLES: I must write you the letter you bespoke, though I confess my not knowing exactly where you are, literally or figuratively, nowadays makes your image a dimmer and so harder mark to shoot at. You are in the hands of many masseurs moulding you. One will tell you one thing, another another. The question for you is whether there is such a thing as being corrected into shape. You've probably thought of that and decided to take the risk. My heart will always be with you hoping for your ultimate success. I cant seem to be bothered about your details any more than about the details of the present political fight. All I care about is who wins. In that respect I have much in common with the stamp-collectivist James Farley. I am waiting to see whether or not we will be engulfed. You must try hard to win if only for my sake. I love a knock out and I hate a referees decision. If I might interpose a suggestion, I still feel that the validity of your figure leaves something to be desired. The validity the wholeness, the slam. I mean of course the implied figure as well as the express. I am always anxious about your subject matter. However delicate, it must be substantial. I dont assume for a moment that your momentousness depends on your way of life. We all have weight of experience whatever we do. We can't escape having. They are fools who seek to have. But the art is to throw your weight into things. It's a lifelong study. To the end some of it gets left out. Otherwise there would be the disillusion of having got to the bottom of life. You understand I am not talking of philosophical depth. Nor of muddy depth. And then there is emotion to remember. You've got to drag and scrape across the heart strings, Mr Israfel. Suppose at this point you decided abruptly to throw all merely acquired skill to the winds or rather let it sink where it wants to sink into the subconscious—out of the mind—trusting it now to have become second nature and set yourself to make people very glad or very sorry. It's worth thinking of. I mean once in a while in the middle of being corrected into shape. You know how I always speak and write, subject to being disregarded in the cause of real art.

Ever yours Robert Frost

As Foster continued the work for his doctorate at Iowa, also doing part-time teaching at the University, he did indeed seem to disregard much that Frost had said to him about the cause of real art. In his letters Foster frankly admitted he was enjoying academic life so much that he hoped Frost would not mind if he became a full-time teacher instead of a full-time poet. He took the regular M.A. and Ph.D. examinations in English at Iowa in 1937, and was permitted to submit a book of poems, *For Any Saint,* in place of a master's thesis. But he disappointed Frost by abandoning the proposed plan for his offering a manuscript volume of lyrics as a substitute for a doctoral dissertation. Instead, by way of compromise, he chose Emerson's theory of poetry as the subject of his prose dissertation, and shortly before Christmas in 1939 Frost wrote, somewhat resignedly, to acknowledge the receipt of Charles Foster's dissertation— and of a new poem.

Dear Charlie: That was a nice reasonable way to get out of it on your doctorate. I liked your part in it, the idea of putting Emerson together some more even as he put himself together. Your justifying preface was good. Be careful lest I come to think you do prose better than poetry.

The last poem you sent lingers in my mind as having yielded too weakly to the easy rhyme. You must yet have it out with yourself there. After all is said, the most important thing about a poem (as it seems to me at the moment) is how willfully gracefully naturally entertainingly and beautifully its rhymes are taken. The poet must give the effect of having had his wayward way with them. Well well here I am laying it down to you again.

Let me rather wish you both a happy Christmas.

EVER YOURS ROBERT FROST

During the next few years, as Foster became more involved with academic matters and apparently less concerned with writing poetry, his correspondence with Frost diminished. In the spring of 1944 he wrote telling Frost that he had accepted an associate professorship in the Department of English at the University of Colorado. He implied that this move would probably cause Frost to lose interest in his career—a career partly represented in character by a scholarly book review, recently written, which he enclosed. Frost replied on May 18, 1944.

DEAR CHARLIE Im glad of where you've risen to in rank and altitude. Boulder is one of my stations. The smartest boy I ever had in high school lives there. His name is John Bartlett. He and his wife Margaret are on here to see their daughter graduate from Wellesley this coming Saturday May 20th. I shall be introducing you to them as another of my favorite children. They are not of your college crowd. They fled education to marry young—didnt prosper, got into health and money troubles and went on the Rockies to perish as it seemed to their friends and relatives. But they saved themselves with a scheme to serve papers and magazines with items and articles about the region. I believe they made a small fortune. Anyway it was enough to make them important people in the town and state and give their five boys and girls a good start. I dont know how well I am going to find them on Saturday. I havent seen them for several years. They are not as young as you folks. They graduated from Pinkerton Academy in Derry New Hampshire in nineteen ten or eleven. They were both in the same class. She was as smart in her way as he was.

You shouldnt write me as valedictorily as that. You are always very interesting to me and I like to hear what you are thinking about. The review of the book on Thoreau shows how easily you handle prose. I keep wondering why you cant make a go of verse. You have had too much advice from me already. I say no more on that subject. But you would think that with all the impulse I know you have and with all the devotion you feel for your Emerson, Thoreau and Dickinson you couldnt help being a poet before it's all over. Do you suppose its because you won't learn to hit the figure right in the middle? Like a person who cant hit a note in the middle with his voice. Perhaps you oversay the metaphor—fetch it too far. Or have I said that before? I really don't care whether you are a success in poetry or not. I can tell from hearsay you are a good teacher and the better for having got your doctor's degree the humane way under Foerster. But neither do I care whether you are a good teacher or not. We're friends. So dont ever speak to me again except as man to man.

I go to Ripton Vermont for the long summer on Sunday. Write me ex tempery if there's anything I say or do you dont like. But I guess I cant get you mad at me at this late date after all you have taken from me in the past. You know I have wanted to help you be what you want to be. Tell me—do I ow[e] you a book or anything?

Ever yours R.F.

Friends they remained, keeping in touch with each other during all the succeeding years of Frost's life. In spite of what Frost had said, however, about not caring what Foster became, the New England poet continued to show his wistfulness. In the spring of 1950, Foster, now a full professor in the Department of English at Grinnell College, wrote to say that he had determined to make one more assault on Parnassus. Frost answered on April 22, 1950.

OLD FAITHFUL By which I mean that though very young and not at all old, you have been faithful a long long time as friendships go. You still take my side after all that has happened in the world since you first wrote me from Lawrenceville about your aspirations in coming to Amherst. It's a great satisfaction to me. I could wish nothing better for myself. And I take your side. I dont need to tell you what I have always wished for *you*. You hint in your letter at fresh departures—fresh assaults on Parnassus—on N'Everest. I wonder what you would consider having made the peak. Signs from a few people unsolicited that they have been having pleasure in your art as of no obligation whatever? Thats the way I feel. But its a hard world to get at the sincerities of. We mustnt look to[o] closely of course Lightly row lightly row as o'er the glassy waves we go. Quotation marks have been fashionably omitted ever si[n]ce I left them out of several poems in A Boys Will. My first book if you remember rightly.

What have you been finding out about your art since I scolded you last? Look here! Do you want to know what I want to see you try your hand at? Tight little bits that shan't look cramped. Stinging little details of nature or human nature. What's the shortest and best thing you ever said? Another Landor would come in fine about now. Did you ever notice how Father Tabb worked away at the hightoned squibb?

Still your teacher! But I must desist. You may be all accomplished. I hope so. You may be sure of yourself. Fine. I dont care too much. I only want you to write poetry if you want to write it. I only want you to succeed with publishers and editors (and public) if you want to succeed with them. You cant fail in character with me. I like the way you have taken your life.

I ought to say I am not very clear about what happened between you and my publishers. They wouldnt let you set me to music on the terms you proposed—was that it? I dont like to ask too much of them or I might speak for you. They are mostly new people to me this year. They have done wonders for my book I like to show some meekness in requital.

Im back at where you expected me to be. But I come rather played out with various excitements. Ive seen George and had your three books from him. I'll sign them. Look for them soon. I see one belonged to Charles Hanson Towne the poet. I see lots of things. You'd think my eyes might not hold out.

My best to you both.

Ever yours RF.

Education by Poetry

A MEDITATIVE MONOLOGUE

Asked to give a talk before the Amherst College Alumni Council in the fall of 1930, Robert Frost chose as his subject "Education by Poetry." The talk was recorded stenographically, and afterwards he revised it for publication in the *Amherst Graduates' Quarterly* of February 1931. It is here reprinted from *Selected Prose of Robert Frost,* pp. 33–46.

I am going to urge nothing in my talk. I am not an advocate. I am going to consider a matter, and commit a description. And I am going to describe other colleges than Amherst. Or, rather say all that is good can be taken as about Amherst; all that is bad will be about other colleges.

I know whole colleges where all American poetry is barred—whole colleges. I know whole colleges where all contemporary poetry is barred.

I once heard of a minister who turned his daughter—his poetry-writing daughter—out on the street to earn a living, because he said there should be no more books written; God wrote one book, and that was enough. (My friend George Russell, "Æ", has read no literature, he protests, since just before Chaucer.)

That all seems sufficiently safe, and you can say one thing for it. It takes the onus off the poetry of having to be used to teach children anything. It comes pretty hard on poetry, I sometimes think—what it has to bear in the teaching process.

Then I know whole colleges where, though they let in older poetry, they manage to bar all that is poetical in it by treating it as something other than poetry. It is not so hard to do that. Their reason I have often hunted for. It may be that these people act from a kind of modesty. Who are professors that they should attempt to deal with a thing as high and as fine as poetry? Who are *they*? There is a certain manly modesty in that.

That is the best general way of settling the problem; treat all poetry as if it were something else than poetry, as if it were syntax, language, science. Then you can even come down into the American and into the contemporary without any special risk.

There is another reason they have, and that is that they are, first and foremost in life, markers. They have the marking problem to consider. Now, I stand here a teacher of many years' experience and I have never complained of having had to mark. I had rather mark anyone for any-thing—for his looks, carriage, his ideas, his correctness, his exactness, anything you please,—I would rather give him a mark in terms of let-ters, A, B, C, D, than have to use adjectives on him. We are all being marked by each other all the time, classified, ranked, put in our place, and I see no escape from that. I am no sentimentalist. You have got to mark, and you have got to mark, first of all, for accuracy, for correctness. But if I am going to give a mark, that is the least part of my marking. The hard part is the part beyond that, the part where the adventure begins.

One other way to rid the curriculum of the poetry nuisance has been considered. More merciful than the others it would neither abolish nor denature the poetry, but only turn it out to disport itself, with the plays and games—in no wise discredited, though given no credit for. Any one who liked to teach poetically could take his subject, whether English, Latin, Greek or French, out into the nowhere along with the poetry. One side of a sharp line would be left to the rigorous and righteous; the other side would be assigned to the flowery where they would know what could be expected of them. Grade marks where more easily given, of course, in the courses concentrating on correctness and exactness as the only forms of honesty recognized by plain people; a general indefinite mark of X in the courses that scatter brains over taste and opinion. On inquiry I have found no teacher willing to take position on either side of the line, either among the rigors or among the flowers. No one is willing to admit that his discipline is not partly in exactness. No one is willing to admit that his discipline is not partly in taste and enthusiasm.

How shall a man go through college without having been marked for taste and judgment? What will become of him? What will his end be? He will have to take continuation courses for college graduates. He will have to go to night schools. They are having night schools now, you know, for college graduates. Why? Because they have not been educated enough to find their way around in contemporary literature. They don't know what they may safely like in the libraries and galleries. They don't know how to judge an editorial when they see one. They don't know how to judge a political campaign. They don't know when they are being fooled by a metaphor, an analogy, a parable. And metaphor is, of course, what we are talking about. Education by poetry is education by metaphor.

Suppose we stop short of imagination, initiative, enthusiasm, inspiration and originality—dread words. Suppose we don't mark in such things at all. There are still two minimal things, that we have got to take care of, taste and judgment. Americans are supposed to have more judgment than taste, but taste is there to be dealt with. That is what poetry, the only art in the colleges of arts, is there for. I for my part would not be afraid to go in for enthusiasm. There is the enthusiasm like a blinding light, or the enthusiasm of the deafening shout, the crude enthusiasm that you get uneducated by poetry, outside of poetry. It is exemplified in what I might call "sunset raving." You look westward toward the sunset, or if you get up early enough, eastward toward the sunrise, and you rave. It is oh's and ah's with you and no more.

But the enthusiasm I mean is taken through the prism of the intellect and spread on the screen in a color, all the way from hyperbole at one end—or overstatement, at one end—to understatement at the other end. It is a long strip of dark lines and many colors. Such enthusiasm is one object of all teaching in poetry. I heard wonderful things said about Virgil yesterday, and many of them seemed to me crude enthusiasm, more like a deafening shout, many of them. But one speech had range, something of overstatement, something of statement, and something of understatement. It had all the colors of an enthusiasm passed through an idea.

I would be willing to throw away everything else but that: enthusiasm tamed by metaphor. Let me rest the case there. Enthusiasm tamed to metaphor, tamed to that much of it. I do not think anybody ever knows the discreet use of metaphor, his own and other people's, the discreet handling of metaphor, unless he has been properly educated in poetry.

Poetry begins in trivial metaphors, pretty metaphors, "grace" metaphors, and goes on to the profoundest thinking that we have. Poetry provides the one permissible way of saying one thing and meaning another. People say, "Why don't you say what you mean?" We never do that, do we, being all of us too much poets. We like to talk in parables and in hints and in indirections—whether from diffidence or some other instinct.

I have wanted in late years to go further and further in making metaphor the whole of thinking. I find some one now and then to agree with me that all thinking, except mathematical thinking, is metaphorical, or all thinking except scientific thinking. The mathematical might be difficult for me to bring in, but the scientific is easy enough.

Once on a time all the Greeks were busy telling each other what the All was—or was like unto. All was three elements, air, earth, and water (we once thought it was ninety elements; now we think it is only one). All was substance, said another. All was change, said a third. But best and most fruitful was Pythagoras' comparison of the universe with number. Number of what? Number of feet, pounds, and seconds was the answer, and we had science and all that has followed in science. The metaphor has held and held, breaking down only when it came to the spiritual and psychological or the out of the way places of the physical.

The other day we had a visitor here, a noted scientist, whose latest word to the world has been that the more accurately you know where a thing is, the less accurately you are able to state how fast it is moving. You can see why that would be so, without going back to Zeno's problem of the arrow's flight. In carrying numbers into the realm of space and at the same time into the realm of time you are mixing metaphors, that is all, and you are in trouble. They won't mix. The two don't go together.

Let's take two or three more of the metaphors now in use to live by. I have just spoken of one of the new ones, a charming mixed metaphor right in the realm of higher mathematics and higher physics: that the more accurately you state where a thing is, the less accurately you will be able to tell how fast it is moving. And, of course, everything is moving. Everything is an event now. Another metaphor. A thing, they say, is an event. Do you believe it is? Not quite. I believe it is almost an event. But I like the comparison of a thing with an event.

I notice another from the same quarter. "In the neighborhood of matter space is something like curved." Isn't that a good one! It seems to me that that is simply and utterly charming—to say that space is something like curved in the neighborhood of matter. "Something like."

Another amusing one is from—what is the book?—I can't say it now; but here is the metaphor. Its aim is to restore you to your ideas of free will. It wants to give you back your freedom of will. All right, here it is on a platter. You know that you can't tell by name what persons in a certain class will be dead ten years after graduation, but you can tell actuarially how many will be dead. Now, just so this scientist says of the particles of matter flying at a screen, striking a screen; you can't tell what individual particles will come, but you can say in general that a certain number will strike in a given time. It shows, you see, that the individual particle can come freely. I asked Bohr about that particularly, and he said, "Yes, it is so. It can come when it wills and as it wills; and the action of the individual particle is unpredictable. But it is not so of the action of the mass. There you can predict." He says, "That gives the individual atom its freedom, but the mass its necessity."

Another metaphor that has interested us in our time and has done all our thinking for us is the metaphor of evolution. Never mind going into the Latin word. The metaphor is simply the metaphor of the growing plant or of the growing thing. And somebody very brilliantly, quite a while ago, said that the whole universe, the whole of everything, was like unto a growing thing. That is all. I know the metaphor will break down at some point, but it has not failed everywhere. It is a very brilliant metaphor, I acknowledge, though I myself get too tired of the kind of essay that talks about the evolution of candy, we will say, or the evolution of elevators—the evolution of this, that, and the other. Everything is evolution. I emancipate myself by simply saying that I didn't get up the metaphor and so am not much interested in it.

What I am pointing out is that unless you are at home in the metaphor, unless you have had your proper poetical education in the metaphor, you are not safe anywhere. Because you are not at ease with figurative values: you don't know the metaphor in its strength and its weakness. You don't know how far you may expect to ride it and when it may break down with you. You are not safe in science; you are not safe in history. In history, for instance—to show that [it] is the same in history as elsewhere—I heard somebody say yesterday that Aeneas was to be likened unto (those words, "likened unto"!) George Washington. He was that type of national hero, the middle-class man, not thinking of being a hero at all, bent on building the future, bent on his children, his descendants. A good metaphor, as far as it goes, and you must know how far. And then he added that Odysseus should be likened unto Theodore Roosevelt. I don't think that is so good. Someone visiting

Gibbon at the point of death, said he was the same Gibbon as of old, still at his parallels.

Take the way we have been led into our present position morally, the world over. It is by a sort of metaphorical gradient. There is a kind of thinking—to speak metaphorically—there is a kind of thinking you might say was endemic in the brothel. It is always there. And every now and then in some mysterious way it becomes epidemic in the world. And how does it do so? By using all the good words that virtue has invented to maintain virtue. It uses honesty, first,—frankness, sincerity—those words; picks them up, uses them. "In the name of honesty, let us see what we are." You know. And then it picks up the word joy. "Let us in the name of joy, which is the enemy of our ancestors, the Puritans . . . Let us in the name of joy, which is the enemy of the kill-joy Puritan . . ." You see. "Let us," and so on. And then, "In the name of health . . ." Health is another good word. And that is the metaphor Freudianism trades on, mental health. And the first thing we know, it has us all in up to the top knot. I suppose we may blame the artists a good deal, because they are great people to spread by metaphor. The stage too—the stage is always a good intermediary between the two worlds, the under and the upper,—if I may say so without personal prejudice to the stage.

In all this I have only been saying that the devil can quote Scripture, which simply means that the good words you have lying around the devil can use for his purposes as well as anybody else. Never mind about my morality. I am not here to urge anything. I don't care whether the world is good or bad—not on any particular day.

Let me ask you to watch a metaphor breaking down here before you.

Somebody said to me a little while ago, "It is easy enough for me to think of the universe as a machine, as a mechanism."

I said, "You mean the universe is like a machine?"

He said, "No. I think it is one . . . Well, it is like . . ."

"I think you mean the universe is like a machine."

"All right. Let it go at that."

I asked him, "Did you ever see a machine without a pedal for the foot, or a lever for the hand, or a button for the finger?"

He said, "No—no."

I said, "All right. Is the universe like that?"

And he said, "No. I mean it is like a machine, only . . ."

". . . it is different from a machine," I said.

He wanted to go just that far with that metaphor and no further. And so do we all. All metaphor breaks down somewhere. That is the beauty of it. It is touch and go with the metaphor, and until you have lived with it long enough you don't know when it is going. You don't know how much you can get out of it and when it will cease to yield. It is a very living thing. It is as life itself.

I have heard this ever since I can remember, and ever since I have taught: the teacher must teach the pupil to think. I saw a teacher once going around in a great school and snapping pupils' heads with thumb and finger and saying, "Think." That was when thinking was becoming the fashion. The fashion hasn't yet quite gone out.

We still ask boys in college to think, as in the nineties, but we seldom tell them what thinking means; we seldom tell them it is just putting this and that together; it is just saying one thing in terms of another. To tell them is to set their feet on the first rung of a ladder the top of which sticks through the sky.

Greatest of all attempts to say one thing in terms of another is the philosophical attempt to say matter in terms of spirit, or spirit in terms of matter, to make the final unity. That is the greatest attempt that ever failed. We stop just short there. But it is the height of poetry, the height of all thinking, the height of all poetic thinking, that attempt to say matter in terms of spirit and spirit in terms of matter. It is wrong to call anybody a materialist simply because he tries to say spirit in terms of matter, as if that were a sin. Materialism is not the attempt to say all in terms of matter. The only materialist—be he poet, teacher, scientist, politician, or statesman—

is the man who gets lost in his material without a gathering metaphor to throw it into shape and order. He is the lost soul.

We ask people to think, and we don't show them what thinking is. Somebody says we don't need to show them how to think; bye and bye they will think. We will give them the forms of sentences and, if they have any ideas, then they will know how to write them. But that is preposterous. All there is to writing is having ideas. To learn to write is to learn to have ideas.

The first little metaphor . . . Take some of the trivial ones. I would rather have trivial ones of my own to live by than the big ones of other people.

I remember a boy saying, "He is the kind of person that wounds with his shield." That may be a slender one, of course. It goes a good way in character description. It has poetic grace. "He is the kind that wounds with his shield."

The shield reminds me—just to linger a minute—the shield reminds me of the inverted shield spoken of in one of the books of the "Odyssey," the book that tells about the longest swim on record. I forget how long it lasted—several days, was it?—but at last as Odysseus came near the coast of Phaeacia, he saw it on the horizon "like an inverted shield."

There is a better metaphor in the same book. In the end Odysseus comes ashore and crawls up the beach to spend the night under a double olive tree, and it says, as in a lonely farmhouse where it is hard to get fire—I am not quoting exactly—where it is hard to start the fire again if it goes out, they cover the seeds of fire with ashes to preserve it for the night, so Odysseus covered himself with the leaves around him and went to sleep. There you have something that gives you character, something of Odysseus himself. "Seeds of fire." So Odysseus covered the seeds of fire in himself. You get the greatness of his nature.

But these are slighter metaphors than the ones we live by. They have their charm, their passing charm. They are as it were the first steps toward the great thoughts, grave thoughts, thoughts lasting to the end.

The metaphor whose manage we are best taught in poetry—that is all there is of thinking. It may not seem far for the mind to go but it is the mind's furthest. The richest accumulation of the ages is the noble metaphors we have rolled up.

I want to add one thing more that the experience of poetry is to anyone who comes close to poetry. There are two ways of coming close to poetry. One is by writing poetry. And some people think I want people to write poetry, but I don't; that is, I don't necessarily. I only want people to write poetry if they want to write poetry. I have never encouraged anybody to write poetry that did not want to write it, and I have not always encouraged those who did want to write it. That ought to be one's own funeral. It is a hard, hard life, as they say.

(I have just been to a city in the West, a city full of poets, a city they have made safe for poets. The whole city is so lovely that you do not have to write it up to make it poetry; it is ready-made for you. But, I don't know—the poetry written in that city might not seem like poetry if read outside of the city. It would be like the jokes made when you were drunk; you have to get drunk again to appreciate them.)

But as I say, there is another way to come close to poetry, fortunately, and that is in the reading of it, not as linguistics, not as history, not as anything but poetry. It is one of the hard things for a teacher to know how close a man has come in reading poetry. How do I know whether a man has come close to Keats in reading Keats? It is hard for me to know. I have lived with some boys a whole year over some of the poets and I have not felt sure whether they have come near what it was all about. One remark sometimes told me. One remark was their mark for the year; had to be—it was all I got that told me what I wanted to know. And that is enough, if it was the right remark, if it came close enough. I think a man might make twenty fool remarks if he made one good one some time in the year. His mark would depend on that good remark.

The closeness—everything depends on the closeness with which you come, and you ought to be marked for the closeness, for nothing else. And that will have to be estimated by chance remarks, not by question and answer. It is only by accident that you know some day how near a person has come.

The person who gets close enough to poetry, he is going to know more about the word *belief* than anybody else knows, even in religion nowadays. There are two or three places where we know belief outside of religion. One of them is at the age of fifteen to twenty, in our self-belief. A young man knows more about himself than he is able to prove to anyone. He has no knowledge that anybody else will accept as knowledge. In his foreknowledge he has something that is going to believe itself into fulfillment, into acceptance.

There is another belief like that, the belief in someone else, a relationship of two that is going to be believed into fulfillment. That is what we are talking about in our novels, the belief of love. And the disillusionment that the novels are full of is simply the disillusionment from disappointment in that belief. That belief can fail, of course.

Then there is a literary belief. Every time a poem is written, every time a short story is written, it is written not by cunning, but by belief. The beauty, the something, the little charm of the thing to be, is more felt than known. There is a common jest, one that always annoys me, on the writers, that they write the last end first, and then work up to it; that they lay a train toward one sentence that they think is pretty nice and have all fixed up to set like a trap to close with. No, it should not be that way at all. No one who has ever come close to the arts has failed to see the difference between things written that way, with cunning and device, and the kind that are believed into existence, that begin in something more felt than known. This you can realize quite as well—not quite as well, perhaps, but nearly as well—in reading as you can in writing. I would undertake to separate short stories on that principle; stories that have been believed into existence and stories that have been cunningly devised. And I could separate the poems still more easily.

Now I think—I happen to think—that those three beliefs that I speak of, the self-belief, the love-belief, and the art-belief, are all closely related to the God-belief, that the belief in God is a relationship you enter into with Him to bring about the future.

There is a national belief like that, too. One feels it. I have been where I came near getting up and walking out on the people who thought that they had to talk against nations, against nationalism, in order to curry favor with internationalism. Their metaphors are all mixed up. They think that because a Frenchman and an American and an Englishman can all sit down on the same platform and receive honors together, it must be that there is no such thing as nations. That kind of bad thinking springs from a source we all know. I should want to say to anyone like that: "Look! First I want to be a person. And I want you to be a person, and then we can be as interpersonal as you please. We can pull each other's noses—do all sorts of things. But, first of all, you have got to have the personality. First of all, you have got to have the nations and then they can be as international as they please with each other."

I should like to use another metaphor on them. I want my palette, if I am a painter, I want my palette on my thumb or on my chair, all clean, pure, separate colors. Then I will do the mixing on the canvas. The canvas is where the work of art is, where we make the conquest. But we want the nations all separate, pure, distinct, things as separate as we can make them; and then in our thoughts, in our arts, and so on, we can do what we please about it.

But I go back. There are four beliefs that I know more about from having lived with poetry. One is the personal belief, which is a knowledge that you don't want to tell other people about because you cannot prove that you know. You are saying nothing about it till you see. The love belief, just the same, has that same shyness. It knows it cannot tell; only the outcome can tell. And the national belief we enter into socially with each other, all together, party of the first part, party of the second part, we enter into that to bring the future of the country. We cannot tell some people what it is we believe, partly, because they are too stupid to understand and partly because we are too proudly vague to explain. And anyway it has got to be fulfilled, and we are not talking until we know more, until we have something to show. And then the literary one in every work of art, not of cunning and craft, mind you, but of real art; that believing the thing into existence, saying as you go more than you even hoped you were going to able to say, and coming with surprise to an end that you foreknew only with some sort of emotion. And then finally the relationship we enter into with God to believe the future in— to believe the hereafter in.

Among the Poems He Left Behind

GROUP THREE

Neither of these poems was published during the lifetime of Robert Frost, and the earlier of the two was never given a title. Three versions of this untitled poem were sent by Frost to his long-time friend Louis Untermeyer: the first, in a letter dated July 7, 1921; the second, in a letter of September 26, 1921; the third—the version used here—in a letter postmarked January 15, 1942. All were published in *The Letters of Robert Frost to Louis Untermeyer,* pp. 130–131, 136, and 331.

"The Offer" was also shared with Untermeyer, in a letter sent on August 20, 1932. Then, years later, when Frost was gathering poems for a new volume, to be called *A Further Range,* he wrote Untermeyer, "I seem to have lost somewhere one whole note-book with the poem in it about proposing to supply the sorrow felt if the storm will supply the tears: Dammit I wonder in whose house I left that privacy lying around. But never mind that now. Can you let me have a copy of the tears poem?" (*The Letters of Robert Frost to Louis Untermeyer,* pp. 228 and 265.)

[TO PRAYER I THINK I GO . . .]

To prayer I think I go,
I go to prayer—
Along a darkened corridor of woe
And down a stair

In every step of which I am abased.
I wear a halter-rope about the waist.
I bear a candle end put out with haste.

For such as I there is reserved a crypt
That from its stony arches having dripped
Has stony pavement in a slime of mould.
There I will throw me down an unconsoled
And utter loss,
And spread out in the figure of a cross.—
Oh, if religion's not to be my fate
I must be spoken to and told
Before too late!

THE OFFER

I narrow eyes and double night;
But still the flakes in bullet flight
More pointedly than ever smite.
What would they more than have me blink?
What is it? What am I to think—
That hard and dry to hard and dry
They may have said for years?
Am I, are they, or both to melt?
If I supply the sorrow felt,
Will they supply the tears?

"... it will always be about equally hard to save your soul."

A LETTER TO *THE AMHERST STUDENT*

> Shortly before his sixtieth birthday, Robert Frost received greetings from the editors of the Amherst College undergraduate newspaper, *The Amherst Student*. He made response to their felicitations in a letter that was published in the *Student* on March 25, 1935, now reprinted from *Selected Prose of Robert Frost*, pp. 105–107.

It is very, very kind of the *Student* to be showing sympathy with me for my age. But sixty is only a pretty good age. It is not advanced enough. The great thing is to be advanced. Now ninety would be really well along and something to be given credit for.

But speaking of ages, you will often hear it said that the age of the world we live in is particularly bad. I am impatient of such talk. We have no way of knowing that this age is one of the worst in the world's history. Arnold claimed the honor for the age before this. Wordsworth claimed it for the last but one. And so on back through literature. I say they claimed the honor for their ages. They claimed it rather for themselves. It is immodest of a man to think of himself as going down before the worst forces ever mobilized by God.

All ages of the world are bad—a great deal worse anyway than Heaven. If they weren't the world might just as well be Heaven at once and have it over with. One can safely say after from six to thirty thousand years of experience that the evident design is a situation here in which it will always be about equally hard to save your soul. Whatever progress may be taken to mean, it can't mean making the world any easier a place in which to save your soul—or if you dislike hearing your soul mentioned in open meeting, say your decency, your integrity.

Ages may vary a little. One may be a little worse than another. But it is not possible to get outside the age you are in to judge it exactly. Indeed it is as dangerous to try to get outside of anything as large as an age as it would be to engorge a donkey. Witness the many who in the attempt have suffered a dilation from which the tissues and the muscles of the mind have never been able to recover natural shape. They can't pick up anything delicate or small any more. They can't use a pen. They have to use a typewriter. And they gape in agony. They can write huge shapeless novels, huge gobs of raw sincerity bellowing with pain and that's all that they can write.

Fortunately we don't need to know how bad the age is. There is something we can always be doing without reference to how good or how bad the age is. There is at least so much good in the world that it admits of form and the making of form. And not only admits of it, but calls for it. We people are thrust forward out of the suggestions of form in the rolling clouds of nature. In us nature reaches its height of form and through us exceeds itself. When in doubt there is always form for us to go on with. Anyone who has achieved the least form to be sure of it, is lost to the larger excruciations. I think it must stroke faith the right way. The artist[,] the poet[,] might be expected to be the most aware of such assurance. But it is really everybody's sanity to feel it and live by it. Fortunately, too, no forms are more engrossing[,] gratifying, comforting, staying than those lesser ones we throw off, like vortex rings of smoke, all our individual enterprise and needing nobody's co-operation; a basket, a letter, a garden, a room, an idea, a picture, a poem. For these we haven't to get a team together before we can play.

The background in hugeness and confusion shading away from where we stand into black and utter chaos; and against the background any small man-made figure of order and concentration. What pleasanter than that this should be so? Unless we are novelists or economists we don't worry about this confusion; we look out on [it] with an instrument or tackle it to reduce it. It is partly because we are afraid it might prove too much for us and our blend of democratic-republican-socialist-communist-anarchist party. But it is more because we like it, we were born to it, born used to it and have practical reasons for wanting it there. To me any little form I assert upon it is velvet, as the saying is, and to be considered for how much more it is than nothing. If I were a Platonist I should have to consider it, I suppose, for how much less it is than everything.

"... content with the old-fashioned way to be new."

INTRODUCTION TO ROBINSON'S *KING JASPER*

The poet Edwin Arlington Robinson died just after he had finished correcting the printer's proofs of his book-length narrative poem called *King Jasper.* Frost, asked to write an introduction for the volume, which was published in 1935, contributed this essay (*Selected Prose of Robert Frost,* pp. 59–67).

It may come to the notice of posterity (and then again it may not) that this, our age, ran wild in the quest of new ways to be new. The one old way to be new no longer served. Science put it into our heads that there must be new ways to be new. Those tried were largely by subtraction—elimination. Poetry, for example, was tried without punctuation. It was tried without capital letters. It was tried without metric frame on which to measure the rhythm. It was tried without any images but those to the eye; and a loud general intoning had to be kept up to cover the total loss of specific images to the ear, those dramatic tones of voice which had hitherto constituted the better half of poetry. It was tried without content under the trade name of poesie pure. It was tried without phrase, epigram, coherence, logic and consistency. It was tried without ability. I took the confession of one who had had deliberately to unlearn what he knew. He made a back-pedalling movement of his hands to illustrate the process. It was tried premature like the delicacy of unborn calf in Asia. It was tried without feeling or sentiment like murder for small pay in the underworld. These many things was it tried without, and what had we left? Still something. The limits of poetry had been sorely strained, but the hope was that the idea had been somewhat brought out.

Robinson stayed content with the old-fashioned way to be new. I remember bringing the subject up with him. How does a man come on his difference, and how does he feel about it when he first finds it out? At first it may well frighten him, as his difference with the Church frightened Martin Luther. There is such a thing as being too willing to be different. And what shall we say to people who are not only willing but anxious? What assurance have they that their difference is not insane, eccentric, abortive, unintelligible? Two fears should follow us through life. There is the fear that we shan't prove worthy in the eyes of someone who knows us at least as well as we know ourselves. That is the fear of God. And there is the fear of Man—the fear that men won't understand us and we shall be cut off from them.

We began in infancy by establishing correspondence of eyes with eyes. We recognized that they were the same feature and we could do the same things with them. We went on to the visible motion of the lips— smile answered smile; then cautiously, by trial and error, to compare the invisible muscles of the mouth and throat. They were the same and could make the same sounds. We were still together. So far, so good. From here on the wonder grows. It has been said that recognition in art is all. Better say correspondence is all. Mind must convince mind that it can uncurl and wave the same filaments of subtlety, soul convince soul that it can give off the same shimmers of eternity. At no point would anyone but a brute fool want to break off this correspondence. It is all there is to satisfaction; and it is salutary to live in the fear of its being broken off.

The latest proposed experiment of the experimentalists is to use poetry as a vehicle of grievances against the un-Utopian state. As I say, most of their experiments have been by subtraction. This would be by addition of an ingredient that latter-day poetry has lacked. A distinction must be made between griefs and grievances. Grievances are probably more useful than griefs. I read in a sort of Sunday-school leaflet from Moscow, that the grievances of Chekhov against the sordidness and dullness of his home-town society have done away with the sordidness and dullness of home-town society all over Russia. They were celebrating the event. The grievances of the great Russians of the last century have given Russia a revolution. The grievances of their great followers in America may well give us, if not a revolution, at least some palliative pensions. We must suffer them to put life at its ugliest and forbid them not, as we value our reputation for liberality.

I had it from one of the youngest lately: "Whereas we once thought literature should be without content, we now know it should be charged full of propaganda." Wrong twice, I told him. Wrong twice and of theory prepense. But he returned to his position after a moment out for reassembly: "Surely art can be considered good only as it prompts to action." How soon, I asked him. But there is danger of undue levity in teasing the young. The experiment is evidently started. Grievances are certainly a power and are going to be turned on. We must be very tender of our dreamers. They may seem like picketers or members of the committee on rules for the moment. We shan't mind what they seem, if only they produce real poems.

But for me, I don't like grievances. I find I gently let them alone wherever published. What I like is griefs and I like them Robinsonianly profound. I suppose there is no use in asking, but I should think we might be indulged to the extent of having grievances restricted to prose if prose will accept the imposition, and leaving poetry free to go its way in tears.

Robinson was a prince of heartachers amid countless achers of another part. The sincerity he wrought in was all sad. He asserted the sacred right of poetry to lean its breast to a thorn and sing its dolefullest. Let weasels suck eggs. I know better where to look for melancholy. A few superficial irritable grievances, perhaps, as was only human, but these are forgotten in the depth of griefs to which he plunged us.

Grievances are a form of impatience. Griefs are a form of patience. We may be required by law to throw away patience as we have been required to surrender gold; since by throwing away patience and joining the impatient in one last rush on the citadel of evil, the hope is we may end the need of patience. There will be nothing left to be patient about. The day of perfection waits on unanimous social action. Two or three more good national elections should do the business. It has been similarly urged on us to give up courage, make cowardice a virtue, and see if that won't end war, and the need of courage. Desert religion for science, clean out the holes and corners of the residual unknown, and there will be no more need of religion. (Religion is merely consolation for what we don't know.) But suppose there was some mistake, and the evil stood siege, the war didn't end, and something remained unknowable. Our having disarmed would make our case worse than it had ever been before. Nothing in the latest advices from Wall Street, the League of Nations, or the Vatican incline me to give up my holdings in patient grief.

There were Robinson and I, it was years ago, and the place (near Boston Common) was the Place, as we liked afterward to call it, of Bitters, because it was with bitters, though without bitterness, we could sit there and look out on the welter of dissatisfaction and experiment in the world around us. It was too long ago to remember who said what, but the sense of the meeting was, we didn't care how arrant a reformer or experimentalist a man was if he gave us real poems. For ourselves, we should hate to be read for any theory upon which we might be supposed to write. We doubted any poem could persist for any theory upon which it might have been written. Take the theory that poetry in our language could be treated as quantitative, for example. Poems had been written in spite of it. And poems are all that matter. The utmost of ambition is to lodge a few poems where they will be hard to get rid of, to lodge a few irreducible bits where Robinson lodged more than his share.

For forty years it was phrase on phrase on phrase with Robinson, and every one the closest delineation of something that *is* something. Any poet, to resemble him in the least, would have to resemble him in that grazing closeness to the spiritual realities. If books of verse were to be indexed by lines first in importance instead of lines first in position, many of Robinson's poems would be represented several times over. This should be seen to. The only possible objection is that it could not be done by any mere hireling of the moment, but would have to be the work of someone who had taken his impressions freely before he had any notion of their use. A particular poem's being represented several times would only increase the chance of its being located.

The first poet I ever sat down with to talk about poetry was Ezra Pound. It was in London in 1913. The first poet we talked about, to the best of my recollection, was Edwin Arlington Robinson. I was fresh from America and from having read *The Town Down the River*. Beginning at that book, I have slowly spread my reading of Robinson twenty years backward and forward, about equally in both directions.

I remember the pleasure with which Pound and I laughed over the fourth "thought" in

> Miniver thought, and thought, and thought,
> And thought about it.

Three "thoughts" would have been "adequate" as the critical praiseword then was. There would have been nothing to complain of, if it had been left at three. The fourth made the intolerable touch of poetry. With the fourth, the fun began. I was taken out on the strength of our community of opinion here, to be rewarded with an introduction to Miss May Sinclair, who had qualified as the patron authority on young and new poets by the sympathy she had shown them in *The Divine Fire*.

There is more to it than the number of "thoughts." There is the way the last one turns up by surprise round the corner, the way the shape of the stanza is played with, the easy way the obstacle of verse is turned to advantage. The mischief is in it.

> One pauses half afraid
> To say for certain that he played—

a man as sorrowful as Robinson. His death was sad to those who knew
him, but nowhere near as sad as the lifetime of poetry to which he
attuned our ears. Nevertheless, I say his much-admired restraint lies
wholly in his never having let grief go further than it could in play. So
far shall grief go, so far shall philosophy go, so far shall confidences go,
and no further. Taste may set the limit. Humor is a surer dependence.

> And once a man was there all night
> Expecting something every minute.

I know what the man wanted of Old King Cole. He wanted the heart
out of his mystery. He was the friend who stands at the end of a poem
ready in waiting to catch you by both hands with enthusiasm and drag
you off your balance over the last punctuation mark into more than you
meant to say. "I understand the poem all right, but please tell me what
is behind it?" Such presumption needs to be twinkled at and baffled.
The answer must be, "If I had wanted you to know, I should have told
you in the poem."

We early have Robinson's word for it:

> The games we play
> To fill the frittered minutes of a day
> Good glasses are to read the spirit through.

He speaks somewhere of Crabbe's stubborn skill. His own was a
happy skill. His theme was unhappiness itself, but his skill was as
happy as it was playful. There is that comforting thought for those who
suffered to see him suffer. Let it be said at the risk of offending the
humorless in poetry's train (for there are a few such): his art was more
than playful; it was humorous.

The style is the man. Rather say the style is the way the man takes himself; and to be at all charming or even bearable, the way is almost rigidly prescribed. If it is with outer seriousness, it must be with inner humor. If it is with outer humor, it must be with inner seriousness. Neither one alone without the other under it will do. Robinson was thinking as much in his sonnet on Tom Hood. One ordeal of Mark Twain was the constant fear that his occluded seriousness would be overlooked. That betrayed him into his two or three books of out-and-out seriousness.

Miniver Cheevy was long ago. The glint I mean has kept coming to the surface of the fabric all down the years. Yesterday in conversation, I was using "The Mill." Robinson could make lyric talk like drama. What imagination for speech in "John Gorham"! He is at his height between quotation marks.

> The miller's wife had waited long,
>   The tea was cold, the fire was dead;
> And there might yet be nothing wrong
>   In how he went and what he said:
> "There are no millers any more,"
>   Was all that she had heard him say.

"There are no millers any more." It might be an edict of some power against industrialism. But no, it is of wider application. It is a sinister jest at the expense of all investors of life or capital. The market shifts and leaves them with a car-barn full of dead trolley cars. At twenty I commit myself to a life of religion. Now, if religion should go out of fashion in twenty-five years, there would I be, forty-five years old, unfitted for anything else and too old to learn anything else. It seems immoral to have to bet on such high things as lives of art, business, or the church. But in effect, we have no alternative. None but an all-wise and all-powerful government could take the responsibility of keeping us out of the gamble or of insuring us against loss once we were in.

The guarded pathos of "Mr. Flood's Party" is what makes it

merciless. We are to bear in mind the number of moons listening. Two, as on the planet Mars. No less. No more ("No more, sir; that will do"). One moon (albeit a moon, no sun) would have laid grief too bare. More than two would have dissipated grief entirely and would have amounted to dissipation. The emotion had to be held at a point.

> He set the jug down slowly at his feet
> With trembling care, knowing that most things break;
> And only when assured that on firm earth
> It stood, as the uncertain lives of men
> Assuredly did not . . .

There twice it gleams. Nor is it lost even where it is perhaps lost sight of in the dazzle of all those golden girls at the end of "The Sheaves." Granted a few fair days in a world where not all days are fair.

> "Well, Mr. Flood, we have the harvest moon
> Again, and we may not have many more;
> The bird is on the wing, the poet says,
> And you and I have said it here before.
> Drink to the bird."

Poetry transcends itself in the playfulness of the toast.

Robinson has gone to his place in American literature and left his human place among us vacant. We mourn, but with the qualification that, after all, his life was a revel in the felicities of language. And not just to no purpose. None has deplored

> The inscrutable profusion of the Lord
> Who shaped as one of us a thing

so sad and at the same time so happy in achievement. Not for me to search his sadness to its source. He knew how to forbid encroachment. And there is solid satisfaction in a sadness that is not just a fishing for ministration and consolation. Give us immedicable woes—woes that nothing can be done for—woes flat and final. And then to play. The play's the thing. Play's the thing. All virtue in "as if."

> As if the last of days
> Were fading and all wars were done.

As if they were. As if, as if!

"... *my life has been a book life.*"

TEN OF HIS FAVORITE BOOKS

"I don't live in a library," Frost told an Amherst College audience on September 28, 1962, "and I am not a terrible reader, but my life has been a book life." (The occasion for this declaration was the announcement of an anonymous gift that was to provide for the construction of Amherst's Robert Frost Library.) Earlier, in an interview with W. G. Rogers, released by the Associated Press on April 3, 1960, he had observed, "Libraries are in the same game I'm in. That's the game of surrounding people with books—getting people coated with books."

Among his many comments over the years on the subject of books—of books in general or on particular books—none is more interesting than what Frost wrote late in 1934, when he was among a group of distinguished individuals asked by the Massachusetts Library Association, "Please choose, and give reasons for your choice, ten books, exclusive of the Bible and Shakespeare, dictionaries, encyclopedias, and other ordinary reference books, that you believe should be in every public library." His answer was included with sixty-odd other responses in a volume entitled *Books We Like* (Boston, 1936), pp. 141–142.

(1) *The Odyssey* chooses itself, the first in time and rank of all romances. Palmer's translation is by all odds the best. As Lawrence in a preface to his own translation describes the author of the original, he is

evidently a man much more like Palmer than like Lawrence. I can permit myself but one translation out of ten books.

(2) *Robinson Crusoe* is never quite out of my mind. I never tire of being shown how the limited can make snug in the limitless.

(3) *Walden* has something of the same fascination. Crusoe was cast away; Thoreau was self-cast away. Both found themselves sufficient. No prose writer has ever been more fortunate in subject than these two. I prefer my essay in narrative form. In *Walden* I get it and always near the height of poetry.

(4) Poe's *Tales*. Here is every kind of entertainment the short story can afford, the supernatural, horrific, pseudo-scientific, ingenious, and detective. (Every kind, I should perhaps say, but the character.)

(5) *The Oxford Book of English Verse* and

(6) Untermeyer's *Modern American and British Poetry* pretty well cover between them the poetry of our race. I am permitting myself two and one half numbers of actual verse in the ten—twenty-five per cent. That doesn't seem for the moment an undue proportion.

(7) *The Last of the Mohicans* supplies us once for all with our way of thinking of the American Indian.

(8) *The Prisoner of Zenda*—surely one of the very best of our modern best-sellers.

(9) *The Jungle Book* (first). I shall read it again as often as I can find a new child to listen to me.

(10) Emerson's *Essays* and *Poems*—the rapture of idealism either way you have it, in prose or in verse and in brief.

On Crudities and Opposites

TWO LETTERS

At an annual dinner of the Poetry Society of America held in
New York City on April 1, 1937, Robert Frost was the guest
of honor. Starting to talk on "Crudities," he combined these
remarks with others on "Opposites." The poet Robert P.
Tristram Coffin, after hearing the talk, wrote to ask if Frost
might be willing to send him a summary of what he had said;
Coffin wished to use parts of the text in a lecture he was
preparing on Frost. In his initial letter of reply Frost was
helpful, and then further promptings from Coffin elicited a
supplementary response. These two communications,
written from Florida, were first published in *Selected Letters
of Robert Frost,* pp. 461–467.

DEAR COFFIN, It is my bad luck I am away off down here where I can't
help you help me. I suppose you have nothing to call you even part way
in this direction till you come to Baltimore for your lectures. I would
venture some way into the cold but I mustn't come so far as to seem
inconsistent to those with whom I have used the cold as an excuse to
stay away from their platforms and dinner tables. A lot would come out
in talk once you got me started with what you happened to remember
of that Poetry Society affair. I'm terrible about my lectures. In my anxi-
ety to keep them as long as possible from becoming part of my literary
life, I leave them rolling round in my head like clouds rolling round in
the sky. Watch them long enough and you'll see one near-form change
into another near-form. Though I am sure they are hardly permissable
on the platform, I continue to bring them there with no more apology
than to a parlor or class room. Their chief value to me is for what I pick

up from them when I cut across them with a poem under emotion. They have been my inner world of raw material and my instinct has been to keep them raw. That can't long retain their state however. The day approaches when they will lose their fluidity and in spite of my stirring spoon become crystal. Then one kind of fun will be over and I shall have to find another to take its place (tennis most likely or hoeing). I thought I was about ready to let them set when I accepted the Harvard invitation to deliver them in writing after delivering them by word of mouth. Something in me still fights off the written prose. The nearest I ever came to getting myself down in prose was in the preface to Robinson's *King Jasper*. That is so much me that you might suspect the application to him of being forced. It was really no such thing. We two were close akin up to a certain point of thinking. He would have trusted me to go a good way in speaking for him particularly on the art of poetry. We only parted company over the badness of the world. He was cast in the mold of sadness. I am neither optimist nor pessimist. I never voted either ticket. If there is a universal unfitness and unconformity as of a buttoning so started that every button on the vest is in the wrong button hole and the one empty button hole at the top and the one naked button at the bottom so far apart they have no hope of getting together, I don't care to decide whether God did this for the fun of it or for the devil of it. (The two expressions come to practically the same thing anyway.) Then again I am not the Platonist Robinson was. By Platonist I mean one who believes what we have here is an imperfect copy of what is in heaven. The woman you have is an imperfect copy of some woman in heaven or in someone else's bed. Many of the world's greatest—maybe all of them—have been ranged on that romantic side. I am philosophically opposed to having one Iseult for my vocation and another for my avocation; as you may have inferred from a poem called Two Tramps in Mud Time. You see where that lands me on the subject of Dante's Beatrice. Mea culpa. Let me not sound the least bit smug. I define a difference with proper humility. A truly gallant Platonist will remain a bachelor as Robinson did from unwillingness to reduce any woman to the condition of being used without being idealized.

But you didn't ask me to distinguish between myself and Robinson. I fell accidentally into a footnote to the *King Jasper* preface in self defence. What you asked for is any recollection I have of my recent talks. I may be able to bring some of them back in detail—give me time. What in the world did I say in New York. Was my subject "Neither or Both." Do you want to show me the notes you made? Is there time? I'm going to hurry this off tonight for a beginning and then if you say so try to tell you a little more. One of my subjects at Harvard was Does Wisdom Matter. I mean in art. Does it matter for instance that I am so temperamentally wrong about Beatrice. You can hear more if it is worth your while. Another subject was The Renewal of Words. Molly Colum had been saying the world was old, people were jaded and the languages worn out. My whole lecture was an answer to her defeatism, though I took good care not to name her—and don't you name her. Poetry is the renewal of words forever and ever. Poetry is that by which we live forever and ever unjaded. Poetry is that by which the world is never old. Even the poetry of trade names gives the lie to the unoriginal who would drag us down in their own powerlessness to originate. Heavy they are but not so heavy that we can't rise under them and throw them off.

Well well well——

SINCERELY YOURS ROBERT FROST

DEAR COFFIN: Your letter brings back my animus of that April 1st. I was gunning for the kind of Americans who fancied themselves as the only Americans incapable of crudity. I started off with some crudity I knew they could join me in laughing at and I ended up with some they might not be so incapable of themselves. But I protested all the way along my love of crudity. I thank the Lord for crudity which is rawness, which is raw material, which is the part of life not yet worked up into form, or at least not worked all the way up. Meet with the fallacy of the foolish: having had a glimpse of finished art, they forever after pine for a life that shall be nothing but finished art. Why not a world safe for art as well as democracy. A real artist delights in roughness for what he can do to it. He's the brute who can knock the corners off the marble block and drag the unbedded beauty out of bed. The statesman (politician) is no different except that he works in a protean mass of material that hardly holds the shape he gives it long enough for him to point it out and get credit for it. His material is the rolling mob. The poet's material is words that for all we may say and feel against them are more manageable than men. Get a few words alone in a study and with plenty of time on your hands you can make them say any thing you please.

You remember the story of the neighbor who asked me how much I got apiece for my books. Then there was the man who after telling me for hours about his big bold business adventures asked me toward morning what I did with myself. I staved off the confession. I likened myself to him in adventurousness. I was a long-shot man too. I liked not to know beforehand what the day might bring forth. And so till he lost patience with me and cried "Shoot!" Well I write poetry. "Hell," he said unhappily "my wife writes that stuff." And it turned out she did. I came on a book of her verse at the house of the President of Sophie Newcomb in New Orleans where she lived and her husband visited. I must tell you the latest. A forty year old telegraph operatress had drawn her own inference from my telegrams. "You write," she said to me one day. "Yes."—"Poetry?" "Yes." "Just the person I'm looking for then. I lost my father a year or so ago and I'd like to get a poem written about him. I'll tell you what I want said." She took paper and pencil.—But how much better or worse was she than the man [Hermann Hagedorn] out of Harvard, New York, real society and literature who came a long way to ask me to write something American to save America? He was sure I could write something really American if I tried. But I must remember to like crudity even in high places and I must be willing to be crude myself for other people's purposes.

In my book of 1923 [*New Hampshire*] I dealt with the crude importunacy of those who would have you a prude or a puke (mewling and puking in the public arms). Choose you this day to be a puke or be disowned by the intelligensia. Fifteen years have gone by and the almost equally disgusting alternatives offered are collectivist or rugged individualist. (Can you bear it?) Here I have to recall myself as a workman to my duty of liking crudity in however amused a way. In this connection I probably told the story of my getting called a counter-revolutionary for not writing my poetry "tendential." By tendential in politics they mean what is sure to happen. After making sure it is going to happen, they don't trust it to happen of itself: they take hold and make it happen. Just so the horsey bets on a sure thing and then does all that in him lies with dope and counter dope, sponges in the nose, bribery and threat to make the sure thing surer. There is a horrid crudity of morals in our idealistic tendential friends. But I must stick to it that I like crudity.

Hegel saw two people marry and produce a third person. That was enough for Hegel—and Marx too it seems. They jumped at the conclusion that so all truth was born. Out of two truths in collision today sprang the one truth to live by tomorrow. A time succession was the fallacy. Marriage, reproduction and the family with a big F have much to answer for in misleading the analogists. Fire flashes from the flint and steel of metaphor and if caught in lint it may be spread, but that is no reason why it should spread to burn the world. That is monomania or monometaphor.

Take Justice and Mercy (you got my pairs of opposing goods exactly). A mind where there was a mind wouldn't think of them as breeding a third thing to live on after they are dead and gone. Justice and Mercy stand each other off and the present stands up between them. Divine Right and Consent do the same with the same result.

They are like the two hands that, by first tightening and then loosening the double string between them, make the tin buzzer buzz like a little buzz saw. You must have played with a tin buzzer on the Kennebeck.

Mind where there was a mind would be ashamed to have been radical when young only to be conservative when old. Life sways perilously at the confluence of opposing forces. Poetry in general plays perilously in the same wild place. In particular it plays perilously between truth and make-believe. It might be extravagant poetry to call it true make believe—or making believe what is so.

Of course use anything you can or will. It's a good idea to leave out people's names.

I thought my Education by Poetry might help. It was taken down without my knowledge.

Ever yours R.F.

Among the Poems He Left Behind

GROUP FOUR

Robert Frost must have had entirely different reasons for never bringing into any of his own volumes either of the poems entitled "Good Relief" and "Winter Ownership." The narrative element in the first was based on an actual experience that had touched the poet deeply while he was in England in 1912. The poem was not completed and published, however, until years later. It was included as a featured component of Lesley Frost's anthology *Come Christmas* (New York, 1935). "Winter Ownership" appeared in the *New York Herald Tribune Magazine* for March 4, 1934.

GOOD RELIEF

Shall we, then, wish as many as possible
As merry Christmases as possible
And charge the limitation up to thought?
No, be the Christmas card with which we greet:
A Merry Christmas to the World in Full.
And as for happiness not being bought—
Remember how two babes were on the street—
And so were many fathers out on strike
The vainest of their many strikes in vain,
And lost already as at heart they knew.
But the two babes had stopped alone to look
At Christmas toys behind a window pane,
And play at having anything they chose.
And when I lowered level with the two
And asked them what they saw so much to like,

One confidentially and raptly took
His finger from his mouth and pointed, "Those!"
A little locomotive with a train.
And where he wet the window pane it froze.
What good did it do anyone but him—
His brother at his side, perhaps, and me?
And think of all the world compared with three!
But why like the poor fathers on the curb
Must we be always partizan and grim?
No state has found a perfect cure for grief
In law or gospel or in root or herb.
'Twas in this very city thoroughfare
I heard a doctor of the Kickapoo
By torch-light from a cart-tail once declare:
The most that any root or herb can do
In suffering is give you Good Relief.

WINTER OWNERSHIP

Who is it gathering snow on lash and lip
    In the dead of the year to the muffled evening goes?
Some owner asserting winter ownership.
    He may be incidentally counting snows,

And has to be out in the snows for the snows to count.
    Full fifty firsts he has kept on nights like this
(To walk a level and yet in courage mount).
    A spill of snow goes down with a sandy hiss

Through a withered-leaf-clad oak. A sudden flight
    Of tiniest birds goes by like a charge of shot,
As if recalled by the storm-made-early night
    From berry and seed to a southern aim forgot.

No danger of his forgetting his aim or quest.
    The muffled evening gives a long-drawn sigh,
So charged with both possessing and being possessed
    He can scarcely resist the impulse to make reply.

Is there some assurance he comes to the woods to beg?
    Why doesn't he enter the woods and say what it is?
The feel of the solid meadow up his leg
    Is enough assurance that what is his is his.

And the snow may have depth to reduce his step to a plod,
    But he somehow gathers the speed to realize
The contour curves of the forest rod by rod
    Along the way it rests its hidden size.

He is content to let it go at a pass—
    As turning dust to dew or brow and lip,
He cuts steps darkly down to the very grass,
    Caressing contour, asserting ownership.

Poverty and Poetry

A TALK

Robert Frost usually began an evening's poetry reading by talking informally on a subject of his choice; then he would read a few poems to illustrate the points he had been making. Here is such a talk given at Haverford College on October 25, 1937, as published, from a stenographic transcript, by the Friends of the Princeton University Library in the quarterly *Biblia* for February 1938.

I gave out a subject, but it never reached you; so I am free to talk about what I please or not talk at all—or read to you. I shall read chiefly.

There's a little matter that has been on my mind. I am often more or less tacitly on the defensive about what I might call "my people." That doesn't mean Americans—I never defend America from foreigners. But when I speak of my people, I sort of mean a class, the ordinary folks I belong to. I have written about them entirely in one whole book: I called it *A Book of People*. But I found as I went around, seeing colleges more than anything else, that one and another spoke or implied something about my people that I didn't care for. I went a long way once to see one or two of my little things acted as if they were plays. They are very short plays, too short to act, but they have something of the dramatic in them. All the actors were cultivated people and they thought the way to represent my three people on the stage was to have them hop a little as if they were going over clods. And one of the actors who acted in the thing—I did not know what to say to him afterwards. I was full of too much to say, and I thought perhaps I would put it this way:

"They are much the same as we are. As a matter of fact," I said—I didn't know just how to make him understand—"as a matter of fact, both of them had been to college."

I don't think he would ever hop for them again. I was a little angry with him, but that was what I had to say to him, because there are people who don't go to college and who don't hop clods.

I spent all that part of my life, over twenty years of it, with just country neighbors around me. Some of them had been educated and some of them hadn't. They were all much the same. I was brought up in a family who had just come to the industrial city of Lawrence, Massachusetts. My grandfather was an overseer in the Pacific Mills. They had just come to the city from Kingston, New Hampshire, up by Exeter.

The other day I was reading a book called *A Proletarian Journey* by a boy named Fred Beal. His family ran into more poverty in Lawrence than I ran into. I ran into some: I don't know how to measure poverty (I'm not boasting). His people went right down and he went to work at fourteen years of age in two of the same mills that I worked in. He talks of himself as a proletarian; he went *radical.* It is a very interesting book to me because he names overseers and men at the mill—and all people I knew. He was twenty years after me. We had memories of the farm and the country that I went back to. I walked out of it all one day.

He uses the word *proletarian* for himself and a great man in Lawrence. The great man was named Wood, of the Wood's Mills—a great figure against Bill Haywood, his antagonist in the big Lawrence strike of 1910–1911, I think. Now Wood was really a proletarian in my use of the word. As the swear-word is, he was really a son of a sea-cook—I mean it literally—a son of a Portuguese sea-cook. He grew up in New Bedford—and rose to be the head of all the woollen mills; the Woollen Association, or whatever they call it.

Then he had the tragedy, after patronizing the poor and doing everything he could for his employees—even giving them escalators in the mills. He got a great strike on his hands and came out very badly in it. He lost the affection of his people and committed suicide afterwards. He was the genuine proletarian, because he came up from nowhere.

Now Fred Beal, who calls himself the same thing, is a Beal and a Hay of New Hampshire. Right away that's something a little different; he never knew the peasant life of Europe. He also counts himself a kin of Hannibal Hamlin, who was Vice-President with Lincoln in his first administration—that is another thing. For no matter how educated or poor a man is, a certain level up there in Vermont and New Hampshire stays about the same. We people just sort of fountain up, jet up out of it.

When I meet very wealthy people, I have to face them. I remember facing once a small group, not a thousand miles from Philadelphia. I did it for a charity-working friend of mine. She told me that the girls I must speak to must be gone for: they were worth at least a million apiece, and I could be rough on them. I knew they were all helping her in her charity work, so you can see my state of mind. I felt cross to be there. I took for my text,

"Let not man bring together what God hath set asunder."

Let the rich keep away from the poor for all of me, as the slang is. Well, that's just the way I feel.

I suppose I take that position as an artist. "You wrote about the poor," they said. I never measured that; I wouldn't have done it if I knew anything was going to be made of it. I didn't do it to get rid of the poor because I need them in my business.

What is the position of poetry toward the poor? I think, if you look back all through the years, you will find that—maybe falsely, hypocritically—poetry has praised poverty. It may be hypocritical because wealth is sour grapes—there is a good deal of that. I've sometimes thought that England was a very convenient place to be an artist in, because you have a whole class there who is poorer than any class here, for an artist to retire into in his poor years. Cabbage, bread, cheese, and tea without milk—he can have that. He can lose himself to his relatives and have that. I am not saying that poverty shouldn't be abolished. I do not know anything about it.

But what *is* the relation of poverty and poetry? I know once in self-defense I did come near to swearing. It says in the Bible, you think—I don't—it says in the Bible that you always have the poor with you. That isn't what it says. It says, "For Christ's sake, forget the poor some of the time." There are many beautiful things in the world beside poverty. I have praised poverty and spoken of its beauty and its use for the arts, but there are other things. I'm not here to dwell with too much emphasis on poverty. I just bring up the little question of the relationship and make a few suggestions, because I run the risk of reading about people—I wouldn't dare say whether they were rich or poor people.

I saw this summer one of the poorest spots in Vermont. I saw an old, old lady who couldn't seem to go on relief because she owned a little house. She hadn't much object in selling the house, because it wouldn't bring much. When she did sell it, she had to give all the money to pay her debts. But even then she couldn't go on relief because they had the record of her having sold a house. They thought she sold it on purpose to go on relief—a very corrupt happening in this impure world. A strange situation: she has a hired man and he is about half her age. And he goes out and earns their living as her hired man. She gives him part of what he earns.

And then I'll just tell you of a charitable act of my own. I don't often do charitable acts; only once in a great while. I went over there just as winter was coming on. The hired man had got hold of an old schoolhouse, long deserted, and had moved it onto an old cellar-hole by an old well. And they were starting to live there. The house was like a hen standing up in the nest; it hadn't settled down on its foundations. It looked kind of cold and windy, and I said:

"You'd better get the wall up under there."

The lady said:

"He is doing it just as fast as he can find the means."

And I said:

"He could raise the means, I guess you know," fidgeting a little, "and I wouldn't take it out in work right away."

He hung his head, and she said:

"James likes to know where he stands."

Of course you know as far as pity is concerned, there's nothing in it. It touches you a little, I suppose, in the middle, like amusement—there's a not unmixed feeling that people have about it. That's the last of a village once quite distinguished. I won't say any more for fear you'll run across it some day. All I say about it is that we're in danger, in our way of thinking that mercy comes first in the world. It comes in, but it comes in second. The thing you are most interested in is justice; all you ask for is justice in the struggle.

I had a boy come to me with poetry the other day. Who is a poor thing? He comes to me with talk about mercy on earth—everything has now gone merciful; kinder times ahead. I let him talk and have it all his own way. That's all right. Finally he came out with the poetry he'd brought. I said:

"You've come for mercy?"

He looked at me for a second, and said:

"No, sir, I just want fairness."

You see, they really have more spunk than you think. I said;

"I thought so."

After I treated him with fairness—and he came out, as it happened, very poorly in my estimation—then I might in mercy carry him home to his mother. It's there, of course. It's part of everything. But there's so much confusion about who is a poor thing, nowadays, that I can't help saying there's not much of that sort of thing around my poor people. [. . .]

All I want to point out is that you can't generalize about things, you can not go around saying things carelessly.

You take the poor women's clubs. All my sophisticated friends make fun of them. I don't suppose women's clubs know how poor they are in the estimation of some of my friends. They think just about the same of women's clubs as they think of Rotary Clubs—I'm betraying them to you. When I get with that kind of people, I feel like telling them about what happened to me in "Terre Hut." (That's what the conductor called it. I'm always picking on dialect, though I never use it.) Well, I went to Terre Hut. Once on a time I knew only the poor farmers in New Hampshire; lately I've got sort of travelled. Before I read to the club there, I was asked what I'd like to see before sentence was pronounced on me by the women's club. I said I'd like to see Eugene Debs. (I thought that would blast them. They were all bankers' wives and such.) They looked at each other rather regretfully:

"Why, you must see him. But you know, he's very ill."

I said:

"I wouldn't want to disturb him. My idea was to disturb you."

And they said:

"Disturb *us?*"

I said:

"I supposed he was an enemy of society."

And they said:

"Why, I suppose so."

And I said:

"I suppose he ruined your city."

They said:

"Well, he has done a good deal of harm. But he's such a nice person. We've just been singing carols to him."

There you are again—just as much blended generosity and largesse as you want to see anywhere—in Terre Hut, in the poor Middle West. One of my friends jokes, "East is East and West is West, but the Middle West is terrible." There's no argument to it. You just can't generalize.

Coming down on the train, a boy just about to get his doctor's degree at Yale told me:

"Anthologies are the worst thing in the world. You don't want to read anthologies, do you?"

I said:

"I've heard that a good many times. I don't want to contradict your teachers."

Poor thing. If anthologies are bad, so is all criticism, for anthologies are just a form of criticism. There's no better way for you to approach Shakespeare's sonnets than through reading the selections Palgrave made of them and the selections Quiller-Couch made of them. It's the example without too many words. Maybe the anthologies are bad; on the other hand, they are good, too. Maybe the poor are unfortunate, but on the other hand, they may be fortunate.

Let me read a poem to you. Here's my last book and it has got a good deal more of the times in it than anything I ever wrote before. And there's a little bit in this one called, "A Drumlin Woodchuck." You see, I had a funny time this year about this book. One well known paper called me a "counter-revolutionary" for writing it. I didn't know who wrote that. But I was called a "counter-revolutionary" with frills—there were some other words with it. In New York, I stood up and said:

"I wish I could think the man who called me that was in this audience. I would like to call him a 'bargain-counter revolutionary'."

I didn't mean any harm; I just meant a little harm. I had word afterward that he knew what I meant. Some go-between, some semi-radical was in the audience. And I'd better look out, because he had a sense of humor, and got the point about the bargain-counter revolutionary. I'd better look out, I'd get a firecracker. I told his friend I had a sense of humor, too: I knew what a firecracker meant. We forgot about it in the family and along about a holiday a box arrived. I never get things in boxes. I didn't think much about it, though. I started to open it, when I noticed that my name was printed by hand. Some people write that way, artists do, you know. Then I noticed up in the corner there was no name. It came from nobody, nowhere. I said to my wife:

"Don't you think we'd better give this back to the postman?"

She said:

"Well, we don't want the whole town to know about it."

So I said:

"I guess we'll take the paper off carefully, so that the jack-in-the-box won't jump out if he's in there."

I took the paper off very carefully. There was a cigar-box. And strangely enough, the seal was broken. There was a very large tack holding it shut. I didn't like the looks of that tack. I said:

"Well, I'm in for it now and might as well see it through. Let's go out in the yard with it. The house might be destroyed."

(We counter-revolutionaries believe in property.) We went out. I tied a large stone securely to it so that it would have some weight. Then I stood off, facing a great big tree of ours, and hurled the thing at the tree—and scattered cigars all over the yard! So whatever's coming to me hasn't come to me yet. [. . .]

The Poet's Next of Kin in a College

A TALK

This talk served as a curtain raiser to an evening's poetry reading at Princeton University on October 26, 1937, and was published as a companion lecture to "Poverty and Poetry" in the February 1938 *Biblia*.

Don't think for a minute that I think it matters much whether a poet has any kin or friends in a college. I suppose that a poet should lead a dog's life for a long, long time; that he should be late in knowing too well that he is a poet. But when it is all over and his diploma rolls away, he looks back sometimes, I suppose, and wonders who was nearest him and who was kindest to him.

Of course the kindest to him will always be the English department, if we are to speak by departments. It was not always so. The English department grows sentimental with age: it is often overly kind. And poets are often spoiled for facing editors, by this over-kindness. The teachers look on themselves as paid to like young writers: they have to like so many per year. Editors are paid to hate new writers. There is quite a gulf to bridge from teachers who love you to editors who hate you. The editors especially hate poetry, because they don't know where to put it. That is one practical reason. Sometimes I get a letter, a kind letter, from an editor who knows me and wants to do something for poetry. He says, have I a long thing that nobody else will take? That shows what they think about each other.

The English department may be the poet's best and surest friend. But I am talking about kin. Who is nearest the poet in age and occupation? He looks around the English department and sees all kinds of teachers.

One you might call the keeper of the texts. That means, of course, very little to a writer. Then there is the person who lectures on literature as representative. That is, he is interested in poetry as it represents its age. If it is a dull age, it should be dull poetry; if it is a rotten age, then it should be rotten poetry; if it is an inscrutable age, it should be inscrutable poetry. That is another concern, I think, that does not matter to the poet at all. He should not be bothered. Then, of course, there is just the general critical approach. That is very dangerous, for the poet—it puts too many words around poetry. For him, the anthology is the best form of criticism to meddle with. It is pure example. I was told, when I was young, let the anthologies alone. You might as well say, let all opinion in poetry alone, for the anthology is the best of all opinionation. It is a good form of criticism, just because it is pure example. But the critical approach is dangerous. It is not the spirit, quite, of the young poet.

Let's leave that department and look at the socio-economic department. That is to blame for the vitiation of much of our poetry today. A poet's main interest is in doing something well. That department's interest is in doing people good, doing the world good. A poet must always prefer to do something well to doing people good. He is lost if he is interested in doing people good. Leave that to the socio-economic department—while it lasts.

Now let us look briefly at science. That might be nearer than most: pure science, because it is nothing if it is not achievement, if it is not creative. Even with young men, it expects something on the ball, something of originality. But science is antagonistic to the English department and has done it much harm. It has introduced scientific methods of criticism. I said to a literary-scientific-research man, recently:

"I suppose poetry is the least of all things given to quotation."

"On the contrary," he replied, after a moment's thought. "It is one texture of quotations. You write it out of all of the books you have ever read, and it is my place to come after you and trace it to its source!"

I didn't write anything for six months after that. It drove me into what I might call deceptions. That's the intrusion of the scientific into the artistic.

I myself, since forty, have had a great leaning toward the philosophy department—but you know that's just letting all my prejudices out. My admiration for philosophy. I'll tell you why. I think that young people have insight. They have a flash here and a flash there. It is like the stars coming out in the sky in the early evening. They have flashes of light. They have that sort of thing which belongs to youth. It is later in the dark of life that you see forms, constellations. And it is the constellations that are philosophy. It is like forcing a too early mathematics on a child, to bring him to philosophy too young. We have system and we have plan all too soon now. You know too well and have convictions too well by the time you are forty. The flashing is done, the coming out of the stars. It is all constellations—night.

You see, I have said that the growth of a poet is through flashes. Sight and insight makes poetry, and that belongs to the beginning poet—the poet coming out. I suppose that poets die into philosophy as they grow older—if they don't die the other way. They die into wisdom. Maybe it is a good way to die.

I will tell you a story, to bring you to the point. One of my great friends was a college president, now gone. He came to me years ago with a boyish interest in poetry, a naïve interest. And this is the way he had come to it. He had looked on poetry as performance. He was a Welshman. His father had made pottery (and poetry) in America, at Utica, New York. His earliest recollection of poetry was sitting with his father, at the close of a prize contest and hearing the prizes awarded for poetry. The judge was an old Welshman, brought over from Wales, to deliver the prizes. The first prize was awarded for a certain poem and the old judge said, "Will the writer of it stand." My friend's father stood up. That was his first encounter with poetry. Performance. Bravo! Victory!

He went afterward to play baseball on a country ball team one summer, and was picked up by some college boys and taken to their college and educated free. I think I am right in saying that he pitched all four years on his college team and only lost two games in four years. From there he went to the Boston Nationals and after one year of some pitching blossomed out into the greatest pitcher in the country. For one year. And then he said to himself: "This ends early—can't last many years—and there is always poetry, which is akin. I'm going back to that." So he went back to college and got some more degrees—and ended up a college president. He came to me in that spirit entirely.

Now don't imagine I don't know all the problems of athletics. But I never look around on athletics in college with anything but an affectionate spirit. Take a boy who is intellectual, who spends his time worrying over the athletes about him. He will never write poetry. If he tries, he will never write anything but criticism. He'll be like a variable approaching its limit; never quite getting there. Poetry is a young thing, as we all know. Most of the poets have struck their notes between the ages of fifteen and twenty-five. That is just the time when you are in college and graduate school. It is in those ten years that you will strike your note or never. And it is very like athletic prowess in that respect. They are very close together.

When I see young men doing so wonderfully well in athletics, I don't feel angry at them. I feel jealous of them. I wish that some of my boys in writing would do the same thing. I wish they would stop grouching at the athletes—leave them alone and do something as well in the arts. Remember, you can't excuse yourself on the grounds of age. Sight and insight. You must have form—performance. The thing itself is indescribable, but it is felt like athletic form. To have form, feel form in sports—and by analogy feel form in verse. One works and waits for form in both. As I said, the person who spends his time criticizing the play around him will never write poetry. He will write criticism—for the *New Republic*!

When one looks back over his own poetry, his only criticism is whether he had form or not. Did he worry it out or pour it out? You can't go back to a tennis game and play it over—except with alibis. You can go back over a poem and touch it up—but never unless you are in the same form again. Yet the great pleasure in writing poetry is in having been carried off. It is as if you stood astride of the subject that lay on the ground, and they cut the cord, and the subject gets up under you and you ride it. You adjust yourself to the motion of the thing itself. That is the poem.

So many ways I have tried to say what I feel. Keeping the thing in motion is sometimes like walking a rolling barrel. Again, a small poem is like the five or six balls a pitcher pitches to a given batter. There is a little system—a little set of pitched balls; a little set of sentences. You make the little set and the coming off is it—long or short. When Poe said that all poems were short, he meant that a long poem was just full of little runs—you could take them out; you could tell where it happened. I've boasted I could tell whether it happened in the morning or midnight—with morning calmness or midnight intoxication! It's different, of course, if a poem is just penned to bother. I can understand that kind, even—if I will be bothered. But all I ask is to be smitten.

This Is My Best

A CHOICE OF SIXTEEN POEMS

In preparing for his 1942 volume *This Is My Best,* the anthologist Whit Burnett asked ninety-three American authors to participate in a game of self-evaluation; each was to choose from his lifetime output a unit that in his opinion represented his creative best, and then to give some comments on the selection made.

Robert Frost picked sixteen poems and arranged them in this order: "The Need of Being Versed in Country Things," "Come In," "The Onset," "Stopping by Woods on a Snowy Evening," "On a Tree Fallen Across the Road," "The Wood-Pile," "Wilful Homing," "A Blue Ribbon at Amesbury," "Two Tramps In Mud Time," "A Prayer in Spring," "Mowing," "A Drumlin Woodchuck," "Sitting by a Bush in Broad Sunlight," "Sand Dunes," "A Soldier," and "The Gift Outright." Here is his commentary on his choices.

It would be hard to gather biography from poems of mine except as they were all written by the same person, out of the same general region north of Boston, and out of the same books, a few Greek and Latin, practically no others in any other tongue than our own. This was as it happened. To show that there was no rule about place laid down, I may point to two or three poems reminiscent of my ten years as a child in San Francisco and a few others actually written in California at the time of the Olympic games. More than a few were written in Beaconsfield and in Ryton, England, where I farmed, or rather gardened in a very small way from 1912 to 1915. My first two books were published in England by the Scotch and English, to whom I am under obligations for life for my start in life. This too was as it happened. I had on hand when I visited England the material of those two books and more than half of another. I had had poems in American magazines, but not many, and my relative unsuccess with magazines had kept the idea of a book from ever entering my head. It was perhaps the boldness of my adventure among entire strangers that stirred me up to try appealing from the editors of magazines to the publishers of books.

I have made this selection much as I made the one from my first book, *A Boy's Will,* and my second book, *North of Boston,* looking backward over the accumulation of years to see how many poems I could find towards some one meaning it might seem absurd to have had in advance, but it would be all right to accept from fate after the fact. The interest, the pastime, was to learn if there had been any divinity shaping my ends and I had been building better than I knew. In other words could anything of larger design, even the roughest, any broken or dotted continuity, or any fragment of a figure be discerned among the apparently random lesser designs of the several poems? I had given up convictions when young from despair of learning how they were had. Nevertheless I might not have been without them. They might be turned up out of the heap by assortment. And if not convictions, then perhaps native prejudices and inclinations. I took thirty poems for *A Boy's Will* to plot a curved line of flight away from people and so back to people. For *North of Boston* I took group enough to show the people and to show that I had forgiven them for being people. The group here given brings out my inclination to country occupations. It began with a farm in the back yard in San Francisco. This is no prejudice against the city. I am fond of several great cities. It is merely an inclination to country things. My favorite implements (after the pen) are the axe and the scythe, both of which besides being tools of peace have also been weapons of war. The Hungarian peasantry under Kossuth carried the scythe into battle in their attempt at independence from Austria, and the axle of an ancient war chariot was prolonged into a scythe at either end. In three of the poems I celebrate the axe, in one the scythe.

"... a matchmaker, matching ideas and matching lines—"

A SELECTION OF COUPLETS

Speaking at Connecticut College on December 8, 1959,
Robert Frost declared:

"In a talk of mine called 'How Can You Tell When You're
Thinking' I've settled it that all there is to thought is feats of
association. [. . .] Now, wouldn't it be a pretty idea to look
at that as the under part of every poem: a feat of
association, putting two things together and making a
metaphor—anything you want to call it, analogy and all the
different words for the same thing—putting this and that
together, to your own surprise, as well as everybody
else's[. . .] . Carry that idea a little further, to think that
perhaps the rhyming, the coupling of lines is an outward
symbol of this thing that I call feats of association. [. . .]

"You got to be in on the coupling of thoughts, and you only
ask to see a pleasant symbol of coupling in the rhymes: the
coupling of lines[. . .] . I'm coupling 'em all the time, for
better or worse. It's as if I, inwardly and outwardly, was a
matchmaker, matching ideas and matching lines—coupling
lines. [. . .]

"Now I'm going to read you poems, and right away you'll notice
me at it, and you mustn't forget that the main thing about the
poem is its carrying through the coupling of the things that
make the idea; but all the time these little couplets are sort of

flung out like smoke rings, you know, to say Isn't it lovely to couple things. And you can carry that very far."

In this section are presented some individual rhymed couplets, as well as passages containing groups of couplets, drawn from among Frost's poems that are not published in full within this volume.

I had for my winter evening walk—
No one at all with whom to talk,
But I had the cottages in a row
Up to their shining eyes in snow.

—*from "Good Hours," lines 1–4*

I gave it the preliminary spin,
And poured on water (tears it might have been);
And when it almost gaily jumped and flowed,
A Father-Time-like man got on and rode,
Armed with a scythe and spectacles that glowed.
He turned on willpower to increase the load
And slow me down—and I abruptly slowed,
Like coming to a sudden railroad station.
I changed from hand to hand in desperation.

* * *

Once when the grindstone almost jumped its bearing
It looked as if he might be badly thrown
And wounded on his blade. So far from caring,
I laughed inside, and only cranked the faster
(It ran as if it wasn't greased but glued);
I'd welcome any moderate disaster
That might be calculated to postpone

What evidently nothing could conclude.
The thing that made me more and more afraid
Was that we'd ground it sharp and hadn't known,
And now were only wasting precious blade.
And when he raised it dripping once and tried
The creepy edge of it with wary touch,
And viewed it over his glasses funny-eyed,
Only disinterestedly to decide
It needed a turn more, I could have cried
Wasn't there danger of a turn too much?
Mightn't we make it worse instead of better?
I was for leaving something to the whetter.
        —*from "The Grindstone," lines 26–34 and 57–75*

"A sigh for every so many breath,
And for every so many sigh a death.
That's what I always tell my wife
Is the multiplication table of life."
        —*from "The Times Table," lines 9–12*

Here further up the mountain slope
Than there was ever any hope,
My father built, enclosed a spring,
Strung chains of wall round everything,
Subdued the growth of earth to grass,
And brought our various lives to pass.
        —*from "The Birthplace," lines 1–6*

He is husband, she is wife.
She fears not him, they fear not life.
—*from "On the Heart's Beginning to Cloud the Mind,"*
        lines 36–37

Petals I may have once pursued.
Leaves are all my darker mood.
—*from "Leaves Compared with Flowers," lines 19–20*

That life is only life forevermore
Together wing to wing and oar to oar.
—*from "The Master Speed," lines 13–14*

Poor egotist, he has no way of knowing
But he's as good as anybody going.
—*from "Waspish," lines 5–6*

From form to content and back to form,
From norm to crazy and back to norm,
From bound to free and back to bound,
From sound to sense and back to sound.
So back and forth. It almost scares
A man the way things come in pairs.
—*from "To a Thinker," lines 9–14*

I own I never really warmed
To the reformer or reformed.
from "To a Thinker," lines 29–30

Never again would birds' song be the same.
And to do that to birds was why she came.
—*from "Never Again Would Birds' Song Be the Same,"*
lines 13–14

No one has ever failed the poet ranks
To link a chain of money-metal banks.
—*from "The Lost Follower," lines 7–8*

The slave will never thank his manumitter;
Which often makes the manumitter bitter.
—*from "The Literate Farmer and the Planet Venus,"*
lines 90–91

And for a moment all was plain
That men have thought about in vain.
—*from "An Unstamped Letter in Our Rural Letter Box,"*
lines 36–37

May I in my brief bolt across the scene
Not be misunderstood in what I mean.
—*from "The Fear of Man," lines 15–16*

Had but Columbus known enough
He might have boldly made the bluff
That better than da Gama's gold
He had been given to behold
The race's future trial place,
A fresh start for the human race.

*　　*　　*

But all he did was spread the room
Of our enacting out the doom
Of being in each other's way,
And so put off the weary day
When we would have to put our mind
On how to crowd but still be kind.
—*from "America Is Hard to See," lines 25-30 and 37–42*

Colonial had been the thing to be
As long as the great issue was to see
What country'd be the one to dominate
By character, by tongue, by native trait,

The new world Christopher Columbus found.
The French, the Spanish, and the Dutch were downed
And counted out. Heroic deeds were done.
Elizabeth the First and England won.
    —from "For John F. Kennedy His Inauguration,"
                                    lines 11–18

I quote him with respect verbatim.
Some quaint dissatisfaction ate him.
                    —from "A-Wishing Well," lines 6–7

It was by having been contrasted
That good and bad so long had lasted.
                    —from "Quandary," lines 5–6

What Became of New England?

A COMMENCEMENT ADDRESS

While making this commencement address at Oberlin
College on June 8, 1937, Robert Frost obliquely explained
his reasons for choosing to speak on the question, "What
Became of New England?" The talk, edited for publication
from stenographic notes, appeared in the May 1938 *Oberlin
Alumni Magazine.*

Friends:

Graduating Class of 1937 and New England—once removed, perhaps,
as Western Reserve; twice removed from Wisconsin; four times
removed, like me, from California; but New England:

I never gave up willingly any love I've had. The poets I cared for
when I was young, I still care for, alon[g]side of poets I liked later. Find-
ing a new doesn't turn me against an old; I stand on the defensive
against anyone who would take the old away from me. I stand on the
defensive lately a good deal for New England. People say to me, "What
has become of New England?"

Twenty years ago, I published a little book, *North of Boston,* that
seemed to have something to do with New England. It got praise in a
way that cost me some pain: it was described as a book about a deca-
dent, lost society.

A distinguished critic (I could name him; he is visiting in this coun-
try now) has said: "The Catholic peasantry of Europe renews itself
through the ages. The Protestants, the Puritan peasantry of New En-
gland, has dried up and blown away in three hundred years." The first
mistake, of course, was the word "peasantry." But let us consider the
other mistake.

Only the other day I picked up a book about Mexico, and there was an analogy between the races that had displaced other races in Mexico and the same thing in New England: "A sharper, shrewder, a more virile population has crowded out the Yankees." Someone had been visiting for a summer there!

You have been reading, probably, a very beautiful book called *The Flowering of New England,* by a friend of mine. I have only one regret, and that is that there is in the end of it a slight suggestion of the Spengler history,—indication of decline. Van Wyck Brook[s]'s next book is going to be called *Indian Summer.* I suppose we'll be even farther down by then.

What was New England? It was the first little nation that bade fair to be an English-speaking nation on this continent. In the first hundred years it had pushed off from England (it had drawn off and been pushed off, both,) into almost a nation, with its capital at Boston. People in Virginia remarked on the rapid development of the little nation.

There was Boston. There was much beautiful architecture, art. Some want to rob the Puritans of art. The Puritans didn't mind a play if it was in a book: Cotton Mather had one of the First Folios of Shakespeare; and you could *read* a play in Boston. There were ten silversmiths in Boston before there was a single lawyer. People forget all those things. I should mention another thing about New England that we have lost. It was the port of entry of our freedom. We call some of the men who came there by the name of "rebels." And what has become of New England that these people should pity us about or taunt us with?

I don't know how much of a fight you make to hang on to what's yours. You're younger than I by a good many years, and I suppose the older one is the harder he hangs on to what he's built into his life. When the meaning goes out of anything, as happens, forms crumble,—formulae crumble. But the whole function of poetry is the renewal of words, is the making of words mean again what they meant.

Let me take one or two illustrations, in politics and religion.

I heard, as I marched in today, two words in the middle of a sentence; I don't know what the rest was. The two words were "divine right,"—words with an ancient history, words with a great history, words that too many people too easily give up. They've been laughed out of their meaning. But before I'd give them up I'd. . . .

In government we have two things: we have the ruler and the ruled. We have two answers: its first answerability is to itself; its second is the consent of the ruled. Consent? How can there be consent without some guidance to consent to? We've had rulers in this country who had nothing within themselves to which to consent,—with one ear to the ground, attempting to find out what people would consent to.

In 1897 I was sitting in a class in college when I heard a man spend quite the best part of an hour making fun of the expression that we are all "free and equal." So easy to dismiss. Let's have a look at it:

All men were created free and equally funny. Before you laugh too much at that, take another look at it: Four hundred years ago the only people who were funny were yokels; now, today, even kings are funny. We've come a long way.

We hear today about the conquest of fear; and we speak lightly of that old thing, "God-fearing man." Fear? Banish fear from your mind! What kind of a God is it that you should fear? One might forget God in a lull of faith. One might forget God, and talk about the highest in himself. I can't imagine any honest man without the fear of finding himself unworthy in the sight of someone else. It might be something you didn't care to call by name.

I don't give up New England too easily. I don't give up these words that I've cared for,—these phrases. I long to renew them. I seek to renew them.

Another one: "a jealous God." In Greenwich Village I've heard two words dismissed, "fear" and "jealousy." And that makes all the

excitement in Greenwich Village. What is jealousy? It's the claim of the
object on the lover. The claim of God is that you should be true to Him,
and so true to yourself. The word still lives for me.

New England, now,—what's become of it? It's not necessarily to be
found in a literature to be restricted to New England. The little nation
that was, and was to be, gave itself, as Virginia gave herself, westward,
into the great nation that she saw coming, and so gave help to America.
And so any of us who are not New Englanders particularly—any writ-
ers we were, any statesmen we were—were to be Americans,—United
States statesmen, United States writers.

And the thing New England gave most to America was the thing I
am talking about: a stubborn clinging to meaning,—to purify words
until they meant again what they should mean. Puritanism had that
meaning entirely: a purifying of words and a renewal of words and a
renewal of meaning. That's what brought the Puritans to America, and
that's what kept them believing: they saw that there was a meaning that
was becoming elusive.

You can get out a theory that meanings go out of things. You can call
it disillusionment. You can get disillusionment of a phrase, such as
"fearing God," and "equality." And then you can form a religion, like
George Santayana. He lets you see that there is nothing but illusion,
and it can just as well be one kind as another: there is the illusion that
you are conscious of, and there is illusion that you become conscious of
later. But you should go right on anyway, because there's no proof: all
is illusion. You grow to be a sad person.

Some people pity a person who loses his hero. Who suffers the
worse, the person who loses his hero, or the lost hero? You must seek
reality forever in things you care for.

Witchcraft was an illusion, wasn't it? And so is all this Industrialism.
And so is the New Deal. You can make it all illusion with a little help of
Santayana. He says right out in his philosophy that there are two kinds

of illusion, two kinds of madness: one is normal madness, the other is abnormal madness!

Let's take one more: "prayer." I'll tell you one of the poems which comes out of the eighteenth century, and ought by rights to be dead by this time:

Strong is the lion—like a coal
His eyeball—like a bastion's mole
    His chest against the foes:
Strong the gier-eagle on his sail,
Strong against tide the enormous whale
    Emerges as he goes.

But stronger still in earth and air,
And in the sea, the man of prayer,
    And far beneath the tide:
And in the seat to faith assigned,
Where ask is have, where seek is find,
    Where knock is open wide.

On a Passage in Paradise Lost

A LETTER

The poet-teacher Wilbert Snow in an article entitled "The
Robert Frost I Knew," published in *The Texas Quarterly* for
Autumn 1968, included a letter he had received from Frost
growing out of a disagreement between them over how to
interpret a celebrated passage in Milton's *Paradise Lost.*
Snow provides this background:

"The entire problem of justice versus mercy intrigued him. In
the 1930s he sat up until well past midnight many times in
our home denouncing mercy and lauding justice. My wife and
I pled the cause of mercy and pointed out the mercies which
filled the pages of the New Testament. He retorted that he
was an 'Old Testament Christian' who feared the softening
effects of mercy."

The passage in *Paradise Lost* on which the Frost-Snow
disagreement centered (Book III, lines 130–134) includes
these lines: ". . . in Mercy and Justice both, / Through
Heav'n and Earth, so shall my glorie excel, / But Mercy first
and last shall brightest shine." Snow, insisting that Milton
favored mercy, precipitated this impatient rejoinder from
Frost, dated January 2, 1938.

BILL BILL Use your brains a moment while we brush up your vocabu-
lary. You simply must not quibble in a serious matter like a win-at-any
cost public debater. Don't pretend you don't know what Milton meant
when he said mercy was always first. You know your Milton and your

Puritanism. He used it in the sense of first aid to what? To the deserving? No, to the totally depraved and undeserving. That's what we are and have been since the day Eve ate the rotten apple. I bet it was rotten. Eve wouldn't have known the difference. It was probably her first apple. (There you get a genuine first) And look what a city person will eat for an apple from never having seen one on a tree. "In Adam's fall We sinned all." Mercy ensued. There could be nothing for us but mercy first last and all the time from the point of view of the religious pessimist. Milton's first is only relative. It is very like Adam and Eve's being first and yet finding the daughters of men as wives for Cain and Abel. There is the presupposition of a whole set up of sin, failure, judgment, and condemnation. Mercy comes in rather late to prevent execution—sometimes only to delay it. It is too easy to understand Milton. He faced and liked the harshness of our trial. He was no mere New Testament saphead. (I should like to think Christ was none; but have him your own way for the time being. You'd better have read up on your Deuteronomy before I see you again.) Milton loved Cromwell for his Ironsides and Michael for licking the Devil. He had a human weakness for success; he wanted the right to prevail and was fairly sure he knew what right was. Within certain limits he believed in the rewards of merit. But after all was said for the best of us he was willing to admit that before God our whole enterprise from the day we put on fig leaves and went to work had been no better than pitiful.

I'm like that with a class in school. I see the boys as comparatively good and bad but taken as a job lot in the absolute so really good for nothing that I can bring myself to mark them with nothing but mercy and I give them all A or at worst B. Your sense of justice is shocked. You can hardly credit my claim to godlike illogical kindness. I have always been a prey to it. The office where justice sits with the scales over her eyes has never approved of me. I never go there except to try to get a scholarship or a fellowship for some poor fool you probably would have flunked out; particularly a Rhodes Scholarship because I'd rather sacrifice a bad man than a good to the seductions of Cecil Rhodes. There I go distinguishing between the good and bad but I don't readily see how I can avoid it, do you old Tops (plural as a praise word)?

Illogical kindness—that is mercy. Only those are likely to act on it who know what it is in all its subordination. It was just and logical that a man's body should be taken in slavery when he went beyond his depth in debt. It was illogical that his creditor couldn't take him in slavery and the state should take him merely as a prisoner. It was another step in illogic when it was decided his person should never again be taken at all. Another when it was decided that he shouldn't be reduced by the sheriff below a certain amount of personal property. At every step there were warnings from the conservative that character would be demoralized by the relaxation of strict logical justice. People would go in debt on purpose it was feared to abuse the rich and thrifty. We are now in our lifetime seeing a great next step taken in this long story of debt—and it will be something if it is all that comes of your New Deal. It is going to be settled once for all that no man's folly or bad luck can ever reduce him to no income at all. A chicken is hatched with enough yolk in its guts to last it several days. Henceforth not only the rich but everybody born is to be sure of at least a few dollars a week as long as he lives. Never more quite down to the quick. That is in America—and while we can afford it. We are all going to fetch in and make that come true. But don't call that social justice. Keep your words in their places. It is illogical kindness. It is mercy. And you and the Lord have mercy on my argument.

EVER YOURS R.F.

The Figure a Poem Makes

AN INTRODUCTION

The first edition of Robert Frost's *Collected Poems,* published
in 1930, contained no prose introduction, but when an
enlarged edition appeared in 1939 it carried this
introductory essay, entitled "The Figure a Poem Makes."
Thereafter Frost consistently included it in other volumes
that constituted comprehensive gatherings of his poetry
(*Selected Prose of Robert Frost,* pp. 17–20).

Abstraction is an old story with the philosophers, but it has been
like a new toy in the hands of the artists of our day. Why can't we have
any one quality of poetry we choose by itself? We can have in thought.
Then it will go hard if we can't in practice. Our lives for it.

Granted no one but a humanist much cares how sound a poem is if
it is only *a* sound. The sound is the gold in the ore. Then we will have
the sound out alone and dispense with the inessential. We do till we
make the discovery that the object in writing poetry is to make all
poems sound as different as possible from each other, and the
resources for that of vowels, consonants, punctuation, syntax, words,
sentences, meter are not enough. We need the help of context—mean-
ing—subject matter. That is the greatest help towards variety. All that
can be done with words is soon told. So also with meters—particularly
in our language where there are virtually but two, strict iambic and
loose iambic. The ancients with many were still poor if they depended
on meters for all tune. It is painful to watch our sprung-rhythmists
straining at the point of omitting one short from a foot for relief from
monotony. The possibilities for tune from the dramatic tones of mean-
ing struck across the rigidity of a limited meter are endless. And we are

back in poetry as merely one more art of having something to say, sound or unsound. Probably better if sound, because deeper and from wider experience.

Then there is this wildness whereof it is spoken. Granted again that it has an equal claim with sound to being a poem's better half. If it is a wild tune, it is a poem. Our problem then is, as modern abstractionists, to have the wildness pure; to be wild with nothing to be wild about. We bring up as aberrationists, giving way to undirected associations and kicking ourselves from one chance suggestion to another in all directions as of a hot afternoon in the life of a grasshopper. Theme alone can steady us down. Just as the first mystery was how a poem could have a tune in such a straightness as meter, so the second mystery is how a poem can have wildness and at the same time a subject that shall be fulfilled.

It should be of the pleasure of a poem itself to tell how it can. The figure a poem makes. It begins in delight and ends in wisdom. The figure is the same as for love. No one can really hold that the ecstasy should be static and stand still in one place. It begins in delight, it inclines to the impulse, it assumes direction with the first line laid down, it runs a course of lucky events, and ends in a clarification of life—not necessarily a great clarification, such as sects and cults are founded on, but in a momentary stay against confusion. It has denouement. It has an outcome that though unforeseen was predestined from the first image of the original mood—and indeed from the very mood. It is but a trick poem and no poem at all if the best of it was thought of first and saved for the last. It finds its own name as it goes and discovers the best waiting for it in some final phrase at once wise and sad—the happy-sad blend of the drinking song.

No tears in the writer, no tears in the reader. No surprise for the writer, no surprise for the reader. For me the initial delight is in the surprise of remembering something I didn't know I knew. I am in a place, in a situation, as if I had materialized from cloud or risen out of the ground. There is a glad recognition of the long lost and the rest follows. Step by step the wonder of unexpected supply keeps growing. The impressions most useful to my purpose seem always those I was unaware of and so made no note of at the time when taken, and the conclusion is come to that like giants we are always hurling experience ahead of us to pave the future with against the day when we may want to strike a line of purpose across it for somewhere. The line will have the more charm for not being mechanically straight. We enjoy the straight crookedness of a good walking stick. Modern instruments of precision are being used to make things crooked as if by eye and hand in the old days.

I tell how there may be a better wildness of logic than of inconsequence. But the logic is backward, in retrospect, after the act. It must be more felt than seen ahead like prophecy. It must be a revelation, or a series of revelations, as much for the poet as for the reader. For it to be that there must have been the greatest freedom of the material to move about in it and to establish relations in it regardless of time and space, previous relation, and everything but affinity. We prate of freedom. We call our schools free because we are not free to stay away from them till we are sixteen years of age. I have given up my democratic prejudices and now willingly set the lower classes free to be completely taken care of by the upper classes. Political freedom is nothing to me. I bestow it right and left. All I would keep for myself is the freedom of my material—the condition of body and mind now and then to summons aptly from the vast chaos of all I have lived through.

Scholars and artists thrown together are often annoyed at the puzzle of where they differ. Both work from knowledge; but I suspect they differ most importantly in the way their knowledge is come by. Scholars get theirs with conscientious thoroughness along projected lines of logic; poets theirs cavalierly and as it happens in and out of books. They stick to nothing deliberately, but let what will stick to them like burrs where they walk in the fields. No acquirement is on assignment, or even self-assignment. Knowledge of the second kind is much more available in the wild free ways of wit and art. A school boy may be defined as one who can tell you what he knows in the order in which he learned it. The artist must value himself as he snatches a thing from some previous order in time and space into a new order with not so much as a ligature clinging to it of the old place where it was organic.

More than once I should have lost my soul to radicalism if it had been the originality it was mistaken for by its young converts. Originality and initiative are what I ask for my country. For myself the originality need be no more than the freshness of a poem run in the way I have described: from delight to wisdom. The figure is the same as for love. Like a piece of ice on a hot stove the poem must ride on its own melting. A poem may be worked over once it is in being, but may not be worried into being. Its most precious quality will remain its having run itself and carried away the poet with it. Read it a hundred times: it will forever keep its freshness as a metal keeps its fragrance. It can never lose its sense of a meaning that once unfolded by surprise as it went.

The Doctrine of Excursions

A PREFACE

There were many reasons for asking Robert Frost to write a preface for an anthology made up of previously unpublished pieces of poetry and prose submitted at the Bread Loaf Writers' Conference. He had been closely related to Middlebury College's Bread Loaf School of English almost from the time of its founding in 1920, and he had helped to formulate many of the ideas on which the Writers' Conference was established six years later. The *Bread Loaf Anthology*, containing his preface called "The Doctrine of Excursions," appeared in 1939.

You who are as much concerned as I for the future of Bread Loaf will agree with me that once in so often it should be redefined if it is to be kept from degenerating into a mere summer resort for routine education in English, or worse still for the encouragement of vain ambition in literature. We go there not for correction or improvement. No writer has ever been corrected into importance. Nor do we go to find a publisher or get help in finding a publisher. Bringing manuscript to Bread Loaf is in itself publication.

A writer can live by writing to himself alone for days and years. Sooner or later to go on he must be read. It may well be that in appealing to the public he has but added to his own responsibility; for now besides judging himself he must judge his judges. For long the public received him not. Then the public received him. When were the public right? Why, when the final authority is his, should he be bothered with any other? The answer is an article in the doctrine of excursions. All we know is that the crowning mercy for an author is publication in some form or other.

Undeniably the best form is a book with a reputable house at the expense of the house. The next best is a book with a reputable house at the expense of the author. Those two constitute publication in the first and second degrees. But there are several humbler degrees, among them the Bread Loaf Conference. It must not be forgotten that much good poetry has never risen above the second degree and some has undoubtedly come out in newspapers that pay nothing for contributions. Publication in book form like this anthology of ours was not contemplated in the original scheme of Bread Loaf and is not of the essence of the institution. It has simply been added unto us as a reward for modesty.

Bread Loaf is to be regarded then as a place in Vermont where a writer can try his effect on readers. There, as out in the world, he must brave the rigors of specific criticism. He will get enough and perhaps more than enough of good set praise and blame. He will help wear out the words "like" and "dislike." He will hear too many things compared to the disadvantage of all of them. A handkerchief is worse than a knife because it can be cut by a knife; a knife is worse than a stone because it can be blunted by a stone; a stone is worse than a handkerchief because it can be covered by a handkerchief; and we have been round the silly circle. All this is as it has to be where the end is a referee's decision. There is nothing so satisfactory in literature as the knock-out in prize fighting.

But more than out in the world a writer has a chance at Bread Loaf of getting beyond this cavil and getting his proof of something better than approval in signs—looks, tones, manners. Many words are often but one small sign. There is the possibility of his winning through to the affections of the affectionate.

Beyond the self-esteem and the critical opinion of others, the scientist has a third proof I have envied for the artist. From the perturbation of a planet in its orbit he predicts exactly where in the sky and at what time of night another planet will be discovered. All telescopes point that way and there the new planet is. The scientist is justified of his figures. He knows he is good. He has fitted into the nature of the universe. A typical play of the eighties had in it a scene from the digging of the Hoosac Tunnel. The engineer had triangulated over the mountains and driven in shafts from opposite sides to meet each other under the middle of the mountain. It was the eleventh hour of the enterprise. There stood the engineer among the workmen in one shaft waiting to hear from the workmen in the other. A gleam of pickaxe broke through; a human face appeared in the face of the rock. The engineer was justified of his figures. He knew he was an engineer. He had fitted into the nature of the universe.

I should like to believe the poet gets an equivalent assurance in the affections of the affectionate. He has fitted into the nature of mankind. He is justified of his numbers. He has acquired friends who will even cheat for him a little and refuse to see his faults if they are not so glaring as to show through eyelids. And friends are everything. For why have we wings if not to seek friends at an elevation?

The Constant Symbol

AN INTRODUCTION

Robert Frost first published "The Constant Symbol" as an
essay in *The Atlantic Monthly* for October of 1946. Later that
year he used it as the introduction to the Modern Library
edition of his *Poems*. It is reprinted in *Selected Prose of
Robert Frost*, pp. 23–29.

There seems to be some such folk saying as that easy to understand
is contemptible, hard to understand irritating. The implication is that
just easy enough, just hard enough, right in the middle, is what literary
criticism ought to foster. A glance backward over the past convinces me
otherwise. The *Iliad, Odyssey,* and *Aeneid* are easy. The *Purgatorio* is
said to be hard. The Song of Songs *is* hard. There have been works
lately to surpass all records for hardness. Some knotted riddles tell
what may be worth our trouble. But hard or easy seems to me of slight
use as a test either way.

Texture is surely something. A good piece of weaving takes rank
with a picture as decoration for the wall of a studio, though it must be
admitted to verge on the arty. There is a time of apprenticeship to tex-
ture when it shouldn't matter if the stuff is never made up into any-
thing. There may be scraps of repeated form all over it. But form as a
whole! Don't be shocking! The title of his first book was *Fragments.*
The artist has to grow up and coarsen a little before he looks on texture
as not an end in itself.

There are many other things I have found myself saying about
poetry, but the chiefest of these is that it is metaphor, saying one thing
and meaning another, saying one thing in terms of another, the pleasure
of ulteriority. Poetry is simply made of metaphor. So also is philoso-

phy—and science, too, for that matter, if it will take the soft impeachment from a friend. Every poem is a new metaphor inside or it is nothing. And there is a sense in which all poems are the same old metaphor always.

Every single poem written regular is a symbol small or great of the way the will has to pitch into commitments deeper and deeper to a rounded conclusion and then be judged for whether any original intention it had has been strongly spent or weakly lost; be it in art, politics, school, church, business, love, or marriage—in a piece of work or in a career. Strongly spent is synonymous with kept.

We may speak after sentence, resenting judgment. How can the world know anything so intimate as what we were intending to do? The answer is the world presumes to know. The ruling passion in man is not as Viennese as is claimed. It is rather a gregarious instinct to keep together by minding each other's business. Grex rather than sex. We *must* be preserved from becoming egregious. The beauty of socialism is that it will end the individuality that is always crying out mind your own business. Terence's answer would be all human business is my business. No more invisible means of support, no more invisible motives, no more invisible anything. The ultimate commitment is giving in to it that an outsider may see what we were up to sooner and better than we ourselves. The bard has said in effect, Unto these forms did I commend the spirit. It may take him a year after the act to confess he only betrayed the spirit with a rhymster's cleverness and to forgive his enemies the critics for not having listened to his oaths and protestations to the contrary. Had he anything to be true to? Was he true to it? Did he use good words? You couldn't tell unless you made out what idea they were supposed to be good for. Every poem is an epitome of the great predicament; a figure of the will braving alien entanglements.

Take the President in the White House. A study of the success of his intention might have to go clear back to when as a young politician, youthfully step-careless, he made the choice between the two parties of our system. He may have stood for a moment wishing he knew of a third party nearer the ideal; but only for a moment, since he was practical. And in fact he may have been so little impressed with the importance of his choice that he left his first commitment to be made for him by his friends and relatives. It was only a small commitment anyway, like a kiss. He can scarcely remember how much credit he deserved personally for the decision it took. Calculation is usually no part in the first step in any walk. And behold him now a statesman so multifariously closed in on with obligations and answerabilities that sometimes he loses his august temper. He might as well have got himself into a sestina royal.

Or he may be a religious nature who lightly gets committed to a nameable church through an older friend in plays and games at the Y.M.C.A. The next he knows he is in a theological school and next in the pulpit of a Sunday wrestling with the angel for a blessing on his self-defensive interpretation of the Creed. What of his original intention now? At least he has had the advantage of having it more in his heart than in his head; so that he should have made shift to assert it without being chargeable with compromise. He could go a long way before he had to declare anything he could be held to. He began with freedom to squander. He has to acknowledge himself in a tighter and tighter place. But his courage asked for it. It would have been the same if he had gone to the North Pole or climbed Everest. All that concerns *us* is whether his story was one of conformance or performance.

There's an indulgent smile I get for the recklessness of the unnecessary commitment I made when I came to the first line in the second stanza of a poem in this book called "Stopping by Woods on a Snowy Evening." I was riding too high to care what trouble I incurred. And it was all right so long as I didn't suffer deflection.

The poet goes in like a rope skipper to make the most of his opportunities. If he trips himself he stops the rope. He is of our stock and has been brought up by ear to choice of two metres, strict iambic and loose

(448)

iambic (not to count varieties of the latter). He may have any length of line up to six feet. He may use an assortment of line lengths for any shape of stanza like Herrick in "To Daffodils." Not that he is running wild. His intention is of course a particular mood that won't be satisfied with anything less than its own fulfillment. But it is not yet a thought concerned with what becomes it. One thing to know it by: it shrinks shyly from anticipatory expression. Tell love beforehand and, as Blake says, it loses flow without filling the mould; the cast will be a reject. The freshness of a poem belongs absolutely to its not having been thought out and then set to verse as the verse in turn might be set to music. A poem is the emotion of having a thought while the reader waits a little anxiously for the success of dawn. The only discipline to begin with is the inner mood that at worst may give the poet a false start or two like the almost microscopic filament of cotton that goes before the blunt thread-end and must be picked up first by the eye of the needle. He must be entranced to the exact premonition. No mystery is meant. When familiar friends approach each other in the street both are apt to have this experience in feeling before knowing the pleasantry they will inflict on each other in passing.

Probably there is something between the mood and the vocal imagination (images of the voice speaking) that determines a man's first commitment to metre and length of line.

Suppose him to have written down "When in disgrace with Fortune and men's eyes." He has uttered about as much as he has to live up to in the theme as in the form. Odd how the two advance into the open pari passu. He has given out that he will descend into Hades, but he has confided in no one how far before he will turn back, or whether he will turn back at all, and by what jutting points of rock he will pick his way. He may proceed as in blank verse. Two lines more, however, and he has let himself in for rhyme, three more and he has set himself a stanza. Up to this point his discipline has been the self-discipline whereof it is written in so great praise. The harsher discipline from without is now well begun. He who knows not both knows neither. His worldly commitments are now three or four deep. Between us, he was no doubt bent on the sonnet in the first place from habit, and what's the use in pretending he was a freer agent than he had any ambition to be? He had made most of his commitments all in one plunge. The only suspense he asks us to share with him is in the theme. He goes down, for instance, to a depth that must surprise him as much as it does us. But he doesn't even have the say of how long his piece will be. Any worry is as to whether he will outlast or last out the fourteen lines—have to cramp or stretch to come out even—have enough bread for the butter or butter for the bread. As a matter of fact, he gets through in twelve lines and doesn't know quite what to do with the last two.

Things like that and worse are the reason the sonnet is so suspect a form and has driven so many to free verse and even to the novel. Many a quatrain is salvaged from a sonnet that went agley. Dobson confesses frankly to having changed from one form to another after starting: "I intended an Ode and it turned to a Sonnet." But he reverses the usual order of being driven from the harder down to the easier. And he has a better excuse for weakness of will than most, namely, Rose.

Jeremiah, it seems, has had his sincerity questioned because the anguish of his lamentations was tamable to the form of twenty-two stanzas for the twenty-two letters of the alphabet. The Hebrew alphabet has been kept to the twenty-two letters it came out of Egypt with, so the number twenty-two means as much form as ever.

But there they go again with the old doubt about law and order. (The communist looks forward to a day of order without law, bless his merciful heart.) To the right person it must seem naive to distrust form as such. The very words of the dictionary are a restriction to make the best of or stay out of and be silent. Coining new words isn't encouraged. We play the words as we find them. We make them do. Form in language is such a disjected lot of old broken pieces it seems almost as nonexistent as the spirit till the two embrace in the sky. They are not to be thought of as encountering in rivalry but in creation. No judgment on either alone counts. We see what Whitman's extravagance may have meant when he said the body was the soul.

Here is where it all comes out. The mind is a baby giant who, more provident in the cradle than he knows, has hurled his paths in life all round ahead of him like playthings given—data so-called. They are vocabulary, grammar, prosody, and diary, and it will go hard if he can't find stepping stones of them for his feet wherever he wants to go. The way will be zigzag, but it will be a straight crookedness like the walking stick he cuts himself in the bushes for an emblem. He will be judged as he does or doesn't let this zig or that zag project him off out of his general direction.

Teacher or student or investigator whose chance on these defenseless lines may seize, your pardon if for once I point you out what ordinarily you would point me out. To some it will seem strange that I have written my verse regular all this time without knowing till yesterday that it was from fascination with this constant symbol I celebrate. To the right person it will seem lucky; since in finding out too much too soon there is danger of arrest. Does anyone believe I would have committed myself to the treason-reason-season rhyme-set in my "Reluctance" if I had been blasé enough to know that these three words about exhausted the possibilities? No rhyming dictionary for me to make me face the facts of rhyme. I may say the strain of rhyming is less since I came to see words as phrase-ends to countless phrases just as the syllables ly, ing, and ation are word-ends to countless words. Leave something to learn later. We'd have lost most of our innocence by forty anyway even if we never went to school a day.

Speaking of Loyalty

A TALK

After Robert Frost revised the recorded text of this talk, given at Amherst College on June 19, 1948, he allowed it to be published in the *Amherst Graduates' Quarterly* for August 1948, under the title "Speaking of Loyalty." His comments about this piece when he sent his revised version to the *Quarterly*'s editor, Professor George F. Whicher, included the following passage:

"[. . .] It hurts like everything not to bring my point out more sharply. Loyalty is simply to those you have given a right to count on you—your country family friends gang church firm or college. The difficult thing is to straighten it out with them God and yourself when your fancy falls aturning. If it is your country in time of war or if it is your gang you are deserting you may get yourself shot. Loyalty is as simple a thing as that." (Original unpublished letter, without date, in the Amherst College Library.)

Charlie Cole [President of Amherst College] and I, and George Whicher, are just back from having inaugurated [Walter Hendricks] the first president of a brand new college [Marlboro]. The extenuating circumstance is that it is a seedling from Amherst College. The chief event of the occasion for me was the history of the founding of Amherst College as told by Charlie Cole, and the analogy he drew between the shoe-string start of this new college on a mountain in Vermont and the shoe-string start of Amherst College a hundred and so many years ago.

My ear is always cocked for anything democratic these days, and the most democratic thing I know about America is shoe-string starts.

I don't know whether or not they have them in other countries to compare with ours, but they move me—whether of an enterprise or of an individual, of a person—these shoe-string starts. I read the obituaries in the *Times* and the *Tribune* for the stories of them.

At the same place, Marlboro College, our national friend—our Vermont lady of the manor—Dorothy Canfield Fisher made an attempt to define democracy in other terms. She would have it that Vermont, anyway, had always had a classless society, whether Massachusetts had or not, or New Hampshire had or not. And her proof of it was that the wife of the first governor of Vermont, Governor Chittenden, always cooked the meal before she sat down at the table with the guests from New Haven and Boston to eat it. And Dorothy Canfield insisted that was still the Vermont way of life. I'm only a bastard Vermonter, and so I don't know. (I had that from Reed Powell [of Harvard Law School] once. He told me I was only a bastard Vermonter. I'm really a Californian.)

I'm here in a sort of grand bath of loyalties. And I'd like to say a little bit in connection with this—the founding of this new college. There someone is starting a new thing to be loyal to. And the one starting it, the president we inaugurated, was of the class, I think, of 1917, Walter Hendricks. He was a Bond Prize winner. I sat on the platform here in 1917 when his oration won the Bond Prize, an oration on "Adventures in Education," and right there he set out to establish something new to be loyal to.

You often wonder about that. There are talkers abroad who confuse the word loyalty, make confusion with the word loyalty. They use Emerson and they use Josiah Royce to prove that you can be as loyal as Benedict Arnold or Aaron Burr, we'll say, and still be a loyal person. Loyal to something else, that's all they mean. The leading article in the *Harper's Magazine* a month or two ago ["Who is Loyal to America?"

by Henry Steele Commager] was written to prove that. I heard a speech like that here many years ago confusing the loyalties. There is loyalty to chemistry, loyalty to physics, loyalty to geography, loyalty to history, and just incidentally, there might be loyalty to Amherst College and, more incidentally still, loyalty to the United States of America. The only hitch is that the United States is in a stronger position than chemistry, physics, or history to compel loyalty.

Most confusing of all there is loyalty to the next thing ahead of you.

> Heartily know
> When half-gods go,
> The gods arrive.

Emerson was the original heretic—the villain of the piece. But you have to ask yourself (without any help from semantics), "What is the meaning of loyalty to the common ordinary person, to me, for instance?"

I had a questionnaire the other day from an editor. He asked, "What in your opinion is the present state of middle-brow literature in America?" That was new slang to me. I'd got behind a little bit, being off in the country. I hadn't heard of "middle-brow" before. What he meant to say was, "You old skeezix, what's the present state of your own middle-brow stuff?" There was something invidious, I am sure, in that. But right away I thought of a way to use it, not here but in verse, in writing. You make it like this:

> High-brow, low brow,
> Middle-brow, and no brow.

There is a refrain for the next poem.

> High-brow, low brow,
> Middle-brow, and no brow.

Now what is the middle-brow attitude toward loyalty? There's the high-brow attitude—that is the one I speak of—Josiah Royce's and

Ralph Waldo Emerson's. That is loyalty, not to your attachment, but to your attractions. The next one is your concern—let's see what comes next—who's the next lady?

> Heartily know
> When half-gods go,
> The quarter-gods arrive.

Emerson says the gods arrive, the whole gods, but you see we don't know that for sure. The loyalty as he defines it could be the loyalty of a quisling. That's loyalty too, to the next thing. But what's my own poor middle-brow, or low-brow notion of loyalty—not no brow, I won't grant that? . . . By the way, I've got a poem I'm going to write about that some day. It begins something like this. It's about the girl Hanno—I don't want to entertain you with too much scholarship, but about the girl Hanno and his sailors captured on the [. . .] coast of Africa, down the Gold Coast, outside the Gates. It's one of those old Polybius stories. And the poem should begin like this:

> She had no brow but a mind of her own,
> She wanted the sailors to let her alone;
> She didn't like sailors, she didn't like men,
> So they had to shut her up in a pen.

And so on, offhand. They found her so incorrigible, or whatever you call it, that they got sick of it in the end. She scratched and bit, I suppose; so they skinned her alive and took her skin back to Carthage and hung it up to Astarte.

Well, to my loyalty question again. When someone asked a mother what service her son had been in, she answered proudly, "In the Intelligentsia." That's the high-brow of it. Nobody can escape it—it's everywhere. I was looking up "potatoes" in the *Columbia Encyclopedia*—I don't know whether you know the great book—but I was looking up "potato" and I stumbled onto "poetry." You know I write verse? I had never read about poetry before, and so I stopped and read about it. And this is what I read. (The same high-brow stuff. I wonder who wrote it. I should like to catch him before I cool off. He put it like this as if to embarrass me in particular.) He said: "Poetry is largely a matter of rhythm and diction; meaning is not essential, and by many is considered detrimental." I quote from memory.

Well, when Dorothy Canfield talked about a classless society in Vermont, you and I know how to shade it—into more or less classless. But there are these classes apparently, anyway: high-brow, low-brow, middle-brow, and no brow. And my view, whatever it is—I suppose it's somewhere between middle and low—about loyalty is just the plain one of her pride in Vermont. It pleases me, for instance, that Vermont after litigation for a hundred years has established it that New Hampshire has no right to tax the wharves of the seaports (or should we say riverports?) on the [. . . Connecticut] River, on her side of the river. It took over a hundred years of litigation to establish that, and even now the line between the two states has to be re-perambulated every seven years so as to keep the feeling open. That's the national feeling for you! That's the patriotism! That's the loyalty on both sides of the river.

A very high official in California, almost the highest, I guess the highest, said to me as a renegade native son—he said, "Why did you leave California?" I told him, "I went out very young. I was carried out screaming." That made it all right. I was on the spot, but I got out all right.

And right here and now I am looking at somebody who is watching me, too. He's from Dartmouth. And he's wondering how I straighten all this out with Dartmouth when I get back there. I remember once, one of the first times I appeared here, years ago, back in 1916 it was, that one of the faculty members, my fellows-to-be, said to me, "From Dartmouth!" he said. "I never saw a Dartmouth man yet who didn't deserve to be shot." We began like that. I was in that transition stage—

it's one of the problems of life—that transition between one loyalty and another, between an attraction and an attachment.

How do you get from an attachment to follow an attraction? It ought to be painful to you, it ought to be, if you're any good. It ought not to be easy. You ought not to do it cheerfully, lightly, the way Emerson talked of doing it. He didn't do it in practice. I know people who do it in practice, however, on his advice.

The loyalty I'm speaking of—I don't know whether I'm permitted here to deal with it in written words of my own—I've written a great deal about it; once away back when I was very young in a stanza I'll venture to say to you.

> Ah, when to the heart of man
> > Was it ever less than a treason
> To go with the drift of things,
> > To yield with a grace to reason,
> To bow and accept the end
> > Of a love or a season?

Even a season—that pain of the end of summer—is in it for me, the person, the place, friendship, parting is such sweet sorrow, and so on. One of the poems I'll say has to do with the breaking off, with the cost of breaking off with one attachment to form another. And then I'll say a couple of short ones just to wind up and say goodbye.

[Mr. Frost then recited "The Gift Outright," which he called "a history of the United States in a dozen lines of blank verse."]

And that, I take it, is the whole thing. Lately I've been thinking more and more about it. All there is is belonging and belongings; belonging and having belongings. You belong and I belong. The sincerity of their belonging is all I have to measure people by. I hate to take great names in vain, but I am tempted to call some men quislings that perhaps some of you would not like to hear me call quislings. Men in great places. I can't quite take them. My namesake anyway, Robert Lee, never came up to Washington to curry favor with those that had licked him. He sawed wood. That was the only thing for him to do when beaten.

You have to ask yourself in the end, how far will you go when it comes to changing your allegiance.

Poetry and School

REMARKS FROM HIS NOTEBOOKS

In its June 1951 number *The Atlantic Monthly* featured the following text by Robert Frost—identified as being "remarks from his Notebooks"—which the magazine characterized, in a prefatory statement, as showing "the glint" of Frost's philosophy.

Why poetry is in school more than it seems to be outside in the world, the children haven't been told. They must wonder.

The authorities that keep poetry in school may be divided into two kinds, those with a conscientious concern for it and those with a real weakness for it. They are easily told apart.

School is founded on the invention of letters and numbers. The inscription over every school door should be the rhyme A B C and One Two Three. The rest of education is apprenticeship and for me doesn't belong in school.

The chief reason for going to school is to get the impression fixed for life that there is a book side to everything.

We go to college to be given one more chance to learn to read in case we haven't learned in High School. Once we have learned to read the rest can be trusted to add itself unto us.

The way to read a poem in prose or verse is in the light of all the other poems ever written. We may begin anywhere. We *duff* into our first. We read that imperfectly (thoroughness with it would be fatal), but the better to read the second. We read the second the better to read the third, the third the better to read the fourth, the fourth the better to read the fifth, the fifth the better to read the first again, or the second if it so happens. For poems are not meant to be read in course any more than they are to be made a study of. I once made a resolve never to put any book to any use it wasn't intended for by its author. Improvement will not be a progression but a widening circulation. Our instinct is to settle down like a revolving dog and make ourselves at home among the poems, completely at our ease as to how they should be taken. The same people will be apt to take poems right as know how to take a hint when there is one and not to take a hint when none is intended. Theirs is the ultimate refinement.

We write in school chiefly because to try our hand at writing should make us better readers.

Almost everyone should almost have experienced the fact that a poem is an idea caught fresh in the act of dawning.

Also that felicity can't be fussed into existence.

Also that there is such a thing as having a moment. And that the great thing is to know a moment when you have one.

Also to know what Catullus means by *mens animi*.

Also to know that poetry and prose too regarded as poetry is the renewal of words.

Emotion emoves a word from its base for the moment by metaphor, but often in the long run even on to a new base. The institution, the form, the word, have regularly or irregularly to be renewed from the root of the spirit. That is the creed of the true radical.

Emotions must be dammed back and harnessed by discipline to the wit mill, not just turned loose in exclamations. No force will express far that isn't shut in by discipline at all the pores to jet at one outlet only. Emotion has been known to ooze off.

Better readers, yes, and better writers too, if possible. Certainly not worse writers as many are made by being kept forever at it with the language (not to say jargon) of criticism and appreciation. The evil days will come soon enough, and we shall have no pleasure in them, when we shall have dried up into nothing but abstractions. The best educated person is one who has been matured at just the proper rate. Seasoned but not kiln dried. The starch thickening has to be stirred in with slow care. The arteries will harden fast enough without being helped. Too many recent poems have been actually done in the language of evaluation. They are too critical in spirit to admit of further criticism.

And this constant saying what amounts to no more than variations on the theme of "I don't like this and I do like that" tends to aesthetic Puritanism. "For goodness' sake," said one teacher to a class, "write for a change about what you are neither for nor against." When one bold boy asked if there could be any such thing, he was told he had flunked the course.

The escape is to action in words: to stories, plays, scenes, episodes, and incidents.

Practice of an art is more salutary than talk about it. There is nothing more composing than composition.

We were enjoined of old to learn to write now while young so that if we ever had anything to say later we would know how to say it. All there is to learning to write or talk is learning how to have something to say.

Our object is to say something that *is* something. One teacher once said that it was something at once valid and sensational with the accent on both. Classmates punish us for failure better than the teachers by very dead silence or exchanging glances at our expense.

One of the dangers of college to anyone who wants to stay a human reader (that is to say a humanist) is that he will become a specialist and lose his sensitive fear of landing on the lovely too hard. (With beak and talon.)

Another danger nowadays to sensitiveness is getting inured to translations. The rarity of a poem well brought over from one language into another should be a warning. Some translation of course in course for utility. But never enough to get broken to it. For self assurance there should always be a lingering unhappiness in reading translations.

The last place along the line where books are safely read as they are going to be out in the world in polite society is usually in so-called Freshman English. There pupils are still treated as if not all of them were going to turn out scholars.

The best reader of all is one who will read, can read, no faster than he can hear the lines and sentences in his mind's ear as if aloud. Frequenting poetry has slowed him down by its metric or measured pace.

The eye reader is a barbarian. So also is the writer for the eye reader, who needn't care how badly he writes since he doesn't care how badly he is read.

It is one thing to think the text and be totally absorbed in it. There is however an ascendancy in the mood to spare that can also think ABOUT the text. From the induced parallel current in the mind over and above the text the notes are drawn that we so much resent other people's giving us because we want the fun of having them for ourselves.

A B C is letters. One Two Three is numbers—mathematica. What marks verse off from prose is that it talks letters in numbers. Numbers is a nickname for poetry. Poetry plays the rhythms of dramatic speech on the grid of meter. A good map carries its own scale of miles.

For my pleasure I had as soon write free verse as play tennis with the net down.

The Prerequisites

A PREFACE

First published in *The New York Times Book Review* of March
21, 1954, "The Prerequisites" was also used as the preface
for a special selection of Robert Frost's poems, entitled
Aforesaid, which was formally published on his eightieth
birthday, March 26, 1954 (*Selected Prose of Robert Frost,*
pp. 95–97).

Some sixty years ago a young reader ran into serious trouble with
the blind last stanza of a poem otherwise perfectly intelligible. The
interest today might be in what he then did about it. He simply left it to
shift for itself. He might see to it if he ever saw it again. He guessed he
was no more anxious to understand the poem than the poem was to be
understood.

He might have gone to college for help. But he had just left college to
improve his mind if he had any. Or he might have gone to Asia. The
whole poem smacked of Asia. He suspected a whole religion behind it
different from the one he was brought up to. But as he was no traveler
except on foot he must have gone by way of the Bering Strait when
frozen over and that might have taken him an epoch from East to West
as it had the Indians from West to East.

The poem was called "Brahma" and he was lilting along on such
lines as the following in easy recognition:

> They reckon ill who leave me out
> When me they fly I am the wings.
> I am the doubter and the doubt
> And I the hymn the Brahmin sings.

which was all very pretty. For Brahma he naturally read God—not the God of the Old Testament nor of the New either, but near enough. Though no special liberal he valued himself on his tolerance of heresy in great thinkers. He could always lend himself to an unsound idea for the duration of the piece and had been even heard to wish people would cling to their heresies long enough for him to go and tell on them.

Success in taking figures of speech is as intoxicating as success in making figures of speech. It had to be just when he was flushed with having held his own with the poem so far and was thinking "good easy man" "What a good boy am I" that the disaster happened. The words were still Brahma's:

> The strong gods pine for my abode
> And pine in vain the sacred seven
> But thou meek lover of the good
> Find me and turn thy back on Heaven.

There he blacked out as if he had bumped his head and he only came to dazed. I remember his anger in asking if anybody had a right to talk like that. But he wasn't as put out as he let on to be. He didn't go back on poetry for more than the particular poem or on that for more than the time being. His subconscious intention was to return on it by stealth some day if only it would stay in print till he was ready for it. All was he didn't want the wrong kind of help. The heart sinks when robbed of the chance to see for itself what a poem is all about. Any immediate preface is like cramming the night before an examination. Too late, too late! Any footnote while the poem is going is too late. Any subsequent explanation is as dispiriting as the explanation of a joke. Being taught poems reduces them to the rank of mere information. He was sure the Muse would thank him for reserving a few of her best for being achieved on the spur of the moment.

Approach to the poem must be from afar off, even generations off. He should close in on it on converging lines from many directions like the divisions of an army upon a battlefield.

A poem is best read in the light of all the other poems ever written. We read A the better to read B (we have to start somewhere; we may get very little out of A). We read B the better to read C, C the better to read D, D the better to go back and get something more out of A. Progress is not the aim, but circulation. The thing is to get among the poems where they hold each other apart in their places as the stars do.

And if he stubbornly stayed away from college and Asia (he hated to be caught at his age grooming his brains in public) perhaps in time college and Asia, even the Taj Mahal, might come to him with the prerequisites to that poem and to much else not yet clear.

Well, it so happened. For the story has a happy ending. Not fifty years later when the poem turned up again he found himself in a position to deal with all but two lines of it. He was not quite satisfied that the reference to "strong gods," plural, was fair poetry practice. Were these Titans or Yidags or, perish the thought, Olympians?—Oh no! not Olympians. But he now saw through the "meek lover of the good" who sounded so deceptively Christian. His meekness must have meant the perfect detachment from ambition and desire that can alone rescue us from the round of existence. And the "me" worth turning "thy back on Heaven" for must of course be Nirvana—the only nothing that is something. He had grown very fastidious about not calling the round of existence a wheel. He was a confirmed symbolist.

"Don't get converted. Stay."

EXCERPT FROM AN ADDRESS

This is an excerpt from a commencement address given by Robert Frost at Dartmouth College in June of 1955. The talk, transcribed from a tape recording of the exercises, was published in the July 1955 issue of the *Dartmouth Alumni Magazine.*

But you came to college bringing with you something to go on with—that was the idea from my point of view: something to go on with. And you brought it with an instinct, I hope, to keep it—not to have it taken away from you, not to be bamboozled out of it or scared out of it by any fancy teachers. I've known teachers with a real hanker for ravishing innocence. They like to tell you things that will disturb you.

Now, I think the College itself has given you one thing of importance I'd like to speak of. It's given you, slowly, gradually, the means to deal with that sort of thing, not only in college but the rest of your life. The formula would be something like this: always politely accept the other man's premises. Don't contradict anybody. It's contentious and ill natured. Accept the premises—take it up where it's given you and then show 'em what you can make of it. You've been broadened and enlarged to where you can listen to almost anything without losing your temper or your self-confidence.

You came from the "Bible belt," say. You were confronted with the fact of evolution. It was supposed to disturb you about your God. But you found a way to say—either with presence of mind, wittily, or slowly with meditation—you found the way to say, "Sure, God probably

didn't make man out of mud. But He made him out of *prepared mud.*"
You still had your God, you see.

You were a Bostonian and you had been brought up to worship the
cod. To you the cod was sacred and her eggs precious. You were con-
fronted with facts of waste in nature. One cod egg is all that survives of
a million. And you said—what did you say? You found something to
say, surely. You said, "Perhaps those other eggs were necessary in order
to make the ocean a proper broth for the one to grow up in. No waste;
just expense." And so on.

I myself have been bothered by certain things. I've been bothered by
rapid reading. All my teaching days I've heard rapid reading advocated
as if it were something to attain to. Yes, sure; accept the premises,
always, as a gentleman. Rapid reading—I'm one of the rapidest of read-
ers. I look on all the reading you do in college—ten times as much a
year as I do in ten years, and I'm a reader—I look on it as simply *scan-
sion.* You're simply looking the books over to see whether you want to
read 'em, later. It comes to that; and accepting it that way. The word's
gone forth, you happen to know probably, that the rapid reading is
going to be played down in the educational world. But it can be
regarded as simple scansion.

What you're doing as a rapid reader is saying, per paragraph, per
paragraph, "Yeah, I know" (two words you see in it)—"Yeah, that's
about 'togetherness.'" "Yeah." And, paragraph by paragraph you say,
"Yes, I know." It doesn't take long to know that that's what it would say
if you read it all. And you can do that by the chapter—the chapter titles.
You say, "Yeah," you know, "I know what that chapter would be." You
can go further than that: "I can tell by the spine of the book." Very rapid
reader.

Always fall in with what you're asked to accept, you know; fall in
with it—and turn it your way. Expression like "divine right."—Divine
right? yes,—if you let me make what I want of it: the answerability of

the ruler, of the leader; the first answerability to himself. That's his divine right. First answerability to his highest in himself, to his God.

Then one more that I'd just like to speak of—you run on to these things all the time. I live on them. I'm going to tell you that every single one of my poems is probably one of these adaptations that I've made. I've taken whatever you give me and made it what I want it to be. That's what every one of the poems is. I look over them. They are not arguments. I've never contradicted anybody. My object in life has been to hold my own *with* whatever's going—not *against,* but *with*—to hold my own. To come through college holding my own so that I won't be made over beyond recognition by my family and my home town, if I ever go back to it. It's a poor sort of person, it seems to me, that delights in thinking, "I have had four years that have transformed me into somebody my own mother won't know." Saint Paul had one conversion. Let's leave it to Saint Paul. Don't get converted. Stay.

This one turns up, too—another expression. They say, "If eventually, why not now?" I say, "Yeah," but also, "If eventually, why now?"

You've got to handle these things. You've got to have something to say to the Sphinx. You see, that's all. And you've been, I'm pretty sure—you've come more and more to value yourself on being able to handle whatever turns up.

What would you say to this one? (You probably haven't encountered it. I have lately.) We hired a Swede to come over here and pass an expert's opinion on our form of government. And after he passed his judgment on it, we invited him back and gave him another honorary degree, just like this. (Never mind his name—we won't go into names—maybe I've forgotten it.) But, anyway, did you hear what his judgment was? That our form of government is a conspiracy against the common man.

You've been enlarged and broadened to where you can listen to anything without getting mad. So have I. But I have to have something to say to that, sooner or later—on the spur of the moment, to show my wit, or at leisure, you know, to show my ability at reasoning, my reasoning powers. Well, the answer to that is that that's what it was intended to be. It was intended to be a conspiracy against the common man. Let him make himself *uncommon*. He wasn't to be put in the saddle. And so on. Now I conclude that.

"... *little observations, little thoughts.*"

APHORISTIC LINES OF POETRY

During an interview with Dr. Jonas E. Salk, recorded in Pittsburgh in May of 1956, Robert Frost declared, "If I went back over what I've written—if it was fine-tooth combed—I'd be picking out those things that I set store by: little observations, little thoughts." On another occasion, before an audience at Boston University, October 30, 1958, he asserted with regard to his poems, "You could find your way through all my poetry with a line in each one of them."

This section is made up of single aphoristic lines, constituting "little observations, little thoughts," chosen from various poems that are not given in full within this volume.

Pressed into service means pressed out of shape.
> —*from "The Self-Seeker," line 149*

The trial by market everything must come to.
> —*from "Christmas Trees," line 24*

Yankees are what they always were.
> —*from "Brown's Descent," line 53*

Where wheels have freshly sliced the April mire.
> —*from "Blue-Butterfly Day," line 8*

But something has to be left to God.
> —*from "Good-by and Keep Cold," line 29*

Blood has been harder to dam back than water.

—from "The Flood," line 1

Over back where they speak of life as staying

—from "The Investment," line 1

But my heart was beginning to cloud my mind.

—from "On the Heart's Beginning to Cloud the Mind,"
line 13

It's knowing what to do with things that counts.

—from "At Woodward's Gardens," line 37

So love will take between the hands a face. . . .

—from "Moon Compasses," line 8

The best way to hate is the worst.

—from "The Vindictives," line 81

Light was a paste of pigment in our eyes.

—from "Iris by Night," line 9

The clover-mingled rowan on the ground

—from "Iris by Night," line 13

Two souls may be too widely met.

—from "A Missive Missile," line 52

And there is always more than should be said.

—from "The Wind and the Rain," line 40

Nor will you find love either, nor love you.

—from "To a Moth Seen in Winter," line 13

Here come more stars to character the skies,

—from "The Literate Farmer and the Planet Venus,"
line 75

Some ignorance takes rank as innocence.

—from "The Literate Farmer and the Planet Venus,"
line 88

There's a lot yet that isn't understood.

—from "The Literate Farmer and the Planet Venus,"
line 136

No place to get lost like too far in the distance.

—from "Too Anxious for Rivers," line 11

Each knows his own discernment best.

—from "An Unstamped Letter in Our Rural Letter Box," line 43

Religious faith is a most filling vapor.

—from "Innate Helium," line 1

I put no faith in the seeming facts of light.

—from "Skeptic," line 4

A man has got to keep his extrication.

—from "From Plane to Plane," line 61

But waste was of the essence of the scheme.

—from "Pod of the Milkweed," line 40

Great is the reassurance of recall.

—*from "A Concept Self-Conceived," line 5*

A King must give his people character.

—*from "How Hard It Is to Keep from Being King When It's in You and in the Situation," line 142*

The only certain freedom's in departure.

—*from "How Hard It Is to Keep from Being King When It's in You and in the Situation," line 194*

The artist in me cries out for design.

—*from* A Masque of Reason, *line 261*

"*Look out I don't spoof you.*"

LETTERS TO AN INCIPIENT BIOGRAPHER

Some rarely revealed sides of Robert Frost's art and personality are illuminated by his letters to Sidney Cox. The two men had first met at Plymouth, New Hampshire, in 1911, while the poet was on the faculty of the Plymouth Normal School, and Cox—much younger than Frost—was teaching in the Plymouth High School. They became close friends, and the correspondence between them began as soon as Frost went to England in 1912.

Not long after he returned to America in 1915, Frost apparently made the initial proposal that Cox might like to assemble and arrange for publication some of the ideas and opinions Frost had casually expressed during their various conversations with one another. Gradually, during the next ten years and more, Cox did prepare a manuscript for such a book. When he submitted it to Frost in 1928, the poet made no immediate reply, but several months later he wrote from England to his friend under date of October 11, 1928 (*Selected Letters of Robert Frost,* pp. 350–351).

SIDNEY, SIDNEY It won't do. You'll say I've been long enough coming to that brief conclusion. I practically had to wait till I had grown into another person so I could see the problem presented with the eyes of an outsider. Looking in on it from another country and from another time with all the disinterestedness possible I find I'm against the book—at least in my lifetime: when I'm off the scene you can decide for yourself. My greatest objection to the book is that it doesn't put you and me in the right personal relation. I think you would realize that if you took time. Your repeated insistence on the fact that you never came to see me except when summoned has the very opposite effect from what you intend. Instead of making us out equals in friendship as I should have thought we were, it puts you in the position of a convenience used and sent for whenever I had anything for you to set down for posterity. I dont like the picture it makes of either of us. It isnt a true picture either. I cant remember exactly when you asked my permission to keep a record of the best of our talks. But I'm sure it was late in our lives. I invited you to visit me and I wrote to you many times before you could have been so self conscious about it all. I might have to search myself for my reason in singling you out for a conversation a year. I can tell you offhand I never chose you as a Boswell. Maybe I liked your awkwardness, naivete and spirituality. We won't strain for an answer. [. . .]

No you'll have to forgive me and be as good friends as if nothing had ever happened, but it wont do. You'll have to reason our relationship on to a better footing than it has apparently been on lately. Let's not be too damned literary.

REALLY FAITHFULLY YOURS ROBERT FROST

Cox was not dismayed by this rebuff, and during the next few years he insisted he was going to revise his manuscript until the poet was satisfied with it. Attempting, apparently, to be more specific in discouraging his friend's tenacity, Frost wrote Cox in April 1932 (*Selected Letters of Robert Frost,* pp. 385–386).

HONESTLY SIDNEY, You are getting out of hand. I'm afraid you aren't going to let yourself be unduly influenced by me any more.

I grow surer I don't want to search the poet's mind too seriously. I might enjoy threatening to for the fun of it just as I might [enjoy threatening] to frisk his person. I have written to keep the over curious out of the secret places of my mind both in my verse and in my letters to such as you. A subject has to be held clear outside of me with struts and as it were set up for an object. A subject must be an object. There's no use in laboring this further years. My objection to your larger book about me was that it came thrusting in where I did not want you. The idea is the thing with me. It would seem soft for instance to look in my life for the sentiments in the Death of the Hired Man. There's nothing to it believe me. I should fool you if you took me so. I'll tell you my notion of the contract you thought you had with me. The objective idea is all I ever cared about. Most of my ideas occur in verse. But I have always had some turning up in talk that I feared I might never use because I was too lazy to write prose. I think they have been mostly educational ideas connected with my teaching, actually lessons. That's where I hoped you would come in. I thought if it didnt take you too much from your own affairs you might be willing to gather them for us both. But I never reckoned with the personalities. I keep to a minimum of such stuff in any poets life and works. Art and wisdom with the body heat out of it. You speak of Shirley. He is two or three great poems—one very great. He projected, he got, them out of his system and I will not carry them back into his system either at the place they came out of or at some other place. I state this in the extreme. But relatively I mean what I say. To be too subjective with what an artist has managed to make objective is to come on him presumptuously and render ungraceful what he in pain of his life had faith he had made graceful. . . .

EVER YOURS RF.

Although this cumulative tension placed a strain on the friendship between the two men, they continued to

(476)

correspond and to see each other occasionally during the next few years. Evidently troubled by a considerable silence, Frost wrote on October 24, 1933, to invite Cox to visit him in South Shaftsbury, Vermont—a letter quoted here from the original in the Dartmouth College Library.

DEAR SIDNEY: Things that did themselves have crowded out the things that needed us to do them. I'm dazed to think how long ago I promised to have you here or up to Franconia. I dont know how you are, but I'm so constituted that I dont seem to mind being neglected by people I am sure feel all right toward me. What do you say to coming down Saturday this week and going back Sunday?—Unless you have a football game to keep you [at Dartmouth].—Be careful what you say against football or any other college athletics. I think that as they are taken so poetry should be taken and not otherwise. So I look on them as a model for our kind and a reproach to the other kind of teachers. But I will excuse you from football this week since it will be me you are deserting it for. Come if you can and will. Come as a friend and equal and dont trouble your head or silly old diary with trying to decide which wants to see the other more. I didnt mean exactly what you thought I did when years ago I was so incautious as to suggest that you might like to turn to account some of the theories of school, life, and art I let fall in talk but was too lazy ever probably to use in writing myself. You took it that I was asking to be Boswellized. That has hurt our relationship a shade if you will forgive my saying so. I meant something the most impersonal. I shouldnt mind a word of credit for an idea of course. A fellow named Gordon Chalmers recently got his doctors degree for a thesis on Thomas Browne and Metaphor at Harvard that really owed a lot more to me than he was generous enough to declare. You'd never treat me that way. In my judgement you wouldnt be treating me much better if you went to the other extreme and brought my name and ways in every other word. Some time you might solve for me the problem of how I was going to tell the world the principles upon which I had composed. I shrink from prefaces as you know. Once in a while it comes over me to wish some friend would do my explaining for me. It shouldnt take much and it might better be based on my talk in general than on particular rambling talks with me. Im just now more or less in trouble with well intentioned people who want to publish stenographic reports of my so called lectures in New York at the New School. I dont want the picturesque setting and charms or uncharms of me. I want the ideas rounded out and rounded up into something more formal than I care to take the responsibility for myself. Enough of this. You'll gather from it more or less why I was against the larger book you sent me for approval. Either the ideas for the ideas' sake and without the dirt and dross of me or no book at all ever while I live or after I die. Try to please me. Gee lets enjoy life. Come for the fun of it when you come.

EVER YOURS ROBERT FROST

Perhaps encouraged more than he should have been by this letter, Cox began to give a new shape to his Frost manuscript, and during the next few years the friendship between the two men did seem to improve. But the poet obviously continued to fear that Cox remained too deeply concerned with intimate biographical details, as is suggested by this extract from a letter he wrote to Cox on January 1, 1937 (*Selected Letters of Robert Frost*, p. 435).

DEAR SIDNEY: [. . .] I'm sorry not to be where I can see something of you in the wild and unharnessed state [of California]. But then I doubt if I should find you very different. You and I are not the kind that can be described as either wild or tame: I always maintain that I would be the same in a society of one as in a society of one hundred and thirty million. My conditioning is all internal. My appetites are checked by each other rather than by anything in my surroundings. Or do I deceive myself? I dont care if I do in this respect. My denial that I am the result of any particular surroundings comes to nothing more than a refusal to think of myself as one who might have been better or worse if I had been thrown with different people in different circumstances. Look out I don't spoof you. About five years ago I resolved to spoil my correspondence with you by throwing it into confusion the way God threw the speech of the builders of the tower of Babel into confusion. My reason is too long to go into tonight[. . .].

EVER YOURS, R.F.

Adamant in his refusal to be discouraged, Cox continued to work on the book, and gradually Frost became reconciled to the inevitability of it, as is indicated by this excerpt from a letter he mailed to Cox on May 18, 1938—a letter now preserved at Dartmouth.

[. . .] I have always hoped you might sometime publicly remember me in writing, but I got discouraged with the way you started off on my having sought you at least as much as you sought me. What the hell has that kind of inferiority superiority got to do with two people like us? Unless I have got him stopped the poetry editor of Time is presently going to deal with me in some such deplorable scandalousness. [. . .] There is only you left to be uniquely mental with me mind to mind. Maybe I ask too much too vaguely. Damn it I dont want to dictate the book. [. . .]

Sidney Cox managed to complete his Frost book shortly before he died in 1952. Several years later, after it had been

accepted for publication by New York University Press, Frost
was embarrassed by the request that he write an
introduction for it. Although he did prepare a first draft, he
held it until he could make certain Cox's widow would
approve of what he had undertaken. On August 21, 1956, he
wrote to Mrs. Cox in a letter also now at Dartmouth.

[. . .] I don't know whether you know what's been going on between me and Wilson Follett, the editor of the New York University Press. He has wrung out of me a preface to Sidney's book which I am not sure it was good taste for me to write. The thing hasn't gone so far that it can't be stopped if I see more reasons against it than for it. To say the least it is very unusual for a man to be prefacing a book about himself. The deciding question is how you feel in the matter, what you want me to do, and what you think Sidney would want me to do.[. . .]

When Frost received word of approval from Mrs. Cox, he
went ahead, and reprinted here is his brief "Introduction" to
Sidney Cox's *A Swinger of Birches: A Portrait of Robert Frost*
(New York, 1957).

This ought to be a good book. Everybody who has seen it in manuscript says it is. The author probably knew me better than he knew himself and consequently contrariwise he very likely portrayed himself in it more than me. I trust it is in my favor. I know he would mean it to be. I don't read about myself well or easily. But I am always happier to hear that I am liked faults and all than that I am disliked. I had to tell Sidney once that I didn't believe it did me the least good to be told of the enemies he had had to defend me from. I have stolen look enough over the edge of the book to see that what went on between us is brought out much as in our correspondence. My letters to him I might mention are on deposit in the Dartmouth College Library. I wish I had kept some of the great letters he wrote me but I am no curator of letters or anything else. He was at his best in his free letters. Yes, and of course in his teaching. A great teacher. He was all sincerity and frankness. He once wrote an article for the *New Republic* about *my* sincerity. I know that because it was in the title. We differed more in taste perhaps than in thinking. But we stood up to each other to support each other as two playing cards may be made to in building. I am a great equalitarian; I try to spend most of my time with my equals. He seemed worried at first lest it should appear I didn't seek him as much as he sought me. He respected me very highly. And he was more serious about such things than I. Not that he lacked a sense of humor. He liked a good story, and I am sure he would have enjoyed my version of our first encounter. It began one evening in 1911 when we met as strangers looking on at a school dance at Plymouth, New Hampshire, where we were both teachers, he in one school, I in another. I didn't know who he was except that he looked very teasably young. He didn't know who I was except, it seems, that I looked too old. By saying something flip-pant about the theme papers he had to hurry away to correct I angered him to the point of his inquiring behind my back if it was because of alcohol I had got no further up in the world at my age. I was thirty-seven. I was just teaching psychology in the Plymouth Normal School. He disdained to speak to me on the street for a while afterwards. But his seriousness piqued the mischief in me and I set myself to take him. He came round all right, but it wasn't the last time he had to make allowances for me. He worked at it devotedly. He must have been about half my age then. He was all of two thirds my age when he died. He was catching up. He was cut off before he came all the way through with himself. But he had made up his mind to much. My heart was in his lit-erary success and I have hopes this is it.

Among the Poems He Left Behind

GROUP FIVE

Robert Frost once complained—half humorously, and half seriously—that he had not been invited to contribute any of his poems to the *Treasury of Ribaldry* edited by Louis Untermeyer. To illustrate what his friend had missed, he rattled off three samples, one of which Untermeyer described (in *The Letters of Robert Frost to Louis Untermeyer,* p. 374) as "not only blasphemous and bawdy but unprintable."

The truth was that Frost never could quite muster courage enough to put into a published book any of his rhymed indelicacies. A thoroughly mild one—an untitled limerick— was added at the page-proof stage to his book *In the Clearing* (1962), but before publication Frost caused it to be deleted. it is quoted here from a typescript preserved within the Dartmouth College Library. A direct example, on the other hand, of Frost's ribaldry is "Pride of Ancestry," reprinted here from *Robert Frost: The Years of Triumph,* p. 473.

[FOR TRAVELERS GOING SIDEREAL . . .]

For travelers going sidereal
The danger they say is bacterial.
I don't know the pattern
On Mars or on Saturn
But on Venus it must be venereal.

PRIDE OF ANCESTRY

The Deacon's wife was a bit desirish
And liked her sex relations wild,
So she lay with one of the shanty Irish
And he begot the Deacon's child.

The Deacon himself was a man of money
And upright life and a bosom shirt;
Which made her infidelity funny
And gave her pleasure in doing him dirt.

And yet for all her romantic sneakin'
Out the back door and over the wall
How was she sure the child of the Deacon
Wasn't the Deacon's after all?

Don't question a story of high eugenics.
She lived with the Deacon and bedded with him,
But she restricted his calesthenics
To the sterile arc of her lunar rhythm.

And she only had to reverse the trick
And let the Irishman turn her turtle
When by his faith as a Catholic
A woman was almost sure to be fertile.

Her portrait hangs in the family gallery
And a family of nobodies likes to think
That their descent from such a calorie
Accounts for their genius and love of drink.

Observations and Declarations of a Poet-Statesman

During the last decade of his life, having attained vast fame as a man of letters, Robert Frost in a sense initiated yet another career, as he gradually became more and more involved in public affairs, and as increasingly his views were sought on public issues.

Beginning in 1954, when the U.S. Department of State sent him as a delegate to the World Congress of Writers at São Paulo, in Brazil, he took on an impressive succession of statesmanly tasks. They included his appointment as Consultant in Poetry to the Library of Congress, and later as the Library's Honorary Consultant in the Humanities; services as an "ambassador of good will" on missions to Great Britain, Israel, Greece, and Russia; as a special pleader for the release of fellow poet Ezra Pound who, charged with treason in World War II, had for many years been confined to a mental institution; and, perhaps most dramatically, as a representative of the arts, participating in the Inauguration of President John F. Kennedy.

The following extracts are intended to be merely representative of the varied statements made by Robert Frost in his capacity as poet-statesman.

The word "freedom" is on everybody's lips. I never have valued any liberty conferred on me particularly. I value myself on the liberties I take, and I have learned to appreciate the word "unscrupulous." I am not a sticker at trifles. If I wrote the history of the world in jail like Nehru twenty years ago I would expect to take many liberties with the story. I should expect to bend the story somewhat the way I wanted it to go. There is a certain measure of unscrupulousness in this. I find the same thing in good scientists. An unscrupulous person for me in science, history or literature is a person who doesn't stick at trifles.

Now the freedom that I am asked to think about sometimes is the freedom to speak—to speak out—academic and in the press, or from the platform like this. I say I have the right to tell anything—to talk about anything I am smart enough to find out about. Second, I am free to talk about anything I am deep enough to understand, and third, I am free to talk about anything I have the ability to talk about. The limitations on my freedom, you see, are more in myself than anywhere else.

The ability to find out, the ability to understand, the ability to express[. . .].

—*from a commencement address at Sarah Lawrence College on June 7, 1956, published in booklet form as* A Talk for Students (*New York, 1956*).

Now there is a word we've had that goes wrong. I don't know whether you have encountered it or not. The word is, "the dream." I wonder how much you have encountered it? I have it thrown in my face every little while, and always by somebody who thinks the dream has not come true. And then the next time I pick it up to knit I wonder what the dream is, or why. And the next time I pick it up, I wonder who dreamed it. Did Tom Paine dream it, did Thomas Jefferson dream it, did George Washington dream it? Gouverneur Morris? And lately I've decided the best dreamer of it was Madison. I have been reading the Federalist papers.

But anyway I am always concerned with the question, is it a dream that's gone by? Each age is a dream that is dying, they say, or one that is coming to birth. It depends on what you mean by an age. Is the age over in which that dream had its existence—has it gone by? Can we treat the

Constitution as if it were something gone by? Can we interpret it out of existence? By calling it a living document, it means something different every day, something new every day, until it doesn't mean anything that it meant to Madison. And this thought occurred to me the other day when I picked it up. Has the dream, instead of having come true, has it done something that the witches talk about? Has it simply materialized?

Young writers that I know—novelists that I know—began as poets, most of them. They began more ethereal than substantial, and have ended up more substantial than ethereal. And is that what has happened to our country? Has the ethereal idealism of the founders materalized into something too material? In South America last year at a convention I heard everybody regretting or fearing or worrying about our materialism. Not for our own sake, but for their sake, because we were misleading them into a material future for the whole world, and anxiety for us. I told them we were anxious about that too. We had scales in our bathrooms to see how material we were getting.[. . .]

Now I know—I think I know, as of today—what Madison's dream was. It was just a dream of a new land to fulfill with people in self-control. In self-control. That is all through his thinking. And let me say that again to you. To fulfill this land—a new land—with people in self-control. And do I think that dream has failed? Has come to nothing, or has materialized too much? It is always the fear. We live in constant fear, of course. To cross the road, we live in fear of cars. But we can live in fear, if we want to, of too much education, too little education, too much of this, too little of that. But the thing is, the measure.

I am always pleased when I see someone making motions like this [gesture of conducting a chorus]—like a metronome. Seeing the music measured. Measure always reassures me. Measure in love, in government, measure in selfishness, measure in unselfishness. [. . .]

—from a commencement address at Sarah Lawrence College on June 7, 1956, published in booklet form as A Talk for Students (New York, 1956).

We ought to enjoy a standoff. Let it stand and deepen in meaning. Let's not be hasty about showdowns. Let's be patient and confident in our country. [. . .]

The question for every man and every nation is to be clear about where the first answerability lies. Are we as individuals to be answerable first only to others or to ourselves and some ideal beyond ourselves? Is the United States to be answerable first to the United Nations or to its own concept of what is right?

> —*as quoted in a Washington column by James Reston,*
> The New York Times, *October 27, 1957.*

DEAR MR. PRESIDENT: To be stood up for and toasted alone in such august company by the ruler of the greatest nation in the world was almost more to me than being stood up for in acclaim by whole audiences of his people and mine. At any rate it left me with less to say for myself on the thrill of the moment and was so like the outcome of a life story, it leaves me with nothing to go on with but possibly some more of the same kind of very quiet poetry that seems to have started all this unquietness. I hope you will accept a book of it from me to take to your farm some day. I am a great advocate of some library in the farm house to mix with the life of the farm. Not that I would underestimate its value in the capitol to mix with the life of the Capitol. Books and paintings and music tend to temper the harshness of politics.

> —*from a letter to President Eisenhower after a White House dinner on February 27, 1958* (Selected Letters, *p. 578*).

I am here to register my admiration for a government that can rouse in conscience to a case like this. Relief seems in sight for many of us besides the Ezra Pound in question and his faithful wife. He has countless admirers the world over who will rejoice in the news that he has hopes of freedom. I append a page or so of what they have been saying lately about him and his predicament. I myself speak as much in the general interest as in his. And I feel authorized to speak very specially for my friends, Archibald MacLeish, Ernest Hemingway and T. S. Eliot. None of us can bear the disgrace of our letting Ezra Pound come to his end where he is. It would leave too woeful a story in American literature. He went very wrongheaded in his egotism, but he insists it was from patriotism—love of America. He has never admitted that he went over to the enemy any more than the writers at home who have despaired of the Republic. I hate such nonsense and can only listen to it as an evidence of mental disorder. But mental disorder is what we are considering. I rest the case on Dr. Overholser's pronouncement that Ezra Pound is not too dangerous to go free in his wife's care, and too insane ever to be tried—a very nice discrimination.

Mr. Thurman Arnold admirably put this problem of a sick man being held too long in prison to see if he won't get well enough to be tried for a prison offense. There is probably legal precedent to help toward a solution of the problem. But I should think it would have to be reached more by magnanimity than by logic and it is chiefly on magnanimity I am counting. I can see how the Department of Justice would hesitate in the matter from fear of looking more just to a great poet than it would be to a mere nobody. The bigger the Department the longer it might have to take thinking things through.

—*Statement in the* Pound *case, April 18, 1958,*
records of the U. S. District Court for the District of Columbia.

I'm not the kind of man who thinks the world can be saved by knowledge. It can only be saved by daring, bravery, going ahead. . . .
—*as quoted in an interview-article by Milton Bracker,*
The New York Times Magazine, *November 30, 1958.*

I have long thought that our high schools should be improved. Nobody should come into our high schools without examinations—not aptitude tests, but on reading, 'riting, and 'rithmetic. And that goes for black or white.

A lot of people are being scared by the Russian Sputnik into wanting to harden up our education and speed it up. I am interested in toning it up, at the high-school level.

If they want to Spartanize the country, let them. I would rather perish as Athens than prevail as Sparta. The tone is Athens. The tone is freedom to the point of destruction. Democracy means all the risks taken—conflict of opinion, conflict of personality, eccentricity. We are Athens, daring to be all sorts of people.

> —*as quoted by Mary McGrory,* Washington Evening Star,
> *December 10, 1958* (*Interviews, pp. 193–194*).

We think that if people were all the same, they wouldn't want to hurt each other. But in the arts, we want all the differences we can get. And in society, too. I don't want to be always meeting people who've been everywhere I've been. I've never been to the Taj Mahal. I want to meet people who have been there. We really want people to be different, even if it means a risk of fighting with each other.

I'm beginning to hate the word "peace," the way it's being thrown around today. The word is becoming spoiled. Everybody wants pieces of peace, but we don't expect to have eternal peace, except in the next world; and we don't know what's going on up there. Or down there. . . . We need enough peace to consolidate our gains.

> —*as quoted by Maurice Dolbier,* New York Herald Tribune
> Book Review, *April 5, 1959* (Interviews, *p. 196*).

The chief guide in the world for us in the long way we've come is some more or less intelligent handling of that inexorable thing in us— Biblical thing, you know—passionate preference for something we can't help wishing were so, wishing were true.

All your guidance in politics, religion, and love is something way at the middle of your heart that you can't help wishing was so. [. . .]

The certainty of conflict is originality, that's all—the bursting power, the bursting energy and daring of man. And it's always there, always there. You can't hope for anything that doesn't include that.

—*as quoted in the proceedings of "The Future of Man," a symposium held at New York City, September 29, 1959* (Interviews, *pp. 209 and 212*).

The world is being offered a choice between two kinds of democracy. Ours is a very ancient political growth, beginning at one end of the Mediterranean Sea and coming westward—tried in Athens, tried in Italy, tried in England, tried in France, coming westward all the way to us. A very long growth, a growth through trial and error, but always with the idea that there is some sort of wisdom in the mob.

Put a marker where the growth begins, at the eastern end of the Mediterranean, and there's never been a glimmer of democracy south of there. Over east, in Asia, there have been interesting ideas, but none bothered by the wisdom of the mob.

Our democracy is like our bill of fare. That came westward, too, with wheat and so on, adding foods by trial and error and luck. I think, when corn comes in good and fresh, what would I have done if Columbus hadn't discovered America?

What is this Russian democracy? Ours, I say, is like our bill of fare—kills a few people every year probably, but most of us live with it. The Russian democracy is like a doctor's prescription or a food fad. That's all there is to that. That finished them off.

I have pretty strong confidence that our kind of democracy is better than a trumped-up kind. I'm pretty sure we're going to win. I'm on our side, anyway.

—*as quoted by Roger Kahn,* The Saturday Evening Post, *November 16, 1960* (Interviews, *pp. 240–241*).

IF YOU CAN BEAR AT YOUR AGE THE HONOR OF BEING MADE PRESI-
DENT OF THE UNITED STATES, I OUGHT TO BE ABLE AT MY AGE TO BEAR

THE HONOR OF TAKING SOME PART IN YOUR INAUGURATION. I MAY NOT
BE EQUAL TO IT BUT I CAN ACCEPT IT FOR MY CAUSE—THE ARTS, POETRY,
NOW FOR THE FIRST TIME TAKEN INTO THE AFFAIRS OF STATESMEN.
I AM GLAD THE INVITATION PLEASES YOUR FAMILY. IT WILL PLEASE MY
FAMILY TO THE FOURTH GENERATION AND MY FAMILY OF FRIENDS
AND WERE THEY LIVING IT WOULD HAVE PLEASED INORDINATELY THE
KIND OF GROVER CLEVELAND DEMOCRATS I HAD FOR PARENTS.

—a telegram to President-elect Kennedy regarding the invitation to
participate in his Inauguration on January 20, 1961
(Selected Letters, *p. 586*).

Hard of course to judge of the importance of an event at the time of
it, but an election like that, an inauguration like this, may well be looked
back on as a turning point in the history of our country, even perhaps
in the history of Christendom. It was such a great jump forward toward
settling it once for all that the church's reformation both from within
and from without had been accomplished; the old agonies and antago-
nisms were over; it was tacitly conceded that our founders were not far
wrong; safety lay in a plurality of denominations and doctrines unen-
forced by secular law. I come fresh to say this from communion with
portraits by Stuart of four of them who are on record to this effect,
Washington, Jefferson, Adams, and Madison, enshrined in a temple on
the North Shore of Massachusetts.

> "How still a moment may precede
> One that may thrill the world forever.
> To that still moment none would heed
> Man's doom was linked no more to sever."

So someone said of the first Christmas of all seven hundred and sixty-three years after the founding of Rome. Such was our gift for Christmas confirmed by vote one hundred and eighty years after the first election.

—from "A New England Tribute," as included in Official Program: Inaugural Ceremonies of John F. Kennedy . . . (Washington, 1961).

At the Inauguration on January 20, 1961, Frost attempted to read, but was prevented from doing so by the glare of sunlight, a dedicatory verse he had written for the occasion, and which he intended to give as a preface to "The Gift Outright," the poem Mr. Kennedy had wished him to say from the Inaugural platform.

As originally published in newspapers immediately after the Inauguration, the rhymed dedication began as follows:

> Summoning artists to participate
> In the august occasions of the state
> Seems something for us all to celebrate.
> This day is for my cause a day of days.
> And his be poetry's old-fashioned praise
> Who was the first to think of such a thing.
> This tribute verse to be his own I bring [. . .]

After leaving Washington, Frost devoted himself to substantial revision and extension of the dedication poem (to which fact he alludes in the April-fifth letter to Secretary of the Interior Udall, below). As finally published, with the title "For John F. Kennedy His Inauguration" in Frost's book *In the Clearing* (1962), the poem was seventy-seven lines in length, ending:

It makes the prophet in us all presage
The glory of a next Augustan age
Of a power leading from its strength and pride,
Of young ambition eager to be tried,
Firm in our free beliefs without dismay,
In any game the nations want to play.
A golden age of poetry and power
Of which this noonday's the beginning hour.

DEAR STEWART: [. . .] That dedication poem goes on being added to in my mind till it threatens to become a history of the United States to rival the one Harry Truman says he is writing. You know one of my missions is to get a secretary of the arts into the President's cabinet but I am as good as in there now with you to talk to. I have been reaching the President through you for some time. Somebody's been telling him our economy is manic. I'd like to tell him that a big vigorous economy like ours can't keep itself from overstocking and so having to have a clearance sale once in so often. That's the kind of figure of speech I'm good at. The beauty of my position is I'm only listened to for amusement. But seriously you have made my life a real party for the last go-down.

—from a letter to Stewart L. Udall,
April 5, 1961 (Selected Letters, *pp. 586–587*).

The Founding Fathers didn't believe in the future. They believed it *in.* You're always believing ahead of your evidence. What was the evidence I could write a poem? [. . .] I just believed it.

The most creative thing in us is to believe a thing in, in love, in all else. You believe yourself into existence. You believe your marriage into existence, you believe in each other, you believe that it's worthwhile going on, or you'd commit suicide, wouldn't you?

(493)

And the ultimate one is the belief in the future of the world. I believe the future *in*. It's coming in by my believing it. You might as well call that a belief in God. This word *God* is not an often-used word with me, but once in a while it arrives there.

—*as quoted by Mark Harris,*
Life, *December 1, 1961*
(Interviews, *p. 271*).

DEAR MR. PRESIDENT: How grand for you to think of me this way and how like you to take the chance of sending anyone like me over there affinitizing with the Russians. You must know a lot about me besides my rank from my poems but think how the professors interpret the poems! I am almost as full of politics and history as you are. I like to tell the story of the mere sailor boy from upstate New York who by favor of his captain and the American consul at St. Petersburg got to see the Czar in St. Petersburg with the gift in his hand of an acorn that fell from a tree that stood by the house of George Washington. That was in the 1830's when proud young Americans were equal to anything. He said to the Czar, "Washington was a great ruler and you're a great ruler and I thought you might like to plant the acorn with me by your palace." And so he did. [. . .]

Forgive the long letter. I don't write letters but you have stirred my imagination and I have been interested in Russia as a power ever since Rurik came to Novgorod; and these are my credentials. I could go on with them like this to make the picture complete: about the English-speaking world of England, Ireland, Canada, and Australia, New Zealand and Us versus the Russian-speaking world for the next century or so, mostly a stand-off but now and then a showdown to test our mettle. The rest of the world would be Asia and Africa, more or less negligible for the time being though it needn't be too openly declared.

Much of this would be the better for not being declared openly but kept always in the back of our minds in all our diplomatic and other relations. I am describing not so much what ought to be but what is and will be—reporting and prophesying. This is the way we are one world, as you put it, of independent nations interdependent—the separateness of the parts as important as the connection of the parts.

Great times to be alive, aren't they?

—from a letter of July 24, 1962, to President Kennedy, responding to an invitation to go to Russia in the fall of 1962 (Selected Letters, *pp.* 589–590).

I went over to Russia to confirm an idea I had, a feeling that Russia was drifting westward. We're rivals, in the end, in everything, war and all, to the end.

One of my greatest experiences was to talk to Khrushchev, to have a heart-to-heart talk with him and to see if he was the man I thought he was. I was there to get some things corrected or confirmed. I got things confirmed but not corrected. [. . .]

We were charmed with each other. I'm very fond of him. He's a lovable man. I could talk out to him and he could talk out to me.

It is a grand time to be alive, to see two rivalries drawing up for the next hundred years in the world and to see them do it in a somewhat civilized way.

Khrushchev and I, we met on the basis of honor and decency in the old-fashioned way, in the way of sports and all the way up. It was a very splendid thing and nothing like it ever happened to me.

—as quoted by W. J. McCarthy, Boston Herald, *January 23, 1963.*

On Extravagance

A TALK

Robert Frost's last talk before a collegiate audience was
given in Dartmouth College's newly opened Hopkins Center
for the performing arts, November 27, 1962. It is here
reprinted from the March 1963 *Dartmouth Alumni Magazine*.

I think the first thing I ought to speak of is all this luxuriance: all in
easy chairs and a beautiful hall—and nothing to do but to listen to me.
Pretty soft, I call it. Pretty soft.

I was so made that I—though a Vermonter and all that—I never took
any stock in the doctrine that "a penny saved is a penny earned." A
penny saved is a *mean* thing, and a penny spent is a generous thing and
a big thing—like this. (It took more than a penny to do this. There's
nothing mean about it.)

And one of the expressions I like best is—in the Bible it is and in
poets—they say, "of no mean city am I." That's a great saying, ain't it?—
to be "of no mean city," like San Francisco or Boston.

People deprecate our beautiful cities, and I go around thinking how
many people living in them must say that: "of no mean city am I." How
splendid. And "of no mean college am I." (Funny for me to be talking
about that.)

And I was thinking—I am going to read to you, of course, principally—
I was thinking of the extravagance of the universe. What an *extravagant*
universe it is. And the most extravagant thing in it, as far as we know, is
man—the most wasteful, spending thing in it—in all his luxuriance.

How stirring it is, the sun and everything. Take a telescope and look
as far as you will. How much of a universe was wasted just to produce
puny us. It's wonderful . . . , fine.

And poetry is a sort of extravagance, in many ways. It's something that people wonder about. What's the need of it? And the answer is, no need—not particularly. That is, that's the first one.

I've always enjoyed being around colleges, nominally as a professor, you know, and a puzzle to everybody as to what I was doing—whether anything or not. (You'd like to leave that to others. Never would defend myself there.) And people say to me occasionally, "Where *does* poetry come in?" Some of you may be thinking it tonight: what's it all for? "Does it *count*?"

When I catch a man reading my book, red-handed, he usually looks up cheerfully and says, "My wife is a great fan of yours." Puts it off on the women.

I figured that out lately: that there's an indulgence of poetry, a manly indulgence of poetry, that's a good deal like the manly indulgence of women. We say that women rule the world. That's a nice way to talk. And we say that poetry rules the world.

There's a poem that says;

> We are the music makers,
> And we are the dreamers of dreams . . .
> World-losers and world-forsakers,

. . . and all that. We are "the makers" of the future. We:

> Built Nineveh with our sighing,
> And Babel itself with our mirth;
> And o'erthrew them with prophesying
> To the old of the new world's worth;
> For each age is a dream that is dying,
> And one that is coming to birth.

That's a big claim, isn't it? An exaggerated claim.

But I look on the universe as a kind of an exaggeration anyway, the whole business. That's the way you think of it: great, great, great expense—everybody trying to make it mean something more than it is.

But all poetry asks is to be accorded the same indulgence that women are accorded. And I think the women, the ladies, are perhaps the go-betweens. They're our ambassadors to the men. They break the poetry to the men.

And it's a strange thing that men write the poetry more than the women; that is, the world's history is full of men poets and very few women. Women are in the dative case. It's to and for them, the poetry. And then for men and the affairs of men through them. (One knows the story that makes an argument that women really run the world in the end, run everything.)

And I'm not defending at all. I just thought one of the figures of poetry—(It's a metaphor, isn't it? You know, various kinds of metaphor.)—but one of the figures you never hear mentioned is just the one extravagance.

This is a little extravaganza, this little poem; and to what extent is it excessive? And can you go with it? Some people can't. And sometimes it's a bitter extravagance, like that passage in Shakespeare that so many make their novels out of: life is "a tale told by an idiot . . . , signifying nothing." That's an extravagance, of course—of bitterness.

People hold you. You say something sad or something pessimistic and something cynical, and they forget to allow for the extravagance of poetry. You're not saying that all the time. That's not a doctrine you're preaching. You loathe anybody that wants you to be either pessimist or optimist. It doesn't belong to it, it doesn't belong at all. Are you happy or are you unhappy? Why are you? You have no right to ask.

The extravagance lies in "it sometimes seems as if." That would be a good name of a book: "it sometimes seems as if." Or it says, "if you only knew." You could put that on the cover of a book. "If only I could tell you," you know. "Beyond participation lie my sorrows and beyond relief"—and yet you're harping on 'em, you see, in that way.

I arrived step by step at these things about it all, myself. I've been think-
ing lately that politics is an extravagance, again, an extravagance about
grievances. And poetry is an extravagance about *grief*. And grievances are
something that can be remedied, and griefs are irremediable. And there
you take 'em with a sort of a happy sadness, that they say drink helps—say
it does. ("Make you happy . . . ," the college song goes, "Make you happy,
make you sad. . . ." That old thing. How deep those things go.)

That leads me to say an extr[avagance]. I think I have right here one.
Let's see it. (It's made out in larger print for me by my publishers.) I
remember somebody holding it up for some doctrine that's supposed
to be in it. It begins with this kind of a person:

> He thought he kept the universe alone;

. . . Just that one line could be a whole poem, you know:

> He thought he kept the universe alone;
> For all the voice in answer he could wake
> Was but the mocking echo of his own
> From some tree-hidden cliff across the lake.
> Some morning from the boulder-broken beach
> He would cry out on life, that what it wants
> Is not its own love back in copy speech,
> But counter-love, original response.
> And nothing ever came of what he cried
> Unless it was the embodiment that crashed
> In the cliff's talus on the other side,
> And then in the far distant water splashed,
> But after a time allowed for it to swim,
> Instead of proving human when it neared
> And someone else additional to him,
> As a great buck it powerfully appeared,
> Pushing the crumpled water up ahead,

And landed pouring like a waterfall,
And stumbled through the rocks with horny tread,
And forced the underbrush—and that was all.

That's all he got out of his longing.

And somebody made quite an attack on that as not satisfying the noblest in our nature or something, you know. He missed it all! [. . .]

But that's just by way of carrying it over from what I was talking. I usually, you know, talk without any reference to my own poems: talk politics or something.

And then, just thinking of extravagances, back through the years, this is one—with a title like this, "Never Again Would Birds' Song Be the Same." You see this is another tone of extravagance:

> He would declare and could himself believe

. . . This is beginning to be an extravagance right in that line, isn't it?:

> He would declare and could himself believe
> That the birds there in all the garden round
> From having heard the daylong voice of Eve
> Had added to their own an oversound,
> Her tone of meaning though without the words.
> Admittedly an eloquence so soft
> Could only have had an influence on birds
> When call or laughter carried it aloft.
> Be that as may be, she was in their song.
> Moreover her voice upon their voices crossed
> Had now persisted in the woods so long
> That probably it never would be lost.
> Never again would birds' song be the same.
> And to do that to birds was why she came.

(They used to write extravagant things to ladies' eyebrows, you know. That's one of the parts of poetry.)

Some people are incapable of taking it, that's all. And I'm not picking you out. I do this on a percentage basis! And I can tell by expression of faces how troubled they are, just about that. I think it's the extravagance of it that's bothering 'em.

Say in a Mother Goose thing like this—another kind of extravagance:

> There was a man and he had nought,
>> So the robbers came to rob him;

. . . naturally. You see, that's an extravagance there:

> There was a man and he had nought,
>> So the robbers came to rob him;
> He climbed up to his chimney-top,
>> And then they thought they had him.
>
> But he climbed down on t'other side,
>> And so they couldn't find him;
> He ran fourteen miles in fifteen days,
>> And never looked behind him.

Now, that's all; if you can't keep up with it, don't try to!

And then, I could go right on with pretty near everything I've done. There's always this element of extravagance. It's like snapping the whip: Are you there? Are you still on? Are you with it? Or has it snapped you off?

That's a very emotional one, and then this is one in thought—a recent one, another kind of tone altogether:

> There was never naught,
> There was always thought.
> But when noticed first

It was fairly burst
Into having weight.
It was in a state
Of atomic One.
Matter was begun—
And in fact complete,
One and yet discrete
To conflict and pair.
Everything was there
Every single thing
Waiting was to bring,
Clear from hydrogen
All the way to men.
It was all the tree
It would ever be,
Bole and branch and root
Cunningly minute.
And this gist of all
Is so infra-small
As to blind our eyes
To its every guise
And so render nil
The whole Yggdrasil.
Out of coming-in
Into having been!
So the picture's caught
Almost next to naught
But the force of thought.

And my extravagance would go on from there to say that people think that life is a *result* of certain atoms coming together, instead of being the *cause* that brings the atoms together. There's something to be said about that in the utter, utter extravagant way.

And then . . . , another one. This is a poem that I partly wrote while I was here at Dartmouth in 1892, and failed with. And I kept a couple of lines of it, and they came in later. You can see what I was dwelling on. I was dwelling on the Pacific Coast—the shore out at Cliff House, where I had been as a child:

> The shattered water made a misty din.
> Great waves looked over others coming in,
> And thought of doing something to the shore
> That water never did to land before.
> The clouds were low and hairy in the skies,
> Like locks blown forward in the gleam of eyes.
> You could not tell, and yet it looked as if
> The shore was lucky in being backed by cliff,
> The cliff in being backed by continent;
> It looked as if a night of dark intent
> Was coming, and not only a night, an age.
> Someone had better be prepared for rage.
> There would be more than ocean-water broken
> Before God's last *Put out the Light* was spoken.

Another one, you see, just the way it *all* is. (Some of them probably more than others.)

And then sometimes just fooling, you know:

> I once had a cow that jumped over the moon,

. . . This poem is called "Lines Written in Dejection on the Eve of Great Success":

> I once had a cow that jumped over the moon,
> Not on to the moon but over.

I don't know what made her so lunar a loon;
All she'd been having was clover.

That was back in the days of my godmother Goose.
But though we are goosier now,
And all tanked up with mineral juice,
We haven't caught up with my cow.

Same thing, you know.

And one of the things about it in the criticism, and where I fail, is in I can enjoy great extravagance—and *abandon*. Abandon, especially when it's humorous. (I can show you other things, too; they're not all humorous.) . . . I can enjoy it. But some of this *solemn* abandon—(I don't know what it is they call 'em, abstract art or something like that.)—I don't keep up with it. You see, I'm distressed a little. . . . You get left behind, at some age. Don't sympathize with me too much!

And then, take a thing like this:

But God's own descent
Into flesh was meant
As a demonstration
That the supreme merit
Lay in risking spirit
In substantiation.

That's a whole of philosophy. To the very limit, you know.

And it comes out. . . . It doesn't mean it's untruth, this extravagance. For instance, somebody says to me—a great friend—says, "Everything's in the Old Testament that you find in the New." (You can tell who he was probably by his saying that.)

And I said, "What *is* the height of it?"

"Well," he said, " 'love your neighbor as yourself.' "

I said, "Yeah, that's in both of them." Then, just to tease him, I said, "But it isn't good enough."

He said, "What's the matter with it?"

"And *hate* your neighbor as you hate yourself."

He said, "Do you hate yourself?"

"I wouldn't be religious unless I did."

You see, we had in an argument—of that kind. . . .

Some people can't go with you. Let 'em drop; let 'em fall off. Let the wolves take 'em.

In the Bible twice it says—and I quote that in a poem somewhere, I think; yes—twice it says, 'these things are said in parables . . .'—said in this way that I'm talking to you about: extravagance said in parable, '. . . so the wrong people won't understand them and so get saved.'

It's thoroughly undemocratic, very superior—as when Matthew Arnold says, in a whole sonnet, only those who've given everything and strained every nerve "mount, and that hardly, to eternal life." 'Taint everybody, it's just those only—the few that have done everything, sacrificed, risked everything, "bet their sweet life" on what they lived. (That's again. . . . What a broad one that is: "You bet your sweet life." That's the height of it all, in whatever you do: "bet your sweet life.") And only those who have done that to the limit, he says, "mount, and that hardly . . ."— they barely make it, you know—". . . that hardly, to eternal life."

I like to see you. I like to bother some of you. What do we go round with poetry for? Go round just for kindred spirits some way—not for criticism, not for appreciation, and nothing but just awareness of each other about it all.

Now I'm going to forget all that, but let me say an extravagance of somebody else, another one beside mine. See how rich this is—not mine at all:

> By feathers green, across Casbeen
> The traveller tracks the Phoenix flown,
> By gems he strew'd in waste and wood,
> And jewell'd plumes at random thrown.

Till wandering far, by moon and star,
    They stand beside the funeral pyre,
Where bursting bright with sanguine light
    The impulsive bird forgets his sire.

Those ashes shine like ruby wine,
    Like bag of Tyrian murex spilt,
The claws, the jowl of the flying fowl
    Are with the glorious anguish gilt.

So fair the sight, so bright the light,
    Those pilgrim men, on traffic bent,
Drop hands and eyes and merchandise,
    And are with gazing well content.

That's somebody else, but that's another example—a rich one, lush, lavish.

Then, another kind of thing—not all my own, you know. Take for just the delight in the sound of the two stanzas that I'll say to you—three stanzas, maybe. The way it changes tune with a passion—a religious passion, I guess you'd call it. This is an old poem—old, old poem. It says:

What if the king, our sovereign lord,
Should of his own accord
Friendly himself invite,
And say 'I'll be your guest tomorrow night,'
How should we stir ourselves, call and command
All hands to work! 'Let no man idle stand!'

'Set me fine Spanish tables in the hall;
See they be fitted all;

. . . then I skip a little, and it says:

> Thus, if a king were coming, would we do;
> And 'twere good reason too;
> For 'tis a duteous thing
> To do all honor to an earthly king,
> And after all our travail and our cost,
> So he be pleased, to count no labor lost.

. . . and then watch this, the extravagance of this:

> But at the coming of the King of Heaven

. . . see, we've talked about the coming of the earthly king:

> But at the coming of the King of Heaven
> All's set at six and seven;
> We wallow in our sin,
> Christ cannot find a chamber in the inn
> We entertain Him always as a stranger,
> And, as of old, still house Him in the manger.

That's just letting go—saying.

Then, another strange one. You could say this is bad, you know; it lets you down too much. (That doesn't; that's great stuff; that lifts you up.) But suppose someone says:

> In either mood, to bless or curse
>   God bringeth forth the soul of man;
> No angel sire, no mother nurse
>   Can change the work that God began.

> One spirit shall be like a star,
>   He shall delight to honor one;
> Another spirit he shall mar:
>   None may undo what God hath done.

(507)

Then go back to just in general. . . . I'll just say 'em, I guess—little ones now. Some old ones I'll mix with some new ones.

The first poem I ever read in public, in 1915, was at Tufts College, and this was it—1915:

[Mr. Frost said "The Road Not Taken."]

Then—that's an old one—then another old one, quite a different tone. This one is more casual talking, this next one:

[Mr. Frost said "Stopping by Woods on a Snowy Evening."]

And that. . . . I won't use the word extravagance again this evening. Swear off. (You know sometimes a talk is just trying to run away from one word. If you get started using it you can't get away from it, sometimes.)

But then a new one. (That's supposed to be a problem poem. I didn't write it for that, but it's supposed to be a problem poem. By analogy you can go off from anything. Someone says that means—"The woods are lovely, dark and deep, / But I have promises to keep"—that means the world is "lovely . . . ," life is "lovely, dark and deep," but I must be getting to heaven. You see it's a death poem. You don't mind that. You shouldn't. Let 'em go!) And then here's a new one. "Away!" this is called, "Away!" Little stanzas, tiny stanzas:

[Mr. Frost said the poem "Away!"]

That's straight goods. They can't do much with that.

And then—just as it happens now; it's nothing to do with anything particular—"Escapist—Never." (These are some of my new ones.):

[Mr. Frost said "Escapist—Never," "Closed for Good," "Peril of Hope," "The Draft Horse," and "One More Brevity."]

I would like to read *part* of something to you that's hard to read. It's in my new book, and I have it here in large print for my eye. . . .

This is in blank verse. You know me well enough to know I've written in nothing but blank verse and rhymed verse. I did write one free verse poem, and I kept it. I thought it was so smart!

A lady said to me one night, "You've said all sorts of things tonight, Mr. Frost. Which are you, a conservative or a radical?"

And I looked at her very honestly and earnestly and sincerely, and I said:

I never dared be radical when young
For fear it would make me conservative when old.

That's my only free verse poem.

This is in blank verse, and the title of it (and the little reading of it's all you're going to get): "How Hard It Is to Keep from Being King When It's in You and in the Situation." It's kind of, in a way, political and invidious—but you wouldn't know who I was driving at, maybe— maybe you would. But it's an old story:

[Mr. Frost read approximately half of the poem.]

. . . And that's where I'll leave it. There's twice as much of it. See the rest of it, how it comes out: how the cook becomes king and the other man wants himself executed, the regular king.

And I guess I've taken my time with you—or let me say one or two little things.

So many of them have literary criticism in them—*in* them. And yet I wouldn't admit it. I try to hide it.

So many of them have politics in them, like that—that's just *loaded* with politics. I got it out of the Arabian Nights, of course, the outline of the story; but it's just *loaded, loaded* with politics. And I've bent it to make it more so, you see. I'm guilty. And all that.

But now this one, speaking to a star up there:

[Mr. Frost said "Choose Something Like a Star."]

By that star I mean the Arabian Nights or Catullus or something in the Bible or something way off or something way off in the woods, and when I've made a mistake in my vote. (We were talking about that today. How many times we voted this way and that by mistake.)

And then see little personal things like this. . . . (Do you know the real motivation probably of it all . . . ? Take the one line in that, "Some mystery becomes the proud." Do you know where I got that? Out of long efforts to understand contemporary poets. You see, let them be mystery. And that's my generosity—call it that! If I was sure they meant anything to themselves it would be all right.)

Now take a little one like this—you see how different my feeling's about it:

> She always had to burn a light
> Beside her attic bed at night.
> It gave bad dreams and troubled sleep,
> But helped the Lord her soul to keep.
> Good gloom on her was thrown away.
> It is on me by night or day,
> Who have, as I foresee, ahead
> The darkest of it still to dread.

Suppose I end on that dark note. Good night.

The Prophets Really Prophesy as Mystics The Commentators Merely by Statistics

LAST POEM

The following poem—the last of Robert Frost's poems to be published during his lifetime—was included in the fiftieth–anniversary issue of the magazine *Poetry* (October–November 1962) and was also printed in booklet form as Frost's 1962 Christmas greeting. The latter was mailed out shortly before the holiday, at a time when the poet was a patient in Boston's Peter Bent Brigham Hospital, where he had undergone surgery on December tenth.

THE PROPHETS REALLY PROPHESY AS MYSTICS THE COMMENTATORS MERELY BY STATISTICS

With what unbroken spirit naïve science
Keeps hurling our Promethean defiance
From this atomic ball of rotting rock
At the Divine Safe's combination lock.

In our defiance we are still defied.
But have not I, as prophet, prophesied:
Sick of our circling round and round the sun
Something about the trouble will be done.

Now that we've found the secret out of weight,
So we can cancel it however great.

Ah, what avail our lofty engineers
If we can't take the planet by the ears,

Or by the poles or simply by the scruff,
And saying simply we have had enough
Of routine and monotony on earth,
Where nothing's going on but death and birth.

And man's of such a limited longevity,
Now in the confidence of new-found levity
(Our gravity has been our major curse)
We'll cast off hawser for the universe

Taking along the whole race for a ride
(Have I not prophesied and prophesied?)
All voting *viva voce* where to go,
The noisier because they hardly know

Whether to seek a scientific sky
Or wait and go to Heaven when they die,
In other words to wager their reliance
On plain religion or religious Science.

They need to crash the puzzle of their lot
As Alexander crashed the Gordian knot,
Or as we crashed the barrier of sound
To beat the very world's speed going round.

Yet what a charming earnest world it is,
So modest we can hardly hear it whizz,
Spinning as well as running on a course
It seems too bad to steer it off by force.

"If only I get well. . . ."

LAST LETTER

Robert Frost died at the Peter Bent Brigham Hospital in
Boston on January 29, 1963. The following letter to his old
friends Professor and Mrs. G. Roy Elliott was dictated shortly
before Frost's death, and the original is now located within
the Robert Frost Library at Amherst College. The two men
had become acquainted shortly after the appearance of
Elliott's article entitled "The Neighborliness of Robert Frost,"
which was published in *The Nation* for December 6, 1919.

The text of the letter is here reprinted from its original
appearance in *Selected Letters of Robert Frost,* p. 596.

OH ROY AND ALMA: How the years have come between us. You were
one of the first that gave me any stature, as they call it nowadays, and
remember I went to see you at Bowdoin on purpose for your kind of
recognition. Things have come out fine for you. I'm sorry you don't go
to Florida any more but that's a small matter. We read each other's
books and we know what we're thinking about. Metaphor is it and the
freshness thereof.

I'm mighty glad you like this poem for Christmas ["The Prophets
Really Prophesy as Mystics . . ."]. Why will the quidnuncs always be
hoping for a salvation man will never have from anyone but God? I was
just saying today how Christ posed Himself the whole problem and
died for it. How can we be just in a world that needs mercy and merci-
ful in a world that needs justice. We study and study the four biogra-
phies of Him and are left still somewhat puzzled in our daily lives.
Marking students in a kind of mockery and laughing it off. It seems as

if I never wrote these plunges into the depths to anyone but you. I remember our first walk to Harpswell together.

This is being dictated to Anne Morrison Gentry who writes shorthand and her mother Kathleen Morrison who devises all my future. They are helping me through these hard days in a grand and very powerful hospital. . . . If only I get well, with their help, I'll go deeper into my life with you than I ever have before.

AFFECTIONATELY, R.F.

A Selected Bibliography

PRIMARY PUBLISHED SOURCES

The Poetry of Robert Frost, edited by Edward Connery Lathem (New York, 1969). The comprehensive, standard edition of RF's poems.

Selected Prose of Robert Frost, edited by Hyde Cox and Edward Connery Lathem (New York, 1966). Contains fifteen of RF's introductions, prefaces, and talks revised by him for publication.

Selected Letters of Robert Frost, edited by Lawrance Thompson (New York, 1964). Letters from 1886 to 1963, with notes and index.

Robert Frost and John Bartlett: The Record of a Friendship, by Margaret Bartlett Anderson (New York, 1963). Includes many letters from RF to Bartlett, 1912 to 1945.

The Letters of Robert Frost to Louis Untermeyer (New York, 1963). Interstitial notes by LU supplement these letters of the interval 1915 to 1962.

Robert Frost: Farm-Poultryman, edited by Edward Connery Lathem and Lawrance Thompson (Hanover, N.H., 1963). The texts of eleven prose contributions made by RF to two New England poultry journals, 1903 to 1905.

Robert Frost and the Lawrence, Massachusetts, "High School Bulletin," edited by Edward Connery Lathem and Lawrance Thompson (New York, 1966). Includes all of RF's contributions to the *Bulletin.*

Interviews with Robert Frost, edited by Edward Connery Lathem (New York, 1966). A selection of over fifty interviews, 1915 to 1962.

REFERENCE WORK

Lathem, Edward Connery, editor, *A Concordance to The Poetry of Robert Frost* (New York, 1971). Entries give for each word indexed (covering all eleven of RF's books, as included in the standard edition of his verse), the full line in which the word appears, a page reference to *The Poetry of Robert Frost,* the title of the poem in question, and an indication of the pertinent line's location within the poem.

Index

About the Author

ROBERT FROST was born in San Francisco in 1874. He moved to New England at the age of eleven and later studied at Dartmouth and Harvard, though he never completed a formal degree. His first professional poem, "The Butterfly," was published on November 8, 1894, in the New York magazine *The Independent*.

The publication of *A Boy's Will* and *North of Boston* established his reputation and by the nineteen twenties he was the most celebrated poet in America. With each new book—including *New Hampshire* (1923), *A Further Range* (1936), *Steeple Bush* (1947), and *In the Clearing* (1962)—his fame and honors (including four Pulitzer Prizes) increased, and in 1958 he was appointed Consultant in Poetry at the Library of Congress. Robert Frost lived and taught for many years in Massachusetts and Vermont, and died on January 29, 1963, in Boston.

"His death improverishes us all; but he has bequeathed his nation a body of imperishable verse from which Americans will forever gain joy and understanding." —JOHN F. KENNEDY